THE GOSPELS
IN CONTEXT

D1331417

THE GOSPELS
IN CONTEXT

Social and Political History
in the Synoptic Tradition

by

Gerd Theissen

Translated by

Linda M. Maloney

T&T CLARK
EDINBURGH

T&T CLARK LTD
59 GEORGE STREET
EDINBURGH EH2 2LQ
SCOTLAND

Copyright © T&T Clark Ltd, 1992

Authorised English translation of *Lokalkolorit und Zeitgeschichte in den Evangelien*
© Vandenhoeck & Ruprecht, Göttingen, 1989

This edition originally published under licence from
Augsburg Fortress
426 South Fifth Street, Box 1209
Minneapolis, MN 55440

All rights reserved. No part of this publication may be reproduced,
stored in a retrieval system, or transmitted, in any form or by any means,
electronic, mechanical, photocopying, recording or otherwise,
without the prior permission of T&T Clark Ltd.

First published 1992
First paperback edition 1994
Latest impression 1998

ISBN 0 567 29602 4

British Library Cataloguing-in-Publication Data
A catalogue record for this book is available from the British Library

Printed and bound in Great Britain by MPG Books Ltd, Bodmin

Dedicated to
GÜNTHER BORNKAMM

Contents

Preface

Historical-critical exegesis has repeatedly been written off as outmoded and inadequate to many theological demands. One often hears that everything that is accessible to this kind of investigation has already been researched and that alternative methods must be employed to make possible new approaches to the text. In this situation, this book intends to show that we can still make new discoveries and advance knowledge within the oldest question posed by historical-critical analysis—that of the dating and localization of texts. I received my inspiration for this book especially from Old Testament scholars: John Strange of Copenhagen awakened my interest in biblical archeology and cultural geography on a study tour of the Near East in 1980. Helga and Manfred Weippert of Heidelberg gave me the idea of comparing precise correspondences in archeological and historical dates with texts for the recovery of the history of their traditions. Finally, I should mention the work of the Fribourg school in iconography, which has few rivals in that aspect of New Testament exegesis. The material on the "reed" (Mt 11:7) was presented as a lecture in Fribourg in 1983, and the positive response I received from Othmar Keel and Max Küchler gave me great encouragement.

A number of previously published essays have made their way into this book: "Das 'schwankende Rohr' (Mt 11,7) und die Gründungsmünzen von Tiberias" (*ZDPV* 101 [1985]: 43–55) is largely identical with chapter 1, section A; the same is true of chapter 2, section A, and "Lokal- und Sozialkolorit in der Geschichte der syrophönizischen Frau (Mk 7,24-30)" (*ZNW* 75 [1984]; 202–25). In addition, sections from "Meer und See in den Evangelien: Ein Beitrag zur Lokalkoloritforschung" (*SNTU* 10 [1985]: 5–25) have been adapted in chapter 2, section D, and chapter 6, section A. The Introduction is an edited form of my programmatic essay, "Lokalkoloritforschung in den Evangelien: Plädoyer für die Erneuerung einer alten Fragestellung" (*EvTh* 45 [1985]: 481–500).

I dedicate the book to Günther Bornkamm, to whom I also dedicated the programmatic article in *Evangelische Theologie* of 1985. His exegetical work has had a lasting impact on the "cultural context" of exegesis in Heidelberg. This book's return to the classic historical statement of the problem also has its origin in that "cultural context."

Abbreviations

Aboth R. Nat.	*Aboth de Rabbi Nathan*
Abr.	Philo *De Abrahamo*
Adv. Haer.	Epiphanius *Adversus Haereses*
Adv. Haeres.	Irenaeus *Adversus Haereses*
Adv. Jud. Or.	John Chrysostom *Oration against the Jews*
AGJU	Arbeiten zur Geschichte des antiken Judentums und des Urchristentums
AJP	*American Journal of Philology*
Ann.	Tacitus *Annals*
ANRW	*Aufstieg und Niedergang der römischen Welt*
Ant.	Josephus *Antiquities of the Jews*
Apoc. Abr.	*Apocalypse of Abraham*
Apoc. Esdr.	*Apocalypse of Esdras*
As. Mos.	*Assumption of Moses*
Asc. Is.	*Ascension of Isaiah*
ASNU	Acta seminarii neotestamentici upsaliensis
ASTI	*Annual of the Swedish Theological Institute*
AThANT	Abhandlungen zur Theologie des Alten und Neuen Testaments
Aug.	Suetonius *Divus Augustus*
b. Abod. Zar.	Babylonian Talmud, *Abodah Zarah*
b. Ber.	Babylonian Talmud, *Berakot*
b. Git.	Babylonian Talmud, *Gittin*
b. Pesah.	Babylonian Talmud, *Pesahim*
b. Qidd.	Babylonian Talmud, *Qiddusin*
b. Sota	Babylonian Talmud, *Sota*
b. Taan.	Babylonian Talmud, *Taanit*
2 Bar.	*Second* (Syriac) *Apocalypse of Baruch*
3 Bar.	*Third* (Greek) *Apocalypse of Baruch*

Barn.	*Barnabus*
BBB	Bonner biblische Beiträge
Bell.	Josephus *Bellum Judaicum*
BET	Beiträge zur evangelischen Theologie
BEvTh	Beiträge zur evangelischen Theologie
BFChTh	Beiträge zur Förderung christlicher Theologie
BGBE	Beiträge zur Geschichte der biblischen Exegese
BHH	B. Reicke and L. Rost (eds.), *Biblisch-Historisches Handwörterbuch*
Bib.	*Biblica*
Bibl. Hist.	Diodorus Siculus *Biblical History*
BIES	*Bulletin of the Israel Exploration Society*
BiKi	*Bibel und Kirche*
BiLe	*Bibel und Leben*
BMC	*British Museum Catalogue of Coins of the Roman Empire*
BZ	*Biblische Zeitschrift*
BZNW	Beihefte zur *Zeitschrift für die neutestamentliche Wissenschaft*
C. Ap.	Josephus *Contra Apionem*
Cal.	Suetonius *Gaius Caligula*
Cant. Rab.	*Canticles Rabbah*
CBNT	Coniectanea biblica, New Testament series
CBQ	*Catholic Biblical Quarterly*
CD	Cairo Damascus Document
Cic.	Plutarch *Cicero*
CIL	*Corpus Inscriptionum Latinarum*
CIS	*Corpus Inscriptionum Semiticarum*
1, 2 Clem.	*1* and *2 Clement*
Contra Cels.	Origen *Contra Celsum*
CPJ	Corpus papyrorum Judaicorum
CSEL	Corpus scriptorum ecclesiasticorum latinorum
De Benef.	Seneca *De beneficiis*
De Praem.	Philo *De praemiis et poenis*
Der. Er. Zut.	*Derek Eres Zuta*
Dial.	Justin *Dialogues*
Did.	*Didache*
Dig.	*Digesta*
Diog. Laert.	*Diogenes Laertius*
DTb	Dalp-Taschenbücher
DTT	*Dansk teologisk tidsskrift*
Eccl. Hs.	Eusebius *Ecclesiastical History*
Eccl. Rab.	*Ecclesiastes Rabbah*

EdF	Erträge der Forschung
EHPhR	*Etudes d'histoire et de philosophie religieuses*
EJ(D)	*Encyclopaedia Judaica,* Berlin
EKK	Evangelische-katholischer Kommentar zum Neuen Testament
Ep.	Pliny the Younger *Epistulae*
Epit.	Livy *Epitomae*
ET	*Expository Times*
EThR	*Etudes théologiques et religieuses*
EvTh	*Evangelische Theologie*
EWNT	H. Balz and G. Schneider (eds.), *Exegetisches Wörterbuch zum Neuen Testament*
Flacc.	Philo *In Flaccum*
FRLANT	Forschungen zur Religion und Literatur des Alten und Neuen Testaments
FTS	Frankfurter theologische Studien
FzB	Forschung zur Bibel
GCS	Griechischen christlichen Schriftsteller
Geogr.	Strabo *Geography*
GLAJJ	M. Stern, *Greek and Latin Authors on Jews and Judaism* (Jerusalem, 1974)
Gos. Thom.	*Gospel of Thomas*
Hebr. Quaest in Gen.	Jerome *Questions on Genesis*
Hermot.	Lucian *Hermotimus, or Concerning the Sects*
Hist.	Tacitus *Histories*
HKNT	Handkommentar zum Neuen Testament
HNT	Handbuch zum Neuen Testament
HThK	Herders theologischer Kommentar zum Neuen Testament
HThR	*Harvard Theological Review*
HUCA	*Hebrew Union College Annual*
ICC	International Critical Commentary
IEJ	*Israel Exploration Journal*
IG	*Inscriptiones Graecae*
Ign. *Eph.*	Ignatius *Letter to the Ephesians*
Ign. *Magn.*	Ignatius *Letter to the Magnesians*
Ign. *Sm.*	Ignatius *Letter to the Smyrnaeans*
Inst.	Quintilian *Institutio oratoria*
JBL	*Journal of Biblical Literature*
JJS	*Journal of Jewish Studies*
Jos.	Josephus
Jos. As.	*Joseph and Aseneth*

JQR	*Jewish Quarterly Review*
JRS	*Journal of Roman Studies*
JSHRZ	Jüdische Schriften aus hellenistisch-römischer Zeit
JSJ	*Journal for the Study of Judaism in the Persian, Hellenistic and Roman Period*
JSNT	*Journal for the Study of the New Testament*
Jub.	*Jubilees*
Jud	*Judaica*, Zurich
KEK	Kritische-exegetischer Kommentar über das Neue Testament (Meyer)
KNT	Kommentar zum Neuen Testament (Zahn)
KP	*Kleine Pauly*
LCL	Loeb Classical Library
Leg. Gai.	Philo *Legatio ad Gaium*
LXX	Septuagint
m. Ker.	Mishnah, *Keritot*
m. Qidd.	Mishnah, *Qiddusin*
Midr. Eccl.	*Midrash Ecclesiastes*
MSSNTS	Monograph Series, Society for New Testament Studies
MT	Masoretic Text
Nat. Hist.	Pliny the Elder *Natural History*
NT	*Novum Testamentum* (Leiden)
NT Suppl.	*Novum Testamentum*, Supplements
NTA	Neutestamentliche Abhandlungen
NTD	Das Neue Testament Deutsch
NTF	Neutestamentliche Forschungen
NTOA	Novum Testamentum et Orbis Antiquus
NTS	*New Testament Studies*
OGIS	*Orientis Graeci Inscriptiones Selectae*
Onom.	Eusebius *Onomastikon*
Oros.	*Orosius*
ÖTK	Ökumenischer Taschenbuchkommentar
p. Abod. Zar.	Palestinian Talmud, *Abodah Zarah*
p. Keth.	Palestinian Talmud, *Kethubot*
p. Kil.	Palestinian Talmud, *Kilayim*
P. Oxy.	*Oxyrhynchus Papyri*
p. Sanh.	Palestinian Talmud, *Sanhedrin*
PEFQSt	*Palestine Exploration Fund, Quarterly Statement*
PG	J. Migne, *Patrologia graeca*
Phil.	Cicero *Orationes Philippicae*

Pirqe R. El.	*Pirqe Rabbi Eliezer*
PJ	*Palästina-Jahrbuch*
PRE	*Pauly's Real-Encyclopädie der classischen Alterthumswissenschaft*
Ps.-Clem. *Hom.*	Pseudo-Clement *Homilies*
Pss. Sol.	*Psalms of Solomon*
QDAP	*Quarterly of the Department of Antiquities in Palestine*
1QpHab	*Pesher on Habakkuk* from Qumran Cave 1
Quaest. Nat.	Seneca *Quaestiones Naturales*
RAC	*Reallexikon für Antike und Christentum*
RE	*Realencyklopädie für protestantische Theologie und Kirche*
REJ	*Revue des études juives*
RHPhR	*Revue d'histoire et de philosophie religieuses*
RQ	*Römische Quartalschrift für christliche Altertumskunde und Kirchengeschichte*
RTL	*Revue théologique de Louvain*
Sat.	Juvenal *Satires*
SBB	Stuttgarter biblische Beiträge
SBLbSt	Society of Biblical Literature Sources for Biblical Study
SBS	Stuttgarter Bibelstudien
SHAWPH	Sitzungsberichte der Heidelberger Akademie der Wissenschaften, Philosophisch-historische Klasse
Sib. Or.	*Sibylline Oracles*
SJ	Studia judaica
SJLA	Studies in Judaism in Late Antiquity
SNT	Studien zum Neuen Testament
SNTSMS	Society for New Testament Studies Monograph Series
SNTU	*Studien zum Neuen Testament und ihrer Umwelt*
Sozom. *Eccl. Hist.*	Sozomen *Ecclesiastical History*
Spec. Leg.	Philo *De specialibus legibus*
StANT	Studien zum Alten und Neuen Testament
STh	*Studia theologica*
StNT	Studien zum Neuen Testament
STö	*Sammlung Töpelmann*, Berlin
StUNT	Studien zur Umwelt des Neuen Testaments
t. Ber.	Tosefta, *Berakot*
t. Hul.	Tosefta, *Hullin*
T. Benj.	*Testament of Benjamin*
T. Levi	*Testament of Levi*

t. Men.	Tosefta, *Menahot*
TDNT	G. Kittel and G. Friedrich (eds.), *Theological Dictionary of the New Testament*
ThB	*Theologische Beiträge*
ThBl	*Theologische Blätter*
ThGl	*Theologie und Glaube*
ThHK	Theologischer Handkommentar zum Neuen Testament
ThLZ	*Theologische Literaturzeitung*
ThViat	*Theologia viatorum*
ThZ	*Theologische Zeitschrift*
Tib.	Suetonius *Tiberius*
TThQ	*Theologische Quartalschrift, Tübingen*
TThZ	*Trierer theologische Zeitschrift*
TU	Texte und Untersuchungen
UTb	Uni-Taschenbücher
Vesp.	Suetonius *Vespasian*
Vit. Ap.	Philostratus *Vita Apollonii*
Vitell.	Suetonius *Vitellius*
WA	Martin Luther, Kritische Gesamtausgabe ("Weimar" edition)
WdF	Wege der Forschung
WKLGS	Wissenschaftliche Kommentar zu lateinischen und griechischen Schriftstellern
WMANT	Wissenschaftliche Monographien zum Alten und Neuen Testament
WUNT	Wissenschaftliche Untersuchungen zum Neuen Testament
y. Ber.	Jerusalem Talmud, *Berakot*
y. Demai	Jerusalem Talmud, *Demai*
ZAW	*Zeitschrift für die alttestamentliche Wissenschaft*
ZDPV	*Zeitschrift des deutschen Palästina-Vereins*
ZNW	*Zeitschrift für die neutestamentliche Wissenschaft*
ZThK	*Zeitschrift für Theologie und Kirche*

INTRODUCTION

Social Context and
Political History in the Study
of the Synoptic Tradition

The study of the Gospels was supported for most of the present century by a "form-critical consensus" that expected to find, behind the written texts as we have them, an oral prehistory that is still recognizable today. But this consensus has been shaken. For some time now, doubts about the existence or the importance of an oral tradition in early Christianity have been on the increase; objections have been raised to the hypothesis of "small units" of tradition; and there is growing skepticism about the possibility of reconstructing preliterary versions of the text.[1] The shattering of old truisms is to be welcomed. Classical form criticism has long since become such shopworn dogma in research and teaching that it suggests a false certainty where, instead, we really need new confirmation and assurance. What is at stake is nothing more nor less than the possibility of a "history of the synoptic tradition"—that is, a historical explanation of the beginning, shaping, and alteration of the most important traditions about Jesus.

---

1. The dissolution of the form-critical consensus began with E. Güttgemanns, *Offene Fragen zur Formgeschichte.* Here, for the first time, we encounter a clear skepticism with regard to the possibility of reconstructing the oral prehistory of texts, and a turn toward the "cohesive text" in its present form. The motifs introduced by Güttgemanns were independently advanced by W. Schmithals in his "Kritik der Formkritik" and *Einleitung in die ersten drei Evangelien,* in which he disputed the existence of any appreciable oral tradition in early Christianity. The Gospels are treated as the expressions of literary theologians. Schmithals does not grant the existence of a cohesive text; instead, he undertakes to reconstruct the original texts through the use of a complicated form of literary criticism. This distinguishes him from the third prominent representative of a retreat from classical form criticism: K. Berger, who in his *Formgeschichte des Neuen Testaments* (Heidelberg, 1984) and *Einführung in die Formgeschichte* calls for a "new form criticism" restricted to the analysis and historical tracing of genre within the framework of the literary history of ancient times. According to Berger, the question of an oral prehistory cannot be coupled with the analysis of genre; it represents a history of transmission and should be pursued by a methodology of its own (e.g., the analysis of verbal relationships and fields). I believe that the critical challenges raised by these three exegetes deserve more respect than they have heretofore received.

1

The studies presented here under the title *The Gospels in Context: Social and Political History in the Synoptic Tradition* are intended to aid in the clarification of the possibilities for a "history of the synoptic tradition" from its oral prehistory to the time when it was written down in the Gospels. It will not be possible to take a position on all the problems treated in form criticism and tradition criticism of the Gospels. The present work is restricted to the elementary framework of questions with which every historical work begins. Regarding the evaluation of sources, it asks: Where and when did the sources originate? A "history of the synoptic tradition" would be impossible if we could not distinguish between earlier and later texts, if the place of origin of the texts remained obscure, and if the history of how the Gospels came to be written were to remain unexplored. Research on cultural and temporal contexts is an effort to localize the individual units of the synoptic tradition and their redaction in time and space, with the aid of the clues they provide about their locality and date.

In this, the presupposition of an oral tradition will still be regarded as valid. We will continue to presume the existence of "small units" or "text segments." However, classical form criticism's confidence in its ability to reconstruct the oral prehistory of the texts in detail will be called into question. Here, a new beginning will be necessary, and the study of cultural context—a type of investigation that was foreign to classical form criticism—is intended to contribute to this new beginning. But first we need to justify the modification or retention of the three fundamental postulates described above.

THE HYPOTHESIS OF AN ORAL TRADITION[2]

The existence of oral tradition is directly witnessed by early Christian writers. The prologue to Luke's Gospel presupposes it when it distinguishes between what eyewitnesses and ministers of the word handed down (παρέδοσαν) and the effort to compile a comprehensive narrative of the events surrounding Jesus (Lk 1:1-4). It is addressed also in the second conclusion of John's Gospel, when the author asserts that there are a great many unwritten traditions about Jesus, only a selection of which is presented in the Johannine Gospel (Jn 21:25). Early in the second century, Bishop Papias of Hierapolis collected oral traditions about Jesus. Surviving samples reveal that there were some quite fanciful traditions afloat. What is important is that Papias placed special value on their oral form, because

---

2. Skepticism in regard to the hypothesis of an oral synoptic tradition is found esp. in Schmithals, *Einleitung in die ersten drei Evangelien*, 298–318. See also H. M. Teeple, "The Oral Tradition That Never Existed."

he did not believe that "things out of books would help me as much as the utterances of a living and abiding voice (τὰ παρὰ ζώσης φωνῆς καὶ μενούσης)" (Eusebius *Eccl. Hs.* 3.39.4).

The hypothesis of an oral tradition is confirmed by comparative history of religions: behind the Mishna, which was codified near the end of the second century C.E. (and the commentaries and collections of parallels that go with it), there is an oral tradition whose *Sitz im Leben* was the rabbinic schools. It differs from the early Christian traditions about Jesus, although there are some points of contact.[3] But it shows that early Christianity arose within a cultural milieu that knew and valued oral traditions.

Moreover, within the synoptic texts we encounter features that are most easily explained in terms of an oral prehistory of the texts: these include the formulaic introductions to the parables, recurrent motifs in the miracle stories, and the simple and straightforward construction of the pericopes. In addition, the sayings tradition in the Gospels is represented as "oral tradition": we never hear of any instruction to write down what Jesus had said.[4] It seems that the disciples are supposed to spread his teaching, but not by means of books: they are to go throughout Palestine (Mt 10:2-6) and the whole world (Mt 28:19-20). This presumes an oral form of transmission of Jesus' message. Jesus says, "Whoever hears you, hears me" (Lk 10:16), and not, "whoever reads you, reads me."

Thus the existence of an oral Jesus tradition should not be doubted, even if it was not present everywhere in early Christianity to the same degree. Paul cites only a few bits of the synoptic tradition (1 Cor 7:10-11; 9:14; 11:23-26). There may be many reasons for this,[5] but the least probable is that the Jesus tradition did not yet exist. In that case one would also have to conclude from the Johannine letters that the Johannine Jesus

---

3. On rabbinic tradition, see B. Gerhardsson, *Memory and Manuscript.* Despite reservations concerning a direct transfer of rabbinic techniques of transmission to early Christianity, we must recognize that we have here a historical analogy to the process of tradition in Christianity's earliest phase. R. Riesner, in *Jesus als Lehrer,* has expanded on Gerhardsson's ideas; his work lends increased probability to the existence of forms of oral tradition that were in general use (in the rabbinic schools as well). It is by no means necessary to accept "conservative" conclusions in order, by way of such analogies, to shed light on the Jesus traditions as well. Within the field of classical antiquity, the nearest analogy would probably be the Socratic tradition. See G. Kennedy, "Classical and Christian Source Criticism," 125–54.

4. In apocalyptic writings, conversely, we find instructions for the writing down of the visions (see, e.g., 2 Esdr 14:24-26), or else celestial books are handed over to the visionary (see *1 Enoch* 82:1-3).

5. For Schmithals (*Einleitung in die ersten drei Evangelien,* 99ff.), the absence of synoptic tradition in Paul is a decisive argument favoring his skepticism toward the hypothesis of an oral tradition. But there is also very little synoptic tradition in the writings of Ignatius of Antioch, although he certainly knew Matthew's Gospel (cf. Ign. *Sm.* 1:1).

tradition did not exist at the time those letters were written. Neither John's Gospel nor its traditions are expressly cited there, although their content is presupposed.

THE HYPOTHESIS OF "SMALL UNITS"

We will also maintain the second basic postulate of form-critical investigation, namely, the notion of small, individual units. By this we do not mean to say that these units were handed down in isolation.[6] What is critical is the fact that they could be separated and reappear, over and over again, in new contexts, as in the case of those "wandering sayings" we find in different places in the Gospels: for example, the saying about the first and the last, which appears in various contexts in Mt 19:30, Mt 20:16, and Lk 13:30 and thereby demonstrates its independence.

It is only on the supposition that there are such units, which have the potential of being extracted from their context, that we can explain why, in the course of textual history, small pericopes such as the apophthegms about the Sabbath-breaker in Lk 6:4 (Codex D) or the story of the adulteress found in Jn 7:52—8:12 (or after Lk 21:28 in the minuscule family 13, or after Lk 24:53 in minuscule 1333[c]) were introduced into the text. We can demonstrate that similar processes were involved in the redaction of the Gospels: for example, when the author of Matthew placed the Our Father within a series of associated rules for religious devotional practice (6:9-13) or when the same author interrupted the Markan connection between the second Passion prediction and the dispute about rank by introducing the pericope about the temple drachma (cf. Mt 17:24-27). The reordering of materials by Matthew and Luke also documents the evangelists' awareness that they were reproducing pericopes transmitted in such a way that they could be isolated, and therefore rearranged.[7] If we also recognize that the synoptic traditions in the *Gospel of Thomas* exist in a sequence that has nothing in common with the ordering in the synoptics, the picture is complete: in the literary tradition as we can observe it, the Jesus tradition is treated as a combination of small, individual units. It is no wonder that the fragments of synoptic tradition in Paul's writings appear in isolation from one another, even though they are embedded in larger contexts within the letters themselves. This "separability" of small

---

6. The oral tradition should not be imagined as a "shapeless chaos of small units" existing side by side and independently of one another. This notion was justly criticized by Berger, *Einführung in die Formgeschichte*, 109.

7. W. G. Kümmel, *Einleitung in das Neue Testament*, 19th ed. (Heidelberg, 1978), 32–33 (*Introduction to the New Testament*, trans. Howard C. Kee from the 17th rev. ed. [Nashville, 1975]), gives a simplified, tabular sketch of the general outlines of the rearrangement.

units with respect to their context in any given case gives us the right to examine each unit separately, even when it has not been handed down in isolation, but rather in differing combinations with other units.

THE POSSIBILITY OF RECONSTRUCTING THE ORAL PREHISTORY OF TEXTS

The strong point of the contemporary critique of classical form criticism is not so much its challenge to oral tradition or the possibility of isolating individual units as its skepticism regarding the chances of reconstructing an oral (or written) prehistory of the texts. There are many reasons for this skepticism.

The literary-critical dissection of various layers in the text—that is, the separation of primary, secondary, and tertiary text elements—can scarcely be carried out without some degree of arbitrariness. The results are contradictory, and often they are equally plausible.[8]

The belief that at the beginning of the tradition there existed those "pure forms" described in our textbooks as models for the various genres has proved to be naive. Equally plausible—or implausible—would be the idea that traditions are ground down through use, so that at the end they correspond more nearly to the norms of the genre than they did at the beginning.[9]

But there is scarcely anyone who believes in consistent tendencies of tradition in one or another of these directions. If we once hoped to be able to conclude from the modification of materials in the written tradition to their transformation in the oral prehistory, we have now become more skeptical: there is not even a moment in the course of the written tradition where we can detect clear and unmistakable tendencies.[10]

Finally, we may observe the progress of disillusionment regarding a reconstruction of the *Sitz im Leben*. It is still true that oral forms maintain their stability when they are used in recurring situations. But we have little concrete information about the situations in which early Christian traditions were used.

---

8. Cf., e.g., the critical challenges to standard literary criticism in K. Berger, *Exegese des Neuen Testaments*, 27–32, under the rubric: "The question of coherence must take priority over those of interruption and tension" (p. 32). W. Schmithals, on the other hand, combines an aversion to classical form criticism with a confidence in the practicability of literary-critical operations that has little chance of fulfillment, as illustrated by his reconstruction of an underlying text in Mark (*Das Evangelium nach Markus*, 44–51).

9. See the just criticism by K. Haacker, "Leistung und Grenzen der Formkritik."

10. This is the conclusion of E. P. Sanders, *Tendencies of the Synoptic Tradition.* Add to this the often fundamental questions about the conflicting character of written and oral tradition; see W. H. Kelber, *Oral and Written Gospel.*

Simultaneously with the crumbling of the form-critical consensus, hermeneutical reflection has rehabilitated the "cohesive text" as the object of exegesis. The new "axiom" is that meaning constitutes itself in the synchronic text, not in the diachronic text.[11] This attention to the cohesive text gains additional weight through the fact that the texts, in their present form, have acquired further meaning in the course of their history and influence, and it is only in this form that they are accessible to verifiable interpretation. Anyone who reconstructs and interprets texts standing behind the text as presently given can never know whether the reconstructed text may not be the product of an (unconsciously) anticipated interpretation.

The turn to the cohesive text is a welcome corrective to traditional exegesis. Of course, we should recognize that this shift is being carried out by exegetes who are protected against false interpretations through their extensive background knowledge regarding the earlier history of texts and their historical contexts. They have internalized the very "historical-critical exegesis" whose one-sidedness they rightly reject. Without knowledge of everything within the context of the texts as they now stand—their prehistory, their situation, the historical associations and presumptions of the period—an interpretation of "cohesive texts" would be arbitrary. It would lack that corrective historical knowledge that shields us from distorting backward projections of our problems and values into the past and at the same time enables us to discover analogies between then and now that make possible an appropriate encounter with the texts. Proponents of a turn to the cohesive text should therefore hold fast to the historical task of illuminating the environment and history of the texts as much as possible. Whether one includes this task in "exegesis" in the narrower sense or distinguishes it as a separate notion is a secondary question.

The study of cultural context and political history in the Gospels is, in any case, a historical undertaking. It does not claim to comprehend the whole content of the texts. Beginning from the premise that the Gospel tradition had a prehistory that can be newly investigated for each "individ-

---

11. This new "axiom" results from a convergence of a variety of initiatives: (1) linguistic models of thought are totally determined by the primacy of the synchronic over the diachronic—the meaning of a word is determined, not by its etymology, but by its current usage; (2) a consistent redaction criticism, when confronted by apparent tensions, doublets, and other contradictory features in the text, will also inquire about their meaning in the text as it lies before us before evaluating them as indicators of the prehistory of the text, because the author who had the last word must have chosen and approved the text in its final form; and (3) reflection on the history of influence must keep in mind that the texts have had their historical impact, not in an original form as reconstructed by modern scholars, but as completed units.

ual unit," it intends to show that we can partly illuminate this prehistory, just as classical form criticism supposed it could. But it is not restricted to the investigation of the (oral) prehistory. Obviously, the written Gospels can also be studied for indications of place and date.

Previous efforts at investigation of the prehistory of the texts have largely been based on observations of internal evidence and the evaluation of these. The "new initiative" here presented, in contrast, starts with the following consideration: now and then, a comparison of the content of a text with external data furnishes us with a control on analysis of internal text features. These are "lucky breaks." We cannot do "cultural context research" on every text and reconstruct the political situation in the same way that we can subject every pericope to text-critical, redaction-critical, or structure-analytical investigation. But we may hope that individual cases will make visible a network of relationships that will permit us some cautious generalizations about the history of the whole Gospel tradition. The questions that can be answered in this way are, by their very nature, quite simple. Was there a Jesus tradition in Galilee? Can it be traced back to the 30s or 40s? Were there some Jesus traditions that were emphasized in Judea? Can all the Gospels be located outside Palestine? Does a combined overview of our results yield the basic contours of a history of the synoptic tradition?

External data that may be used to shed light on synoptic texts are, first of all, the materials of political history. No matter how intensively the political history of the New Testament has been examined, this work often remained isolated from the interpretation of New Testament texts. There are practical reasons for this. Only a few points exist at which events in the political world intrude into the "text world" of the New Testament, and even there it is disputed whether they really form a background to the texts. This is true even of the greatest political crisis of the first century of our era: the civil wars of 68–69 C.E. and the concurrent Jewish war. For the most part, they are seen as being reflected in the Gospels—especially in the synoptic apocalypses. But there are still some who would date the Gospels before this crisis.[12] So it happens that, in spite of all efforts, the general history of that period and the history of early Christianity have few points of contact. And yet they do exist. A series of factors combine here to produce a "blunting effect" that causes those things that, in reality, shaped the texts and their host communities to appear only indistinctly within the texts.

---

12. See esp. J.A.T. Robinson, *Redating the New Testament*, 13–30, 86–117.

To begin with, we need to keep in mind that what we encounter in texts are not historical events, but interpretations of them. These interpretations follow traditional schemata of apprehension and evaluation. They often intrude so far into the foreground as to awaken the suspicion that we have to do here only with the reproduction of *topoi* and traditions, and not with reactions to concrete situations. The proof that the situation has left its mark usually consists in demonstrating selection and modification of traditional motifs in a text that correlate in a more than accidental way with a situation that admits of reconstruction.

Further, the traditions and interpretations contained in the texts are the expression of limited social perspectives. The host groups of early Christian texts lived in a special world of meaning—removed from the centers of power in Hellenistic-Roman society. They encountered the events of political history as recipients, not as actors. The motives and perspectives of the ruling class were foreign to them. The Qumran community is analogous. We are certain that its texts reflect the political history of Palestine, but that history appears in a perspective that is shattered by sectarianism. The historical connections that appear in the books of the Maccabees or in Josephus are our objective presuppositions, but they cannot be reconstructed from the Qumran texts.

Finally, we need to reckon with a third "blunting factor" that obscures the political history behind the New Testament texts. Even when politics and current events have demonstrably affected the life of early Christian groups, we cannot always count on finding corresponding indications in the texts, because they consciously exclude a good deal. It is striking that in early Christian texts stemming from the first century of our era we hear nothing specific about the Neronian persecution of Christians, although most primitive Christian texts were written after those events. If Tacitus had not reported them (*Ann.* 15.44) it would be very audacious to postulate their existence on the basis of early Christian texts.[13]

In the studies that follow, two major historical crisis situations will, among other factors, play a prominent role: on the one hand, the critical moment under Gaius Caligula when, in the year 40 C.E., he proposed to erect his own statue in the temple at Jerusalem; and, on the other hand, the major political upheaval in the years 68–70 and the Jewish war. I believe that both these periods of political crisis have more powerfully shaped the history of the synoptic tradition than has heretofore been supposed, even when they are reflected only indirectly in the text. If it can

---

13. The first echoes of Nero's persecution are to be found in *1 Clem.* 6.1–2; *Asc. Is.* 4.2–3; *Acta Pauli* 11.1–17. Cf. W. Rordorf, "Die neronische Christenverfolgung."

be shown that both have influenced the synoptic texts, a "history" of these texts stretching over several decades would be visible to us.

The placement of texts within the history of their time is the alpha and omega of historical-critical research and therefore requires no long methodological justification. With localization it is a different story, so long as no direct statements about the place of their origin have been transmitted. While in questions of date we can exclude all earlier time periods by setting a terminus a quo, the matter of location offers a bewildering variety of possibilities if one particular place of origin seems out of the question. That the Gospels were not written in Palestine can be demonstrated on good grounds. But for that very reason we are in the dark here. The delimitation of possible places of origin is more difficult than the limiting of possible times of writing. Even when we can determine that there is a great degree of familiarity with a particular place, that does not mean that the text must have originated there. Consequently, a more thorough discussion of the methodological problems connected with research on cultural context and efforts to localize texts is called for at this point.

The evidence is decisive here as well. What has happened in times past can never be directly observed. It must be retrieved from the witnesses now at hand. In addition to literary sources, there are material remains, including the land in which those earlier events took place—Palestine and the eastern Mediterranean as the locale for the beginnings of Christianity—plus all the artifacts stemming from that time—coins, inscriptions, monuments. I understand the investigation of cultural context to mean the effort to evaluate biblical texts in terms of localizable data, in such a way that text and land, including the archeological remains found there, shed light on one another.

The relationship of the texts to "localizable data" may be determined in several ways. Cultural context can consist in the objective shaping of texts by geographically determinable situations—even when the texts themselves contain no statement or description of place. For example, in Mt 23:29 the "graves of the prophets" are mentioned: familiarity with these could be presumed only in Palestine.[14] But frequently the texts also contain explicit statements of location. That does not mean that they must have been created at the place named. Just as important for their localization is their "local perspective," that is, the question whether a text regards Palestine from an Eastern or from a Western perspective, or whether a "centered" perspective is discernible, from which we could conclude to a

---

14. Cf. J. Jeremias, *Heiligengräber in Jesu Umwelt.*

location in the middle, between the places mentioned. This investigation of "local perspectives" also enables us to say something, even where we find no concrete localizations. So we will never be able to say precisely where the Gospels were written. But we can probably discover the perspective from which they regard Palestine, the place where the events they describe took place.

Investigation of cultural context must also distinguish among localizable data having different structures. In most cases we cannot locate our texts in a concrete "there and then." We must be content to indicate typical place-connections, for example, impressions left by certain regions or types of landscape: sea and land, desert and rivers, mountains and plains, city and country. We would often be happy if we at least knew whether our texts are native to the coastal cities of the Mediterranean or to cities in the interior, whether they come from a large city or from villages remote from the center.[15] Where we must be content with such generalized associations, we may limit the concept of "cultural context" and speak of "cultural milieu."

We may distinguish two possibilities within the category of "cultural milieu": physical milieu (such as desert and mountains) and social milieu (such as city and country). But this distinction can seldom be carried out in a consistent manner. Wherever we encounter the shaping influence of landscapes in history, we are not dealing with "natural landscapes," but with regions that, in the course of struggles over natural resources lasting many centuries and resulting in their division among groups and societies, were created on and around the natural resources: boundaries, relationships of population groups, transportation routes, and settlements are all the precipitates of a long history of work and conflict. Cultural context is always at the same time "social context." If we want to place special emphasis on this social aspect, we can limit the general concept of "cultural context" a second time and speak of "social context" as a special form of "cultural milieu."

A third distinction is related to the meaning of the "time factor" in studies of cultural context. At first glance, locality and landscape appear to be a relatively "timeless" realm, within which the "time-conditioned" events take place. But that is a false impression. Places and landscapes bear the mark of history. Even the physical face of a landscape is the result of a history, and its cultural form is still more the outcome of changes over

---

15. Thus, *Didache* is usually located in country districts. The direction to the apostles to stay only one day in a place would be unrealistic for large or middle-sized cities, according to K. Wengst, ed., *Didache*, 32–33. Conversely, G. Schöllgen ("Die Didache") suggests some doubts about this widespread assignment of the text to a rural setting.

time. "Cultural context" is therefore always, at the same time, "historical context." We know localities and landscapes only in the form they had at a particular epoch. This is as true of structural factors such as the route of a boundary or the location of a town as it is of unique situations that make possible the localization of texts.

One last distinction should be made among "cultural context," "local tradition," and "local archeological remains." A local tradition is always a text, and local archeological remains are always material objects (or possibly inscriptions as vehicles of texts). "Cultural context" refers to the internal shaping of texts by places, while "local tradition" refers to the places where a tradition was handed down. Not all traditions that have a cultural context need be local traditions of those places that have left their mark on them; they could also have been handed down in other places or spread throughout a whole region. And theoretically it could be the case that a local tradition would reveal no particular influence of the place where it was handed down.

For Palestine, many local traditions have been retained. The reports of pilgrims from the Byzantine era to the Middle Ages give a vivid picture of the things that were being told at the localities of the biblical happenings, centuries after those events took place.[16] In most cases it can no longer be determined whether a pious fantasy that longed for concrete vividness connected the events known from the Bible with particular places, or whether there was an independent local tradition about them. Often it is impossible to prove that a local tradition goes back to pre-Byzantine times, before there was a pilgrim trade requiring biblically colored local traditions that had to be created for purposes of edification, if they did not already exist.

Local archeological remains and local traditions should be evaluated independently of one another.[17] Only then is it sometimes possible, with the aid of archeological discoveries, to lend some probability to the pre-Byzantine existence of a local tradition. But at that point we still have not arrived at the historical events spoken of in the New Testament. Let me illustrate this with an example: With the help of archeological finds, we can trace a local tradition about "Peter's house" to pre-Byzantine times.[18] The pilgrim Egeria writes (at the end of the fourth or beginning of the

---

16. See H. Donner's translations, *Pilgerfahrt ins Heilige Land.* An encyclopedic collection of essays on local traditions in New Testament localities can be found in J. Finegan, *Archeology of the New Testament.*

17. On the methodical evaluation of archeological findings, see the summary by O. Keel and M. Küchler, *Orte und Landschaften der Bibel* 1:348–78.

18. Cf. Riesner, *Jesus als Lehrer,* 438–39; idem, "Die Synagoge von Kafarnaum"; idem, "Neues von den Synagogen Kafarnaums."

fifth century) of a church in Capernaum that incorporates the walls of Peter's house (CSEL 39 [1898]: 122–23). Excavations show that, beneath a basilica dating from the fifth century and a church from the fourth century, there really is a first-century private house that may have been used by Jewish Christians as the gathering place of a house church. So, have we found "Peter's house" (Mk 1:29)? Or did a Christian community in Capernaum trace their place of assembly to Peter on the basis of the biblical reports? Can we be sure that Peter's home was really in Capernaum? This corresponds to what the Synoptics say, but contradicts Jn 1:44, according to which Peter and Andrew came from Bethsaida!

Approaches to evaluation of Gospel texts in terms of historical and cultural context have a common problem of method: they leave the world within the text in order to look "outside." But not every text contains a "window," and not every "window" provides a view. Thus the preferred themes in cultural- and historical-context research on the Gospels seem a bit fortuitous. Nevertheless, in the course of research several focal points have emerged. The following sketchy overview of some older and more recent contributions makes no pretension to completeness. It is intended to make clear that the studies in this book are rooted in a larger tradition of research, even if that tradition may have been somewhat off the beaten track. That is not true of all biblical exegesis. In Old Testament research, the study of political history, territorial history, and biblical archeology has always had a respected place. Within New Testament exegesis, however, they led a kind of shadow-existence, partly because the history of early Christianity seemed to have unfolded in relative isolation from larger historical events, partly because it left few archeological traces, and partly because most of the indications of place in the Gospels had fallen under the suspicion of being "fictional." Since K. L. Schmidt's demolition of the geographic and chronological indications in his *Rahmen der Geschichte Jesu*[19] it has been regarded as historically naive to search for "Jesus' places and paths"[20] or to trust the evangelists to have accurate ideas of geography. We do, of course, inquire about the theological importance of the land for the Gospels and for the gospel.[21] Something similar may be said about political history: the renewal of theology in the first half of the twentieth century caused interest in the actual historical contexts of the New Testa-

---

19. Cf. K. L. Schmidt, *Der Rahmen der Geschichte Jesu.* He concludes: "Only occasionally, on the basis of reflection on the internal character of a story, will we be able to fix it somewhat more exactly in time and place" (p. 317). This is just what the study of cultural context aims to do.

20. G. Dalman, *Orte und Wege Jesu.*

21. W. D. Davies (*Gospel and Land,* 366ff.) distinguishes four theological attitudes to the land of Palestine: rejection, spiritualization, historical concern, and sacramental concentration.

ment to retreat into the background. It was more often to be found among "conservative" exegetes who resisted letting the historical Jesus disappear into a cloud of kerygmatic witnesses. This has changed in the past two decades, and we cannot fail to perceive a backlog of interest in cultural and political history.

The works briefly described in the pages that follow can be divided into four groups. Many of them were intended to be direct or indirect contributions to the search for the historical Jesus. A second group tried to illuminate the history of traditions in the Gospel texts. A third group was concerned with the cultural and political backgrounds of the Gospel redaction. As a fourth group we may summarize the attempts to write a history of early Christianity based on religious geography and some first steps in using political history to the same end.

Contributions to the Search for the Historical Jesus

Despite all historical skepticism, it seems assured that Jesus began his activity in Galilee and ended it in Jerusalem. Here we have two foci for the study of cultural context.

W. Bauer has already pointed out that a certain disengagement may be detected in the Jesus traditions as regards the cities: the Hellenistic towns of Sepphoris and Tiberias are not mentioned in it, but neither are the Jewish Jotapata and Tarichea.[22] Sepphoris is only six kilometers from Nazareth. In 1984, R. A. Batey published two essays[23] in which he interpreted some features of the Jesus tradition in terms of this local background: Sepphoris was destroyed by Quintilius Varus in 4 B.C.E. and the inhabitants were sold into slavery as punishment for the rebellion of Judas of Galilee. The city was rebuilt by Herod Antipas and served as his residence until he founded Tiberias circa 19 or 20 C.E. The question arises whether Joseph, a craftsman (τέκτων), together with his son Jesus, might have been acquainted with the life of the Herodian upper class in Sepphoris that Jesus, as a disciple of the Baptizer, so sharply criticized. Did the theater at Sepphoris already exist, although the first certain evidence of it is from the second century? In that case, there could be a concrete experience behind the polemic use of the concept ὑποκριτής (actor) as a metaphor for "hypocrite"! All these questions are justified, even though we may never be able to answer them to complete satisfaction. We still acquire

---

22. W. Bauer, "Jesus der Galiläer." S. Freyne, *Galilee,* offers a summary work on the Galilean cultural context. See also W. Bösen, *Galiläa als Lebensraum und Wirkungsfeld Jesu.*

23. R. A. Batey, "'Is Not This the Carpenter'"; idem, "Jesus and the Theatre." A predecessor is S. J. Case, "Jesus and Sepphoris."

some plausible hypotheses with which to make it understandable that Jesus maintained his distance from the "cities," despite his geographic proximity to them.

Among the Galilean villages, it is especially Capernaum that emerges prominently in the Jesus traditions. We hear several times of Jesus' "house" there (Mk 2:1; 3:20; 9:33). R. Riesner thinks that the reference may be to Jesus' "school" (= house for teaching).[24] He bases this suggestion also on the archeological discoveries mentioned previously, showing that in Capernaum a Byzantine basilica stood over the remains of a private house from the first century C.E.

For Jerusalem, we would refer to the works of J. Jeremias. He not only studied the cultural and political history of "Jerusalem in the time of Jesus,"[25] but also devoted brief essays to concrete place designations in the Gospels such as "Golgotha"[26] and "Bethesda."[27] The excavation of the double pool of Bethesda was for him a confirmation of the historicity of Jn 5:2-9. More recent research by A. Duprez has added a correction to Jeremias's confident affirmation:[28] the double pool of Bethesda envisioned in Jn 2:9 would not have served any therapeutic purpose, but this could have been the case with a subterranean bath that lay nearby; in Jn 5:2-9 two adjoining places have been fused into one. Here investigation of cultural context would shed more light on the tradition-historical background of Jn 5:2-9 than on its historical context. But that is precisely what makes it fruitful.[29]

Political history can contribute only indirectly to research on the historical Jesus. In the reports about Jesus, two figures drawn from political history appear: the Roman prefect Pontius Pilate and the Jewish tetrarch Herod Antipas, about whom we also learn something from other sources. The more nearly the Gospel reports correspond to the contemporary

---

24. Riesner, *Jesus als Lehrer,* 438–39.

25. J. Jeremias, *Jerusalem zur Zeit Jesu.*

26. J. Jeremias, "Golgotha." R. Riesner ("Golgotha und die Archäologie") gives a summary of research to date.

27. J. Jeremias, *Die Wiederentdeckung von Bethesda.*

28. A. Duprez, *Jésus et les dieux guérisseurs.*

29. More recent contributions to the local history of Jerusalem deal with the early Christian period. R. Riesner ("Essener und Urkirche in Jerusalem"), on the basis of new archeological discoveries, has located the center of the original community on the southwest hill of Jerusalem, not far from the Gate of the Essenes, which in the meantime has been found and excavated. Archeological findings at the so-called "Tomb of David" on the southwest hill point to a Jewish-Christian sacred building from the epoch of Aelia Capitolina, possibly on the site where the original community used to assemble. The nearness to the "Gate of the Essenes" would be historically important if we could suppose that there had been an Essene community near such a gate. In that case there would have been a nearby "model" for early Christian love-communism. Here again, a glimpse of the concrete past is fascinating, but nothing can be concluded with certainty.

picture that emerges from other sources, the more trust we can place in their historicity. This convergence of concrete historical interest and search for the historical Jesus is especially evident in the work of E. Stauffer[30] and often leads to overdrawn conclusions. Newer contributions are more modest in their claims. The work of H. W. Hoehner on Herod Antipas[31] and of J.-P. Lémonon on Pilate[32] have developed the source material with care.

Contributions to Tradition History

The search for direct historical confirmation of the Gospel reports in sources external to the text has probably done more damage, in the eyes of critical-minded exegetes, to their value in the search for cultural context and political history than is really deserved; but skepticism about a direct historical application of the traditions is justified. First of all, we should say that it is our task to clarify the sources themselves before we can draw conclusions from them about the events reflected there. But the more skeptical one is about an immediate historical application of the traditions, the more important it will be to localize the texts themselves and to ask where and when they were handed down. The search for cultural context can contribute something to this tradition-historical clarification of the sources.

We find the first efforts toward a locally oriented history of traditions especially in the work of E. Lohmeyer.[33] He found in the Gospel of Mark a theological contrast bound up with the landscapes of Galilee and Judea: Galilee appears as the land in which salvation is revealed, while Jerusalem is the home of opposition to Jesus. He connected this opposition with two original communities in Jerusalem and Galilee, to which he attributed different types of Christology and eucharistic traditions: Galilee honored Jesus as the Son of man, while Jerusalem hailed him as Messiah. In Galilee the Lord's supper was celebrated as a breaking of bread, whereas in Jerusalem it was a meal commemorating his death. Although these theses have not prevailed, it remains our responsibility to explore the post-Easter impact of the history of Jesus in Galilee and to remain open to the possibility that there were several "original communities." Lohmeyer's initiative was carried on by G. Schille and É. Trocmé.

---

30. Cf. E. Stauffer, *Christus und die Caesaren*; idem, *Jesus: Gestalt und Geschichte.* Stauffer placed too much confidence in historical research when he proposed to call it "realistic theology" in contrast to "kerygmatic theology." See idem, "Entmythologisierung oder Realtheologie?"

31. H. W. Hoehner, *Herod Antipas.*

32. J.-P. Lémonon, *Pilate.*

33. E. Lohmeyer, *Galiläa und Jerusalem.* The research of R. H. Lightfoot (*Locality and Doctrine in the Gospels*), undertaken independently of Lohmeyer, points in the same direction.

After the 1920s, when K. Kundsin interpreted the references to place in the Gospel of John as indications of the history of the Christian community and mission,[34] Schille, in the 1950s and 1960s, extended this idea to the synoptic tradition.[35] He regarded localized miracle stories as founding legends of early Christian communities, and thus as documents of "the church's beginnings." Blind Bartimaeus before Jericho was, so to speak, the first convert in that city. The miracles in the Acts of the Apostles, so often told in connection with the founding of church communities, were the model for this kind of etiologic interpretation. In this way, Schille arrives at three regions in Palestine having original Christian communities: to the Galilean communities he attributes older miracle stories, vocation narratives, and the *kyrios* Christology; in the Judean communities he localizes the sayings tradition and the Son of man title; and in the communities of the Jordan Valley he thinks he can locate the pre-Pauline hymns connected with baptism and the Son of God title. Rightly enough, this analysis was not accepted. But it has one advantage: it does not distinguish Palestinian and extra-Palestinian traditions by the use of pure intellectual-historical criteria such as "Jewish" and "Hellenistic." The latter distinction shaped most of the work on a "history of the synoptic tradition" since R. Bultmann. But it has only limited usefulness, because Palestine was under intensive Hellenistic influence for three centuries (M. Hengel).[36]

Trocmé is also a disciple of Lohmeyer.[37] It was his opinion that the miracle stories collected by Mark are the expression of a quasi-animistic mentality in the rural border regions between Syria and Palestine, while the ethically oriented sayings tradition belongs to the urban mentality of Jerusalem. His student, K. Tagawa, concretized these reflections:[38] his explanation for the localities mentioned in the miracle stories is that the author of Mark found the stories in the places where he locates them. Because most of these place indications point to Galilee, it would follow that the miracle stories were a specifically Galilean tradition.

We must admit that, however plausible the general notion of a locally grounded tradition is, the attempts thus far made to render it concrete are not very persuasive. More successful have been the efforts to illuminate the course of synoptic tradition in light of political history. We can mention only a few examples: G. Hölscher gave classic shape to the thesis that the source behind Mark 13 originated in the crisis brought on by

34. K. Kundsin, *Topologische Überlieferungsstoffe im Johannes-Evangelium.*
35. G. Schille, "Die Topographie des Markusevangeliums"; idem, *Anfänge der Kirche.*
36. M. Hengel, *Judentum und Hellenismus.*
37. É. Trocmé, *La formation de l'Evangile selon Marc*, 37–44.
38. K. Tagawa, *Miracles et Évangile.*

Caligula in 40 or 41.[39] G. Zuntz even wanted to date the whole of Mark's Gospel in the year 40 because of chapter 13.[40] But the reference to the Caligula crisis is disputed: P. Bilde, the Danish expert on Josephus, emphatically rejected it.[41] A second example is the dialogue with the sons of Zebedee (Mk 10:35-45). The martyr's death of James predicted there (*ex eventu?*) occurred during the reign of Agrippa I (41–44 C.E.; cf. Acts 12:2). This pericope is related to a datable event.[42] A methodically exemplary instance of the use of political history to clarify the history of tradition is O. H. Steck's analysis of Mt 23:34-36.[43] The murder of the Zechariah mentioned there could originally have been that of the last prophet named in the historical books of the Old Testament, in 2 Chr 24:20ff. In Matthew (and only there) it has become an event in the time of the Christian community. Here it probably refers to Zachariah, son of Baris (Baruch), who was murdered by the Zealots in 67 or 68 C.E. (cf. *Bell.* 4.335).

Contributions to Redaction Criticism

Despite intensive research, we still do not know exactly where and when the Gospels were written. Introductory works describe the various attempts to locate them. Here I will mention only a few of the newer contributions whose thoughtful argumentation commands respect. J. Zumstein[44] has revived the thesis that Matthew's Gospel originated in Antioch, where Jewish and gentile Christians lived together from the beginning, a circumstance that is said to explain the existence of Jewish and gentile Christian tendencies side by side in that Gospel. H. D. Slingerland[45] has defended the thesis of a Transjordanian origin for Matthew's Gospel, because for this evangelist Judea lies "beyond the Jordan" (Mt 19:1). Hengel[46] gives a series of attractive arguments for locating Mark's Gospel at Rome, where he thinks it was written after Nero's persecution (Mk 13:12) and before the destruction of the temple, circa 68 or 69 C.E. He has also shown the probability that the author of Luke-Acts made a visit to Jerusalem, for he has a detailed knowledge of the layout of the temple (see, e.g., Acts 21:34-35). In my opinion, however, he need not necessarily have been a com-

---

39. G. Hölscher, "Der Ursprung der Apokalypse Mk 13."
40. G. Zuntz, "Wann wurde das Evangelium Marci geschrieben?"
41. P. Bilde, "Afspejler Mark 13."
42. Cf. E. Schwartz, "Über den Tod der Söhne Zebedäi."
43. O. H. Steck, *Israel und das gewaltsame Geschick der Propheten*, 26–33, 50–53, 282–83.
44. J. Zumstein, "Antioche sur l'Oronte et l'évangile selon Matthieu."
45. H. D. Slingerland, "Transjordanian Origin of St. Matthew's Gospel."
46. M. Hengel, "Entstehungszeit"; idem, "Der Historiker Lukas." On Luke, see also H. Klein ("Zur Frage nach dem Abfassungsort der Lukasschriften"), who thinks that the Lukan writings originated in Caesarea.

panion of Paul on his last journey: many Jews and God-fearers visited the temple before its destruction. The author of Luke-Acts could have been one of them, or could have been closely associated with some such Jerusalem pilgrims. But of course he himself could also have been in Jerusalem. Finally, we should mention a new theory about John's Gospel: K. Wengst located it in the area controlled by Herod Agrippa II after the Jewish war, among other reasons because at the time the Fourth Gospel was written it was only there that Jews still had political power and thus could appear in that Gospel as representatives of a hostile outside world.[47]

As far as Mark's Gospel is concerned, the timing of its redaction by reference to political history has a long tradition. A connection with the Jewish war is usually presumed. Either the evangelist is writing in Rome (Hengel)[48] or in Palestine (W. Marxsen)[49] shortly before the destruction of the temple, or, as most exegetes think, he knows of the destruction of the temple in the year 70 C.E. But one seldom finds an interpretation of the whole of Mark's Gospel as a response to the war crisis. There are beginnings in that direction in the work of S.G.F. Brandon, when he reads Mark as an apology of Roman Christians who are attempting to distance themselves from Judaism in face of the hatred of the Jews evoked by the war.[50] A location of the other two Gospels in reference to political history is more difficult. W. Stegemann's effort to connect Luke-Acts with the repressive religious politics of Domitian, in light of the legal situation presupposed in the conflict scenes in Acts, is impressive.[51] Regarding Matthew's Gospel, we might mention W. D. Davies's thesis that the Sermon on the Mount is a response to Jamnia, that is, a Christian reaction to the new organization of Judaism in the Jamnian school after the catastrophe of 70 C.E.[52]

Contributions to the History of
Early Christianity

It seems reasonable to proceed from datable or localizable complexes of tradition to a comprehensive picture of the beginnings of Christianity.

---

47. K. Wengst, *Bedrängte Gemeinde und verherrlichter Christus.*

48. Hengel ("Entstehungszeit," 1ff.) seems to me persuasive in seeing a connection between the crisis situation of the years 68–70 and the origin of Mark's Gospel, a connection that would still have existed if the Gospel were written somewhat later.

49. W. Marxsen, *Der Evangelist Markus.*

50. S.G.F. Brandon, *Trial of Jesus of Nazareth.* Brandon's other work is also worth noting for its description of the interaction of political history and that of early Christianity. Cf. idem, *Fall of Jerusalem;* idem, *Jesus and the Zealots.*

51. W. Stegemann, "Zwischen Synagoge und Obrigkeit" (Habil, Heidelberg, 1982).

52. W. D. Davies, *Setting of the Sermon on the Mount.*

The broadest proposal in this direction was offered by H. Koester and J. M. Robinson in *Trajectories through Early Christianity*.[53] This project was carried out by Koester in his major work in 1980.[54] There he shows how early Christianity bloomed in successive stages in a variety of local centers: first in Syria, then in the Aegean region, in the late second century in Egypt, and later in North Africa, while Rome was significant for the history of early Christianity from an early date. In this same field of research on the beginnings of Christianity, F. Vouga presented an outline of a theological geography of the early movement.[55] He distinguished four groups: the Jewish Christians of Jerusalem, the Hellenists, the Palestinian itinerant charismatics, and another Palestine movement of apocalyptically oriented prophets. K. Berger also suggested a geographically oriented theological history of early Christianity.[56] He proposes that there were several theological centers besides Palestine, especially Damascus (Gospel of John), Ephesus (Colossians, Pastorals, Barnabas) and Rome, to which he attributes both the common material basic to a number of New Testament writings and certain clearly localizable writings.[57] Remarkably enough, there are no proposals for a history of early Christianity in which political-historical aspects give fundamental shape to the whole. Political history often appears only as a general background against which early Christianity stands out. The reciprocal influences that certainly existed between it and early Christian history remain unclear. Here is a task for the future.

Once the method and theme of a cultural-historical and political-historical study of the Gospels have been laid out, we will be better able to determine their relationship to other exegetical approaches. As emphasized previously, the study of cultural context and political history in the Gospels makes no comprehensive hermeneutical claim. It does not aim to determine the meaning of the text itself, but instead to identify the context in which its meaning becomes visible, vital, and often, for the first time, unambiguous. In order to make its contribution clear, we will discuss the evaluation of texts in terms of cultural context and political history with reference to two dimensions that are present in every work of exegesis. The first dimension is determined by the polarity of generalization

---

53. H. Koester and J. M. Robinson, *Trajectories through Early Christianity*.
54. H. Koester, *Einführung in das Neue Testament*.
55. F. Vouga, "Pour une géographie théologique."
56. Berger, *Einführung in die Formgeschichte*, 186–202.
57. An overview of work on local history can be found in several reference works. Two deserve special mention because they document the reawakened interest in local studies: Finegan, *Archeology of the New Testament;* and Keel and Küchler, *Orte und Landschaften der Bibel,* which will long remain a standard work in biblical scholarship.

and individualization, the second by the distinction of questions that are immanent to the text from those that transcend the text. An exegesis generalizes when it formulates its results with the aid of a "net" of general categories. Paradigmatic for generalizing exegesis are grammatic analyses and textual linguistics, as well as all interpretations that make use of general theoretical models. On the other hand, an exegesis individualizes when it analyzes texts as historically unique events, for example, tradition-historical work on concrete texts aimed at detecting their unique history.

The contrast of text-immanent and text-transcending interpretation overlaps with the polarity of generalizing and individualizing exegesis. A text can be examined as a literary phenomenon, to uncover its structures, images, and statements in such a way that these alone, through their mutual relationships, permit us to recognize a meaningful "world" therein. Or it can be located within its real life-context, in space and time, in history and society, so that we can interpret it as the expression of a historically shaped and fully rounded life. In doing so, we leave the world immanent to the text and order the text within a more comprehensive "real world."

Undoubtedly, the study of cultural context and political history belongs among the individualizing and text-transcending approaches: place and time are something unique and individual; geography and archeology lead us beyond the world within the text. It is impossible to exploit the entire meaning of texts in this way. Other approaches must come into play, as illustrated in Table 1.

The studies that follow seek to substantiate two common hermeneutical insights. First, text-immanent analyses need to be enhanced by text-transcending approaches. If we restrict ourselves, as happens in many form-critical and tradition-historical studies, to the analysis of layers, forms, and intentions, many of our results remain arbitrary. We will only begin to trust such analyses if they are now and again substantiated by proofs external to the text—at least in the present state of our knowledge, which is characterized by the crumbling of the "form-critical consensus."

Still more important is the second hermeneutical insight: the individualizing approach characteristic of the study of cultural context and political history can be renewed and deepened by integrating it with the generalizing approach. An integration with social history will be especially fruitful in this regard. When we have learned, through the study of social history, how important the coordination of texts with surviving structures is, we will recognize also in our study of cultural context how important it is to be able to perceive the urban or rural milieu, the typical phenomena of distance and proximity. A style of historical writing that is oriented to individual events and persons may regard such a general orientation

TABLE 1

	Text-immanent	*Text-transcending*
individualizing	e.g., history of traditions	e.g., cultural context and political history
generalizing	e.g., structuralism	e.g., social history

to milieus and typical situations as a deficit of historical perception. But for a social history oriented to structures and types of conflicts, this method yields important insights.

After this sketchy overview of the method, theme, and hermeneutic of our approach, we may conclude by introducing the studies on cultural context and political history in the Gospels that make up this book. The starting point is always a simple inquiry about the indications of date and place in the texts. Through connections between text-internal data, it should be possible to date and locate texts more precisely. The method uses limited, individual probes, but we expect that a collective view of many single points will yield a picture of overarching developments. Ultimately, the following investigations are conceived as a partial contribution to a "history of the synoptic tradition" from its beginnings to the various written versions in the Gospels.

The first part is devoted to the "small units" in the synoptic tradition. Not all of these can be analyzed. Our starting point will, in each case, be a specimen study of examples from the logia and narrative traditions, to be followed by a brief examination of the remaining logia and narrative corpus with a view to temporal placement and local connection, to allow us to judge whether the specimen example permits generalizing conclusions or not.

The second part is concerned with "large units" in the synoptic tradition, that is, with texts that were originally created as complex compositions. Here the synoptic apocalypse will serve as an example of sayings tradition and the Passion story as an example of narrative tradition. Although, in my opinion, we can trace the origins of some of the smaller units back to Galilee and its vicinity—this is a thesis of Part I—the two "major units" here studied are traceable to Jewish communities and were shaped in different ways by their closeness to or distance from the Caligula crisis of 40 C.E.

The subjects of the third part are the "Gospel redactions." Their location also can, within limits, be more precisely determined. We must do without concrete place names, but a designation of the general perspective may well be possible. A hypothesis will emerge, according to which Mark's Gospel partakes of the perspective of Palestine's neighbors (and thus originated neither in Palestine nor in Rome, but in the vicinity of Palestine). For Matthew's Gospel an Eastern perspective is probable, for Luke's a Western view. None of the three Gospels, then, would have originated in Palestine, although they contain materials of Palestinian origin. But all are shaped, in different ways, by their closeness to and distance from the Jewish war of 66–74 C.E.

We will conclude with a summary of the results of these investigations for a "history of the synoptic tradition." Let me emphasize at the outset that studies in cultural context and political history are only a small part of the reflections that will be necessary in order to pursue form criticism and tradition history in the present—not by reiterating the fundamental assumptions formulated a half-century ago, but by critically reviewing and reformulating them.

PART I

SOCIAL CONTEXT AND POLITICAL HISTORY IN THE SMALL UNITS OF THE SYNOPTIC TRADITION

1

The Beginnings of the
Sayings Tradition in Palestine

Most modern readers simply imagine Jesus' words as being spoken in the Palestinian milieu, and for a long time this conception was generally undisputed among scholars as well. Adolf von Harnack characterized the traditions collected in Q as speeches and sayings of Jesus with "an almost exclusively Galilean horizon."[1] Q itself was composed "obviously in Palestine," and the "Jewish-Palestinian horizon"[2] was traceable to the authentic proclamation of Jesus. But Julius Wellhausen, although he regarded the Sayings Source as later than Mark's Gospel and was more skeptical about the authenticity of the traditions collected in it, also believed it had been written in Jerusalem; he conceded only that in Q the horizon was broadened: "In Q Jesus rises above the Jewish horizon which contains him in Mark."[3] Siegfried Schulz's analysis of the Sayings Source arrives at a different result. Certainly there are a few old traditions that are at home in the "border regions of Palestine and Transjordania,"[4] but the bulk of the material belongs within a newer layer of traditions from Syrian gentile Christian communities. Among the latter traditions are the judgment on John (Mt 11:7-11 par.), the sign of Jonah (Mt 12:38-42 par.), the saying about the "pilgrimage of nations" (Mt 8:11-12 par.), and the lament over the Galilean cities (Mt 11:21-24 par.)—traditions with a recognizable local perspective. In view of the fact that scholarship has yielded so many contradictory results, it will be worthwhile to make a systematic evaluation of as many local clues as possible in order to arrive at a more precise determination of the native places and ancestry of individual traditions.

---

1. A. von Harnack, *Beiträge zur Einleitung in das Neue Testament* 2:121.
2. Ibid., 2:172.
3. J. Wellhausen, *Einleitung*, 165.
4. S. Schulz, *Q*, 166.

THE "SHAKEN REED" IN MT 11:7 AND THE
FOUNDATION COINS OF TIBERIAS

According to Mt 11:7, Jesus calls to the people who are going out to the Baptizer in the desert: "What did you go out into the wilderness to look at? A reed shaken by the wind?" It had to be immediately evident to the first addressees and tradents what was meant by the "reed in the wind." For us, though, it is a riddle. Basically, there are two interpretations possible: either the "shaken reed" is to be taken literally, in which case the actual landscape of Palestine is reflected in this saying, or else this is an image that needs to be interpreted on the basis of the fund of imagery in the traditions available at that time.

In principle, a literal interpretation is possible: there were reeds both in the Jordan meadows and on the borders of Lake Gennesaret. They could grow to a height of five meters.[5] In that case, there would be two possible interpretations of Mt 11:7. A wavering reed is something common in the Jordan desert. But the people going out to John had not come to see something ordinary; instead, they were going into the desert, the traditional place of divine revelation,[6] to encounter a prophet.[7] In this interpretation, the people's expectations would be accepted and affirmed by the rhetorical question. Another possible reading looks toward a critical evaluation: the movement aroused by the Baptizer had subsided. "His word and deeds had no lasting effect. It was as if they had only been looking at a reed moved by the wind, or as if they had run after a person in a magnificent robe."[8]

Both interpretations are unsatisfying. That the "shaken reed" refers exclusively to the realities of the Palestinian environment is unlikely in view of the second question: "What then did you go out to see? Someone clothed in soft robes?" This question is formally parallel to the first, but its content would be in contrast to it, for (literally understood) the former would be asking about something that is actually found in the Jordan desert, and the latter about the sort of person who is certainly not to be found there.[9]

---

5. Cf. G. Dalman, *Orte und Wege Jesu*, 91.
6. That the desert is the place of God's revelation is something established since the Old Testament exodus and wilderness traditions. For the New Testament period, we may refer to the Qumran community, which interpreted Isa 40:3 in terms of its desert life (1QS8.12–14); consider also the prophets proffering signs and announcing a renewal of God's saving deeds in the wilderness (Jos. *Bell.* 2.250; 7.438).
7. E. Klostermann defends this interpretation (*Das Markusevangelium*, 96).
8. A. Schlatter, *Der Evangelist Matthäus*, 362.
9. F. Bleek had already come out against the literal interpretation: "Only then one would expect something else to be mentioned in the following verse that one could really anticipate finding in the desert, which is not the case; also, the ὑπὸ ἀνέμου σαλευόμενον would be a

Consequently, there have been repeated attempts at a metaphorical interpretation. The most likely possibility is to see in the "shaken reed" a reflection of wavering human beings. So Lucian, in his dialogue *Hermotimus, or Concerning the Sects*, speaks of those who, lacking judgment, are at the mercy of their teachers. He warns a student: "You will be like water spilled on a table, running whithersoever someone pulls you by the tip of his finger, or indeed like a reed [καλάμῳ] growing on a river bank, bending to every breath of wind, however slight the breeze that blows and shakes it [διασαλεύσῃ αὐτὸν]" (*Hermot.* 68). Older exegetes thought concretely, in Mt 11:7, of the wavering of the Baptizer, who in the preceding pericope sent to ask whether Jesus is really the one who is to come, an interpretation that became questionable as a consequence of form-critical recognition of the original isolation of synoptic pericopes.[10]

Thus, if we cannot interpret the image from the literary context of Matthew's Gospel, we must have recourse to the image itself and the traditional meaning attached to it. In the tradition accessible to us, it appears in two ways: as image of judgment and as fable.

The swaying of the reed can, in Jewish and Old Testament tradition, be an image for God's act of judgment that shakes and shatters human beings. So in Ahijah's prophecy against Jeroboam we read: "the Lord will strike Israel, as a reed [LXX: ὁ κάλαμος] is shaken in the water; he will root up Israel out of this good land that he gave to their ancestors" (1 Kgs 14:15). The Ptolemaic king Philopator is punished by God because he entered the temple: "[God] shook him on this side and that as a reed [ὡς κάλαμον] is shaken by the wind" (3 Macc 2:22). If the servant of God does not break a "bruised reed" (Isa 42:3) that is a sign that he protects those who are already injured. Should the "shaken reed" in Mt 11:7 be understood, then, as an image of judgment?[11] In that case, the only possible interpretation would be: Surely you did not go out into the desert to see God's prophet himself become a "shaken reed"—the same person who is proclaiming judgment on others!

---

superfluous addition" (*Synoptische Erklärung der drei ersten Evangelien*, 447–48.). But the parallelism of the first and second questions is also introduced as an argument for the literal interpretation. Thus A. Plummer (*Critical and Exegetical Commentary on St. Luke*, 204) concludes from the fact that ἄνθρωπον is unmetaphorical that the reed must also be intended literally. The "emblematic" reading presented here is intended precisely to overcome this alternative of literal or metaphorical interpretation.

10. This interpretation from the context is still defended today by W. F. Albright and C. S. Mann, *Matthew*, 136. J. Wellhausen had already rejected this opinion, saying, "Otherwise we would have to think of the Baptizer's wavering in regard to Jesus; but a real connection with 11:2-6 is unlikely" (*Das Evangelium Matthaei*, 52).

11. E. Schweizer (*Das Evangelium nach Matthäus*, 169) points to 1 Kgs 14:15 and 3 Macc 2:22 as parallels to this use of the image of the "shaken reed," but then adopts the usual interpretation: John the Baptizer was not a weather vane or a weakling.

The interpretation of the image as fable is more common. One version of Aesop's fable of the tree and the reed says:

> An Oak that grew on the bank of a river was uprooted by a severe gale of wind, and thrown across the stream. It fell among some Reeds growing by the water, and said to them, "How is it that you, who are so frail and slender, have managed to weather the storm, whereas I, with all my strength, have been torn up by the roots and hurled into the river?" "You were stubborn," came the reply, "and fought against the storm, which proved stronger than you: but we bow and yield to every breeze, and thus the gale passed harmlessly over our heads."

This fable is current in many variations, including three in the corpus of Aesop alone. Trees (*Reed* 179c), oak (*Reed* 17), and olive tree (*Reed* 179b) are contrasted with the acquiescent reed. The fable later appears in Babrios (no. 36) and Avian (no. 16). It has even penetrated the rabbinic tradition (*b. Taan.* 20[b]; cf. *Der. Er. Zut.* 4; *Aboth R. Nat.* 41). Many exegetes see in Mt 11:7 a reference to this fable tradition: the Baptizer is no wavering reed who accommodates himself to circumstance. He shows steadfastness even against princes. This interpretation has most recently been defended by D. Flusser: "When Jesus . . . spoke about the reed shaken by the wind, he was referring to courtiers who live in the houses of kings and wear soft garments (Mt 11:7-9; Lk 7:24-26). He is thinking of the tetrarch's court and John the Baptizer and applying the Aesopian fable of the oak and the reed to them. The Baptizer is the oak, the courtiers are the reed."[12] But this interpretation is not fully satisfying either: the fable clearly gives a positive evaluation of the wavering reed, and sees the resistant oak negatively. Is John the Baptizer being represented as a blinded, stiff-necked person who is responsible for his own demise? That is scarcely imaginable.

The Reed as Emblem of Herod Antipas

In the following pages we will attempt to get beyond the alternative of literal or metaphorical interpretation by means of an "emblematic interpretation." The reed appears on Herod Antipas's first coins, which he had minted for the founding of his capital city, Tiberias (ca. 19 C.E.).[13]

---

12. D. Flusser, "Das Wesen der Gleichnisse," 52. T. Zahn (*Das Evangelium des Matthäus*, 421) had already said the same. For the translation of the Aesopian fable, see *Aesop's Fables. A New Translation by V. S. Vernon Jones, with an Introduction by G. K. Chesterton and Illustrations by Arthur Rackham* (New York, 1939), 36. Note the remarkable interpretation of C. Daniel, "Les Esséniens." The reed (*qane*) would refer to the Zealots. A Zealot is a *qanna*. The Zealots were attacked by their enemies in the desert, that is, shaken by the wind!

13. On the founding of Tiberias, see M. Avi-Yonah, "The Founding of Tiberias"; H. W. Hoehner, *Herod Antipas*, 91–100. Particularly for the dating of its founding, see Y. Meshorer, *Jewish Coins*, 74.

Coins are the oldest means of mass communication—in antiquity the only medium through which powerful political figures could reach almost all their subjects. The images on coins reflect political programs. Is this true also of the plant motifs on the coins of Herod Antipas? Certainly it is, in the broader sense that the tetrarch of Galilee and Perea, by his choice of this motif, depicted himself to his subjects as a pious Jew: the Old Testament–Jewish prohibition of images forbade representations of animals and human beings.[14] His coins show three types of plants.

The first (and oldest) type of coin[15] very probably shows a reed (*Canna communis*) on the obverse (Fig. 1). It was minted only for the founding of Tiberias and later disappeared. The second type of coin[16] is attested from the years 26–27 C.E. Unmistakably, Antipas has moved to a new vegetable emblem, probably a palm tree (Fig. 2). From the last year of Antipas's reign (39 C.E.) comes a third type of coin.[17] It represents a palm branch (Fig. 3).

For us, the first coin is especially interesting. Does the reed we find there throw new light on the "reed in the wind" in Mt 11:7? Or is this a reed at all? W. Wirgin has argued against it,[18] saying that the foundation coins from Tiberias depict a laurel branch like those the emperors from Augustus to Nero held in their hands during their triumphal processions. After Nero, the laurel was replaced by a palm branch. However we interpret the foundation coins of Tiberias, a change of symbols in the triumphal processions after Nero (54–68 C.E.) certainly cannot explain the change of emblems on Antipas's coins between 19 and 30 C.E. Chronology is against it. Besides, an interpretation of the plant motif on Antipas's oldest coins as a laurel branch is scarcely tenable: Tiberias's designers depicted laurel crowns on the reverse of some coins, and in so doing showed leaves of a very different shape.[19]

Furthermore, a mosaic from the Byzantine Basilica of the Multiplica-

---

14. Herod Antipas adhered to the prohibition of images on his publicly circulating coins. But there were animal images in his palace—an offense to strict believers. Josephus therefore received orders from Jerusalem to destroy that palace, but a more radical party got there ahead of him (*Vita* 65–66).

15. This type is found in several variants; cf. the illustrations in Meshorer, *Jewish Coins*, nos. 63, 64, and 65; see also F. A. Madden, *Jewish Coinage*, 97, no. 1, the source of the drawing reproduced here. A. Kindler (*The Coins of Tiberias*) unfortunately does not treat this type of coin.

16. Photographs in Meshorer, *Jewish Coins*, nos. 66–73. The drawing is from Madden, *Jewish Coinage*, 97, no. 2.

17. Photographs in Meshorer, *Jewish Coins*, no. 75. Drawing from Madden, *Jewish Coinage*, 99, no. 6.

18. W. Wirgin, "A Note on the 'Reed' of Tiberias." In contrast, Meshorer (*Jewish Coins*, 73–75) interprets it as a reed, as does M. Avi-Yonah in his "Prolegomenon" to Madden's *Jewish Coinage*, xxix—differing from Madden who thinks of it as a palm branch (p. 97).

19. Cf. Madden, *Jewish Coinage*, 98, no. 5.

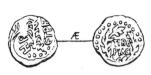

FIGURE 1

FIGURE 2

FIGURE 3

tion of the Loaves on the north shore of Lake Gennesaret reveals how an artist working in that landscape pictured reeds (Fig. 4).[20] Certainly, the artist could have come from Egypt; the Nilometer on the mosaic shows a familiarity with Egyptian motifs.[21] However, the choice of a maritime or river landscape in a church on the shore of Lake Gennesaret could be inspired by the Galilean landscape. The similarity of the plants on the foundation coins of Tiberias to the reed on the mosaic is striking. Here, as there, the heads of the rushes are missing.

We will therefore assume that the interpretation of the emblem on the coins as a reed is the most likely one. There are four reasons why the choice of such a motif would at least be understandable.

1. Reeds are a common submotif on the coins of cities located on rivers. They appear as an attribute of a river god.[22] When Antipas set up his first mint, he would probably have had to call on experienced minters. Reeds were part of their repertoire. Because they had to work on orders from a Jewish prince and images of gods were excluded from the start, a secondary image could easily have become the coins' primary motif.

---

20. The mosaic comes from the end of the fourth or beginning of the fifth century. Cf. J. Finegan, *Archeology of the New Testament*, 48ff. A basic source is A. M. Schneider, *Die Brotvermehrungskirche in et-Tabga.* Cf. also S. Loffreda, *Die Heiligtümer von Tabgha.*

21. Josephus also attests to a local tradition, according to which a powerful spring on the north shore of the Galilean Sea, called Capharnaum, was connected with the Nile: "Some have imagined this to be a branch of the Nile, from its producing a fish resembling the *coracin* found in the lake of Alexandria" (*Bell.* 3.520).

22. Cf. E. Demole, *Fluss- und Meergötter,* nos. 18, 162, 205, and frequently elsewhere. Less fruitful is F. Imhoof-Blumer/O. Keller, *Tier- und Pflanzenbilder auf Münzen und Gemmen des Klassischen Altertums* 10:10, 19:63.

FIGURE 4

2. Antipas could model himself on his brothers, who had begun issuing their own coinage long before. Coins of Archelaus come from the years 4 B.C.E. to 6 C.E.; those of Herod Philip begin in the first year of our era and extend to his last year (34 C.E.). But Antipas began minting only when he had already been reigning for twenty years (in the years 18–20 C.E.). His brothers always chose motifs that were characteristic of their territory. Seven of Archelaus's coin styles bear symbols of seafaring.[23] Only Archelaus had access to the sea, with the port of Caesarea (and a smaller one at Joppa) at his disposal. Philip placed a (pagan) temple on his coins,[24] very probably the temple of Augustus at Paneas, the token of his capital, which he called "Caesarea Philippi." Because he ruled considerable gentile terri-

---

23. Meshorer, *Jewish Coins,* 69, cf. nos. 56–60.
24. Ibid., nos. 76–84.

tories, he could dare to use pagan symbols. In contrast, Herod Antipas, the only son of Herod the Great, who reigned over purely Jewish territory, held strictly to the prohibition of images. He chose a plant motif characteristic of his new capital at Tiberias: a reed like those that grew on the banks of the "Lake of Tiberias."[25]

3. The harmless reed was also a good political choice. Herod Antipas ruled over geographically separate districts: between Galilee and Perea lay a strip of Hellenistic republican cities. This splitting of his territories was a clever move in the division of the land after Herod's death: while the other two sons governed regions that were geographically united but ethnically divided (among Samaritans, Jews, and Syrians), Antipas's territory was ethnically homogeneous but geographically divided—a political problem for him. Herod Antipas had to look for an emblem that would unite the two parts of his realm. They were joined together geographically by the Jordan, which flows through the Lake of Galilee and forms the western border of Perea. A "reed" could be understood both in Galilee and in Perea as a native symbol.[26]

4. One could object that a reed is much too modest a plant to carry so much weight in the choice of a motif. Nevertheless, the reed appears in two descriptions of Palestine by ancient authors. Thus it was regarded by those outside Palestine as especially characteristic of that country. Strabo describes the land through which the Jordan flows in these words: "It also contains a lake, which produces the aromatic rush and reed [κάλαμον]; and likewise marshes. This lake is called Gennesaritis" (*Geogr.* 16.2.16).[27] It is possible that Strabo here confuses the swampy Lake Huleh with Lake Gennesaret. But we ought to consider that he distinguishes lake and swamps and calls the lake "Gennesar," which can only be the Lake of Galilee. Pliny the Elder, in discussing various kinds of reeds (*harundo*), singles out for special mention those of Judea and Syria, which are used for cosmetic and therapeutic purposes: "et quo plura genera faciamus,

---

25. Ibid., 75: "Antipas looked for a special design to symbolize the foundation of Tiberias and found it in the reed, the characteristic vegetation of the region of Tiberia." The later coins from Tiberias also reveal an unmistakable local context. Kindler *(Coins of Tiberias)* gives a survey of these emblems. If the goddess Hygeia (nos. 3b and 16) and the god Serapis (no. 15) appear here, the motivation is the healing springs of Hammath near Tiberias; anchor (no. 5) and galley (no. 10) are related to the Lake of Galilee.

26. When Antipas later replaces the reed emblem with palm branches and palm trees, he again chooses a plant that is found in both parts of his land. Palms are attested on the banks of the Dead Sea (Pliny the Elder *Nat. Hist.* 5.15). In Egeria's account of her pilgrimage to the Holy Land in 385–88 C.E., "many palm trees" are mentioned on the north side of the Lake of Galilee (*Peregrinatio ad loca sancta*, ed. Geyer, 113).

27. *The Geography of Strabo*, with an English translation by H. L. Jones (vols. 1–6, 8) and W.H.S. Jones (vol. 7), 8 vols. (Cambridge, Mass., and London, 1917–32). The text, with translation and extensive commentary, can also be found in M. Stern, *GLAJJ* 1:288–89.

ille, quae in Iudaea Syriaque nascitur odorum unguentorumque causa, urinam movet cum gramine aut apis semine decocta; ciet et menstrua admota" ("To increase the number of the various reeds there is that which grows in Judea and Syria and is used for scents and unguents; boiled down with grass or celery seed this is diuretic, and when made into a pessary acts as an emmenagogue"; *Nat. Hist.* 24.85).[28]

The choice of the vegetation motif "reed" on Antipas's first coins would, then, be quite logical: it deals with a well-known attribute of Palestine, especially of the Jordan Valley. It unites the two separated parts of the country and grows on the border of the Lake of Galilee, where Herod Antipas founded his capital city—the city whose founding was the reason and occasion for his first coinage.

Herod Antipas—The Shaken Reed?

What does the reed emblem on the foundation coin of Tiberias have to do with the "shaken reed" in Mt 11:7? The connection would exist if Jesus' word about the "shaken reed" referred to Herod Antipas, the Baptizer's opponent. We will now examine this from numismatic, literary, and historical evidence. I believe that it can be shown as probable, from all three perspectives, that the "reed shaken by the wind" refers to Antipas.

The Numismatic Evidence

The reed and Herod Antipas could readily be associated because of the foundation coins of Tiberias, since on those coins the reed emblem replaces the usual heads of the coining monarchs and rulers. The legend punched around the reed's image, HPΩΔ(OY) TETPA(PXOY),[29] would have deepened and cemented this association. It says that the coin belongs to Antipas, the ruler—but in place of his head, there is the image of a reed.

But can we presuppose that the simple people of Palestine would have connected the emblems on the obverse of coins with the rulers who had them minted? I think there can be no doubt of it. The point of the controversy story about the census (Mk 12:13-17) is based on just this connection. And this same close identification is presupposed in the coinage of other Herodian rulers. Herod Philip's oldest coin is especially revealing here. It shows the head of Augustus, but with a totally unsuitable legend: (ΦI ΛI ΠΠ)OY TETPA(PXOY).[30] Nothing could better express the established expectation of seeing the coining monarch depicted on the obverse than this mis-coinage from Herod Philip's mint. No less revealing

---

28. Cf. Stern, *GLAJJ* 1:496.
29. Meshorer, *Jewish Coins,* 133.
30. Ibid., no. 76.

are the coins of King Agrippa I, who ruled all Palestine from 41–44 C.E. In heavily gentile Caesarea he, as the first Jewish ruler, had coins made bearing his own portrait,[31] while on other coins he shows the head of the emperor Claudius.[32] But in deference to his Jewish subjects he had another type of coin made for his Jewish territories, on which a canopy has replaced his portrait.[33] The canopy represents a personal attribute of Oriental potentates: the king probably appeared under such a canopy when he was in Jerusalem.

If a personal attribute can replace a portrait, then conversely everything that appears in place of the usual portrait can be regarded as a personal attribute, even if it is otherwise intended by the coining monarch. People would have bestowed minute scrutiny and comment on the first coins of Antipas to appear in the country. Would not some wit have made a joke: look at Antipas, the wavering reed? There were enough reasons to ridicule Antipas. The founding of his capital city, Tiberias, was not uncontroversial. It was laid on unclean ground. The city's population was, at least partly, of dubious background (*Ant.* 18.36–38). The city remained a foreign body within Galilee. The Jesus traditions have nothing to say about it. Therefore, it would be understandable if the foundation coins of the city were the subject of critical comment.

There is a revealing analogy to the use of figures on coins as code names for rulers in the Book of Daniel. In Dan 7:7 the fourth beast symbolizes the Seleucid kingdom. Its horns depict the various Seleucid rulers. These horns are found on coins from the time of Seleucis I Nicator and Antiochos I Soter.[34] If the horns on Seleucid coins could become symbols of the Seleucids, it is also possible that the "reed" on Herod Antipas's coins could become an ironic name with which to ridicule this Herodian ruler.

The Literary Evidence

Does the literary tradition in Mt 11:7-9 also give good reason to think of Herod Antipas in connection with the "shaken reed"? We need to begin with some observations on the form of the brief apophthegm. Matthew

---

31. Ibid., nos. 85, 90, 92, 93.

32. Ibid., nos. 86, 87, 89.

33. Ibid., no. 88 A and B. On these coins, see J. Meyshan, "The Canopy Symbol on the Coins of Agrippas I."

34. Cf. S. Morenz, "Das Tier mit den vier Hörnern." I am grateful to O. Keel and M. Küchler for this reference to the Seleucid coins.

11:7-9 consists of three parallel rhetorical questions.[35] The first two are to be answered "No!" and the last "Yes!"—whereby the truth is more than is stated by a simple affirmative answer to the question. The Baptizer is not only a prophet; he is more than that.

> 1. What did you go out into the wilderness to look at?
>   A reed shaken by the wind?
>   ....

> 2. What then did you go out to see?
>   Someone dressed in soft robes?
>   Look, those who wear soft robes are in royal palaces.

> 3. What then did you go out to see?
>   A prophet?
>   Yes, I tell you, and more than a prophet.

Furthermore, there is a slight asymmetry between the first and second questions.[36] The hearers themselves must infer what opinion is being rejected. The following restatement of the logion may make this clearer.

What addition do we have to supply to the first question? And why is it not stated openly? From an analysis of the literary structure of the logion we observe that, if the first two questions are formally parallel to one another, it may be inferred that their content also corresponds! But if "those who wear soft robes" are to be sought in royal palaces, must not the same be true of the "shaken reed"? Is Jesus here referring to a "wavering" person in the royal palace at Tiberias?[37]

It could be objected that the Matthean version seems to speak of more than one royal palace (οἴκοι in the plural). This objection can be answered: On the one hand, the Lukan parallel (Lk 7:25) speaks of βασιλεῖοι, a

---

35. The Old Testament quotation in Mt 11:10 is an obvious secondary addition: (1) it also occurs, independent of this pericope on the Baptizer, in Mk 1:2; (2) it is lacking in the parallel passage in the *Gospel of Thomas;* and (3) it gives the saying a new accent—the Baptizer is made a forerunner of Jesus, corresponding to the Christian conception of him.

36. P. Gaechter writes, "The second half of v. 7, which is to be expected by analogy with vv. 8 and 9, has been lost in the oral tradition" (*Das Matthäus-Evangelium,* 363). But there could have been a plausible motive for keeping the reference to the territorial ruler shadowy.

37. N. Krieger's ("Ein Mensch in weichen Kleidern") supposition that the Baptizer has formerly lived at Antipas's court is a bit far-fetched.

concept that even in the plural form refers to *one* palace (cf. *Ant.* 13.136, 138; *C. Ap.* 1.140; Philo *Flacc.* 92). On the other hand, it is entirely reasonable to speak of royal palaces in the plural, for these, in contrast to most private houses, were made up of several buildings. Therefore, Josephus refers to Antipas's palace in Tiberias as οἶκοι, that is, "houses" (cf. *Vita* 66).

A second objection could be attached to the mention of "kings" in the plural: first, Herod Antipas was only a tetrarch; second, there seems to be a reference to several "kings." But this objection is also invalid: the Herodians were called "kings," first and last. The New Testament is a good example of this: Herod Antipas is called a "king" in Mk 6:14, 22, 26-27. Lysanias, the ruler of Abilene, was also only a tetrarch (Lk 3:1); still, Josephus calls his territory a "kingdom" (*Bell.* 2.215). Philo, a contemporary of Antipas, even speaks of "the king's [i.e., Herod's] four sons, who in dignity and good fortune were not inferior to a king" (*Leg. Gai.* 300), although the statement includes at least two sons of Herod who were not even tetrarchs.

Therefore, Mt 11:7ff. can certainly refer to the royal palace at Tiberias. Flusser is correct in looking there for the answer to what Jesus meant with the image of the "shaken reed"! Nevertheless, he thinks of courtiers and not of Antipas himself.[38] The second question refers to "someone" (ἄνθρωπον) in the singular. Here only one person can be intended. Similarly, κάλαμον in the parallel initial question may refer to a single person.

If the "shaken reed" is a reference to Herod Antipas, we can explain some of the formal oddities of the pericope. It would certainly not have been opportune to mention the powerful ruler of the country by name. Therefore, the first rhetorical question, in contrast to the two that follow, remains unanswered. The hearers filled it in for themselves: "Did you go out into the wilderness to see a reed shaken by the wind?"—"Of course not: we were not seeking Herod Antipas, but his prophetic opponent!" The shift from singular to plural between the second rhetorical question and its answer can be similarly motivated: the question is about *a* person (singular!) in soft robes, but the answer speaks in the plural of those who wear soft raiment in royal palaces. Here again it would not be opportune to give a direct name to the one who is being ironically attacked. The plural answer clouds the reference to a particular person.

Thus we come to the following conclusion: on the basis of the literary

---

38. Cf. Flusser, "Das Wesen der Gleichnisse," 52. Daniel's opinion (in "Les Esséniens") that the people in "soft robes" who are to be found both in the desert and in royal palaces are Essenes can scarcely be verified. On the contrary, Gaechter is correct when he writes, "With 'royal palaces' Jesus is referring rather openly to Herod Antipas" (*Das Matthäus-Evangelium*, 363).

evidence it is possible for the "shaken reed" to refer to Herod Antipas. In combination with the results of the numismatic analysis, this possibility becomes highly probable.

The Historical Evidence

Abusive names such as "shaken reed"—a name in which there could also be an echo of admiration and respect—do not stick unless they are apt characterizations of the person in question. We must therefore consider whether the behavior of Antipas, as we know it, could have been interpreted as a clever adaptation to changing circumstances. Despite the poverty of resources, I think there are enough indications to make it probable that Antipas could have been regarded as a master of judicious accommodation—and at the same time as a man who wavers.

In Herod's second will, Antipas was named as his successor (*Ant.* 17.146);[39] in fact, he replaced the unlucky Antipater, who was executed shortly before Herod's death. Immediately after the execution, however, Herod changed his will yet again (*Ant.* 17.188)—this time to the disadvantage of Antipas, who was now limited to Galilee and Perea, while the greater part of the land was to go to Archelaus. Antipas challenged the will in Rome, at first with apparent success. Eventually Archelaus won out, but Antipas was able to hold on to his territories. We can justly assume that Antipas understood how to adapt himself to the changing constellations, whether in the mistrust-laden atmosphere of the Herodian court at the end of Herod's reign or in Rome at the court of Augustus.

We may regard as a further sign of clever adaptability his political survival for such a long period after the fall of his brother Archelaus (6 C.E.), even though every opposing group within the land must have had before it the tempting spectacle of Archelaus's fate: he was deposed because of accusations by his subjects (cf. *Ant.* 17.342–44; *Bell.* 2.111). It is very hard to tell how much Antipas himself was involved in bringing about his brother's downfall! Still, Strabo reports (16.2.46) that both Philip and Antipas were accused at the same time and maintained themselves only with great difficulty.[40] Dio Cassius (55.27.6), on the other hand, traces the accusation against Archelaus to his brothers.[41] However that may have been, Antipas showed a talent for political survival.

This is also true in the case of the fall of Sejanus (31 C.E.). It is possible that Antipas had been on good terms with this man who, for a time, was so powerful within the empire. At least his nephew Agrippa, later King

---

39. On Herod's various wills, see Hoehner, *Herod Antipas,* 18–19.
40. Cf. the text and commentary in Stern, *GLAJJ* 1:294ff.
41. Ibid. 2:364–65.

Agrippa I, was successful in denouncing him for having conspired with Sejanus against Tiberius (*Ant.* 18.250).

Antipas survived a further crisis in 36–37 C.E. He had repudiated his Nabatean wife, who then fled to her father: after this, Antipas had to reckon with a hostile neighbor to the south. In 36 a conflict broke out over boundaries. Antipas suffered a catastrophic defeat (*Ant.* 18.113–15). The Syrian legate, Vitellius, had to intervene to stabilize the critical situation along the border. Antipas had, very shortly beforehand, deeply offended this same Syrian legate (*Ant.* 18.105). Nevertheless, he managed to work with him: they went up together to one of the feasts at Jerusalem (*Ant.* 18.122).

What can be seen positively, from one point of view, as clever accommodation, could look like wavering from another perspective! Had not Herod Antipas "wavered" between two capital cities: his old residence at Sepphoris and the new foundation at Tiberias? Did not he also waver between two women? Although Herodias made the repudiation of the first wife a condition of her marriage contract, Antipas did not dare communicate the situation to his first wife (*Ant.* 18.111). Thus she was able to evade banishment by fleeing beforehand! According to the synoptic tradition (Mk 6:20), Antipas even had a good relationship with John the Baptizer, the very prophet whom he had executed. The popular tradition in Mark 6 reveals a "wavering" prince. It may have legendary features, but is certainly historical in showing that Antipas had the reputation of being a "waverer." Josephus also depicts him as a hesitant man in reference to his attempt to obtain the royal title for himself in Rome: only the insistence of the ambitious Herodias caused him to summon the courage to do it (*Ant.* 18.245–46). In this, his hesitancy was much cleverer than Herodias's pressure. His reaching for the royal title became a trap for him: he was denounced before the emperor for having a secret cache of weapons, and so was banished.

Therefore, it is historically quite conceivable that Herod Antipas, on the basis of his first coinage, got the name "wavering reed" or "shaken reed"—a title of ridicule and recognition. Jesus describes him at another point as a "sly fox" (Lk 13:32). Both attributes point in the same direction. Possibly it was that kind of slander—started by the first coin—that caused Antipas to change the emblem. On his later coins, the reed has vanished. In place of the "shaken reed" appears the sturdy palm tree!

Consequences for the Interpretation of Mt 11:7-9

If the "shaken reed" refers to Herod Antipas, both the literal and the metaphorical interpretation would be correct: the emblem on the coin intends to represent reeds in a literal and concrete sense, but as an emblem of Antipas it acquires an ambiguous relationship to the Herodian prince in which all possible associations in the realm of fable and historical tradition could find their resonance. Anyone who was willing could see in Herod Antipas, the addressee of the Baptizer's prophetic preaching of judgment, a "shaken reed" that would be shattered by the blows of fate to be sent from God. Or, in light of the well-known fable tradition, one could see in him a clever politician who adapted himself to all possible circumstances, a contrast to the uncompromising figure of the Baptizer. The decisive point is that these associations were first invoked by the appearance of the coin.

Certain consequences result both for the location of Mt 11:7-9 within the development of tradition and for the understanding of the content of the pericope.

First, the tradition must have arisen within Palestine. It could only be understood in the area where the foundation coins of Tiberias circulated, and in fact these were current in daily use, in a copper form, only in Antipas's territories.[42] We must look there for the source of the tradition. Familiarity with the Palestinian environment is also revealed by the combination of "reed" and "wilderness," or "desert." This seems paradoxical at first, because "reeds" make us think of watery places and "desert" of waterless regions. But the southern Jordan Valley offers both together: a barren desert and, like a long, sinuous oasis in the middle of it, the green river meadows of the Jordan.[43]

EXCURSUS
John as Desert Preacher and Jordan Preacher

The location of the Jordan Baptizer in the wilderness, which has been retained in the synoptic tradition, presumes a great deal of familiarity with the Palestinian environment. In fact, the expression ὁ βαπτίζων ἐν τῷ ἐρήμῳ (Mk 1:4) contains an initial contradiction for the reader: Where could anyone baptize in the desert? The characteristic feature of a desert is its lack of water.

Luke already saw the problem. He changed Mk 1:4 in such a way that desert and Jordan are separated. First he tells us that the Baptizer received the word of God in the desert (Lk 3:2). Only then does he "go" into the region of the Jordan (3:3). The commissioning by God in the wilderness and the carrying out of the assignment by preaching the "baptism of repentance for the forgive-

---

42. Meshorer writes: "The places where the coins of Antipas have been found are limited to the northern regions of the Land of Israel. No coins of his are known to have been found in the region of Judaea. This significant fact seems to indicate that these coins were intended solely for the local need of Antipas' tetrarchy" (*Jewish Coins*, 75).

43. On what follows, see C. C. McCown, "The Scene of John's Ministry."

ness of sins" are located separately. The narrative following the baptism of Jesus is similarly designed; Jesus is driven away from the Jordan into the desert. Luke says expressly that Jesus turned away from the Jordan (ὑπέστρεψεν ἀπὸ τοῦ Ἰορδάνου) and was led by the Spirit in the wilderness (Lk 4:1). Again he separates the river region and the wilderness.

Matthew solved the problem differently. He also avoids saying that John baptizes in the desert. Instead, he says that John was "preaching in the wilderness," concretely, in the "wilderness of Judea" (Mt 3:1). The Judean wilderness is west of the Jordan, between the mountain ridge and the Dead Sea. If Matthew has correctly located the wilderness of Judea, the Baptizer was not yet anywhere near the Jordan when he was preaching. Thus Matthew can describe the crowds coming to him somewhat differently from Mark: "Then the people of Jerusalem and all Judea were going out to him, and all the region along the Jordan" (Mt 3:5). If, against Mark, there are also people from the Jordan region coming out to the Baptizer (ἐξεπορεύετο), he cannot be at the Jordan itself. Matthew apparently imagines that the crowd afterward goes with the Baptizer to the Jordan to be baptized (3:6), even if he does not say so directly. The identification of the mountain wilderness of Judea with the place of the Baptizer's preaching, and the removal from the Jordan which that necessitates, is also apparent from Mt 4:1, for after his baptism Jesus is "led up" (ἀνήχθη) by the Spirit "into the wilderness," that is, into the mountain wilderness where one finds those stones that Satan expects Jesus to turn into bread. The evangelist seems to have an accurate idea of the relationship between the "wilderness of Judea" and the "Jordan." The wilderness is "higher up" than the Jordan Valley.

Both Matthew and Luke separate "wilderness" and "Jordan," each in his own way. Luke's presentation is very general, while Matthew thinks, with geographical accuracy, of the mountain wilderness of Judea! Modern exegetes have followed them, shrewdly postulating in Mk 1:4 a combination of two competing traditions: one about the baptizer in the wilderness, developed out of Isa 40:3; and another (historically accurate) about the baptizer on the Jordan. When the author of Mark's Gospel combines the two, he seems "not to have a clear notion of the geography."[44] R. Bultmann adopted K. L. Schmidt's opinion.[45] W. Marxsen developed it into a far-reaching redaction-critical theory.[46] But the "unclear notions of geography" are in this case those of the modern exegetes, because the Jordan's course carries it through a desert that borders directly on a narrow, green river meadow. The tradition in Mk 1:4 about a "baptizer in the desert" can only come from people who are acquainted with this unusual local situation. This tradition assuredly arose in Palestine.

P. Vielhauer has already noted that the tradition about a baptizer in the desert corresponds to the concrete circumstances and is also confirmed by Mt

---

44. So K. L. Schmidt, *Der Rahmen der Geschichte Jesu*, 21.
45. Cf. R. Bultmann, *Die Geschichte der synoptischen Tradition*, 261.
46. So W. Marxsen, *Der Evangelist Markus*, 17–18.

11:7-10,[47] for here it is clearly presumed that the Baptizer is in the wilderness. Jesus asks the crowds going out to the Baptizer why they are going into the wilderness. This mention of the locale, together with other indications, enables us to locate the tradition in Palestine.

But Mt 11:7 not only can be located in terms of tradition criticism; we can also give it a tentative date. We may begin from the founding of the city of Tiberias (ca. 19 C.E.) as terminus a quo. At that point it became possible, because of the newly minted coins, to connect the "reed" and the Herodian tetrarch. Certainly, once issued, the coins circulated for a long time. However, because another type of coin is in evidence by 26–27, the traditions will have arisen in the 20s. A terminus ante quem is, probably, the death of the Baptizer. The pericope does not presume his execution; or, to put it more cautiously, it can easily be imagined during the Baptizer's lifetime. The redactors of the Gospels sensed that also, and placed the saying within their compositions at a time before the Baptizer's execution. The result of these considerations is that the tradition probably arose in Palestine in the 20s, that is, exactly at the time and in the region in which Jesus was active. In my opinion, the most likely possibility is that it really comes from Jesus. The unusually high praise of the Baptizer also speaks in favor of this. The early Christian community, of course, claimed him as a prophet of Jesus, but here he is placed above all the prophets.

The tradition, in this interpretation, also throws new light on Jesus' message: Mt 11:7-9 would originally have been much more closely linked to the antithesis between Antipas and the Baptizer, between the royal palace and the wilderness prophet, than appears at first glance. The contrast is formed by two stages of relationship. On one side is the cleverly adaptive politician; on the other is the prophet uncompromisingly proclaiming his message. On one side is the luxury of a small Hellenistic power elite, whose clothing already distinguishes it from other people;[48] on the other is the ascetic wilderness prophet with his emphatically simple and archaic dress.[49] In these words of Jesus we sense that two different social worlds in Palestine are in collision here. The Baptizer's criticism of Antipas's marriage also fits into this picture: what Herodias did, when she actively initiated her divorce and demanded the dismissal of another wife before her remarriage, could have been felt in Palestine to be a violation

---

47. P. Vielhauer, "Tracht und Speise Johannes des Täufers," 53–54.
48. On the sumptuous clothing in Tiberias, cf. the episode Josephus depicts there (*Vita* 334–35): a soldier is seen wearing a gorgeous robe that he stole at the plundering of Tiberias and is scourged as punishment.
49. Cf. Vielhauer, "Tracht und Speise Johannes des Täufers," 47–54.

of ancestral custom—and not only by so blunt a prophet as John the Baptizer.[50] Basically, however, Herodias (and Antipas) did nothing but what was common custom in Rome and Greece. There a wife could also take the initiative in a divorce. Monogamy was a matter of course. The Baptizer's protest against Antipas and his marriage to Herodias is thus part and parcel of a popular reaction against the advance of "foreign" customs in the Herodian upper classes: their conformist behavior, their luxury, and their family life meet with rejection among the common people. John the Baptizer is the mouthpiece of this native opposition and reaction.

Our thesis, that the polemic contrast of prophet and royal palace was originally of far greater importance in shaping the tradition than is evident today, is indirectly confirmed by the *Gospel of Thomas*. Here the polemic accent has been better retained, even though it is now completely reinterpreted in terms of the contrast between the true Gnostic and the "great ones" of this world:

> Jesus said:
> Why did you go out into the field?
> To see a reed that is shaken by the wind?
> And to see a man clothed in soft raiment?
> [Lo, your] kings and your great ones
> are they who are clothed with soft raiment,
> and they [shall] not be able to know the truth!
> (*Gos. Thom.* 78)

In the synoptic development of the tradition, the point has been displaced. A combined scriptural citation is attached to the saying; it has also survived in Mk 1:2 independently of this particular tradition:

> This is the one about whom it is written,
> "See, I am sending my messenger ahead of you,
> who will prepare your way before you."
> (Mt 11:10)

The contrast between prophet and prince is replaced by the relationship of John and Jesus, the precursor and the figure announced by him. It is highly probable that this represents an initial Christian displacement of the accent.

---

50. Cf. the critical judgment of Josephus, a member of the upper class, in *Ant.* 18.136: Herodias *deliberately* broke ancestral custom through her marriage!

ISRAEL AND THE NATIONS:
PALESTINE-CENTERED CULTURAL PERSPECTIVES
IN THE SAYINGS OF JESUS

Our ability to demonstrate a local flavor in Mt 11:7-10 rests on accidentally preserved material remains, the coins of Herod Antipas, and the incidental mention of the wilderness. The question arises: If fortunate circumstances enable us to prove that a traditional saying has been shaped by the local situation in Palestine, should we not also expect this to be possible with regard to other Jesus traditions? The problem is only how we can raise this possibility to the level of probability.

We will restrict ourselves for the present to words drawn from the Sayings Source, because they belong to the same strand of tradition in which Mt 11:7-10 has come down to us. Certainly words of Jesus have reached us through other channels. This is evident from the double traditions in Q and Mark as well as the logia in the *Gospel of Thomas*. But in the Sayings Source we have a wealth of Jesus sayings that have a common tradition history and that were collected, at the latest, at the moment when an unknown person wrote them down in the first century of our era. Further words of Jesus drawn from Mark and from Matthew's and Luke's special material can be added at a second level—in the case of sayings in the Matthean and Lukan *Sondergut,* one can never be sure whether they might have been in the Sayings Source and omitted by Matthew or Luke. All the logia being investigated have in common their interest in the relationship of Israel to the Gentiles.

One saying of Jesus puts so much emphasis on a concrete "here" that it positively demands that we ask about its implicit local-cultural perspective. It is a word of judgment against this generation, which reads as follows in Luke:[51]

> The queen of the South will rise at the judgment
> with the people of this generation
> and condemn them,
> because she came from the ends of the earth
> to listen to the wisdom of Solomon,
> and see, something greater than Solomon is here ($\tilde{\omega}\delta\epsilon$)!
> The people of Nineveh will rise up at the judgment
> with this generation
> and condemn it,
> because they repented at the proclamation of Jonah,
> and see, something greater than Jonah is here [$\tilde{\omega}\delta\epsilon$]!"
>
> (Lk 11:31-32)

---

51. For an analysis, see Schulz, *Q,* 250–57; for a further, careful discussion of all the problems, see J. S. Kloppenborg, *"Literary Genre,"* 156–65.

This double word of judgment is now closely connected with the preceding saying about the sign of Jonah. But the connection is not original.[52] The new context of the word of judgment has had the effect, in Matthew, of causing the order of the sayings to be reversed: Matthew first mentions the Ninevites in connection with Jonah, contrasting them with "this generation," and thus establishes a clearer sequence of ideas. But the original order in Luke also makes sense.[53] It corresponds to the chronological order and contains an intensification: the queen of the South was attracted by something positive, while the Ninevites turned away from something evil. The queen was a single person, the Ninevites a whole nation.

We want to pay special attention to the twice-emphasized "here," which is certainly not to be understood in a local or spatial sense, yet contains a local component. Two points of reference are mentioned: the land of the queen, who is drawn by Solomon's wisdom, and Nineveh. Because the queen is said to be "of the south," the reader inevitably connects Nineveh with the north. On the one hand, the mysterious "king of the north" (Dan 11:6, 8, 11, etc.) would correspond to "queen of the south"; on the other hand, Nineveh is traditionally connected with the north. Therefore, Zephaniah prophesies the destruction of the Ethiopians in the south and then continues: "And [Yahweh] will stretch out his hand against the north, and destroy Assyria; and he will make Nineveh a desolation, a dry waste like the desert" (Zeph 2:13). North and south are joined by different "movements": the queen came to Solomon from the south; Jonah went north to the Ninevites. Jesus, speaking the logion, is set between north

---

52. The following arguments speak in favor of this: the preceding "demand for a sign" is found in Mk 8:11-12 independently of the words of judgment that here follow; on the other hand, similar words of judgment, in which pagan readiness for conversion is set up as a model, could exist as an independent tradition (cf. Mt 11:20-24; Lk 10:13-15). Added to this, there is some minor tension with the preceding context: (1) according to Lk 11:29-30, the audience for whom the sign of Jonah is postulated is the same as this "evil generation," while according to Lk 11:31-32 the audience for Jonah's message is contrasted with this evil generation—the former repented, but the latter will be condemned because they did not repent; (2) if the two logia had originally belonged together, one would expect in Luke (as in Matthew) an immediate connection of the Jonah-image with the saying about the "sign of Jonah." The independence of the two traditions is even clearer if G. Schmitt ("Das Zeichen des Jona") is correct in supposing that in Lk 11:29 an apocryphal tradition about a sign of Jonah against the city of Jerusalem has been adapted (*Vitae Prophetarum* 6), for then the sign in Lk 11:29-30 would be connected with Jerusalem, while in Lk 11:31-32 Jonah is clearly connected with Nineveh. However, the reference to the apocryphal tradition is only a possibility.

53. Luke had a reason for retaining the original sequence: Lk 11:30, in contrast to Mt 11:40, speaks of "this generation." The subsequent words of judgment serve the polemic against "this generation"—even in the original sequence. So A. Vögtle, *Das Evangelium und die Evangelien*, 116–19.

and south: the twice-repeated "here" could lie topologically in the middle, in Palestine. The saying incorporates a Palestine-centered local perspective, or, stated more cautiously, it can be understood from such a local perspective without doing violence to it.

The same is true of the saying about the "pilgrimage of nations," which would better be called the saying about the "thronging of those from afar into the reign of God,"[54] because it must remain open whether Jews, Gentiles, or both together are entering into God's rule. The decisive point is that those who are near will be excluded, while those from afar will be included.

This logion stands, in both Matthew and Luke, in a context that is not original. In Mt 8:11-12 it interrupts the story of the centurion from Capernaum. Taking up the positive example of this one Gentile, it promises the Gentiles entry into the reign of God and threatens the "heirs of the kingdom" with exclusion. In this way Matthew's Gospel warns both Jews and Christians, who are also "children of the kingdom" (Mt 13:38) and whose entry into the rule of God is uncertain (Mt 7:21-23).[55]

In Lk 13:28-29, the logion follows a scene in which Jesus, as eschatological judge, refuses people who take pride in their acquaintance with the earthly Jesus. Here, logically, the threat of exclusion comes first and only then is the promise uttered (reversing the original order?): "Then people will come from east and west, from north and south, and will eat in the kingdom of God" (Lk 13:29). Here those who are shut out include followers of Jesus, and those who come in their place are Gentiles, even though this is not expressly stated.

We may doubt that the original tradition thought exclusively of Gentiles,[56] but we cannot give definite proof.

---

54. For a reconstruction of the original form, see Schulz, *Q*, 323–30. According to this, Matthew retained the earlier form of the logion, but it is precisely the description of those approaching as πολλοί and of those close by as "children of the kingdom" that could come from Matthew, because the latter description is also redactional at Mt 13:38.

55. Matthew's critique of Israel, in my opinion, clearly implies a warning to Christians: the Sermon on the Mount, which precedes this, had shown that if their righteousness does not exceed that of the scribes and Pharisees, they will not enter the reign of God (5:20). Even Christian prophets and charismatics will be excluded if they do not do Jesus' will (7:21-23). The readers perhaps do not (yet) know that Christians, too, are "children of the kingdom" (Mt 13:38), but the application of the same phrase to Jews and Christians cannot be accidental.

56. This is an almost universal consensus. Cf., e.g., the fundamental study by J. Jeremias, *Jesu Verheissung*, 47–62. The religious-historical material collected by Jeremias is reviewed by D. Zeller in "Das Logion Mt 8,11f/Lk 13,28f," but Zeller does not discuss the possibility that we find here the additional motif of the gathering of those scattered and that those who are rushing into the reign of God could be both Jews and Gentiles.

1. The motif of the eschatological thronging to Jerusalem is attested in two forms: as "pilgrimage of the nations" (Isa 2:2-4; Mic 4:1-4) and as "gathering of the scattered" (Isa 43:1-7; Ps 107:3; Bar 4:36-37; 5:5-9; *T. Benj.* 9:2; Philo *De Praem.* 165). The two motifs are often combined: the Gentiles in the end-time journey to Jerusalem bring the dispersed Israelites with them as their gifts (Isa 66:12, 20; *Pss. Sol.* 17:31; and perhaps Isa 60:4); or the return of the scattered, which has been made possible through the Israelites' repentance, is completed by the conversion of all Gentiles (Tob 13:1-5, 11; 14:4-7). In other words, most texts expect an assembling of both scattered Jews and converting Gentiles in the end time.

2. The saying of Jesus mentions the quarters from which the distant will approach: east and west (Mt 8:11) or all four directions (Lk 13:28-29). It can be no accident that these four quarters are found especially in Old Testament and Jewish texts on the "gathering of the scattered": Isa 43:5-6;[57] Ps 107:3; Bar 4:36-37; 5:5. Is the primary idea behind the Jesus logion the return of the twelve tribes?

3. The saying about "judging the twelve tribes" (Mt 19:28; Lk 22:28-30) could favor this interpretation. It presumes a return of the scattered Jews. But in the Lukan version it connects this return especially with the expectation of a banquet in the reign of God: "so that you may eat and drink at my table in my kingdom, and you will sit on thrones judging the twelve tribes of Israel." The banquet with Abraham, Isaac, and Jacob (Mt 8:11-12) could also have been, at one time, the festival of reunited Israel.

What is decisive is that in all the Old Testament and Jewish traditions the motif of the approach of those from afar—whether Gentiles, Jews, or both—serves as a confirmation of the ancient promises to Israel. Here, on the contrary, a hope of salvation is turned into a threat: those who are near, those for whom the promise was originally intended, will be excluded.

Can we come to a closer definition of this "nearness?" When the logion speaks of the four points of the compass, it gives the "reign of God" spatial dimensions. It is localizable, but is not located—presumably because it is taken for granted that it is in Palestine. Both traditions incorporated in the logion, in fact, contain a Palestinian perspective. The expectation of an eschatological meal can sometimes be connected with Zion, as in the

---

57. W. Grimm ("Zum Hintergrund von Mt 8,11f/Lk 13,28f") sees in Isa 43:1-7 the background for Mt 8:11-12.

apocalypse in Isaiah: "On this mountain the Lord of hosts will make for all peoples a feast of rich food" (Isa 25:6).[58] The motif of the approach of the people at the end time is regularly connected with Zion.[59] What is new in the Jesus-logion is the combination of these traditions, which possibly is found also in Mt 19:28 and Lk 22:28-30.

The question is whether these expectations were as closely connected with Zion in the Jesus tradition as in the previous traditions, or whether the location "in the reign of God" consciously leaves everything open. The anticipated reign of God is scarcely marked by the perspectives of Jerusalem. It "seems to be made for hungry people, lepers, with little money, but who evidently have no needs at the national level."[60] Exalted cultural requirements will not be fulfilled there. Liturgical dreams of a cultic closeness to God are missing. The satisfaction of all longing is a good meal in the reign of God, not pictured as a sacrificial meal in the temple, but as a banquet among the family patriarchs.[61] Salvation means being close to Abraham, Isaac, and Jacob, none of whom had any relationship to Jerusalem. Therefore it may be that the Jesus movement, with its roots in rural Galilee, took a tradition that concentrated on Jerusalem and broadened it to include all Palestine.

The two previous examples allow only indirect conclusions about the location of the speaker. But in the woes spoken over the cities of Galilee (Mt 11:20-24; Lk 10:13-16), the point of view is made more specific by the use of local names (Table 2).

The Matthean version contrasts the Galilean cities, on the one hand, with Tyre and Sidon in the northwest, and, on the other hand, with the land of Sodom to the south. The three cities that are directly addressed lie in the middle, which indicates a standpoint located between two counterposed reference points; and in my opinion this is all the more probable when this "middle"—as in the logia discussed above—is not more closely described. But only Matthew refers to Sodom.[62] Probably he added it in the interests of paralleling the two parts of the logion, and in so doing had

---

58. However, this expectation is also found, independent of this localization, in *1 Enoch* 62:14 and 1QSa 2.11ff.

59. Jeremias writes: "At every point, without exception, where we encounter the idea of the eschatological pilgrimage of the nations in the OT, the goal of the pilgrimage is the place of divine revelation, the holy mountain of God, Zion" (*Jesu Verheissung*, 51).

60. C. Burchard, "Jesus von Nazareth," 33–34. This insight is sharply stated in these terms: "The reign of God is not an empire; it is a village" (p. 34).

61. So N. A. Dahl: "The meal in the kingdom of heaven is regarded not so much as a sublime counterpart of the sacrificial meal in the Temple, but rather like shared meals in the family and in religious societies" (*Matteusevangeliet* 1:113).

62. For a reconstruction of the Q version, see Schulz, *Q*, 360–66; A. Polag, *Fragmenta Q*, 46–47.

TABLE 2
Woes Spoken Over the Cities
of Galilee

Mt 11:20-24	Lk 10:13-16
Then he began to reproach the cities in which most of his deeds of power had been done, because they did not repent.	
"Woe to you, Chorazin!	"Woe to you, Chorazin!
Woe to you, Bethsaida!	Woe to you, Bethsaida!
for if the deeds of power done in you had been done in Tyre and Sidon, they would have repented long ago in sackcloth and ashes.	for if the deeds of power done in you had been done in Tyre and Sidon, they would have repented long ago, sitting in sackcloth and ashes.
But I tell you, on the day of judgment it will be more tolerable for Tyre and Sidon than for you.	But at the judgment it will be more tolerable for Tyre and Sidon than for you.
And you, Capernaum, will you be exalted to heaven? No, you will be brought down to Hades.	And you, Capernaum, will you be exalted to heaven? No, you will be brought down to Hades."
For if the deeds of power done in you had been done in Sodom, it would have remained until this day. But I tell you that on the day of judgment it will be more tolerable for the land of Sodom than for you."	

recourse to part of the mission discourse (Mt 10:15; Lk 10:12), in which hostile cities are equated with Sodom and Gomorrah.[63] The same saying from the mission discourse stands directly before this threat to the Galilean cities in Luke (cf. 10:10-12), a logical connection that probably existed in the Sayings Source. Matthew disconnected the sayings when he separated

---

63. D. Lührmann (*Redaktion*, 62) attributes the location of Lk 10:12/Mt 10:15 as a connector between the mission discourse and the woes to the redaction of Q. He also assigns Lk 11:30 and Mt 12:40 to this redaction.

the "woes against the cities of Galilee" from the mission discourse. He adds a narrative introduction that creates a new "context" for the logion (Mt 11:20) and adds the comparison with the fate of Sodom in order to retain the associative framework that existed in the Sayings Source. Luke probably gives us the logion as a whole in the more original form.

We are interested particularly in the three Galilean towns. Of these, Bethsaida is best known.[64] It was elevated to "city" status by Philip and named "Julias" in honor of the emperor Augustus's daughter (*Ant.* 18.28). In the New Testament, we encounter it as a "village" (cf. Mk 8:22, 26). Because no coins from this city have survived, we can doubt whether it really was a "polis."[65] Josephus's formulation is interesting: "He [i.e., Philip] raised [it] to the status of city by adding residents and strengthening the fortifications [καὶ τῇ ἄλλῃ δυνάμει]" (*Ant.* 18.28). We could interpret that to mean that this town had only two marks of a city: a relatively large population and fortifications. Perhaps it was a "polis" with limited rights. But it was well enough known for Josephus (*Vita* 399; *Ant.* 18.28; *Bell.* 2.168), Pliny the Elder (*Nat. Hist.* 5.71), and Ptolemy (*Geogr.* 5.16.4) to mention it.

Chorazin, on the other hand, is a relatively unknown place.[66] Apart from this verse, it is not mentioned in contemporary literary sources. Eusebius was the first to report (*Onom.* 333) on Chorazin as a ruined town near Capernaum. Archeological digs at Chirbet Keraze (Chorazin), three kilometers northwest of Capernaum, have uncovered the remains of a synagogue built of black basalt, with sculptures; it should be dated to the fourth century C.E. The town may also have been mentioned by Rabbi Jose (ca. 150 C.E.).[67] In *Menahot* 85a, we have his saying: "They would have brought [the meal-offering] even from the wheat of Karzaim and of Kefar Achim, if only they had been nearer to Jerusalem." Kefar Achim is otherwise unknown, but could be the same as Kefar Nahum (Capernaum). Then we would have proof outside Mt 11:20-24 for the close relationship

---

64. On Bethsaida, see C. Kopp, *Die Heiligen Stätten*, 230–43; E. Schürer, *History of the Jewish People* 2:171–72.

65. Cf. A.H.M. Jones, "Urbanization of Palestine," 80. E. Schürer (*Geschichte* 2:208) refers the status of Bethsaida as a polis to *Ant.* 20.8.4 (= 20.159), but this is an error; Josephus is there distinguishing a polis called Julia from fourteen surrounding villages, but he obviously refers to Julias in Perea, the former Betharamphtha (*Ant.* 18.27), which he clearly distinguishes from Bethsaida (Julias; *Ant.* 18.28). Schürer's error was not corrected in the new edition by G. Vermes and F. Millar (*History of the Jewish People* 2:172). It is found in many reference works, e.g., A. Fuchs, "Βηθσαϊδά(ν)"; M. Enslin, "Bethsaida."

66. See Kopp, *Die Heiligen Stätten*, 243–46; B. Reicke, "Chorazim." The dating of the synagogue to the second or third century should be corrected. It belongs to the fourth century; cf. P. Kaswaldek, "Corazim."

67. H. Strack and P. Billerbeck, *Kommentar zum Neuen Testament* 1:605.

of the two towns. But the parallel passage in the Tosefta, *Menahot* 9:2 (525) reads "Barchaim" instead of "Karzaim," so that we cannot be sure whether the latter is really named here.

Capernaum is known to us from the Gospels.[68] Josephus uses the name once for a spring at the northern end of the Lake of Galilee (*Bell.* 3.519), but that is a secondary application of the name, for Kefar Nahum means literally "Nahum's village." In *Vita* 403 he further relates that in that region he had a fall in some swampy ground and hurt himself, so that he was brought into the village "Cepharnocus."[69] This can only be Capernaum. The only rabbinic references, interestingly enough, point to the existence of "minim" (Jewish Christians?) in Capernaum at the beginning of the second century: they convert a Jew, who then demonstratively breaks the Sabbath by riding on a donkey, but later is won back to orthodox Judaism (*Midr. Eccl.* 1.8 [9ᵃ]; and, with reference to this episode, 8:26 [38ᵃ]).[70]

As far as local perspective is concerned, it is significant that the two towns of Chorazin and Bethsaida are closely related to one another and appear in contrast to Tyre and Sidon as another pair of connected towns.[71] In the first four decades of the first century C.E., they were separated by a political frontier: Chorazin (like Capernaum) was in the territory of Herod Antipas (4 B.C.E.–39 C.E.), while Bethsaida belonged to Philip (4 B.C.E.–34 C.E.). The boundary vanished at the Jordan and was artificially drawn, since Jews on both sides of the border considered themselves united. This was clear also in the course of history: on the one hand, this unity was recognized "from above" when Nero conveyed lands on both sides of the Jordan to Agrippa II as his "kingdom" in 54 C.E.; on the other hand, it was demonstrated "from below" in the Jewish war (66–70 C.E.) when the Jewish population in both districts adopted the same rebellious attitude. The mention of both cities in a logion that goes back to the first half of the century clearly reflects a popular sense of belonging together that long outlasted artificial political boundaries.[72]

---

68. On Capernaum, see Kopp, *Die Heiligen Stätten,* 215–30; W. Nauck, "Kapernaum."

69. The manuscript tradition diverges here. Another reading is "Kapharnomon" (καφαρνώμων).

70. Both passages speak of "minim" in Capernaum. These need not be Jewish Christians, since demonstrative breaking of the Sabbath is not necessarily characteristic of Jewish Christian observance. Basically, "minim" are any kind of heretics.

71. Tyre and Sidon are always mentioned together: cf. Isaiah 23; Jer 47:4; Ezekiel 26–28; Zech 9:2-4; Joel 3:4; see also Ezra 3:7; 1 Chr 22:4; Jdt 2:28; 1 Macc 5:15.

72. This is probably why John's Gospel can speak simply of "Bethsaida in Galilee" (Jn 12:21). Kopp remarks correctly: "So also popular speech probably took no account of the constantly shifting boundaries, any more than it recognized the pagan renaming of its cities. The residents of the original Bethsaida were bound by a thousand ties to the mother-province; they spoke the same dialect and lived in the same way on and out of the 'Sea of Galilee'" (*Die Heiligen Stätten,* 235).

The second remarkable feature of this saying against the Galilean cities is the prominent place given to Capernaum, which emerges even more clearly in Luke than in Matthew: the very point of the saying, in Luke, is the accusation against Capernaum. It is attacked in images that, in the Old Testament, are directed against sinful Babylon (cf. Isa 14:11, 13, 15) and proud Egypt (Ezek 31:14-18): a tiny, unimportant fishing village is assailed like the great powers of the ancient Orient! This Capernaum must be worse than Chorazin and Bethsaida, for there still seems to be hope for those two: the cities that are compared with them, Tyre and Sidon, were still in existence. Here perhaps the last word is not yet spoken. For Capernaum, on the other hand, catastrophe is predicted. What a "small world" is visible here!

The word of warning is frequently interpreted as post-Easter prophecy looking back to Jesus' completed work.[73] But the content of the tradition does not coincide with the post-Easter picture of Jesus' activity in Galilee that has been handed down to us: no miracles of Jesus at Chorazin are reported. Jesus' activity in Galilee is described as successful. But in particular, in a retrospective view of the life of Jesus, his rejection would scarcely be seen as culminating in Capernaum, but rather in Jerusalem, the place of his execution. It is thus rather certain that no complete picture of Jesus' work is presumed here; instead, concrete experiences connected with a small section of Galilee are being assimilated—whether it is Jesus reflecting on his miracles in these places, or whether early Christian itinerant charismatics are dealing with their rejection in those towns. The local perspective is Galilean. We are looking at a very limited world in which small towns, otherwise insignificant, are places of decisive importance.

---

73. Bultmann (*Die Geschichte der synoptischen Tradition*, 118) offers three arguments against the authenticity of the saying: First, it looks "back on Jesus' activity as something already completed." But it is only in the Matthean version, which Bultmann (probably wrongly) considers the original, that there is a clearly retrospective look to Jesus' activity (Mt 11:20); and even this look back does not encompass the whole of Jesus' life, but only his Galilean activity. Second, the logion "presuppose[s] the failure of the Christian preaching in Capernaum." It is true that it presumes the failure of a movement of conversion in Chorazin, Bethsaida, and Capernaum. The demand for conversion is already present with John the Baptizer. What is characteristic of Jesus is that he raises this demand in populated areas. Deeds of power (δυνάμεις) had already attracted people's attention to Jesus himself (Mk 6:2, 14); it was not first aroused by his followers (Mt 7:22). The representation of Gentiles as better fits well in Jesus' preaching (cf. Mt 12:41-42). An ὀνειδίζειν like that referred to in Matthew's introduction to this saying (11:20) is also attested for Judas Galileus: Ἰουδαίους ὀνειδίσας ὅτι Ῥωμαίοις ὑπετάσσοντο μετὰ τὸν θεόν (Jos. *Bell.* 2.433). In Mt 11:20-24 indications of a specifically Christian preaching are lacking. Third, it would have been difficult for Jesus to imagine that Capernaum could be exalted to heaven by his activity. If the occasion of Capernaum's pride really was Jesus' work there, the saying would be hard to understand in a post-Easter situation. Or were the people in Capernaum proud of a man executed on a cross?

We can limit the dating even further. The saying does not presuppose any Christian communities in Tyre and Sidon. Their conversion is played up as an unreal possibility against the Galilean cities. But in the fifties, at the latest, there was a Christian community in Tyre. Paul visited it on his last journey to Jerusalem (Acts 21:3-6). There were also Christians in Sidon whom Paul was permitted to visit when he was being conducted to Rome (Acts 27:3). The saying in Mt 10:20-24 should predate the existence of these communities.

In some further logia in Q, persecuted early Christian prophets are placed in the series of the Old Testament prophets.[74] It is said of them: "in the same way they persecuted the prophets who were before you" (Mt 5:12//Lk 6:22-23). Their opponents are threatened that the killing of the prophets (or the righteous) from Abel to Zechariah will be revenged on this generation (Lk 11:49-51//Mt 23:34-36). These words naturally would have been most impressive in the place where, according to the belief of the time, the prophets had been killed, that is, in Palestine. But they need not have been spoken there. Paul formulated similar sayings about the killing of the prophets in the Aegean region (1 Thess 2:14-16). Therefore, we must look for additional indications of locality. We find them in the saying about the graves of the prophets:

> "Woe to you, scribes and Pharisees, hypocrites!
> For you build the tombs of the prophets
> and decorate the graves of the righteous, and you say,
> 'If we had lived in the days of our ancestors,
> we would not have taken part with them
> in shedding the blood of the prophets.'
> Thus you testify against yourselves,
> that you are descendants of those who murdered the prophets."
> (Mt 23:29-31; cf. Lk 11:47-48)

In its content and tradition history, this saying belongs among the other words about the prophets. It is interesting that here there is still a reference to something that is presupposed as a certainty in the other sayings: the continuity of killing of prophets from the ancestors to the present. This continuity is not seen (differently from 1 Thess 2:14-16 and Mk 12:1-12) in terms of the present generation's involvement in the death of Jesus, but instead is founded on the existence of popular veneration of the graves of prophets and holy people: the acceptance of the past expressed here is made an accusation against the addressees, although they defini-

---

74. Cf. O. H. Steck, *Israel und das gewaltsame Geschick der Propheten*, a fundamental study of the Deuteronomic tradition of the killing of the prophets up to and including New Testament times.

tively distance themselves from the persecution of the prophets. In my opinion, such a saying only makes sense in a place where there are graves of prophets and holy people, that is, in Palestine.[75] The hearers must be acquainted with local customs surrounding the graves and the veneration of holy persons.

Besides the traditions from the Sayings Source that have been discussed here, in which a Palestinian local perspective is evident, there are also some sayings in Matthew's and Luke's special material that deserve mention. They are all to be found in the mission discourses of Matthew and Luke. For this reason, they are important for the whole sayings tradition: in the mission discourse we find the rules of those itinerant preachers who carried on Jesus' message. In their preaching, the words of Jesus were heard (Lk 10:16), which can also be interpreted to mean that they were handing on the words of Jesus (and possibly other Jesus traditions).

Luke is the only author who gives the puzzling injunction "Greet no one on the road!" (Lk 10:4). The saying could have been in Q, for Matthew has a clear motive for omitting it. For him, greeting one another is part of the Christian ethos: "And if you greet only your brothers and sisters, what more are you doing than others? Do not even the Gentiles do the same?" (Mt 5:47). Only Matthew has this concretization, an explication of the commandment of love of enemies. Given this injunction in an earlier part of the Gospel, Matthew cannot cope with a saying that forbids greeting, and so omits it. But Luke may have understood its original meaning: it is really about a "prohibition of visiting." Early Christian wandering preachers should not visit their relatives and friends during their travels, something that would keep them from their task. But in a place where one has relatives, it would be impolite to stay with someone else. If this interpretation by B. Lang is correct,[76] then the logion is unmistakably tied to the Palestinian situation. Where would the early Christian itinerant preachers find their relatives and friends if not in the vicinity of their home towns?

The mission discourse in Matthew retains two pieces of Matthean special material that place local limits on the activity of early Christian itiner-

---

75. Cf. J. Jeremias, *Heiligengräber in Jesu Umwelt*.

76. B. Lang, "Grussverbot oder Besuchsverbot?" In this Lang adopts an interpretation already found in G. L. Hahn, *Das Evangelium des Lucas* 2:34–35. Two arguments are important here: (1) in Luke, ἀσπάζομαι can indicate a (relatively long) stopping with friends (Acts 18:22; 21:7; 25:13); (2) it is regarded as impolite not to visit one's relatives when one comes to their town. When Lucius, in Apuleius's *Metamorphoses* (2.3), does not stop with his aunt, and then happens to meet her, he has to give her express assurance: "As often as I have occasion to pass by your house I will come and see how you do." I. Bosold (*Pazifismus und prophetische Provokation*, 84–85) offers another interpretation: non-greeting is said to be a provocative symbolic action.

ant charismatics. The first introduces the mission discourse and names the addressees of the mission:

> "Go nowhere among the Gentiles,
> and enter no town of the Samaritans,
> but go rather to the lost sheep of the house of Israel."
> (Mt 10:5b-6)

The second reassures the disciples in the face of the persecutions they are to expect. It does not so much name addressees of the mission as indicate refuges to which the persecuted disciples can flee:[77]

> "When they persecute you in one town [lit. "this city"], flee to the next;
> for truly I tell you,
> you will not have gone through all the towns of Israel,
> before the Son of man comes."
>
> (Mt 10:23)

The content of a third saying could place it in the same group. It speaks of the purpose of sending messengers to Israel: the twelve tribes are to be reassembled and governed by the twelve disciples.

> "At the renewal of all things,
> when the Son of man is seated on the throne of his glory,
> you who have followed me will also sit on twelve thrones,
> judging the twelve tribes of Israel."
> (Mt 19:28; cf. Lk 22:28-30)

The concentration on Israel connects all three sayings. The mission to the "lost sheep" (without a shepherd) corresponds to the judging of the twelve tribes (by new "shepherds"). The Parousia of the Son of man is expressly mentioned in two of the logia. All three establish a close relationship between the disciples and Israel.

---

77. Interpretation of the passage varies: τελεῖν is taken either as "completion of the missionary work" or "end of flight." For the discussion, cf. H. Hübner, art. "τελέω," *EWNT* 3:830–32; M. Künzi, *Naherwartungslogion*, 178 etc. The variation may be explained by the fact that the broader context of the mission discourse indicates a missionary task, but the immediately preceding context, as well as the first part of the saying, speaks of persecution. A further factor is that τελεῖν with accusative object (as in Mt 7:28, 13:53, 19:1; 26:1) points to the completion of an action, while the meaning "completion of a journey" would be unusual. But the Greek interpreters, who were closer to the language of Matthew than we are, consistently think of the flight of the disciples (cf. Künzi, *Naherwartungslogion*, 178). Thus in my opinion there is no compelling philological reason to see any great tension between v. 23a (flight) and v. 23b (missionary work) and to divide the logion into two independent sayings (against W. G. Kümmel, *Verheissung und Erfüllung* [Zürich, 3d ed. 1956], 55–60). An opposition in the meanings of "flight" and "mission" would, moreover, be an artificial construction in light of the historical reality! The flight of the Hellenists from Jerusalem led to the Samarian and gentile mission (Acts 8:1ff.). Paul, as missionary, was often "on the run" (cf. 2 Cor 11:30-33). Even Matthew connects the sending of messengers to Israel with flight and persecution (Mt 23:34-36).

The third saying clearly comes from the Sayings Source, but the origins of the other two are disputed. Were they in Q?[78] Are they taken from a pre-Matthean special tradition?[79] Or did the evangelist himself (or his school) formulate them?[80]

Only one thing is certain: Luke would have had every reason to eliminate them, had he found them in Q. In Luke, Jesus travels through Samaria (Lk 9:51ff.) and warns against the very expectation of the immediate end that is expressed in Mt 10:23 (Lk 21:8). From the probability that Luke *would have* dropped these sayings, of course, it does not follow that he really *did* strike them, because we do not know whether he found them in Q.

We can further surmise that the author of Matthew did not create the two sayings. Of course, it is often proposed that they correspond to his specific idea of Jesus: in his lifetime Jesus was sent only to Israel (cf. Mt 15:24); after Easter he turns to all nations (Mt 28:18-19). This does not mean to deny that Matthew arranged the sequence of a particular and a universal mission in this way. But it is slightly different to say that he created this tension. It should be recalled that in the mission discourse Jesus says nothing about his own mission; he only speaks of the mission of his disciples. Matthew is thinking of their post-Easter mission when he takes up portions of the synoptic apocalypse—predictions regarding the time after Jesus' death—from Mark 13 and includes them in the mission discourse (Mt 10:17-22 = Mk 13:9-13). Matthew would scarcely have understood the mission discourse in a "historicizing" way, as a collection of instructions that, so far as Mt 10:5-6 and 10:23 are concerned, apply only to Jesus' lifetime. It is Matthew who does not put these instructions of Jesus in a narrative about a pre-Easter mission—unless one wants to see in the introductory remark "these twelve Jesus sent out" (10:5) an indication of such an account. It is also Matthew who emphasizes that everything Jesus taught during his lifetime is still valid after Easter (Mt 28:18-19). I think there can be no doubt that the instructions of Jesus in Mt 10:5-6 are in force until the Parousia, until "the Son of man comes" (10:23). But this limitation of the disciples' mission to Israel, valid also for the period after Easter, is clearly in tension with the order for a universal mission. This means we ought to reckon with the fact that Mt 10:5b-6 and 10:23 were

---

78. H. Schürmann in particular has pleaded the case for the affirmative in studies of great subtlety: "Mt 10,5b-6 und die Vorgeschichte des synoptischen Aussendungsberichtes"; idem, "Zur Traditions- und Redaktionsgeschichte von Mt 10,23." See the other authors cited in Polag, *Fragmenta Q,* 45, 61.

79. So Dahl, *Matteusevangeliet* 1:136, 139. He correctly surmises that both logia come from the same tradition.

80. So, most recently, J. Gnilka, *Das Matthäusevangelium,* 361–62, 374–75.

not created by Matthew, but taken over by him, especially since the thematically related logion Mt 19:28 is clearly pre-Matthean.

Both of the Israel logia reveal a limited local perspective. The sending to "the house of Israel" means the people of Israel (cf. Mt 2:6; 19:28), not necessarily limited to Palestine because there could also be lost sheep from Israel outside its boundaries. However, the exclusion of Gentiles and Samaritans shows that Matthew is referring to Jewish-populated Palestine.[81] The following words point to a rural area because they mention cities and villages together (10:11).

The second saying also suggests a restricted area. The strange statement about "this city" is remarkable, and remains opaque for us. It must once have referred to one particular city, but which one is not evident from the context. If they are persecuted in "this city," they are to flee to "the next." Until the Parousia, there will always be a Jewish city that welcomes Christian missionaries. That kind of confidence belongs to an early period, when a mission was still being pursued in Israel with a certain degree of optimism.

How did Matthew himself account for the saying? "Israel," for him, is first of all Jewish-populated Palestine, "the land of Israel," or particularly Archelaus's territory (2:20, 21). But in 10:23, Matthew may be thinking of a larger area, for immediately beforehand he has spoken of persecutions in councils and synagogues and by governors and kings (10:17-18). But there were governors and kings in the whole eastern empire: in Nabatea, Chalcis, Cilicia, Commagene, Adiabene. The plural indicates an area larger than Palestine, where there was only one governor and one king at a time (Agrippa I and II), although it must be noted that people could refer to a tetrarch as "king" (cf. Mk 6:14). The application to regions beyond Palestine is also evident from the fact that the missionaries are to give witness before "the Gentiles," which shows that not only Jews are in view (Mt 10:18). In addition, it is important to Matthew that, in 10:1ff., those twelve apostles are sent out who will one day judge the twelve tribes of Israel (Mt 19:28), thus including also the scattered tribes of the Diaspora outside

---

81. Jeremias (*Jesu Verheissung*, 16–17) goes still further: he regards πόλιν as the mistranslation of an Aramaic word that means "province" without specific reference. Originally, the land of Samaria must have been intended: "The instruction not to go to Samaria cuts off the south from [the disciples], and the order not to go to the gentiles eliminates the other three points of the compass: they should restrict themselves to Galilee" (p. 17). It is true that the road to Judea and Perea leads, for a short distance, through gentile territory. Galilee and Perea are not contiguous regions. But even in Scythopolis, whose territory had to be crossed, there were Jews (cf. Jos. *Bell.* 2.466ff.). And surely no one who heard this saying would have supposed that the "lost sheep of the house of Israel" were only in Galilee.

Palestine. Matthew 4:24 already points beyond Palestine: before Jesus' fundamental teaching in the Sermon on the Mount, people from "all Syria" are coming to him. The region where, in the evangelist's understanding, "Israel" is to be sought in 10:23 could thus be larger than Palestine. Either it includes all of Syria—the rabbis could define Eretz Israel in this broader sense[82]—or the whole Diaspora.[83] Matthew can take over the saying if, within his environment, (1) he only knows Christian communities in which there are both gentile and Jewish Christians and (2) he knows of Jewish communities in which no Christian missionaries have yet been active and where Christians have not yet found "refuge." It is not unthinkable that at the end of the first century C.E. a Christian would have had such a picture of the spread of Christianity. But in the pre-Matthean tradition, Mt 10:23 could well have referred to a much more limited area. We find ourselves near "this city," which is most certainly to be sought in Palestine.

If the two sayings about Israel (Mt 10:5, 23) come from pre-Matthean tradition, their *Sitz im Leben* is probably to be found in those groups that appear at the apostolic council as representatives of the mission to Israel. Peter is their leading figure. The two sayings about Israel would have entered Matthean tradition by way of Petrine groups. That is historically possible, for at other points as well Matthew has special material in which Peter has a prominent place: the saying about primacy (Mt 16:18-19), the Matthean version of the stilling of the storm (14:22-33), and the pericope about the temple drachma (17:24-27). If Matthew's special material reached him at other points from those groups, why not here as well? The content of both sayings fits admirably with the little we know about these people: they were itinerant preachers who considered themselves dedicated to Israel. They distinguish themselves from the Hellenists, whose mission brings them also to Samaritans (Acts 8:3ff.) and Gentiles (Acts 11:20). Their center (and "home base") was the Jerusalem community. The city of Jerusalem could be the reference of the puzzling ἐν τῇ πόλει ταύτῃ (10:23), especially since we know of conflicts there between the authorities and early Christian missionaries (Acts 12:1ff.) and since Peter left the city in the wake of such a conflict (Acts 12:17). The search for the lost sheep of Israel would fit within their program. (That much later we meet Peter as "shepherd" of the sheep [Jn 21:15-17] could, of course, be coincidental.) Added to this is the fact that the circle of the Twelve, associated with Peter, is also closely bound up with "Israel." The number twelve

---

82. Cf. O. Keel and M. Küchler, *Orte und Landschaften der Bibel* 1:262–68.

83. So G. Strecker, *Der Weg der Gerechtigkeit*, 41–42: Matthew is thinking of "all the cities of the earth where Jews dwell."

would already point to that, even if it were not directly established by the logion Mt 19:28. Thus, it is probable that all three sayings about Israel stem from the itinerant charismatic circle of the Twelve, in which Peter had a dominant position. Matthew 10:5 and 10:23 would then have played a role in the early period of the Petrine mission to Israel.

Thus we have been able to point out a whole series of logia that reveal a Palestinian and often even a Galilean cultural context. It is true that the demonstrations have varying degrees of plausibility. But on the whole, the result may be regarded as established: parts of the sayings tradition were influenced by localities in Galilee (or in Palestine). This result may sound trivial, since Jesus came from Galilee and all the sayings we have examined are attributed to him. No wonder that here and there a Galilean cultural context glimmers through! But the insight seems less trivial if we consider that in one of the most thoroughgoing analyses of the sayings tradition the greater part of the logia discussed are attributed to Syrian communities outside Palestine.

For the "localizing" of logia a further observation is important, namely, that the sayings tradition had as its primary (if not only) *Sitz im Leben* the early Christian itinerant charismatics.[84] Through words of judgment against "this generation" and woes against places that refuse them, they took control of their own situation of rejection and homelessness. In the contrast between ascetic desert prophets and the luxuries of court life they saw reflected the opposition between their own lives and those of "normal people." In the sayings about Israel, they recovered their own self-understanding: as itinerant messengers to Israel, which must be called to conversion before the end that is soon to break upon it. This *Sitz im Leben* of the sayings tradition that emerges in the words about discipleship and in the mission discourse is not the special object of this investigation, but it has a fundamental importance for it: it makes it impossible to locate the traditions about place in a single locality such as Jerusalem. Wandering preachers have their home bases, of course, but they carry traditions to many places. They are responsible for the spread of those traditions. Insofar as Jesus traditions were transmitted by them, they are a priori not bound to a specific place, but only to a region. The center of early Christian itinerant preachers was, in the earliest period, Palestine. But there were also Jewish communities in the neighboring regions of Syria. An advance of Jesus traditions into these nearby areas is probable from the

---

84. I hold to my thesis about wandering radicals, even if it would have to be formulated differently at the present time. Cf. the original expression in G. Theissen, "Wanderradikalismus."

start, but should not lead us to deny the Galilean-Palestinian stamp of many sayings. The way in which the situation in the border region between Syria and Palestine affected the Jesus tradition is better investigated, I think, in the narrative tradition rather than in the sayings tradition. It is to the narrative tradition that we now turn.

2

Crossing Boundaries in the Narrative Tradition

Although the sayings and narrative materials are part of the same stream of synoptic tradition, we must expect to find that they were transmitted under differing conditions. For Jesus sayings, Jesus is supposed to be the author. But the fact is that stories about Jesus are always composed by someone else. Not one of them can claim Jesus as its author. The early Christian transmitters of these stories were probably aware of that fact: within the history of the tradition as we can reconstruct it, they made fewer changes in the words of Jesus than in the stories. And even within the stories, words of Jesus are more "stable" in the retelling than is the narrative content.

Add to this a further difference: sayings and collections of sayings were most often handed on by people who were convinced of their value, that is, by adherents who found instructions for their own lives in these words. But stories, including summary reports about someone's teaching, are interesting to all those who want to form a picture of a historical personage: adherents, outsiders, and opponents. For example, Josephus offers us a summary report about the Baptizer (*Ant.* 18.116–19), in which his teaching is sketched in very general terms, lacking the preaching of eschatological judgment. However, the Baptizer's words have been preserved only in the Gospels—assembled by people who saw in him a significant prophet. Another example is James, the brother of the Lord. Christian tradition has preserved a pseudepigraphal letter from him containing his teaching. Josephus also speaks of him, but from his brief report we cannot even detect that James was a Christian. Josephus is interested only in the circumstances and consequences of his execution, and is silent about James's convictions (*Ant.* 20.200ff.). Of course, we cannot formulate any "law" from these two examples. Those who, as outsiders, want to refute a teaching will be interested in it for that reason and may even repeat it word for word, as Origen does in *Contra Celsum*. There were certainly sayings about

Jesus that circulated among his enemies: the word about the temple is brought against him in his trial before the Sanhedrin (Mk 14:58). But there is a certain probability that stories enjoy a wider circle of tradents and addressees than do sayings and instruction. In the process, the element of the story that seems remarkable or unusual will probably reach the "outside" most rapidly: scandalous facts such as being executed as a criminal, or marvelous things such as healings and exorcisms.

The name of this chapter, "Crossing Boundaries in the Narrative Tradition," has a double reference. In some narratives the local border situation between Palestine and the neighboring regions is especially evident. The story of the Syrophoenician woman will be investigated as an example. Beyond this, the narrative tradition reveals a crossing of social boundaries: not only disciples and followers of Jesus, but the whole people tell about Jesus and John. Matthew 11:18-19 refers directly to this kind of popular fame: the Baptizer is seen as an ascetic, Jesus as a "glutton and drunkard." Therefore our second step will be to analyze a narrative tradition about the Baptizer that was probably not handed on by Jesus' followers: the court legend of his execution. Finally, there will be a summary discussion of the conditions for the transmission of miracle stories and apophthegms.

THE STORY OF THE SYROPHOENICIAN WOMAN AND THE BORDER REGION BETWEEN TYRE AND GALILEE

In Mk 7:24-30, a foreign woman who asks for help for her sick daughter is rejected by Jesus with the words, "Let the children be fed first, for it is not fair to take the children's food and throw it to the dogs" (Mk 7:27). Jesus' answer is morally offensive. It is as if a doctor would refuse to treat a foreign child. Moreover, Jesus' response is an exegetical problem: the bread metaphor does not fit the woman's request. Jesus is not being asked for food, but for his help as a physician and exorcist.

Matthew already sensed this second problem. In his version, Jesus responds to the woman's petition with the more appropriate image of a shepherd: "I was sent only to the lost sheep of the house of Israel" (Mt 15:24). Only then does he add the saying about food being thrown to the dogs (15:26). The "exegetical" problem—the tension between the request and the bread metaphor—is thus blunted. But the moral problem becomes more acute, for in Matthew the "dogs" in Jesus' metaphor are clearly Gentiles, that is, those who do not belong to the house of Israel. In particular, we no longer find it said here that they are to have their turn later. Mark 7:27a is dropped. The insulting nature of Jesus' refusal is revealed even more clearly. Then, as now, to call someone a "dog" was an insult.[1] Of course, it is possible to think of faithful house pets.[2] These got the table scraps (*Jos. As.* 10:13), and the diminutive κυνάριον applies to them. But that does not make the image any nicer: the association of dogs with Gentiles gives it a negative tone in any case. We only need think of sayings such as: "Anyone who eats with an idolater is like someone who eats with a dog; as the dog is uncircumcised, so is the idolater" (*Pirqe R. El.* 29).[3]

New Testament exegesis has taken different routes in an effort to make sense of Jesus' offensive saying. We may distinguish three types of interpretation: biographical, paradigmatic, and salvation-historical.

The biographical interpretation of the pericope is seldom found today. Here the offensiveness of Jesus' attitude is felt more powerfully than in modern exegesis, which quickly inclines to trace the pericope to discussion within the Christian communities. So J. Weiss[4] asks of Mt 7:27: "How does [Jesus], with his direct, unprejudiced ways, arrive at such an idea?" He can only explain Jesus' attitude thus: he has been disappointed by his own people and has withdrawn to a lonely place. The gentile woman's cry for help has made the paradox of the situation clear to him: "He no longer can or will help his people, and immediately the needs of foreigners are pressing upon him! The unnatural character of the moment quickly forms itself into a parabolic image for him. It is a hasty word and does not mean that he will not help." This explains nothing: disappointment at his own people could just as well lead him to turn toward foreigners. Apart from that, we have to ask why the episode was handed down. Must it not express something independent of a single biographical situation?[5]

---

1. "Dog" is a dirty word: a comparison with this animal is regarded as degrading (cf. 1 Sam 17:43; Isa 56:10-11); "dog" symbolized what is despicable (Eccl 9:4; 1 Sam 24:14; 2 Kgs 8:13; Prov 26:11). The New Testament continues this way of speaking: the fact that Lazarus cannot even keep the stray dogs away from him is a sign of his deep misery (Lk 16:21). What is holy may not be thrown before dogs and swine (Mt 7:6). Opponents and heretics are made contemptible by being called "dogs" (2 Pet 2:22; Phil 3:2; Rev 22:15; Ign. *Eph.* 7:1). See also O. Michel, "κύων"; S. Pedersen, "κύων."

2. Examples of positive references to dogs are Epictetus *Dissertationes* 4.1.111: the "little dog" is among the things from which it is hard to separate ourselves. In Tob 5:17 [6:2] the κύων τοῦ παιδαρίου accompanies the parents as they say farewell to their son. The distinction between one's own house pets and unfamiliar strays is important precisely in the question of table scraps. Aseneth throws her idolatrous food out the window onto the street with the words: "my royal dinner and my fatted beasts have I given to the [strange] dogs" (*Jos. As.* 10:14, cf. 13:8). For some general material on the ambivalent attitude to dogs in antiquity, see W. Richter, "Hund."

3. K. Tagawa (*Miracles et Évangile*, 118–19) opposes the identification of Gentiles with dogs, since it is always found as an explicit comparison among the rabbis, never as a metaphor. But in my opinion the instances cited by P. Billerbeck (*Kommentar* 1:724–26) are clear enough to equate dogs with Gentiles in the context of this story.

4. J. Weiss, *Die drei ältesten Evangelien*, 128.

5. Another example of biographical interpretation is I. Hassler, "Incident of the Syrophoenician Woman": Jesus winked when he made his refusal, and so on!

(2) Paradigmatic interpretation sees the behavior of the Syrophoenician woman as an example of faith that is attacked and tested, that holds fast to Jesus even against appearances.[6] This interpretation can be maintained at both the traditional and redactional levels: the rejection by the wonder-worker of the woman petitioner is the heightening of a traditional motif, that of "impeded approach," that we find in many miracle stories. E. Haenchen sees here "the primitive notion"[7] that the wonder-worker has only a limited amount of healing capacity, which belongs to the Jews. The gentile woman is trying to get some of this power applied to her own case. Her persistent importunity is the expression of a common belief in miracles. What this interpretation sees as a variation on a traditional motif could have been given a new meaning in Mark. Two interpreters see this specifically Markan idea in the depiction of faith in Jesus. Thereby the accent can lie on the *fides quae*, the hidden dignity of Jesus (B. Flammer),[8] or on the *fides qua*, the testing of the faith of the petitioning woman (K. Tagawa).[9] Both suppose that the story originally had a different meaning and was intended to legitimate the gentile mission. This is disputed by J. Roloff, for whom the story was, from the beginning, about tested faith.[10] All these paradigmatic interpretations are undoubtedly correct on one point: the Syrophoenician woman is one of the great symbols of tested faith. But the "testing" of that faith happens in a concrete historical context: between Jesus and the woman stand the barriers that separate Jew and Gentile. Every interpretation must keep that in mind.

(3) This is the point at which the salvation-historical interpretation begins. R. Pesch expresses a broad consensus when he writes, "The pericope documents the early Christian struggle to overcome a particularism about salvation that was derived from Israel's preeminence."[11] The sharp rejection comes not from Jesus, but from an early Christian group that wanted to bar Gentiles from access to the community; in fact, it appears that two opinions are at odds here. In v. 27b, "It is not fair to take the children's food and throw it to the dogs," we have what sounds like complete rejection of Gentiles. But the preceding phrase, "Let the children be fed first" (v. 27a), seems like a (secondary) relativizing of the rejection: the absolute "no" becomes a "not for the moment." This kind of temporal priority of Jews before Gentiles corresponds to early Christian ideas as found in Paul (e.g., Rom 1:16), but also independent of Paul (Acts 13:46).[12] *and elsewhere*

Two questions remain. First, why should an early Christian group attribute

---

6. The high point of this interpretation is Luther's sermon on fasting, WA 17/2, 200–204.

7. E. Haenchen, *Der Weg Jesu*, 274.

8. B. Flammer, "Die Syrophönizerin."

9. Tagawa, *Miracles et Évangile*, 120.

10. J. Roloff, *Das Kerygma*, 159–61.

11. The salvation-historical interpretation is represented by, among others, R. Pesch, *Das Markusevangelium*, 390; J. Gnilka, *Evangelium nach Markus* 1:290.

12. The salvation-historical interpretation sees the pericope as evidence of the struggle about accepting Gentiles. W. Schmithals (*Das Evangelium nach Markus* 1:351–56) contradicts the consensus that the story is about acceptance of Gentiles in Christian communities. The

to Jesus an opinion that it has rejected, if it wants to combat that opinion in the minds of other Christians? Roloff is right to express doubt about the customary derivation of the pericope from community debates. A fundamental refusal of the gentile mission, he says, is not to be found anywhere in the New Testament, and the pericope is trying to make intelligible the historical attitude of Jesus precisely in its contrast to the post-Easter situation.[13]

The second question is evoked by the incongruence of the request and its refusal. Why is a petition for healing answered by a rejection that speaks of food? E. Lohmeyer correctly asks, "Is the rescue of a sick child, even a foreigner, to be regarded as a refusal of bread to others?"[14] We can answer this question with two considerations. First, the food metaphor could be conditioned by the fact that common meals often occasioned a debate on the relationship between Jews and Gentiles (cf. Gal 2:11-14). A later version of the pericope, in the Pseudo-Clementine *Homilies*, shows that it really could be understood in that way:[15] "There is among us one Justa, a Syro-Phoenician, by race a Canaanite, whose daughter was oppressed with a grievous disease. And she came to our Lord, crying out, and entreating that he would heal her daughter. But he, being asked also by us, said: 'It is not lawful to heal the Gentiles, who are like to dogs on account of their using various meats and practices, while the table in the kingdom has been given to the [children] of Israel.' But she, hearing this, and begging to partake like a dog of the crumbs that fall from the table, having changed what she was, by living like the [heirs] of the kingdom, she obtained healing for her daughter, as she asked" (Ps.-Clem. *Hom.* 2.19.1–3).

Perhaps even Mark wanted the story understood in that way. The narrative about the Syrophoenician woman stands, in Mark, between the first and second feeding stories. In the context we often encounter the key word ἄρτος (6:35ff., 52; 7:2, 5, 27; 8:4ff., 14-17) as well as the associated χορτασθῆναι (6:42; 7:27; 8:8). In addition, the first feeding takes place in Jewish territory (6:35ff.), the second in that of the Gentiles (8:1ff.). It is easy to conclude that the successive feedings of the "children" and the "dogs," the Jews and the Gentiles (Mk 7:27) are related in the redactional context to the order of the two feedings.[16] One can thus readily imagine that the pericope was secondarily applied to the relationship of Jews and Gentiles in Christian communities—and in the process the saying about bread was connected with the problem of food laws. But it is

---

gentile mission is already recognized in the Markan community. In the situation after the Jewish war it is a question of accepting the πρῶτον of the Jews, as the Syrophoenician Gentile so admirably does.

13. Roloff, *Das Kerygma*, 156–61, esp. nn. 200, 201.

14. E. Lohmeyer, *Markus*, 145.

15. On this late "retelling," see W. Bauer, *Das Leben Jesu*, 346–47.

16. Cf. E. Wendling, *Die Entstehung des Markusevangeliums*, 81; K. Kertelge, *Die Wunder Jesu im Markusevangelium*, 156. Even if one does not regard the embedding of the story in its context in this light, a connection with the context remains: the teaching about clean and unclean things (7:1ff.) is now being practiced for the first time. Cf. T. A. Burkill, "Syrophoenician Woman," esp. 29; A. Pilgaard, *Jesus som undergører i Markusevangeliet*, 98–101.

scarcely imaginable that the saying was formulated with an eye to that problem, for the order it emphasizes—first the children, then the dogs; first the Jews, then the Gentiles—has nothing to do with the community problem of common meals. Here the situation was that everyone had the same rights and all sat at table together. Besides, one must ask: Would it not have been much simpler to tell a story about Jesus' eating with "unclean" people in order to have a legitimating model for shared meals among Jewish and gentile Christians? Why should anyone create a complex concealment of these problems within a miracle story? Why should anyone attribute an attitude of rejection to Jesus, when what was at stake was the establishment of an attitude of acceptance within the community?

Let us summarize our brief survey of the three types of interpretation of Mk 7:24-30. We find an effort throughout to interpret Jesus' rejection of the petitioning woman in such a way that it loses its offensiveness, either by tracing it biographically to an (unprovable) momentary mood of Jesus, by interpreting it symbolically as a test of faith, or by regarding it as the expression of an element of salvation-historical symbolism—the opening of the church to the Gentiles. None of these approaches is persuasive. The difficulty remains: How can one refuse a request for the healing of a child by saying that children are to be preferred to dogs? How can we avoid being caught in the contradiction that children are given a higher value within the image presented, but in reality a suffering child is being denied help? This is the point at which the search for cultural context begins. It may be able to offer a new impulse toward understanding the pericope. Jesus' cynical response can more readily be understood if we keep in mind the historical situation of the region in which the story is located.[17] Jesus' rejection of the woman expresses a bitterness that had built up within the relationships between Jews and Gentiles in the border regions between Tyre and Galilee. The first tellers and hearers of this story would have been familiar with the situation in this region, so that, on the basis of that familiarity, they would have felt Jesus' sharp rejection of the woman seeking his help to be "true to life."

Thus it is our task to investigate the relationship of Jews and Gentiles in the border regions of Tyre and Galilee. We will consider six different aspects:

1. The ethnic relationships in this region: What peoples lived there?

---

17. Burkill ("Syrophoenician Woman") and Gnilka (*Evangelium nach Markus* 1:290) suppose that Jesus' journey into the region of Tyre was spun out of the characterization of the woman as a "Syrophoenician."

2. The cultural and linguistic circumstances: What languages were spoken? What cultural influences crossed paths there?
3. The social status of Hellenistic Phoenicians in the Phoenician city-states: Was there a hierarchical order between the "Greeks" and the natives?
4. The economic conditions in the border region between Tyre and Galilee: Were there economically determined relationships and dependencies among the various population groups?
5. The political power-relationships between the city-state of Tyre and the Jewish "hinterland": What structurally determined conflicts of interest can be demonstrated?
6. The social-psychological aspects of the relationship between Jews and Gentiles, that is, stereotypes and prejudices on both sides.

Even with all that, the pericope about the Syrophoenician woman will not be "interpreted." We will only have created the preconditions for an interpretation of this miracle story. We will have to content ourselves, at the end of this section, with a brief look at the consequences of the investigation for the exegesis of the story.

Ethnic Relationships in
the Border Region between Tyre and Galilee

According to Mk 7:24, Jesus is in "the region of Tyre."[18] This means the rural surrounding territory that belonged to every ancient city-state. We have an inscription from the neighboring city of Ptolemais that expressly mentions this "pagus vicinalis."[19] For Tyre we have literary evidence of a rural territory. Josephus mentions it expressly in *Bell.* 3.38 in describing the boundaries of Galilee: "on the north Tyre and its dependent district [Τυρίων χώρα] mark its limits." We also hear about villages belonging to Tyre (*Bell.* 2.588), including Kedasa or Cydasa near the Galilean border (*Bell.* 2.459; 4.105). According to synoptic tradition, Jesus never visited the city itself, but only its rural territories—just as, according to Mk 3:8, the crowd thronging to him does not come from Tyre itself, but from

---

18. The preferred reading of the Textus Receptus (𝔐) and, most recently, H. Greeven, *Synopse der drei ersten Evangelien*, μεθορί (= border, territory surrounded by frontiers), makes this still clearer. Another interesting reading is the peculiar ὄρη (Minuscule 565), reminiscent of the hill country on the border between Tyre and Galilee.

19. Cf. M. Avi-Yonah, "Newly Discovered Latin and Greek Inscriptions," 86–87, no. 3. The inscription reads: "PAGO VICINAL(I)," as if it were a dedication. It presumes a contrast with the *pagus urbanus*.

the vicinity (περὶ Τύρον καὶ Σιδῶνα).[20] This restriction to the countryside is all the more astonishing because, at the time when the synoptic tradition was being shaped and the Gospels written, there was already a Christian community in Tyre (cf. Acts 21:3-6), and it would have been natural either to connect Jesus with the city or to associate the residents of the city with Jesus. The restriction of Jesus to the rural area may thus correspond to the real pre-Easter situation.

What we can know about the population of this region also speaks in favor of this conclusion. Not only in Tyre itself, but also in the countryside there must have been Jewish villages, places that were still deeply rooted in the native Jewish culture. From these villages came some of the most faithful followers of John of Gischala, one of the instigators of the Jewish revolt. In *Bell.* 2.588, Josephus writes about the rise of this revolutionary leader. At first he was a solitary figure, but later he acquired followers: "He ended by mustering a band of four hundred men, for the most part fugitives from the region of Tyre and the villages in that neighborhood [ἐκ τῆς Τυρίων χώρας καὶ τῶν ἐν αὐτῇ κωμῶν]." Later, John and his associates defend the outer court of the temple against the besieging Romans. We have to suppose that he and his followers were convinced adherents to the Jewish faith, just as it is often the case that the most fanatical nationalists come from border regions or from abroad. In *Vita* 372, Josephus describes John's disciples again: "John was left with no more than his fellow-citizens and some fifteen hundred foreigners from the Tyrian metropolis [ἐκ τῆς Τυρίων μητροπόλεως]." This would indicate that his foreign adherents had fled to Galilee from the city of Tyre itself.[21]

At a later time, as well, Jewish villages are presumed in the Tyrian region. The tractate *Demai* of the Jerusalem Talmud discusses fruits that possibly have not been tithed—an acute problem for these Jewish villages in "foreign territory" (cf. *Y. Demai* 1.3 [22d]). Finally, we should mention the synagogue in Akziv (in the South Tyrian region on the Mediterranean coast) for which there is a literary witness from the second half of the first century.[22]

---

20. The redactional alteration in Lk 6:17 to "the coast of Tyre and Sidon" is typical. Luke seems to view Palestine from a Mediterranean perspective.

21. Some Jews would have been living in the Phoenician regions for a very long time. We hear of an immigration to Phoenician territory in the early Hellenistic period: after Alexander's death, Jews fled to Phoenicia before the Syrian-Ptolemaic wars (Jos. *C. Ap.* 1.194). On Jews in Tyre, see also *Bell.* 2.478.

22. Cf. F. Hüttenmeister and G. Reeg, *Die antiken Synagogen in Israel*, 7–8; see also *Atlas of Israel* 9:9B, in which Jewish settlements from ancient times are indicated in the south Tyrian region.

The author of Mark, of course, understood Jesus' "journey" into the Tyrian region as an "excursion into gentile territory." Before the pericope on the Syrophoenician woman there is discussion of the question of ritual cleanliness, at the end of which Jesus (in a private teaching session) completely accepts the point of view of the gentile Christians that all foods are clean (cf. Mk 7:19). After the pericope there is a journey to the Decapolis (7:31), that is, into "gentile country." Anyone who looks closely at the geographical relationships will discover that, both in the rural hinterland of Tyre and in the territory of the Decapolis, Jesus could find Jews living next to Syrians and Phoenicians.[23] Thus the "journey into gentile territory" described by Mark only touches places where Jews lived. This favors the idea that Mark gave an entirely new meaning to some of the place-designations he received from tradition: Jesus' going to the places mentioned gives the appearance of a mission to the Gentiles, of whose legitimacy and necessity Mark is convinced (cf. Mk 13:10).

Cultural Circumstances in
the Border Region between Tyre and Galilee

Three different cultural "worlds" met in this region. On the one hand, there was the longstanding contrast between Phoenician and Jewish culture. On top of this was imposed a Hellenistic culture that undoubtedly made a much greater impact in the cities than in the hinterland, in which we may include the Jewish-populated areas of Palestine. The meeting of these three cultures is still visible in our pericope. The woman who comes to Jesus is characterized in Mk 7:26 as ʽΕλληνίς Συροφοινίκισσα τῷ γένει, whereby, as in the following examples, an invariable factor (origin)[24] is combined with a variable aspect (culture or place of residence):

> Jos. *Vita* 427:
> Josephus's third wife is characterized as a γυναῖκα κατῳκηκυῖαν μὲν ἐν Κρήτῃ, τὸ δὲ γένος᾽ Ἰουδαίαν. She lived in Crete, but her origins were Jewish.
> Jos. *C. Ap.* 1.179–80:
> Aristotle conducts a dialogue with a Hellenized Jew who is a "Greek"

---

23. This simple fact needs to be reemphasized. Pesch (*Das Markusevangelium*, 387), for example, thinks that the region of Tyre is "gentile territory." M. Avi-Yonah correctly states the contrary: "The territory of Tyre included quite a number of villages inhabited by Jews" (*Holy Land*, 130).

24. In the examples that follow, γένος indicates ethnic origin. Acts 4:36 and 18:2 prove that this word can also refer to geographical origin: Barnabas is a Levite (i.e., of Jewish origin in the ethnic sense) from Cyprus: Κύπριος τῷ γένει (Acts 4:36).

not only in language, but also in thought: τὸ μὲν γένος ἦν Ἰουδαῖος ἐκ τῆς κοίλης Συρίας . . . Ἑλληνικὸς ἦν οὐ τῇ διαλέκτῳ μόνον, ἀλλὰ καὶ τῇ ψυχῇ.

Philo *Abr.* 251:

Philo characterizes Hagar as "an Egyptian by birth, but a Hebrew by her rule of life": γένος μὲν Αἰγυπτίαν, τὴν δὲ προαίρεσιν Ἑβραίαν.

As in Mk 7:26 (and Acts 4:36; 18:2) the characterization of the person is always in two parts. This two-part way of describing someone speaks against the idea that the two characterizations in Mk 7:26 were added by the redactor.[25] They could well be traditional. Matthew also combines two aspects in his version of the pericope—that is, ethnic and local origin— when he speaks of a "Canaanite woman from that region" (Mt 15:22). The Pseudo-Clementines refer to a "Syro-Phoenician, by race a Canaanite" (Ps.-Clem. *Hom.* 2.19.1), thus combining the Markan and Matthean versions.

What can we gather from the designation Ἑλληνίς? We can presume at least that the Syrophoenician woman knew Greek, but probably also that she was thoroughly integrated in Greek culture. That is at least the interpretation given by the Pseudo-Clementines. There the Syrophoenician woman buys Clement's two brothers:

"Now the woman who bought us was a proselyte of the Jews, an altogether worthy person, of the name of Justa. She adopted us as her own children, and zealously brought us up in all the learning of the Greeks. But we, becoming discreet with our years, were strongly attached to her religion, and we paid good heed to our culture, in order that, disputing with the other nations, we might be able to convince them of their error. We also made an accurate study of the doctrines of the philosophers, especially the most atheistic,—I mean those of Epicurus and Pyrrho,—in order that we might be the better able to refute them" (Ps.-Clem. *Hom.* 13.7.3–4).

This is certainly a novelistic composition, but it well illustrates what one could expect, in the third century C.E., of a "Greek woman of Syrophoenician origin." Knowledge of Greek in no way excluded a familiarity with Aramaic. The second description of the woman as a Syrophoenician could also be intended to make it clear how a "Greek woman" could communicate with an itinerant Jewish preacher from the hinterland. We have proof that the Tyrian population was bilingual well into New Testament times. According to Josephus (*Ant.* 8.144; cf. *C. Ap.* 1.116), Menander of Ephesus

---

25. L. Schenke (*Die Wundererzählungen des Markusevangeliums*, 255) and H. J. Klauck (*Allegorie und Allegorese*, 273) regard "Greek" as a redactional addition. D. Koch (*Die Bedeutung der Wundererzählungen*, 87) leaves open the question of which of the two designations is secondary. A. Dermience ("Tradition et rédaction," 29) considers the second designation redactional.

translated Tyrian sources into Greek. Inscriptions in two languages have been preserved from Phoenician colonies: from Delos there are Tyrian inscriptions from the fourth and first centuries B.C.E.,[26] and from Athens there are Sidonian inscriptions from the fourth or third century.[27] If the native language was maintained even in foreign parts, how much more may one expect to find a living Phoenician language among all parts of the population in the homeland. With the aid of this native language, a Syrophoenician could converse quite well with a Jew: Palestinian Aramaic and Phoenician are so closely related that at one point Josephus can simply interpret an ancient author's mention of the "Phoenician language" as referring to the language of the Jews (C. Ap. 1.173).

The Syrophoenician woman is thus a Hellenized Phoenician who runs across a Galilean prophet in the rural territory belonging to Tyre. Here two different "social worlds" meet. Their distance may be illustrated by Josephus's note on Zebulon, a small city on the border between Ptolemais and Galilee: Cestius Gallus burned it down "although he admired its beauty, with its houses built in the style of those at Tyre, Sidon, and Berytus" (Bell. 2.504). These houses built in Hellenistic style evidently appear as foreign bodies among the simple dwellings in Galilean villages. We may imagine the Syrophoenician woman in similar fashion: a strange appearance in the rural hinterland of her city, in a place where many Jews still lived.

Social Status and Hellenistic Culture in the Phoenician City-States

The characterization of the Syrophoenician woman as a "Greek" gives us a valuable indication of the social class to which the tellers and hearers of the story assigned her. Knowledge of Greek language and culture point to a member of the upper class, since Hellenization had first affected the people of higher status everywhere.[28] And for a long time there would be many among the simple people who did not understand Greek:[29]

1. During the reign of Diocletian, an official in Scythopolis translates the homily during worship from Greek into Aramaic, but only because otherwise some people would not have understood anything.[30]

---

26. CIS 1, no. 114. On this, cf. E. Schürer, Geschichte 3:97ff. On an inscription from the first century, cf. R. Dussaud, "Inscription phénicienne."

27. Cf. CIS 1, nos. 115–21.

28. Avi-Yonah writes, "The coastal Philistines and Phoenicians became hellenized, at least as far as their upper classes were concerned" (Holy Land, 213).

29. On what follows, see Schürer, Geschichte 2:85 n. 243.

30. Cf. B. Violet, ed., Die palästinischen Märtyrer des Eusebius von Cäsarea, 4. Procopius has

2. In Jerusalem, the preaching text and homily are translated from Greek into "Syrian" (i.e., Aramaic) and Latin. A travel journal reports that there is always someone there "qui siriste interpretatur propter populum, ut semper discant." If the translation is done "propter populum," this certainly means the simple, uneducated people.[31]

3. In Gaza, ca. 400 C.E., a local boy speaks only Aramaic. His mother affirms that neither she nor her child can speak Greek.[32]

Certainly, knowledge of Greek had also penetrated the lower classes: otherwise, the Greek inscriptions in Palestine forbidding grave-robbing would make no sense.[33] But an ordinary woman with little knowledge of Greek would no more be described as a "Hellene" than a German with average English skills would be called an "Anglophile." For the hearers and readers of Mk 7:24-30, a "Hellene" was certainly someone above average. This is true for the Pseudo-Clementines as well. They turn her into a wealthy woman: she buys shipwrecked boys as slaves and gives them a Greek education (Ps.-Clem. *Hom.* 13.7.3–4). Rejected by her pagan husband, she remains alone, but gives her daughter in marriage to a poor Christian (a πένης; *Hom.* 2.20.2). The story of her family is supposed to demonstrate that for the sake of the faith one must be prepared to give up status and riches. As we have said, all this is novelistic coloring. But the story of the Syrophoenician woman apparently aroused fantasies in that direction.

In addition, there is a second, very modest indication that the Syrophoenician woman was relatively affluent. Mark speaks in this story of a κλίνη, not a κράβαττος ("mattress," "straw tick"; cf. Mk 2:4, 9, 12; 6:55; Jn 5:8ff.). He thus chooses the more elevated expression: κράβαττος was regarded as vulgar. The Atticist lexicographer recommends σκίμπους.[34] Sozomen gives us an anecdote about a Cyprian bishop who was publicly criticized by another bishop for having substituted the stylish word σκίμπους for κράβαττος in the text, "Stand up and take your mat and

---

three offices in the church: he is lector, "in another place (office) he translates Greek into Aramaic," and he is also an exorcist. This is the Syrian text. In the Greek tradition this part is missing.

31. S. Silviae, "Peregrinatio ad loca sancta," 99.

32. Cf. H. Grégoire and M. A. Kugener, eds., *Marc le diacre,* ch. 68, 55. Note the legendary motif here: the fact that a child who only speaks Syriac should prophesy in Greek is regarded as a great miracle.

33. I am thinking of the well-known Nazareth inscription. On this, cf. B. M. Metzger, "The Nazareth Inscription Once Again," in *Jesus und Paulus. Festschrift für W. G. Kümmel* (Göttingen, 1975), 221–38.

34. *Phrynichus* 44. Cf. W. G. Rutherford, *The New Phrynichus,* 137–38. We should, however, mention that in another part of the pericope Mark uses another word rejected by Phrynichus, κυνάριον, instead of his recommended κυνίδιον (cf. *Phrynichus* 50).

walk." "Are you supposed to be better than the one who said κράβαττος, since you are ashamed to use that word?" he asked him (Sozom. *Eccl. Hist.* 1.11.23.40–24.5). Therefore, when Mark avoids the familiar word κράβαττος, which he had used before not only in a traditional miracle story, but also in a redactional summary (6:55), the word choice could be an indication of the "better economic circumstances" of the Syrophoenician.[35]

We can go one step further: if the Syrophoenician is a "Greek," this probably says something about her legal status as well. In the Hellenistic city-states the "Greeks" made up the free citizenry. Education and civic status were closely connected. The gymnasium was the precondition for full citizenship. H. Bengtson therefore surmises that "Hellenes" refers to "all the men and women in the Syrian/Phoenician cities who belonged to the privileged upper class of civic society, the 'Hellenes,' without regard to their ethnic origin or descent. When the Gospel of Mark 7:26 speaks of a 'Greek woman' who is Syrophoenician by birth, the only explanation for this contrast is that the woman belonged to the privileged group of 'Hellenes' although she was by birth a Syrophoenician."[36] As a "Hellene" she was one step further removed from the inhabitants of the Jewish hinterland than as a Syrophoenician.[37]

Economic Conditions in
the Border Regions of Tyre and Galilee

The distance between Tyre and the partly Jewish population of its hinterland was exacerbated by economic factors. Tyre was a rich city, its wealth

---

35. Cf. Gnilka, *Das Evangelium nach Markus* 1:293. In addition, we should note that Mark knows the word κλίνη. But there is a motive for using it in 4:21 and 7:4 because a lamp can be placed under a bed, but not under a mattress (4:21). Similarly, it is easier to "wash" a standing bed (7:4). We cannot read too much into the choice of words. It is only important in connection with the characterization of the Syrophoenician woman as a "Greek."

36. Thus H. Bengtson, "Syrien in der hellenistischen Zeit," 252.

37. Based on an analysis of the associations of the word "Syrophoenician," Dermience ("Tradition et rédaction," 21–22) arrives at a quite different result. He points out that "Syrophoenix" as a feminine form is found nowhere outside the New Testament, and the masculine form appears first in two Latin authors (Lucilius, fragments 496–97; Juvenal *Sat.* 8.159). For these authors the concept is definitely deprecating. It follows that "on peut déduire que le féminin évoquait une femme peu recommandable, voire une prostituée" ("one may conclude that the feminine form evokes a woman with little to recommend her, that is, a prostitute"; p. 23). But I think that is an invalid conclusion. The negative associations in the Latin authors are related to conduct in business (cf. Lucilius, fragments 496–97: "and this damned skinflint, this Syrophoenician, what did he usually do in such a case") and should be treated as expressions of Roman prejudice. The Romans (and in part the Greeks as well) looked down on Orientals. The philosopher and rhetor Eunapios from Asia Minor (fourth century C.E.), on the contrary, praises the Syrophoenicians for their pleasant conversation (*Vitae Sophistarum* 496).

based on metal work, the production of purple dye (cf. Pliny *Nat. Hist.* 5.17.76; Strabo *Geogr.* 16.2.23), and an extensive trade with the whole Mediterranean region.[38] Its money was one of the most stable currencies in circulation at this period; it survived for decades without significant devaluation.[39] This was certainly one reason why the temple treasury was kept in Tyrian coin, even though this meant accepting the fact that coins of Tyre depicted the god Melkart.

But Tyre had a problem: its rural territory was limited by natural factors.[40] Tyre was on an island, and the nearby strip of coast suitable for farming was narrow. For agricultural products, the city depended on imports, and this dependence was a constant in the city's history. We find indications of this situation even in the Old Testament: Solomon sent wheat and oil to Hiram of Tyre (1 Kgs 5:11). Josephus writes still more plainly that Solomon every year sent "grain and wine and oil" to King Hiram "of which, because . . . he inhabited an island, he was always particularly in need" (*Ant.* 8.141; cf. 8.54). According to Ezekiel, Judea and Israel sent wheat, olives and figs, honey, oil, and balm to Tyre (Ezek 27:17). No wonder that a drought in Palestine also led to famine in the region of Tyre and Sidon (1 Kgs 17:7-16).

We can gather some additional details from the imperial decrees concerning the Jews collected in *Ant.* 14.190–216. There we read of the annual exports of wheat from Joppa to Sidon (*Ant.* 14.206). Still more important is the pledge "that the children [of Hyrcanus] shall rule over the Jewish nation and enjoy [καρπίζωνται] the fruits of the places given to them" (*Ant.* 14.196). This guarantee applies to all Judea and Galilee, but Sidon, Tyre, and Ascalon are mentioned as typical places in which the decree is to be publicly posted (*Ant.* 14.197), as though this were particularly necessary to make plain to those cities that they do not have a claim to the produce of the Jewish territories. This is still clearer in the second decree. It contains, among other things, the statement that all the "places, lands and farms, the fruits of which the kings of Syria and Phoenicia, as allies of the Romans, were permitted to enjoy by their gift [καρποῦσθαι], these the Senate decrees that the ethnarch Hyrcanus and the Jews shall have" (*Ant.* 14.209). The "kings of Syria and Phoenicia" can only be dynasties in the Hellenistic cities "liberated" by Pompey.[41] They had a fundamental interest

---

38. For the history of Tyre, see W. Flemming, *History of Tyre;* N. Jidejian, *Tyre through the Ages.*

39. A. Ben-David (*Jerusalem und Tyros,* 8) speaks of the "uniquely solid value" of Tyrian coins, which he represents with a graph on p. 14.

40. On this, see S. Freyne, *Galilee,* esp. 114–21.

41. E.g., the tyrant Marion in Tyre, who briefly seized some Galilean territory ca. 43 B.C.E. (cf. *Bell.* 1.238–39; *Ant.* 14.298).

in the agricultural produce of their hinterland. The most significant evidence of this dependence of Tyre and Sidon on the agricultural produce of rural Galilee is in the New Testament itself. Under Agrippa I (41–44 C.E.) there was danger of all-out economic warfare:

> Now Herod [Agrippa I] was angry with the people of Tyre and Sidon. So they came to him in a body; and after winning over Blastus, the king's chamberlain, they asked for a reconciliation, because their country depended on the king's country for food. (Acts 12:20)

By contrast, relations with Berytus were less tense: Agrippa II donated grain and oil to that city (*Ant.* 20.212). We hear more about exports from Galilee to the Hellenistic coastal cities at the time of the Jewish war. For example, grain belonging to the emperor was stored in a village in upper Galilee (*Vita* 71). We hear about Queen Berenice's grain supplies in Besara (*Vita* 119). In both cases it was intended for export. Rabbinic sources confirm these exports of grain.[42] They mention donkey caravans bringing grain from the interior to Tyre (*Y. Demai* 1.3; *Cant. Rab.* 5.14). In Tyre there was a big grain market (*p. Abod. Zar.* 4.39d).

Archeological digs have also confirmed the close ties between Galilee, especially upper Galilee, and Tyre. In contrast to lower Galilee, the northern part of the province was entirely oriented to the Phoenician coastal cities.[43]

In short, Tyre was a wealthy city that needed to buy agricultural produce from the hinterland. When "normal" means were insufficient, one had to resort to bribery in order to achieve one's ends (cf. Acts 12:20). The Galilean hinterland and the rural territory belonging to the city (partly settled by Jews) were the "breadbasket" of the metropolis of Tyre. In the crises of supply that occurred periodically[44] it was clear from the start who had the upper hand: Tyre was financially powerful enough to buy grain for itself in crisis situations. But even in "normal" times the farmers in the territory inhabited by Jews would often, and justly, have had the feeling of having to produce for the rich city-dwellers while they themselves lived in want.

---

42. Cf. A. Ben-David, *Talmudische Ökonomie* 1:239–43, on commerce with the Hellenistic cities: "Tiberias, Sepphoris, and Arab, a tiny spot near Sepphoris, are mentioned as grain markets, together with independent Tyre, the terminus of the grain road from Galilee by way of Kesib and the place where Jewish donkey-driver traders (Heb. *Chamaroth Be-Zor*, i.e., donkey-drivers in Tyre) bought grain" (p. 186).

43. E. M. Meyers, "The Cultural Setting of Galilee." R. S. Hanson ("Tyrian Influence in the Upper Galilee") gives proof of this economic orientation of upper Galilee to Tyre in coin discoveries from the region of Meiron: "For the 1st century C.E., coins from Tyre account for almost half of our total supply" (p. 53).

44. Only a few of the regional supply crises are known to us. J. Jeremias (*Jerusalem zur Zeit Jesu*, 157–61) has collected evidence of the times of want in Jerusalem that we are aware of.

Thus the rural Jewish population in the hinterland of the Hellenistic cities shared the general fate of the whole country: in the struggle over food waged between city and country, they usually got the short end of things. According to Galen, a shortage of food is often a problem in the countryside. He writes about famines:

> The city people who, as is customary, store up enough food in summer to last the whole year, take all the wheat from the fields together with the barley, beans and lentils, and leave for the country people nothing but the remaining pulses, although they themselves even take the greater part of that, too, into the cities. The country people then, when they have used up their winter supplies, have only unhealthful nourishment through the entire summer. In that period these country people eat the shoots and suckers of unhealthful plants. (Galen *De probis pravisque alimentorum succis* 1.6.749–50)

In this situation, Jesus' words in Mk 7:27 have a powerful impact: "Let the children be fed first, for it is not fair to take the children's food and throw it to the dogs."[45] This saying, which at first is so offensive, would have to awaken the following associations: "First let the poor people in the Jewish rural areas be satisfied. For it is not good to take poor people's food and throw it to the rich Gentiles in the cities."

Let us be clear: we are not saying that Jesus' words had that intention. The denotative kernel of this saying only maintains that, just as one prefers children to dogs, so his first concern is for the Jews. But surrounding this denotative kernel is an associative field conditioned by the historical situation. It is evoked by the choice of image: when people mentioned food in the border regions of Tyre and Galilee, and also spoke of children (= Jews) and dogs (= Gentiles), they simultaneously addressed the general economic situation, determined by a clear hierarchy that was just as clearly reversed by Jesus' words. Perhaps Jesus, in replying, was able to make connections with a well-known saying shaped by this situation.

The Political Relationships in the Border Regions between Tyre and Galilee

Commerce was only one means of securing the city's agricultural supply. Another was territorial expansion, whether by peaceful or hostile methods.

---

45. The introduction in v. 27b, οὐ γάρ ἐστιν καλόν, is reminiscent of the "Tobspruch" in the wisdom tradition. "Tobsprüche" have the structure: "Better . . . than." In Mk 7:27 the structure is not linguistically developed, but could be surmised as a "deep structure." The sense of the saying is: "It is better to feed the children than the dogs under the table." To that extent it sounds like a "Tobspruch." On this genre, see G. F. Snyder, "Tobspruch in the New Testament." Burkill ("Syrophoenician Woman," 175–76) takes it to be a proverb like "charity begins at home." The origin of the whole tradition history would be a corresponding Jewish-Christian logion in v. 27b, secondarily implanted in a miracle story and then, in a third step, weakened by v. 27a.

This kind of territorial expansion to the south and southeast was all the more logical because Tyre had no "natural" borders with Galilee.[46] The lands of these Jewish and gentile regions merged gradually into one another. The temptation to expand at the expense of the Jewish hinterland was powerful.

Even in the Old Testament we read of a Tyrian expansion to the south: Hiram of Tyre bought twenty Galilean cities from Solomon. Josephus says that he found proof of this sale in the city archives of Tyre (*C. Ap.* 1.110; cf. 1 Kgs 9:10-14). In the Persian period the southward expansion was carried further.[47] The Persians divided the Palestinian coastal region alternately between Sidon and Tyre.

This expansion of the Phoenician coastal cities of Sidon and Tyre to the south sometimes had lasting success. Josephus speaks of Mount Carmel, "a mountain once belonging to Galilee, and now to Tyre" (*Bell.* 3.35). He also describes Kedasa (Cydasa), at the time of Jonathan (152–143 B.C.E.), as a town between the land of Tyre and Galilee (*Ant.* 13.154).[48] During the Jewish war, however, it was clearly in Tyrian territory. Josephus describes it as a "village of the Tyrians, always at feud and strife with the Galilaeans" (*Bell.* 4.105).

Tyre's policy, shaped by its own interests, of seeking as far as possible to exercise control over the territory that supplied its agricultural products was difficult to carry out in Roman times. It is true that the Romans declared Tyre autonomous (Strabo *Geogr.* 16.2.23)[49] and Mark Antony refused to give it to Cleopatra (*Ant.* 15.95), but Augustus had consciously promoted the establishment of a large, contiguous Jewish territory under Herod. This strengthened Jewish neighbor made any expansion to the southeast more difficult. Additionally, in 20 C.E. Augustus temporarily effected a constitutional degradation of Tyre and Sidon, probably because of internal anarchy (cf. *Dio Cassius* 54.7.6; Suetonius *Augustus* 47).[50] The

---

46. Freyne writes: "Finally we reach the northern boundaries of Galilee, and it is significant that the physical features here are much more complex and that no outstanding natural boundary suggests itself to mark off the region in any particular direction. Perhaps we should not then be surprised to find that the political boundaries have apparently reflected this confusion of nature" (*Galilee,* 8). On Tyre's expansionist drive, he writes: "Tyre . . . has a history of personal encroachment into Galilean territory from the days of Solomon to Caesar. Thus it poses the threat not of the invader but of the permanent aggrandizer" (p. 120).

47. On what follows, see Avi-Yonah, *Holy Land,* 30–31.

48. Cydasa is also mentioned in the Zenon papyri as Kydisos (PCZ 59004 = CPJ, no. 2a), but I do not think that establishes that Cydasa belonged to Tyre in the third century (against Avi-Yonah, *Holy Land,* 130), although it is historically probable.

49. This probably could not be done without bribing the Roman general Scaurus, in whose honor the Tyrians made an inscription. On this interesting story, see Jidejian, *Tyre through the Ages,* 102–3.

50. Cf. ibid., 88.

only opportunities for expansion lay in the east. Such an expansion is attested only for the neighboring city of Sidon, which in the first century had a common border with Damascus (cf. *Ant.* 18.153).

Although King Herod had known how to keep on good terms with Tyre, the other Herodian princes lived in tension with that city. Herod Agrippa, while still a "private citizen," had supported the interests of Damascus against Sidon (*Ant.* 18.153–54). As king he carried on a veritable economic war against Tyre and Sidon (Acts 12:20). Herod Agrippa II was even denounced by the Tyrians as "enemy of their own and of the Romans" before Vespasian in 67 C.E. (*Vita* 407). Such tensions were not merely the result of personal animosities; they reflect an unavoidable conflict of interests. The Herodians stood in the way of Tyrian expansion to the south. Over a long period of time this expansion had been successful. Tyre originally extended only to the so-called "Tyrian ladder," a point at which the mountains come close to the sea. In the rabbinic sources, however, Wadi Qarn has become the boundary.[51]

Social-Psychological Relationships in the Border Regions between Tyre and Galilee

Economic dependence, political expansionism, and cultural distance provided a fertile soil for aggressive prejudices on both sides.

There is a whole series of texts indicating that the Tyrians were especially hostile to Jews. Josephus writes, "the Egyptians, the whole race without exception, and among the Phoenicians the Tyrians, are notoriously our bitterest enemies" (*C. Ap.* 1.70). This statement could be accurate as regards the Tyrians. Whereas, at the beginning of the Jewish war, the Sidonians took no action against their Jews (*Bell.* 2.479) and Berytus provided a refuge for King Agrippa II and his sister Berenice (*Vita* 49; 357), the Tyrians rained violence on their Jewish minority (*Bell.* 2.478), even though the attacks on Jews in their city were not so excessive as those in Scythopolis and Caesarea.

It was not the first time that there had been such assaults. As early as the reign of the tyrant Marion, Jewish property in Tyre had been seized and Jewish people enslaved. After his victory over Cassius, Mark Antony ordered the return of the Jews' property and the release of those enslaved (*Ant.* 14.313, 317, 321).

The attacks at the beginning of the Jewish war led to further actions against the rebellious Jews. A Tyrian army appeared before Gischala and

---

51. Cf. Avi-Yonah, *Holy Land,* 129–30. Based on inscriptions, he dates the moving of the boundary southward to the third century C.E.

burned the town (*Vita* 44)—possibly in reprisal for the destruction of Tyrian Kedasa (*Bell.* 2.459). There was also an anti-Jewish flavor in the Tyrians' maligning of King Agrippa II when Vespasian arrived in the East: their "βλασφημεῖν . . . τὸν βασιλέα" (*Vita* 407) is probably only a special instance of a regular defamation of Jews. In short, we can apply to Tyre what Josephus says about the Hellenistic cities and their soldiers: "Further auxiliaries in very large numbers were collected from the towns; these, though lacking the experience of the regulars, made good their deficiency in technical training by their ardour and their detestation of the Jews" (*Bell.* 2.502).

Fear and suspicion of the Jews were also active in the Christian community at Tyre. When Paul stopped there on his last journey, the Christians urged him not to go on to Jerusalem (Acts 21:3-6).

> There are some indications that the prejudices were not less grievous on the other side. It is from this very borderland between Galilee and the Hellenistic Mediterranean cities that we hear of rebel groups that, we may suppose, conducted raids on the "Greeks" and Syrians. John of Gischala is one example of these. We can gather more precise details about the region of Zebulon, that is, the borderland between Ptolemais and Galilee. In the so-called "bandit war," Varus sent troops from Ptolemais into this region to fight the insurrectionists (*Ant.* 17.288–89; *Bell.* 2.68). This was repeated under Cestius at the beginning of the Jewish war (*Bell.* 2.503). The bandit chief "Jesus," who would fight against Josephus, was active in this region (*Vita* 104–5). I think that the activities of this kind of rebel are an indication of hostility toward the Hellenistic cities—a hostility that had a long tradition. Prophetic sayings against foreigners were familiar; they condemned Tyre as a rich and godless city (cf. Amos 1:9-10; Isaiah 23; Jer 25:22; 47:4; Ezekiel 26–28; Joel 3:4; Zech 9:2). The synoptic prophetic saying in Mt 11:21-24 carries on this tradition: "Woe to you, Chorazin! Woe to you, Bethsaida! For if the deeds of power done in you had been done in Tyre and Sidon, they would have repented long ago in sackcloth and ashes." The addressees are tiny Galilean towns; Chorazin is almost completely unknown. It is true that one can see the saying as a sign of the tendency to play off foreign cities against local towns with regard to their morality; but it is presupposed as a matter of course that Tyre and Sidon are regarded by the audience as being just as repugnant as Sodom and Gomorrah. It is only in this light that the saying gains its aggressive sharpness: the Galileans are no better than these despicable cities. (It is also notable that the saying talks of the "land" of Sodom, not the city. This facilitates an understanding of the saying in terms of the rural conditions of the audience.)

In summary, the story of the Syrophoenician woman is much easier to understand, it seems to me, if the tellers and hearers were acquainted with the situation in the border regions of Galilee and Tyre. Aggressive prejudices, supported by economic dependency and legitimated by religious traditions, strained the relationships between the more thoroughly Hellenized Tyrians and the Jewish minority population living either in Tyre or in its vicinity, partly in the city and partly in the countryside. The economically stronger Tyrians probably often took bread out of the mouths of the Jewish rural population, when they used their superior financial means to buy up the grain supply in the countryside. It is possible that there was a common saying that condemned this situation: should one take food away from one's own children and give it to the dogs (i.e., the pagans)? In that case, what is special about the story in Mk 7:24ff. is that, from the start, the power relationships are different. A representative of the Hellenized class, which normally gave the tone to everything, comes begging the help of an itinerant preacher and exorcist from the Jewish hinterland. She begs help from a member of a group that otherwise always gets the short end of things. She is sharply reminded of the normal situation of dependency. Would it not be just, at the very least, not to distribute one's own gifts to strangers? Behind Jesus' cynical words there lies a bitterness grounded in real relationships.

This study of the cultural context reveals that the story is probably Palestinian in origin. It presupposes an original narrator and audience who are acquainted with the concrete local and social situation in the border regions of Tyre and Galilee. As a result, it now appears more difficult to trace the origins of the story exclusively to early Christian debates about the legitimacy of the gentile mission—debates we read about in Jerusalem, Caesarea, and Antioch. Something more concrete is at stake. In principle we cannot exclude the possibility that the story has a historical core: an encounter between Jesus and a Hellenized Syrophoenician woman.

Our study of the cultural context concludes with this observation. It does not claim to be an exhaustive exegesis of the story of the Syrophoenician woman. But in conclusion we may ask whether something has not emerged in this study that will be helpful for the deeper understanding of this pericope. If the considerations developed here are correct, the miracle would not consist in healing someone far away, but in the overcoming of an equally divisive distance: the prejudice-based distance between nations and cultures, in which the divisive prejudices are not simply malicious gossip, but have a real basis in the social, economic, and political relationships between two neighboring peoples. The Syrophoenician woman accomplishes something that for us today seems at least as marvelous as the miracle itself: she takes a cynical image and "restructures" it in such a way that it permits a new view of the situation and breaks through walls that divide people, walls that are strengthened by prejudice. How does she accomplish that restructuring?

Two aspects should be emphasized. On the one hand, the woman picks up the positive image of the children in the saying in Mk 7:27 and "plays off" this positive value against the factual devaluation of the need of her own child. Behind the sharp refusal, she can hear a positive attitude to children expressed in the image. And when she acts on behalf of a child, she is only putting into practice what is praised in the image within the saying. In formal terms, she plays off the image against the content.[52]

At the same time, she succeeds in giving a positive value to the abusive word "dog." Presumably, she can draw support from positive traits associated with dogs. Although in all cultures these animals serve to enrich the repertoire of human invective, they are also praised, and justly so, for a positive characteristic: their enduring fidelity. A rabbinic anecdote may serve to illustrate that this characteristic of dogs was known and valued:

> Once, when some shepherds were milking, a snake came and drank from the milk. The dog had been watching the snake, and saw that the shepherds were sitting down to partake of the milk; he began to bark at them, but they paid no attention; finally he got up, drank the milk, and died. They buried him and put up a memorial to his faithfulness. To this day it is called "the dog's monument." (*Peshitta* 79b)

The woman not only evokes the image of the faithful dog in her clever reply, she behaves like a "devoted dog." She believes that, despite his refusal, Jesus can and will help her daughter. Jesus expressly recognizes this attitude: "For this saying, you may go your way; the demon has left your daughter" (Mk 7:29). But the modern reader is no less impressed by the fact that, along with this demon, the equally threatening demon of prejudice between the members of different nations and cultures was "driven out."

---

52. The woman's answer has parallels in Judg 1:7 and Philostratus *Vit. Ap.* 1.19. In Judg 1:7 King Adonibezek, who is being besieged by the Israelites, boasts that seventy kings with their thumbs and their great toes cut off used to pick up scraps under his table—a symbol of the most thorough degradation of the enemy. According to W. Storch ("Zur Perikope von der Syrophönizierin"), the point is that although the Syrophoenician woman is one of the "dogs" (i.e., the enemies of the people of God), even dogs like Adonibezek gave the same food to their prisoners as to their children. I doubt that the audience of this story had such acute biblical associations in mind, and I think it impossible that they would have expected a non-Jewish woman to have such a thorough knowledge of biblical history. It is possible that the woman's answer adopts a more general kind of expression: Philostratus speaks of the crumbs that are thrown to the dogs as a way of saying that Damis collected even the incidental words of Apollonius. He uses the image as a comparison: he acted like the dogs who feed on the remnants of the meal. An image that serves Philostratus as an illustration of exemplary behavior furnishes a negative portrait of begging in the Jewish wisdom teacher Pseudo-Phocylides: "Do not eat what falls from the table of the others! Instead, eke out your living from your own possessions, without reproach" (155f.).

THE LEGEND OF THE BAPTIZER'S DEATH:
A POPULAR TRADITION TOLD FROM
THE PERSPECTIVE OF THOSE NEARBY?

We can say with a degree of certainty that the story of the Syrophoenician woman was narrated by people who knew the border region between Tyre and Galilee. The area where it was originally handed down can be located. Is that a singular piece of luck? Or do other stories about Jesus contain indications of the place and time of their transmission? One problem is that we can compare traditions about Jesus only in a limited sense with stories about other people of that time. Tales of rabbinic teachers were handed down under different conditions and permit no direct analogies. There is only one exception: the court legend[53] about the death of the Baptizer. It was retained, together with the Jesus traditions, in Mk 6:17ff. If we could shed some historical light on the environment in which it was transmitted, that might in turn illuminate the Jesus material in which it is embedded and in which it has been handed down. Perhaps in this way we will learn more about the channels of tradition from which the author of Mark has gathered material.

Josephus has retained a competing story about the Baptizer's death (*Ant.* 18.116–19) that in many respects corresponds better to the historical event: it attributes to Herod Antipas a political motive in executing John. A comparison of the two traditions about the Baptizer can make clear the interests that have shaped the Baptizer legend in Mark's Gospel.[54]

---

53. R. Bultmann (*Die Geschichte der Synoptischen Tradition*, 328–29) classifies Mk 6:14ff. as a "legend." K. Berger (*Formgeschichte des Neuen Testaments*, 334) calls it a "report of martyrdom" belonging at the same time to the genre of "court tales" (cf. Daniel 3–4; Esther; 1 Esd, etc.). M. Dibelius (*Überlieferung*, 80) names it an "anecdote." Lohmeyer (*Markus*, 121) refers to it as a "novella." Others presuppose a development of the story that changed its genre. J. Gnilka ("Das Martyrium Johannes"; cf. idem, *Das Evangelium nach Markus* 1:245–46) thinks that an original sketch of the martyr has been overlaid with the popular motif of the vengeful woman. First, it seems clear to me that this is not a typical story of martyrdom. In Jewish martyr stories the sufferings of the martyrs, accepted for the sake of their faith, are depicted (cf. 2 Macc 6:18-31; 7; *Bell.* 2.152–53). In the Hellenistic acts of the martyrs the defense of the martyrs before their judges is described. Both elements are lacking in Mk 6:14ff. Second, it is not a typical legend of a holy man. No use is made of the various opportunities to portray his exemplary piety. Of course it is presupposed that he is "a righteous and holy man" (Mk 6:20), but this is not developed in the narrative. Josephus, who calls him a "good man" (*Ant.* 18.117), gives a vivid illustration of the reasons why he deserves this description. Third, the category "anecdote" is also too general. It does not compass the milieu that shapes the whole story: this is a court anecdote. The term "court legend" is intended to convey that we are dealing with a court anecdote about intrigue and the misuse of power in which, in contrast to comparable court tales (Herodotus *Histories* 9.108–13; Plutarch *Artax* 17), a "holy man" is the victim. Characterizing it as a "court novella" would not reflect this feature.

54. Of course, the Baptizer tradition in Josephus *Ant.* 18.116ff. is itself not free of bias. The eschatological character of the Baptizer's preaching is downplayed, and the interpretation of his baptism sounds as if Josephus was at pains to correct a massive sacramental misunderstanding.

Let us give a brief sketch of the background of the two traditions. Herod Antipas had—perhaps at the urging of Augustus—married the daughter of a Nabatean king, a diplomatic countermove to check the expansionist drive of the Nabateans.[55] This expansionism is well attested. Aretas III (ca. 85–60 B.C.E.) moved on Damascus in about the year 85 and besieged the Jewish king Alexander Jannaeus (*Ant.* 13.392; *Bell.* 1.103). Obdoas II (29–9 B.C.E.) bought the Auranitis circa 21 or 20 B.C.E. for fifty talents. Augustus promised that region to Herod I, but the Nabateans maintained their claim to it (*Ant.* 15.352; *Bell.* 1.398). A marriage between a Herodian and a Nabatean woman curbed a swelling conflict. After the dissolution of the marriage, the Nabateans revived their old claims. They demanded "Gamala"[56] (probably after Philip's death in 34 C.E.) and subjected Antipas to a disastrous defeat (*Ant.* 18.114). At the same time, Paul attests that they moved on Damascus in about 36 C.E. (2 Cor 11:32), which became possible after the defeat of Antipas.[57]

Antipas's marriage to Herodias was also accompanied by domestic political difficulties: it transgressed Jewish law (cf. Lev 18:16; 20:21). Antipas thus fell into the same shadow as his brother Archelaus (4 B.C.E.–6 C.E.). The latter had married Glaphyra, a wife of his dead brother Alexander, even though Alexander had children with her (and thus the exception in Deut 25:5-6 did not apply). In order to make this marriage, Archelaus had also divorced his previous wife, Mariamne. The people disapproved of his behavior. Josephus tells a "court legend" (*Ant.* 17.350ff.) that attributed Glaphyra's sudden death to this offense against the law: her first husband, Alexander, is supposed to have appeared to her in a dream, bitterly reproached her, and announced that he would make her his wife again—that is, by calling her out of this life. This story would scarcely have been told by the Sadducee-minded upper classes (cf. Mk 12:18ff.); it breathes a Pharisaic spirit, since the expectation of a life after death is simply presumed. Thus Archelaus's behavior had already provoked criticism among the people. Everyone knew that, soon afterward, Archelaus was deposed by the emperor at the insistence of his Jewish and Samaritan subjects. Herod

---

55. Cf. Schürer, who writes: "Certainly there were also political motives that moved him to marry the daughter of the Arabian king. He believed that this would be more effective than any fortifications in securing his land against Arab attacks; and it may have been Augustus himself who urged him to make the marriage" (*Geschichte* 1:433; cf. idem, *History,* 342). Augustus gave his support, on the whole, to marriage connections between his client kings (Suetonius *Augustus* 48).

56. The mss. of *Ant.* 18.113 read "Gamala," "Gamalitidis," etc. Editors often conjecture "Gabala" (cf. Josephus, *Ant.* [LCL] 9:80–81). I do not think that is necessary. Gamala was in Philip's territory, thus precisely in the region that the Nabateans had bought in 21 or 20 B.C.E., but had not been able to take possession of. Now they could make their demands effective. Probably they raised the claim only after Philip's death in 34 C.E. The war with Antipas took place in 36 C.E. The large number of deserters from Philip's territory shows that not everyone was convinced of the superiority of Antipas's claims.

57. On the appearance of Nabateans in Damascus in the 30s, cf. R. Wenning, *Die Nabatäer,* 25. This supplements N. Hyldahl ("Paulus og Arabien"), who supposes a Nabatean military advance on Damascus after the Nabatean war.

Antipas's marriage to Herodias some twenty years later could also have undermined his legitimacy in the eyes of the people. Keeping the fate of Archelaus in view, his critics might have endangered his position.

This combination of external and internal political problems was threatening to Antipas. He had to anticipate that his opponents, both inside and outside, might unite against him. His defeat by Aretas in 36 C.E. gave a portent of this constellation: Josephus traces it to deserters from Antipas's army, men from Philip's territory (*Ant.* 18.114). The Baptizer, too, as the voice of an internal popular opposition, could easily be associated with the Nabateans, for he was working not far from them. His preaching made use of wilderness typology (Isa 40:3 = Mk 1:3). Josephus does not attribute the arrest of the Baptizer to his general impact. Instead, he expressly says: "When others too joined the crowds about him [καὶ τῶν ἄλλων συστρεφομένων] . . . Herod became alarmed. Eloquence that had so great an effect on [the people] might lead to some form of sedition" (*Ant.* 18.118). The Baptizer must suddenly have found a greater resonance beyond his previous following, probably due to his criticism of Herod Antipas's "marriage politics." But we are less interested in reconstructing the historical circumstances than in detecting the conditions under which the story of the Baptizer's death was handed down.[58]

This much appears certain: the legend was not shaped by scribal groups. Either its authors were unacquainted with the precise requirements of the law that Herod had violated in marrying Herodias or they were not interested in them, because the Baptizer's reasons for criticizing the marriage are formulated in the most general terms: "It is not lawful for you to have your brother's wife" (Mk 6:18). That is not wrong, but it ought to be stated more precisely: "It is not lawful for you to marry your brother's wife while he is still alive." Had he died childless, it would even be obligatory for his brother to marry his widow (Deut 25:5-6; Mk 12:19). One might say that such distinctions are too subtle to be retained in the tradition.[59] But this very subtlety can be found in Josephus, not in his remarks on the Baptizer, but in a longer excursus on the Herodian family (*Ant.* 18.27ff., 142): "Ἡρωδιὰς ἐπὶ συγχύσει φρονήσασα τῶν πατρίων Ἡρώδῃ γαμεῖται τοῦ ἀνδρὸς τῷ ὁμοπατρίῳ ἀδελφῷ διαστᾶσα ζῶντος" ("Herodias, taking it into her head to flout the way of our [ancestors], married Herod, her husband's brother by the same father . . . ; to do this she parted from a living husband"; 18.136). In the educated upper classes, people told the story of

---

58. On the history of Herod Antipas, cf. E. Schürer, *History of the Jewish People* 1:340–53; H. W. Hoehner, *Herod Antipas*.

59. Mark 12:19 and parallels show, however, that precise legal regulations were discussed in early Christian tradition: the institution of levirate marriage was well understood in early Christianity.

Herod Antipas's marriage together with a rather precise legal opinion on it. Herodias also appears more active in this tradition. It is she, not Antipas, who intends to abrogate the traditional laws. She insists, as a condition of her marriage, that Antipas's first wife, the daughter of the Nabatean king, be sent away (*Ant.* 18.110). In other words, she actively obtains her own divorce and refuses to enter into a polygamous marriage. In both cases she is acting according to patterns of behavior that were a matter of course in Greece and Rome.[60] "To flout the ways of our ancestors" means adopting progressive "Western" norms.[61]

But Mk 6:17ff. is ignorant of Herodias's initiative (although she appears as the driving force behind the proceedings against the Baptizer), nor is the offense against the law given a precise juristic description. Both of these circumstances indicate that what we have here is a popular tradition: the people could scarcely imagine that a woman would take as much initiative in obtaining her own divorce as was possible in the upper classes. Nor were the fine points of the legal situation important to them.

Was this story told by the Baptizer's disciples, then?[62] Perhaps in the circle of his disciples who buried his body afterward (Mk 6:29)? That is improbable, because all the characteristic notes of the Baptizer's preach-

---

60. G. Delling ("Ehehindernisse") does not mention marriage with a brother's divorced wife as one of the impediments recognized in Greece and Rome.

61. Although the Herodians' frequent marriages between uncles and nieces were not contrary to Jewish law, they probably offended against the more rigorous interpretation of those laws by some of the pious. Among the marriages between uncle and niece that are attested are Herodias's marriages to Herod and Antipas (both half brothers of her father, Aristobulus); Salome's marriage to Philip, a half brother of her father, Herod; and the marriage of Berenice to Herod of Chalcis, a full brother of Agrippa I. According to Lev 18:12-13, only marriages between aunt and nephew were forbidden, not those between uncle and niece. The Essenes demanded equal treatment in these cases: the forbidden grades of kinship were to be the same for men as for women (cf. CD 5.9–11). In this view, Herodias's first marriage would already have been offensive.

62. Thus, though tentatively, Bultmann: "The story is then perhaps an indication of a branch of Baptistry on Hellenistic soil" (*Die Geschichte der Synoptischen Tradition*, 329). So also H. Windisch, "Zum Gastmahl des Antipas"; Pesch, *Das Markusevangelium* 1:343. This thesis is emphatically affirmed by K. Berger, *Exegese des Neuen Testaments*, 220–21. Mark 6:17ff. represents a world contrary to the Baptizer's preaching. The Baptizer is killed by the thing against which his message was directed: drunken carousing (cf. Mt 11:18), wine, and a foolish oath: "The report of the Baptizer's death is thus a theological bequest from the Baptizer movement" (p. 221). The decisive arguments against this attractive thesis are to be found as early as Dibelius (*Überlieferung*, 78–79). The Baptizer vanishes in Mk 6:17ff.: "only the dead man's head appears in the scene" (p. 79). A story concerned with the Baptizer would describe his death. Nor is the point the "contrast between the villainous king and the Baptizer," for then we would expect "that the person of the preacher of repentance would be interjected into the picture of the sensual carousing of the lascivious court, clad in ascetic-prophetic garments and with words of the most threatening possible import on his lips. But the narrator makes no such attempt" (p. 79). In fact, the story hastens over the religious point of departure—criticism of Antipas's marriage—to get to the "religiously irrelevant banquet scene" (p. 78 n. 3).

ing are missing: his proclamation of judgment, his call to conversion, and his demand that people be baptized and live righteous lives. Also lacking is any portrayal of the Baptizer as a prophet or martyr. What great possibilities his followers would have had for depicting his steadfastness! What a chance they would have missed for placing some "last word" in his mouth! The Baptizer community would certainly have been interested in his deportment at the last hour of his life. If they had no information about it, it would have been easy to depict the death of the prophet with the typical features of the Jewish martyr tradition.

The things that speak against the story's being a tradition from the Baptizer's community also speak against it as a specifically Christian tradition. Besides, there is nothing here to point to the Baptizer as a precursor of Jesus. Nothing connects his death with Jesus' execution. There is not a trace of the reflection of Christian groups about the Baptizer.[63]

Thus, Mk 6:17ff. is a popular folk tradition about the death of the Baptizer[64] that may even have been accessible to non-Jews. At any rate, specifically Jewish features retreat into the background. We have indications of the existence of such traditions. Josephus reports that Herod Antipas's defeat by the Nabatean king Aretas was interpreted as punishment for his execution of the Baptizer (*Ant.* 18.116, 119). This interpretation was plausible at the time: according to Mk 6:17ff., the Baptizer had attacked that very divorce that led to the enmity between Antipas and Aretas, the king of the Nabateans. The repudiation of the first wife demanded by the marriage contract had to be understood as a cancellation of friendly relations between the rulers of Galilee and of the Nabateans and thus was the occasion of the war in which Antipas was so

---

63. Hoehner (*Herod Antipas*, 303–6) thinks of a community tradition. He mentions two possibilities: Joanna, the wife of Chuza, could have told the story to Peter, who could have handed it on to Mark, or Menahem could have brought it to the community at Antioch, from whom Mark would have gotten it. But here again, Dibelius already saw the decisive point: Mk 6:17ff. "has no evangelistic interest. All the gospel reports about the Baptizer depict him in light of the greater one who comes after him. Here every trace of relationship to the matter the evangelists really wanted to pursue is lacking. That is remarkable, to say the least" (*Überlieferung*, 78).

64. Dibelius (*Überlieferung*, 78) appreciates the closeness to the "novellas," but finds that Mk 6:17ff. lacks a purpose appropriate to that form. Therefore, he also holds for a popular tradition. "The way in which he [i.e., John] disappeared from public view evidently led to all sorts of rumors among the people" (p. 86). Lohmeyer emphasizes still more decidedly that Mk 6:17ff. "is a popular ballad made up of many well-known motifs. . . . The story has nothing in common with Jewish or early Christian piety; it is 'pagan,' although acquainted with matters Jewish" (*Markus*, 121–22). He therefore looks for its origins in Jewish circles that had accommodated themselves to their Hellenistic milieu. Gnilka also favors popular tradition: "This story, transmitted in isolation, is to be approached neither as Christian nor as a tradition of the Baptizer's disciples, but as a tale circulating among the people. . . . It could have been the purpose of the story to stigmatize the godless doings of the powerful, and concretely of Herod Antipas and his court, through this recollection" (*Das Evangelium nach Markus* 1:246).

decisively defeated. Josephus first reports that "some of the Jews" had regarded the destruction of his army as God's just punishment (*Ant.* 18.116). Later he attributes this view to "the Jews" as a whole (*Ant.* 18.119). In both cases, he witnesses to the existence of popular traditions about the Baptizer and his death.[65]

The stories behind Josephus's remarks would scarcely have been the same as the legend recorded in Mk 6:17ff. There is nothing here about divine punishment. Instead, what dominates the story is the legendary motif of the free request.[66] For example, we find this motif in traditions about Caligula and his circle as well. Its surprising result is connected, even fifty years after these events, with a banquet given by Agrippa for Gaius Caligula, in which the latter is supposed to have permitted Agrippa a wish, which Agrippa used to request the rescinding of the order to rededicate the Jerusalem Temple in honor of the emperor. It is historically correct that the intervention of Agrippa I contributed to a good outcome in that case, but the form of his intervention is legendary. The legendary reshaping of events was done in the place where the events occurred: Josephus wrote his *Antiquities* in Rome, where the legendary banquet is supposed to have taken place. In Mk 6:17ff. we are dealing with a similar legendary retelling of events. Did it also happen at the place where they occurred?

Doubts may rightly be raised, for there is a series of remarkable displacements. According to Josephus, the Baptizer was imprisoned and executed at Machaerus in the southern part of Perea (*Ant.* 18.119).[67] But a reader of Mk 6:17ff. who has no preconceptions could only think of the capital city of Galilee as the location of the occurrence. That is where the "leading men of Galilee" gather. Nothing is said about Perea, although it was part of Herod's realm. This "northward displacement" corresponds to the historical events. The territory of Agrippa I, as it existed at the time of

---

65. Mark 6:14-15 also attests to the existence of "popular traditions" about the Baptizer: so Dibelius (*Überlieferung,* 86) who speaks of "popular rumor."

66. This motif is witnessed by Herodotus (*Histories* 9.108–13): Xerxes promises his lover Artayante that he will fulfill her every request (ἐκέλευσε αὐτὴν αἰτῆσαι ὅ τι βούλεται; 9.109). In the Book of Esther the motif appears three times (5:3; 5:6; 7:2). There we also find the offer of half the kingdom (cf. Mk 6:23). The circulation of the motif in contemporary Jewish culture is attested by Josephus (*Ant.* 18.289–97): Gaius permits Agrippa I a request, which the latter uses to ask the rescinding of the order to desecrate the temple by establishing the cult of the emperor there.

67. R. Riesner ("Johannes der Täufer auf Machärus") sees no contradiction between Josephus's tradition and Mk 6:17ff. The Gospels say nothing about the place of execution. A banquet would also be possible in Machaerus because two large dining halls (*triclinia*) have been found there. Cf. F. Manns, "Marc 6,21-29 à la lumière des dernières fouilles du Machéronte." I think, however, that Mk 6:17ff. unmistakably thinks of a place in Galilee. For the author of Mark this is quite clear.

the writing of Mark's Gospel, had, in relation to Antipas's realm, transferred its center northward. Only a small part of Perea was under Agrippa's rule, but in return he possessed Abilene, that is, the territory north of Palestine that had belonged to Lysanias (*Ant.* 20.138; cf. 19.275), and Chalcis with its capital at Arcea (*Bell.* 7.97).

An accommodation to changes taking place between 30 and 70 is evident at another point as well. Antipas is not called "tetrarch," his real title, but "king."[68] He never possessed that title; in fact, it was in attempting to have it bestowed on him by the emperor that he fell into disfavor and was deposed. But the Herodians who followed him, Herod of Chalcis (41–48 C.E.), Agrippa I (41–44 C.E.), and Agrippa II (54–ca. 90?), were all kings. Agrippa II even called himself "the great king" because he ruled several kingdoms (in northern Palestine and in Lebanon). His sister, Berenice, appears as "βασίλισσα μεγάλη" (*OGIS* 428). The fact that Antipas appears as "king" in Mk 6:17ff. could well be a trace of narrators in whose environment Herodians were "kings" quite as a matter of course.

A third change from the real situation is no less revealing: Herodias, before her marriage, had been the wife of an otherwise unknown Herod (*Ant.* 18.136), but in Mk 6:17 her first husband is called "Philip."[69] This can only mean Philip the tetrarch, who is mentioned fleetingly at Mk 8:27 in connection with his capital city, Caesarea Philippi. The confusion is understandable: Philip was the best-known of Herod's sons, next to Antipas. Both of them had long reigns (4 B.C.E.–34 C.E. in one case; 4 B.C.E.–39 C.E. in the other). They were neighbors. A tradition about a marriage between Antipas and his brother's wife would sooner or later

---

68. Luke 3:1 and Mt 14:1 correct Mark by using the proper title "tetrarch." But Matthew, following his source, then shifts back to "king" (cf. 14:9). As "king" he appears in Justin *Dial.* 49.4 and *Gospel of Peter* 1:2. But at Antioch, Herod Antipas was still known as "tetrarch" at the beginning of the second century (Ign. *Sm.* 1:2—by way of Matthew's Gospel?). Confusion of titles is not only found in popular tradition; it happens to historians also. Josephus mentions the "ethnarch" Archelaus among the "kings" (*Ant.* 17.354; cf. Mt 2:22). We also read, in Josephus *Vita* 52, of a tetrarch named Soemus, whose grandson Varus was βασιλικοῦ γένους. This tetrarch is called "rex" by Tacitus (*Ann.* 12.23): "Ituraeique et Iudaei defunctis regibus Sohaemo atque Agrippa provinciae Suriae additi." Pilate had, according to the Caesarea inscription, the title "praefectus Iudaae" (cf. Schürer, *History of the Jewish People* 1:358 n. 22), but Tacitus calls him "procurator," apparently an anachronistic application of the title that was borne only later, by his successors.

69. The traditional harmonizing of the names in Josephus and in Mk 6:17ff. is given detailed foundation by Hoehner (*Herod Antipas,* 131–36). The otherwise unknown "Herod," who according to Josephus was Herodias's husband, is supposed to have had Philip as a second name. But it is highly unlikely that Herod I had given the same name to two of his sons. It is true that we have a number of cases in which brothers concurrently bore the name "Herod." But that is the family name (cf. Schürer, *History of the Jewish People* 1:344 n. 19). This harmonizing does not shed much light on the Markan text because Mark certainly was not thinking of some Herod Philip, but of Philip the tetrarch, whose name he mentions in passing (Mk 8:27). For him, in any case, a confusion existed.

have to have been connected with Philip as *the* well-known brother of Antipas. At the same time, we may presume that Philip was known especially in northern Palestine and the adjoining Syrian territories.

A fourth shift away from historical reality consists in the transfer of the major responsibility for the Baptizer's execution to Herodias. She appears as a bloodthirsty plotter. Even Matthew did not want to believe that; he attributes an intention to kill the Baptizer to Herod Antipas himself. He does not explain Antipas's hesitation to carry out his intention by means of the ruler's secret sympathy with the Baptizer (as in Mk 6:20), but credits it to the Baptizer's popularity among the people, which the prince had to take into account (Mt 14:5).[70] Matthew thus comes closer to the historical reality than does Mark. However, we have evidence from a later period that Herodian women involved themselves in legal affairs and so made decisions about the life and death of prisoners. Agrippa II is present at the trial of the apostle Paul, but so is his sister, Berenice (Acts 25:13ff.; 26:30). The same Berenice intervenes successfully with her brother Agrippa II to save the life of a condemned man, Justus of Tiberias (*Vita* 343, 355). Quintilian (*Inst.* 4.1.19) even counts her among those who were *quidam rerum suarum iudices,* and thus at the very least exercised great influence over legal proceedings. The idea that Herodian women influenced court processes and executions could, on the basis of such episodes, have fixed itself in the popular mind, the only difference being that in Mk 6:17ff. a nefarious influence is attributed to them. Here prejudice possibly influenced the imagination.[71] On this point, too, we can say that in the second half of the first century C.E. such a picture of a Herodian woman was more

---

70. The Matthean version corrects Mark very obviously at the points where the latter is too much at odds with historical reality: (1) Herod Antipas is correctly called "tetrarch" (Mt 14:1), and only later, in harmony with Mark, is he called "king"; (2) he gives a more realistic account of the ruler's motive for the killing—Antipas's fear of the Baptizer's influence among the people is stated here (cf. Mt 14:5), as it is by Josephus (*Ant.* 18.118); and (3) the dancing daughter becomes Herodias's daughter. Matthew does not correct the confusion of Herodias's first husband with Philip. Only Codex D and part of the Latin textual tradition omit the name. Matthew's changes in the Markan text are interesting because they show that a text that is secondary from a literary-historical point of view can be more "historical" in some details than a text that is primary from the literary standpoint.

71. An analogous case of shifting the supposed reasons for a political murder from political to private motives is the death of Caecina at Rome in 79 C.E. Suetonius reports: "Among these [i.e., those whose punishment Titus publicly demanded] was Aulus Caecina, an ex-consul, whom he invited to dinner and then ordered to be stabbed almost before he left the dining-room; but in this case he was led by a pressing danger, having got possession of an autograph copy of an harangue which Caecina had prepared to deliver to the soldiers" (Suetonius *Titus* 6.2). But the *Epitome de Caesarum* reports of the same events: "Caecinam consularem adhibitum cenae, vixdum triclinio egressum, ob suspicionem stupratae Berenicis uxoris suae iugulari iussit" (10.4). Here the accusation of a sexual relationship with Berenice, Titus's mistress, is made the cause of Caecina's murder.

likely to be plausible in northern Palestine and southern Syria—places where Herodians ruled.

A fifth change in the real situation can be seen in the matter of the dancing daughter.[72] According to the best-attested reading, she is a daughter of Herod whose name is "Herodias" (cf. Mk 6:22, codices B, D, et al.), but in the rest of the story she is a daughter of Herodias (see also Mt 14:6). A number of manuscripts have corrected Mk 6:22 accordingly. Every reader will spontaneously understand the story to be speaking of a daughter of Herodias from her first marriage. Because the mother–daughter relationship is a fixed part of the story, we may regard it as traditional. It is only in Mark's version that the three principal characters in the game of intrigue against the Baptizer all, through secondary alterations, are made to bear the name "Herod" or its feminine form, "Herodias," as if the very naming was meant to signal that such stories were typical of the Herodian royal house and particularly of its women. It may therefore be presumed that the traditional story spoke of a daughter of Herodias. We learn her name from Josephus: it was Salome (*Ant.* 18.136). Her biography connects her with northern Palestine and Chalcis: she first married Philip, the tetrarch of Trachonitis; after his death in 34 C.E., she married Aristobulus, the son of Herod of Chalcis. Would it not have been in the region of her holdings, among her subjects and neighbors, that people would most likely have had a motive for spreading stories such as that in Mk 6:17ff., which placed her in an unfavorable light?

EXCURSUS:

Chronology plays a role in the assessment of the court legend in Mk 6:17ff. According to Mk 6:20ff., Salome was a "girl." Herodias's second marriage and the Baptizer's end must have happened in the (late?) 20s because, according to Mark's Gospel, the activity, arrest, and death of the Baptizer precede Jesus' end (ca. 30 C.E.). Q takes a similar view of the succession of the Baptizer and Jesus (cf. Mt 11:12, 16-19).

On the other hand, some have suggested a later dating for the Baptizer's execution.[73] Salome would then have been much older, and would even have been a widow. Josephus tells us that many Jews interpreted Antipas's defeat by the Nabateans in 36 C.E. as God's punishment for executing the Baptizer (*Ant.* 18.116–19). Could two such events, coupled by the idea of retribution, have been as much as ten years apart? Must they not have followed immediately on

---

72. On the problem of the identity of the dancing daughter, see the extensive treatment by Hoehner (*Herod Antipas*, 151–54). Justin also calls the dancing daughter a "niece" of Herod, thus regarding her as a daughter of Herodias from her first marriage (*Dial.* 49.4).

73. Thus W. Schenk, "Gefangenschaft und Tod des Täufers."

one another? Not necessarily! In Lk 11:51, an eschatological punishment is proclaimed for a murder that was several hundred years in the past. In Mt 22:7, Jesus' death and the destruction of Jerusalem are related to one another despite an interval of forty years between the two events. But a "delayed" reaction of the Nabatean king is also historically plausible: Josephus reports that the dissolution of the marriage was only the "start" of the quarrel (*Ant.* 18.113) and distinguishes this from the immediate occasion of the war, which was a dispute over Gamala. Because Gamala was in Philip's territory, the dispute could only have broken out after his death in 34 C.E. The death, together with the neutralization of the Roman protective power by the Parthians, offered the Nabatean king his chance for "revenge"—all the more so because he had well-founded claims to Philip's territories (*Ant.* 15.352). It is plausible that he would have waited a long time for such an opportunity.

But independently of a late dating of John the Baptizer's death, it is often supposed that Salome had already married in the 20s, and in any case that she was by no means a young girl.[74] What do we know about her age? She was born between 5 C.E. (at the earliest) and 20 C.E. (at the latest). On the one hand, we can date the birth of her mother, Herodias, between 10 and 7 B.C.E.,[75] and we must allow at least thirteen to fifteen years before her marriage and the birth of a child. On the other hand, Salome's birth could not have occurred later than 20 C.E. because she married Philip, who died in 34 C.E., and she must have been at least thirteen years old at her marriage. If we suppose a fairly early year for her birth, it would be plausible that Salome had already been married to Philip in the 20s and that Mk 6:20ff. must be an imaginative construct for that reason. But this is by no means conclusive. Josephus, in fact, relates the events of her life in this sequence: "after her birth" her mother was divorced from her first husband; then she married Philip, who died childless; Salome then married Aristobulus and bore him three sons: Herod, Agrippa, and Aristobulus (*Ant.* 18.137). If we interpret this sequence chronologically, a late dating for Salome's birth is more probable: the divorce takes place not long after her birth. Salome was still a child when she came to the court of Antipas. Only after that did she marry Philip. The marriage would have been politically motivated: because of the tensions between Antipas and the Nabateans, the Galilean prince attempted to forge closer ties with his neighbor, Philip. The fact that Philip was much older than his niece (and wife), Salome, was understandable in a political marriage.[76] But the age discrepancy between the young wife and her husband

---

74. Thus D. Lührmann, *Markusevangelium*, 114: Salome had been married for a long time, or was already a widow.

75. Herodias was the daughter of Herod's son, Aristobulus, who was executed in 7 B.C.E., so the latest possible date for her birth would be 7 or 6 B.C.E. On the other hand, she was the younger sister of Agrippa I, who died in 44 C.E. at the age of 54 (*Ant.* 19.350), and thus was born in 10 B.C.E. So she could not have been born ca. 14 B.C.E. (against E. Klostermann, *Das Markusevangelium*, 58).

76. Philip may have been born ca. 23 or 22 B.C.E. He must already have been a young man when he began his reign in 4 B.C.E. If Salome was born ca. 15 C.E., she would have been

could have led to the popular notion that Salome, as Mk 6:17ff. presumes, was Philip's daughter. The fact that the marriage was childless would have supported the mistaken supposition.

After Philip's death, Salome married Aristobulus,[77] a son of Herod of Chalcis (d. 48 C.E.). Nero made Aristobulus ruler over Armenia Minor in 54 C.E. Circa 72 or 73, Chalcis appears under Aristobulus's dominion (*Bell.* 7.226). Perhaps Vespasian, after incorporating the kingdom of Armenia Minor within a Roman province, had given him his paternal inheritance as compensation. Three sons are attested, and a coin of the parents survives, with a portrait of Aristobulus and Salome. Since Aristobulus appears alone on his coins after 64 C.E., it is possible that Salome died before 64.[78]

In a final, sixth point, we can recognize a secondary enrichment of the motifs in the court legend in Mk 6:17ff.: the appearance and dancing of a king's daughter at a feast is a legendary motif, apparently designed to attribute "shady morals" to the Herodian women. When women are mentioned at men's banquets, the idea of sexual contact is always present.

Cicero, in his second speech against Verres, attacks the loose living of the accused: he is said to have resided at Lampsacos with a respected citizen, Philodamus, for the purpose of seducing his host's daughter. To forestall this, Philodamus waited on him personally. When they were at a banquet and had drunk a lot of wine, Rubrius, Verres's associate and accomplice, asked that the daughter be brought out.

> The respectable and already elderly father received the rascal's suggestion with astonished silence. As Rubrius persisted, he replied, in order to say something, that it was not the Greek custom for women to be present at a men's dinner party [*negavit moris esse Graecorum ut in convivio virorum accumberent mulieres*]. (*In Verrem* 2.1.26 §66)

The father persists in refusing to call in his daughter. It comes to a violent quarrel in which a slave is killed. The citizens of Lampsacos are alarmed by all this, and even threaten to kill Verres.

In Terence's comedy *Eunuchus*, we find the same combination of motifs. The unsuccessful suitor of the courtesan Thais, a type of the miles gloriosus, wants to bring an innocent girl to a banquet in order to make the courtesan jealous. He had previously given her the girl as a slave. But Thais wants to protect the girl, whose true identity she knows. The following dialogue ensues: " 'Boy, bring us Pamphila to entertain us.' Thais

---

nearly forty years younger than her first husband. But the discrepancy in age would still have been notable if she had been "only" thirty years his junior.

77. On Aristobulus, see R. D. Sullivan, "Dynasty of Judaea," 319–21.

78. Cf. A. Reifenberg, *Ancient Jewish Coins*, nos. 71–73. But Reifenberg doubts whether no. 73 may not belong to Aristobulus's son of the same name (see p. 25).

rages: 'Never again shall that one come to table.' The soldier insists; now the row begins" (Terence, *Eunuchus* 4.1.10–12). Later the soldier, with quite transparent motives, asks that the girl be returned to him (4.7).

Another suggestive text is the court novel about the banquet of the Macedonian king Amyntas, who had to entertain an embassy from Persia.

> After dinner, while the wine was still going round, one of the Persians said: "At important dinners like this, my Macedonian friend, it is our custom in Persia to get our wives and mistresses to come and sit with us in the dining-room. You have welcomed us kindly, provided us with an excellent dinner, and offered earth and water to our King Darius; come then—won't you do as we do?" "Gentlemen," Amyntas replied, "what you mention is by no means the custom in Macedonia; with us, men and women are kept separate. However, you are our masters, and, as you ask for this favor, you shall not be refused." Amyntas sent for the women, and they came in and sat down in a row opposite the Persians, who, finding them very charming, remarked to Amyntas that such an arrangement was by no means a good one: it would surely have been better for the women not to have come at all if, instead of sitting beside them, they merely intended to sit opposite. It was a painful thing only to be allowed to look at them. Amyntas could not avoid taking the hint; he told the women to move over and sit with the guests, and as soon as they did so, the Persians, who were very drunk, began to touch their breasts, and even, in some cases, to try to kiss them. (Herodotus *Histories* 5.18)

Amyntas's son overcomes the Persians by a trick. He promises that the women will be available for their pleasure, but first they are to bathe. The "women" who return are really disguised young men, who kill the Persians with their concealed daggers.

The story of Odatis, the king's daughter, also belongs in this series. Her father refuses to give her to the man she loves. Instead, at a banquet at which the great men of the kingdom are assembled, she is to choose one of them as her husband by handing him a cup of wine. Weeping, she goes out and sends for her beloved. When he rushes to her side, she gives him the goblet and he carries her away (Athenaeus *Deipnosophistarum* 13.35–36). Here also the appearance of a royal daughter before drinking men signifies a sexual relationship, this time legitimated by marriage.[79]

It is simply taken for granted, in Mk 6:17ff. also, that women (and young girls) are not present at men's banquets. The dancing girl has to

---

79. Windisch in particular refers to this story ("Zum Gastmahl des Antipas," 73ff.) to support the historicity of Mk 6:17ff. But in this story, too, the appearance of the king's daughter is unusual: it serves to emphasize her humiliation. Herodotus *Histories* 2.121.5 is not a parallel. There an Egyptian king sends his daughter into a brothel to discover the culprit who had stolen a body; she is to give herself to any man, but first she is to ask him about the cleverest and wickedest thing he has ever done. Herodotus emphasizes that he does not believe this story.

leave the room in order to speak to her mother. Not even the wife of the ruler is present at his birthday celebration (Mk 6:24). The motif of dancing has no parallels.[80] It takes the place of directly sexual motifs in the parallels that have been cited. The evident background for this motif is the fact that at symposia, hetaerae could be present, playing the flute and dancing[81]—but not honorable women.

Often enough a violent quarrel is associated with such feasts, usually with the purpose of protecting the threatened morals of the women present (see Herodotus *Histories* 5.18–20; Cicero *In Verrem* 2.1.66ff.). But now and then the women themselves initiate the idea of executing someone (Esther 5–7; Herodotus *Histories* 9.108–13)—sometimes merely out of a desire for a gruesome experience, as was the case with the mistress of L. Quinctius, who was expelled from the Senate. The accusation against him was that

> in Placentia, he had taken a woman with a bad reputation, but with whom he was terribly in love, to his banquet. There, in order to plume himself before this whore, he told her, among other things, how cleverly he had conducted his investigations and how many men he had in prison, sentenced to death, whom he would have decapitated with the axe. The woman reclining at his right said that she had never seen anyone's head cut off with an axe, and she would very much like to see it. Her lover submitted to her will, ordered that one of those unfortunates should be brought in, and had his head cut off. It was a wild and gruesome deed. . . . At a meal, where it was customary to offer part of the food and drink to the gods and to call down blessings on one another, a human being was slaughtered like a sacrificial animal and the table sprinkled with his blood, all as a show for a brazen whore who was lying on the consul's breast! (Livy *Epit.* 39.43.2–4)[82]

In fact, Mk 6:17ff causes the Herodian women to appear in a bad light, and in so doing is certainly unjust to them. We must include this story

---

80. G. Dalman ("Zum Tanz der Tochter der Herodias") points to "well-bred" dancing of women in front of men in Palestine as he knew it. But even this does not make the king's dancing daughter any more plausible: Mk 6:17ff. presumes that she thrilled the drunken court, which she could not have done with decent, well-bred movements.

81. Cf. F. Weege, *Der Tanz in der Antike*, 118ff. J. Gnilka writes: "If a folk tradition developed the image of the dancing daughter of Herodias, this is probably a sign of the bad reputation of the royal house in the eyes of the people" ("Das Martyrium Johannes des Täufers," 89).

82. Livy retells this story in a completely different version: L. Quinctus persuaded a young male prostitute to travel with him from Rome to Gaul. To compensate him for missing the gladiatorial games in Rome, he murdered before his eyes, with his own hands, a respectable Gaul who had deserted to the Romans and turned to him for protection (Livy *Epit.* 39.42.8–12). The connection of sex with bloodthirstiness is also found in the traditions about Alexander Jannaeus: "While he feasted with his concubines in a conspicuous place, he ordered some eight hundred of the Jews to be crucified, and slaughtered their children and wives before the eyes of the still living wretches. This was the revenge he took for the injuries he had suffered; but the penalty he exacted was inhuman for all that" (*Ant.* 13.380–81).

within the body of malicious gossip that pursued a number of Herodian women in the first century.

The Acts of the Pagan Martyrs, stemming from Alexandria in the first to second century C.E.,[83] reflect the contrast between Jews and Greeks in the Egyptian capital and show how Greeks combine anti-Jewish with anti-Roman attitudes. Thus, in the *Acta Isidori* (Resc. A, col. 3.1.11–12 = CPJ 2, no. 156d) the accused attacks the emperor as follows: "I am neither a slave nor the son of a songstress, but a gymnasiarch of the famous city of Alexandria. You, however, are the despicable son of the Jewess, Salome." Claudius, the son of Drusus and Antonia minor, is here defamed as the illegitimate child of Salome. She was a sister of Herod I, with good connections to the Julio-Claudian imperial house, especially the empress Livia, to whom she bequeathed her possessions in Palestine after her death in about 10 C.E. (*Ant.* 18.31). Josephus depicts her as an intriguer who brought about the deaths of her sister-in-law Mariamne and the latter's sons, Alexander and Aristobulus. At any rate, she did not enjoy a very high reputation among the Jews' Alexandrian neighbors.[84]

But there were other ugly rumors as well. When Herod Agrippa I died suddenly at Caesarea in 44 C.E., the non-Jewish residents of the city celebrated his death with obscene festivals: "They hurled insults, too foul to be mentioned, at the deceased; and all who were then on military service— and they were a considerable number—went off to their homes, and seizing the images of the king's daughters carried them with one accord to the brothels, where they set them up on the roof and offered them every possible sort of insult, doing things too indecent to be reported" (*Ant.* 19.357).[85] There can be no doubt that here young Herodian women were being jeered at as prostitutes. The women in question were three of Agrippa's daughters: Berenice, then sixteen years old and married to Herod of Chalcis; ten-year-old Mariamne; and six-year-old Drusilla. Both of the younger daughters had already been promised by their father to future husbands (*Ant.* 19.355). The libertinistic aura can scarcely be traced to these young princesses. It had already been attached to the Herodian women before this.[86]

---

83. Cf. H. A. Musurillo, *Acts of the Pagan Martyrs.*

84. There may be a defamatory reference in *Acta Isidori* 1.18 = CPJ 2, no. 156b, where Agrippa I is denounced as a "three-obolus Jew." Prostitutes are often classified according to price, e.g., as "quadrantaria" (Quintilian *Inst.* 8.6.53; cf. Plutarch *Cic.* 29).

85. That a Herodian prince, popular among the Jews, had images made of his daughters and thus broke the second commandment, may seem astonishing. But Agrippa I often had his own portrait placed on his coins, if only those that were not minted in Jerusalem. Cf. Y. Meshorer, *Jewish Coins,* 78–80, 138–41; J. Meyshan, "The Coinage of Agrippa I," *IEJ* 4 (1954): 186–200.

86. Parallel to this taunting of Agrippa I after his death in Caesarea was the jeering of

One of these three Herodian women, Berenice, had to struggle against malicious gossip all her life.[87] As a young girl she was married, or betrothed, to the son of the Alexandrian alabarch (*Ant.* 19.276–77). After his death she was the wife of Herod of Chalcis, who died in 48 C.E. She then lived as a widow for a long time, at the court of her brother, Agrippa II. Here she became the subject of gossip: "But when a report gained currency that she had a liaison with her brother, she induced Polemo, king of Cilicia, to be circumcised and to take her in marriage; for she thought that she would demonstrate in this way that the reports were false" (*Ant.* 20.145). But the marriage was soon dissolved: "Berenice, [because] of licentiousness, according to report, deserted Polemo" (*Ant.* 20.146). Here, δι' ἀκολασίαν can refer either to Polemo's behavior or to that of Berenice. After the divorce, she lived at her brother's court again.

In Acts 25:22ff., Agrippa II and Berenice appear together. They are regarded as "king and queen" (cf. Jos. *Vita* 48, 180) and they act in concert.[88] When King Agrippa was "denounced" by the Tyrians in 67 C.E. (*Vita* 407–8), the old rumors about their incestuous relationship may have played a role. Then, during the Jewish war, there occurred the famous love affair between Titus and Berenice, who was more than ten years his senior. Josephus maintains a decorous silence about this, but it was known in Rome (cf. Tacitus *Hist.* 2.2; Suetonius *Divus Titus* 7.1; Dio-Xiphilinus 66.15.3ff.).[89] Titus might have married Berenice, but when she turned up in Rome in the year 75 and even began living with Titus, there was strong resistance to the marriage of the new emperor-designate to the princess from the East. In this context, the old gossip about Berenice's incestuous relationship with Agrippa II was revived (Juvenal *Sat.* 6.156–60).[90] For political reasons, Titus had to terminate the relationship.

---

him, ca. 38 C.E., during his stay in Alexandria (cf. Philo *Flacc.* 25ff., esp. 36–39). The Greeks "spent their days in the gymnasium jeering at the king and bringing out a succession of gibes against him. In fact they took the authors of farces and jests for their instructors and thereby showed their natural ability in things of shame" (*Flacc.* 34).

87. On Berenice, see Sullivan, "Dynasty of Judaea," 311–12. T. Mommsen (*Römische Geschichte* 5:540 [= 3d ed., 7:239]) is not unimpressed by the negative propaganda directed against her when he writes, "In addition . . . Berenice, a small-time Cleopatra, with what remained of her well-worn charms, held captive the heart of the conqueror of Jerusalem."

88. Berenice is always called "queen" in the sources; cf. Jos. *Vita* 119; Tacitus *Hist.* 2.81; *IG* 3.556. In an inscription in Beirut, Berenice is even called "regina" by her brother Herod II. Cf. G. H. Macurdy, "Julia Berenice," 253: she exercised a kind of co-dominion with her brother.

89. For a critical analysis of the sources and the political background of the controversy over Berenice, see J. A. Crook, "Titus und Berenice."

90. Macurdy is probably correct in thinking "that the story of her alleged incest, which is so prominent in all discussions of her, rests on prejudiced evidence and could easily arise from the events of her early life which led to her participation in her brother's power" ("Julia Berenice," 253).

We can locate Mk 6:17ff. within the context of these rumors about the libertinistic morals of Herodian women. Dancing Salome fits well with a Berenice who is supposedly living in an incestuous relationship and with the Herodian princesses who are symbolically placed in a brothel. It was probably the undoing of the Herodian women that they behaved in a more "emancipated" manner than the people, just as the Herodian upper class in general distanced itself from the strict customs of its ancestors. Probably their lives were no more corrupt than those of other members of their class. But there were groups that needed the image of the wicked Herodian women—groups among the simple people of Palestine, but especially among the Jews' nearest neighbors; we can locate denunciations of Herodians and Herodian women particularly in the territories adjoining Palestine: Alexandria, Caesarea, and Tyre. The non-Jewish neighbors of the Palestinian Jews needed to distance themselves from the Jews and to make the Jewish royal house look ridiculous. The story about the death of the Baptizer could also have been taken up eagerly in these neighboring territories. We can still surmise how this happened. Some indications point to the northern neighbors of Palestine. As wife of the tetrarch Philip, Salome was known there as daughter-in-law of the king of Chalcis and as queen of Armenia Minor. If it is the case that Salome's husband (or son?) Aristobulus received the little kingdom of Chalcis ca. 72, there would have been an immediate occasion for reviving old tales about the family. Inaccurate reporting of family relationships, the blurring of the political and religious dimensions of the Baptizer's execution, the adaptation of the situation to the changes and displacements that had occurred in northern Palestine—all these would be understandable in that region. Our surmise is therefore that an anti-Herodian perspective from a neighboring territory dominates this story. The evangelist Mark found it in the form of a popular tradition somewhere in the vicinity of Palestine, probably not far from those regions that in the second half of the first century were still ruled by male and female Herodians.

However, we should emphasize that malicious gossip about Herodian women is also readily imaginable in the capital of the world empire, Rome, especially because Titus had a relationship with one of these Herodians. The "propaganda" against a possible marriage with her could make good use of any defamatory material against Herodian women. But this location of the legend about the Baptizer's death, however well it may fit the traditional placing of Mark's Gospel at Rome, is improbable. Josephus records in the *Antiquities* what people at Rome knew about the Baptizer and the Herodian house. Nowhere does he connect the death of the Baptizer with intrigues by Herodian women. For him, the Baptizer's execution is politically motivated. It takes place at Machaerus. The responsible Herodian is a "tetrarch," not a king, and the family relationships are differently described.[91]

CONDITIONS FOR TRANSMISSION OF
THE MIRACLE STORIES

If the story about the Baptizer's death is a common folk tradition, and not handed down solely by his followers and those of Jesus, the question arises: Is this Baptizer legend the only popular tradition in the Gospels? Would there not also have been stories among the Jesus traditions that had traveled outside the circle of his closest associates? Miracle stories[92] are the most likely candidates, for here we find direct indications that they were widely told. From a form-critical point of view, these indications have differing characteristics.

1. In the expository part of a miracle story, the appearance of the one seeking help is sometimes motivated by his or her having heard about Jesus' marvelous deeds. For example, the woman with the issue of blood has suffered a long time from her illness. "She had heard about Jesus, and came up behind him in the crowd" (Mk 5:27). The Syrophoenician woman also "heard" about Jesus, although he wanted to remain hidden (Mk 7:25). In Luke, the centurion from Capernaum sends for Jesus after having "heard" about him (Lk 7:3; cf. Jn 4:47). It is taken for granted that during Jesus' lifetime people were telling stories about his deeds.

---

91. Lohmeyer seeks the origins of Mk 6:17ff. "in Jewish circles, such as those in Rome . . . that have already accommodated themselves to the hellenistic milieu" (*Markus*, 121). But in his personal copy he corrects "Rome" to "Syria." Cf. idem, *Das Evangelium des Markus: Ergänzungsheft*, 11.

92. Now and then the existence of a special genre of "miracle stories" is disputed. Thus M. Dibelius (*Formgeschichte*, 34ff., 66ff.) distinguishes between "paradigms" and "novellas." But we must note that the "novellas" consist exclusively of miracle stories (see the list on p. 68) and are specifically defined by being oriented to the miraculous; he includes among the "paradigms" five miracle stories whose point is more in the saying than the deed. This division of the miracle stories has seized upon a matter of content that is important for the history of tradition, as we will show in what follows: "miracles" were handed down as popular and as community traditions, and we cannot draw a sharp line between the two. The denial of the existence of an ancient genre of "miracle stories" is otherwise motivated in K. Berger, "Hellenistische Gattungen im Neuen Testament," 1212–18; idem, *Einführung in die Formgeschichte*, 76–84. According to Berger, miracle stories are distributed among several genres, none of which is constituted by the miracle itself. In my opinion we can say, as regards the New Testament, that here it is not modern consciousness that began to collect reports about Jesus' miraculous deeds. The Synoptics already speak of δυνάμεις (Mt 11:20, 23; Mk 6:2, 14), and John of σημεῖα (Jn 2:11, etc.). Under these headings, they collect phenomena that we most often find related in "miracle stories." But it is especially the stereotypical motifs and structures of these stories that show they belong together. That elements from other genres may appear in them is not to be denied.

2. Notices about the spread of these tales, standing at the end of the miracle stories, confirm this picture: "At once his fame began to spread throughout the surrounding region of Galilee" (Mk 1:28).[93] The leper who had been healed "went out and began to proclaim it freely, and to spread the word" (Mk 1:45). The eyewitnesses of the exorcism at the sea "ran off and told it in the city and in the country" (5:14). Later, the healed man himself takes on this role: "And he went away and began to proclaim in the Decapolis how much Jesus had done for him" (Mk 5:20). In this, the tellers of Jesus' miracles defy his express wishes: "Then he ordered them to tell no one; but the more he ordered them, the more zealously they proclaimed it" (Mk 7:36).[94] Similarly, the order to keep silent in Mt 9:30-31 is violated: Jesus wishes that no one should know of the healing of the two blind men, "But they went away and spread the news about him throughout that district." Two analogous passages in Acts confirm that it was a general presupposition that miracles would be spontaneously recounted (cf. Acts 9:42; 19:17).

3. Of particular interest are those cases within apophthegms (another genre of Jesus tradition) in which knowledge of Jesus' miracles is presumed. We hear of Jesus' native town that he could do no miracle there (Mk 6:5). But the rumor of his miracles had already reached the town before he got there. For that reason the crowd can cry in astonishment, "What deeds of power are being done by his hands!" (Mk 6:2). According to Mk 6:14, even Herod Antipas must have heard about Jesus' miracles. Otherwise, he would not fear that Jesus might be the resurrected Baptizer, and therefore "these powers are at work in him." In response to the Baptizer's question, his messengers are even entrusted directly with stories of Jesus' miracles: "Tell John what you hear and see: the blind receive their sight, the lame walk, the lepers are cleansed, the deaf hear, the dead are raised, and the poor have good news brought to them" (Mt 11:4-5).

4. Finally, we should also mention the summaries. There, the thronging of crowds to Jesus from Galilee, Jerusalem, Idumea, Perea, Tyre, and Sidon is explained by their "hearing all that he was doing" (Mk 3:8).[95] In

---

93. Mark 1:28 can be understood to say that Jesus' reputation spread in nearby parts of Galilee or in the regions bordering on Galilee. That in fact, according to Mark, his reputation extended to neighboring regions is shown by Mk 3:7-8.

94. U. Luz ("Das Geheimnismotiv") has made an illuminating distinction between "miracle secrets" that are violated and "the secret of Jesus' person," which is respected.

95. In this summary Mark mentions, in addition to the core Jewish areas of Galilee and Judea, the neighboring regions as well: Idumea in the south, and Tyre and Sidon in the north. The fact that he does not include the Decapolis in the east at this point is probably conditioned by the story found at Mk 5:1ff., which presumes that Jesus is unknown when he appears in the Decapolis.

the other miracle summaries (Mk 1:32-34; 6:53-56) it is not expressly said that people came in hordes to Jesus because they had heard of his miraculous deeds, but it is implicitly presupposed.

Of course, we cannot directly discern from such statements the conditions under which miracle stories were transmitted. But we retain the picture the evangelists had of them. From this picture we can infer back to the circumstances at the time of the evangelists, and from there to earlier times. Thus we will analyze this picture more closely in light of three questions. Who tells about Jesus' miracles? What form do the stories take? Where are they told?

Who Tells about Jesus' Miracles?

Three roles are mentioned in the texts. For the most part, it is the witnesses of the event who circulate an anonymous rumor about Jesus' unusual deeds. Less often, the person who has been cured announces the healing performed (Mk 1:45, 5:20).[96] In one instance (Mk 5:20), the healed person's witness is in competition with a more general rumor (5:14). Twice, the "tradition process" is traced directly to Jesus: he instructs the Baptizer's emissaries to tell of his miracles (Mt 11:5), and he gives the cured man in Mk 5:19 a "commission to proclaim." It is all the more notable that Jesus' disciples are never directed to *report* about Jesus' miracles. Their task is to *perform* miracles (Mt 10:8; Lk 10:9). However, the disciples are entrusted with the task of handing on Jesus' words (Mt 10:7; 28:19).

What conclusions can we draw from these narrative roles within the text about the circumstances of transmission at the time of the evangelists? If the evangelists trace anonymous tradition to eyewitnesses, they of course are making an inference. But the starting point for this inference must be a tradition that existed outside their own communities as well. Mark 5:1-20 is especially informative: the bearers of the common rumor about Jesus "flee" from him. On the basis of their reports, Jesus is asked to leave the country (5:14). This presupposes a negative picture of Jesus—a picture that certainly would not have been retained in the Christian community. In Mk 5:1-20, a positive tradition competes with this image: the man who has been healed spreads that tradition throughout the whole of the Decapolis. The existence of two competing traditions can be interpreted in two ways. In the eyes of the one telling the story, it could be a case of two Jesus traditions existing outside the Christian community, each of which was

---

96. D. Zeller ("Wunder und Bekenntnis") assumes that the healed persons themselves are the first to tell the miracle stories. His essay is a model of good method: the roles of the narrators immanent to the text must be the starting point for the search for the historical narrators.

partly negative and partly positive. Jesus traditions with a positive coloration existing outside the community are attested by the pericope about
the "strange exorcist" (Mk 9:38-40) who is driving out demons in Jesus'
name (and therefore must have heard something about Jesus' exorcisms),
but does not belong to the Markan community. "He is not following us,"
the disciples complain (Mk 9:38-39). Nevertheless, he has a positive attitude toward Jesus.

A negative picture of Jesus' miraculous deeds existing outside the circle
of his followers can be inferred from the pericope about Beelzebul: if
Jesus' opponents think they can detect the work of Satan behind his exorcisms, they must have heard about the exorcisms themselves (Mk 3:22).
This is particularly true in Mark, in which, unlike in Q (Mt 12:22-30; Lk
11:14-23), the discussion about Beelzebul is not occasioned by an exorcism. Instead, Jesus' opponents come from Jerusalem and therefore cannot be eyewitnesses of the exorcisms described in the earlier chapters.
They are reacting to reports about Jesus. Thus, there is considerable evidence that Mark presumes Jesus to have both a positive and a negative
reputation outside the Christian community.

However, the parallel existence of the two "forms of tradition" in Mk
5:1-20 could also be explained through the competition of popular and
community traditions. The commission to the healed man to proclaim the
news of his healing sounds like a Christian commission to preach: "Tell
them how much the Lord has done for you, and what mercy he has shown
you" (5:19). The center of attention here is not the miraculous event, but
God's action and God's mercy revealed in it. This commission legitimates
a miracle tradition such as we might expect to find within the community
itself. But the carrying out of the commission is different: "And he went
away and began to proclaim in the Decapolis how much Jesus had done
for him; and everyone was amazed" (Mk 5:20). Here the religious interpretation is obscured; the verb κηρύσσειν intimates it. But it may say nothing more than ἀπαγγέλλειν in 5:14, 19. Thus we could understand the
conclusion of the miracle story in this way: Jesus really commissions the
man he has cured to proclaim the work of God, but in fact he only spreads
the word about the remarkable deeds of Jesus. In that case, Mk 5:1-20
would give us indications of a common popular tradition about Jesus'
miracles that was partly negative (5:14; cf. 5:16) and partly positive (5:20)
in tone, and yet fell short of Jesus' real intention (5:19). This common
popular tradition is traceable both to the eyewitnesses of the miracle and
to the testimony of the man healed.

We can still discern transitional moments between the message Jesus
desired to give and the fame that spread without his wishing it. Neither of
the cured people who appear in Mark as transmitters of miracle stories is

among Jesus' intimate disciples, but both are called followers of Jesus. Jesus sends both of them "away." The leper who has been cured is supposed to go to the priest, declare himself clean, and do everything necessary to return to the "normal" world. The healed man of Gerasa explicitly asks to be allowed to remain with Jesus. Against his wishes, he is sent "home," in order to tell his friends about Jesus' action. Both are sent back to "normal" life. Their illnesses brought them social isolation, and their return to life is a demonstration of health. But Mark also recognizes another possibility: of blind Bartimaeus we read that "he followed [Jesus] on the way" (Mk 10:52). He is the only healed person the miracle story tells us became a "follower" in the narrower sense. In him we may discern the role of the early Christian itinerant charismatic, and in the other cured people the role of the nonitinerant sympathizers who were the basis of the local church communities. The news about Jesus' miracles, arising in such circles, made its way beyond them, but its spread among the people was not entirely dependent on such "sympathizers."

In Mark we can still detect a definite tension between this generally circulating tradition about the miracles and Jesus' own intention—that is, the miracle tradition in which the community recognized its own special convictions. This tension is evident in the "miracle secret."[97] Jesus did not want his miracles to be told, but his wish could not prevail. It is true that the miracle secret corresponds to certain traditional elements—an aura of secrecy is part of the miracle—but it receives a new accent in Mark.[98] In Mk 1:44 the command of silence could originally have applied up to the point of the priest's declaration that the man was clean. Now it is formulated without limit, and it is immediately violated. The violation (Mk 1:45) could be traceable to Markan redaction. In Mk 5:19, sending the man home would originally have served to demonstrate his healing. Mark, in a redactional addition, has the healed man preach in the Decapolis instead of going "home." In this way, a secondary limitation on further telling of

---

97. The different forms of the "secret" can be distinguished in Mark by the length of time after which each secret is revealed. The miracle secret is violated immediately. The secret about Jesus' person is revealed at Jerusalem paradoxically: here the Markan Jesus speaks openly of himself as "Son of God" (Mk 12:6; 14:61-62). But the secret teaching "in the house" is maintained as secret: it addresses problems of the post-Easter communities. The different spans of time probably correspond to a different "radius of transmission." Jesus was widely known and admired as a miracle-worker. His claim to be the messenger and Son of God was a stumbling-block outside the Christian community. But much of his teaching was community tradition that was only handed on within the group.

98. In *Urchristliche Wundergeschichten,* 143ff., I have shown that the motifs of silence and secrecy are part of the traditional language of miracle and magic. This does not exclude the possibility of Mark's having made a new and unique use of the traditional language at his disposal. "Redaction" is, in this case, the application of an existing repertoire of motifs to a new situation.

the event is insinuated into the command to "go home," and the preaching in the Decapolis appears as a violation. The contradiction between Jesus' desire to keep the event secret and a miracle tradition that had spread everywhere is clearest in Mk 7:36: "Then he ordered them to tell no one; but the more he ordered them, the more zealously they proclaimed it."

Thus, the situation of the tradition as Mark found it would have been as follows: the Markan community found traditions about Jesus circulating beyond its own circle, among all the people. In order to adopt them as its own, the community had to attribute historicity to these traditions, making them testimony of Jesus' activities. To explain their "foreignness" to the community, it at the same time had to deny authenticity to the process by which the traditions were created: it was contrary to Jesus' wishes that these miracle stories were circulating among the people. Thus the Markan command to keep the miracles a secret would be an accommodation between popular and community traditions, that is, between two forms of tradition whereby miracle stories were handed down.[99]

Martin Dibelius posited two comparable forms of tradition: on the one hand, paradigms that were conceived entirely for a religious purpose; on the other hand, novellas in which the miracle itself is the object of the story. The former would have been handed on by the "preachers" of the gospel, the latter by the "storytellers" in the community.[100] Dibelius locates both these forms of tradition in the Christian community. For him, the

---

99. The interpretation of the secrecy motif in Mark as the attempt at a synthesis between different traditions has a long history. W. Wrede (*Das Messiasgeheimnis in den Evangelien*) saw it as an accommodation between post-Easter faith in the Messiah and the nonmessianic traditions about the life of Jesus. Bultmann (*Die Geschichte der synoptischen Tradition*, 372–73) interprets Mark as a refutation of the Hellenistic kerygma about Christ by means of the tradition of the history of Jesus. E. Schweizer's "Zur Christologie des Markusevangeliums" (in his *Neues Testament und Christologie im Werden*, 86–103) may serve as an example of the exegesis that finds in the motif of secrecy an accommodation between the miracle traditions and those of the Passion. To this idea of a "synthesis" of particular types of interpretation can be opposed another that discerns a polemic in the secrecy motifs. According to this view, the evangelist takes up the miracle stories in order to neutralize them. So T. J. Weeden, "Die Häresie." In order to locate my proposed interpretation of the command of secrecy in miracle stories within previous research, let me emphasize that (1) I am not attempting an interpretation of all the secrecy motifs in the Gospel, but only of the command of secrecy in the miracle stories, and (2) this interpretation is only intended to explain the occasion for a secrecy motif, not its intention and function in Mark. Thus this interpretation can be combined with others.

100. Cf. Dibelius, *Formgeschichte*, 66ff. Zeller ("Wunder und Bekenntnis," 206) is correct in pointing to an internal tension in Dibelius's concept: on the one hand, the miracle stories are said to have a missionary function among people who are accustomed to the miraculous deeds of gods and prophets; on the other hand, they are assigned a social function that is located within the Christian community because the role of the community's teachers is carried out inside the community itself.

acceptance of the novellas, with their secular coloration, was a first step in earliest Christianity's accommodation to the "world." But if we take the secular character of the so-called novellas seriously, we must see not only their content as secular, but also the people who handed them down. Their "tellers" are not a special group within the Christian community, but people in the community at large who have a special talent for story-telling, independent of their closeness to or distance from the Christian group. Clearly, miracle stories were also told within the Christian community. But they had a form that made them readily accessible beyond the group of the followers of Jesus.

What Forms Did the Miracle Stories Take?

To this point we have simply assumed that when the "rumor" about Jesus' deeds spread across the land, it was in the form of miracle stories of the type found in the Synoptic Gospels. But could summary accounts not have fulfilled the function ascribed to this report, namely, astonishing and attracting people? Were they necessarily those typically stylized miracle stories we find in Mark's Gospel? Here a comparison with contemporary miracle traditions can be helpful.

Josephus, in his description of King Solomon in the *Antiquities*, praises the king's power of exorcistic healing. This power is still said to be widespread in the author's own time. To support this assertion, he tells the following story:[101]

> I have seen [ἱστόρησα] a certain Eleazar, a countryman of mine, in the presence of Vespasian, his sons, tribunes and a number of other soldiers, free men possessed by demons, and this was the manner of the cure: he put to the nose of the possessed man a ring which had under its seal one of the roots prescribed by Solomon, and then, as the man smelled it, drew out the demon through his nostrils, and, when the man at once fell down, adjured the demon never to come back into him, speaking Solomon's name and reciting the incantations which he had composed. Then, wishing to convince the bystanders and prove to them that he had this power, Eleazar placed a cup or foot-basin full of water a little way off and commanded the demon, as it went out of the man, to overturn it and make known to the spectators that he had left the man. (*Ant.* 8.46–48)

Josephus names himself as a witness of this.[102] The event described

---

101. On the interpretation, see D. C. Duling, "Eleazar Miracle and Solomon's Magical Wisdom."

102. Ἱστόρησα can mean "I have seen it" or "I have experienced it"; cf. ibid., 21. Since Josephus, after his capture during the Jewish war, belonged to Vespasian's inner circle, he could have been an eyewitness. He is writing at Rome, and could scarcely risk telling a false story for which surviving witnesses of the Jewish war could have marked and punished him as a liar.

must have happened in 67 or 68 C.E. Josephus writes of it about 25 years later. There is no reason to doubt that a Jewish exorcist had astonished the officer corps of the Roman army with his powers at some point during the Jewish war. The story as told is a typical miracle tale, its teller an eyewitness.

Tacitus tells of two miraculous healings by Vespasian at Alexandria, supposed to have taken place in 70 C.E. These are also brief stories, not summary reports on Vespasian's healing powers.[103] At the conclusion of the story, Tacitus affirms that he received it from eyewitnesses: "Both facts are told by eye-witnesses even now when falsehood brings no reward" (*Hist.* 4.81.3). Tacitus wrote ca. 104–110 C.E., when the Flavian house was already a thing of the past. There is no reason to doubt that he had interviewed eyewitnesses.

The miracle stories in Josephus and Tacitus are comparable to early Christian miracle stories in the process of transmission: for both historians, there is a period of some 25 to 35 years between the events described and their writing. That corresponds to the interval between Jesus' activity and the writing of Mark (ca. 30–35 years). In addition, it is a question of short stories, not summary accounts. Eyewitnesses are the source of the tradition. In no case is there a narrative told without purpose: Josephus desires to "proclaim" the superior wisdom of Solomon; the tradition recorded by Tacitus is supposed to justify the rule of Vespasian, who, as a usurper, lacked legitimacy.

Just as large groups of people told stories about Vespasian's miracles— for only in that way could they fulfill their propaganda function—so people in Jesus' region must have told stories about his miracles at an early date. The character of many miracle stories is not specifically "Christian." Nowhere do we find an Amen-saying of Jesus, although this solemn formula would be quite plausible as an introduction to a word of healing power. The notion of discipleship is wholly lacking (with the exception of Mk 10:52). We hear nothing about the end of the world. "Faith" consists in a generalized trust in Jesus' miraculous power. Only those few miracle stories that Dibelius counts among the paradigms have a characteristically

---

103. On this miracle story, see Berger, *Einführung in die Farmgeschichte,* 79. In this case, the miracle takes place in the framework of an audience scene. The concept of "petitio" is appropriate here: the traditional motif of the request to the wonder-worker appears in the form of a petition presented during an audience. But it is clear from the story itself how far the horizon of experience of a normal audience has been stretched. Vespasian at first refuses. On the background of this miracle by Vespasian, cf. H. Schwier, "Theologische und ideologische Faktoren im ersten jüdisch-römischen Krieg (66-74 n.Chr.) im Zusammenhang mit der Zerstörung des Jerusalemer Tempels" (Diss., Heidelberg, 1988), 308–10.

Christian content:[104] the healing of the paralytic testifies to Jesus' power to forgive sins (Mk 2:1-12), the healing of the withered hand to the relativizing of the Sabbath commandment (Mk 3:1-6), the healing in the synagogue to the new teaching with power (Mk 1:21-28), and the cure of the blind man from Jericho to the empowerment for discipleship (Mk 10:46-52).

However, because the line between paradigms and novellas is fluid, as Dibelius's distinction between pure and impure paradigms shows, it is inappropriate to make the presence or absence of specifically Christian motifs the basis for classifying stories in one or another genre. They are always miracle stories—sometimes in a form shaped by Christian tradents, at other times in a form in which they circulated among all the people and were accessible to them.

Where Were the Miracle Stories Told?

If we suppose that a considerable number of the miracle stories were also popular tradition, we will already have set limits to their spread. In all probability, they were told in the Syrio-Palestinian region. From there they could have penetrated other areas: as the traditions of disciples and communities they would have spread, with the communities themselves, into new regions. But as popular tradition they would have been related mainly in Palestine and the neighboring territories.

The analysis of the story of the Syrophoenician woman revealed that the tellers of this tale were acquainted with the border regions of Tyre and Galilee. Are there other miracle stories in which we can discover likely local ties of this type? We could name three stories connected with the "sea" of Galilee: the stilling of the storm (Mk 4:35-41), the healing of the Gerasene demoniac (Mk 5:1-20), and the walking on water (Mk 6:45-52). It is remarkable that in these stories Lake Gennesaret is called "sea." In all three tales this designation belongs to the traditional part of the miracle story. Even in ancient times, a critic of Christianity found this designation disturbing: probably it was Porphyry, whose skeptical objections to the historical reliability of the Gospels have been preserved for us by Macarius Magnes.[105]

> In any case, those who describe the true conditions of those places, say that there is no sea [θάλασσαν] there, but instead a small lake [λίμνην], created

---

104. Cf. Dibelius, *Formgeschichte*, 40.
105. On Macarius Magnes, who wrote an "Apology" ca. 400 C.E., cf. B. Altaner and A. Stuiber, *Patrologie*, 332–33. That he is opposing the criticism of Christianity raised by the neoplatonist Porphyry (ca. 234–301/305) is indicated also by Jerome's refutation of Porphyry. Still, some scholars identify the anonymous critic with Hierocles (cf. M. Stern, *GLAJJ* 2:425–26 n. 8).

by a river at the base of the hill country in the region of Galilee near the city of Tiberias—a lake that can be crossed in only two hours in small boats made of a single log, and that is not large enough either for waves or for storms. Mark has thus gone beyond the truth. (Macarius Magnes *Apokritikos* 3.6)[106]

What for Porphyry was an opportunity to dispute the historical truth of the Gospel accounts is, for modern historical-critical research, an indicator of the conditions under which the Gospel texts came into being. The designation of a small lake as a "sea," something quite unusual in Greek, points to the linguistic and local connections of the Gospel traditions. On the one hand, we can discern the Semitic language background; on the other hand, we encounter here the locally limited world of ordinary people from Galilee, for whom a lake could easily become a "sea."

The first argument was already used by Jerome against Porphyry. In his exegesis of Gen 1:10 he wrote:

> Et congregationes aquarum vocavit maria. Notandum quod omnis congregatio aquarum, sive salsae sint sive dulces, iuxta idioma linguae hebraicae maria nuncupentur. Frustra igitur Porphyrius evangelistas ad faciendum ignorantibus miraculum eo, quod dominus super mare ambulaverit, pro lacu Genesareth mare appellasse calumniatur, cum omnis lacus et aquarum congregatio maria nuncupentur. (*Hebr. Quaest. in Gen* 1:10)[107]

Hebrew *yam* can mean both "sea" and "lake." With very few exceptions,[108] it is translated in the Septuagint only with θάλασσα, even where clearly an inland body of water is meant, such as the Dead Sea (cf. Gen 14:3; 4 Kgs 14:25; Joel 2:20) or Lake Gennesaret (Num 34:11; Josh 12:3; 13:27). In the Babylonian Talmud the "seas" of Ps 24:2 are interpreted to mean minor lakes and the "great sea":[109] "The verse [Ps 24:2]: For he hath founded it [the land of Israel] upon the seas and established it upon the floods speaks of the seven seas and four rivers which surround the land of Israel. And these are the seven seas: The Sea of Tiberias, the Sea of Sodom, the Sea of Chelath, the Sea of Chiltha, the Sea of Sibkay, the Sea of Aspania and the Great Sea" (*Baba Bathra* 74b). The

---

106. In the same way, Porphyry remarks specifically on the exorcism in Mk 5:1ff. that this is a lake (λίμνη) and not a deep sea (θάλασσα). Macarius Magnes *Apokritikos* 3.4 (= *GLAJJ* 2:478–79, no. 465c).

107. The Byzantine theologian Theophylact of Achrida (died ca. 1108) still found it necessary, in his *Enarratio in Evangelium Joannis*, to defend the New Testament usage: θάλασσαν δὲ λέγει τὴν λίμνην· τὰ γὰρ συστήματα τῶν ὑδάτων, θαλάσσας ἐκάλεσεν ἡ θεία Γραφή (cf. J. Migne, *PG* 123:1284), VI B.

108. Exceptions are *yam* as the western (2 Chr 4:4) or "molten sea" in the temple (2 Chr 4:2), or the "sand of the sea" (Job 6:3).

109. Parallel passages mentioning these and some other seas are *p. Kil.* 9.32c and *p. Keth.* 12.35b. On the various attempts at identification, see P. Billerbeck, *Kommentar,* 185. Even such small lakes as Semechonitis or Phial could be described as "yam" (sea).

New Testament θάλασσα is thus to be understood against the background of Semitic linguistic usage. Insofar as we encounter it in the Gospels, we can see it as an indication of the fact that they were written in a region where Semitic languages directly or indirectly contributed to the shaping of vocabulary. This points to the eastern part of the Roman Empire: either the Gospels were written there, or their authors came from there, or the traditions incorporated in them were native to that region.

Our second consideration points in the same direction. The designation of a lake as "sea" can be taken as an indication of a limited horizon of life. For small farmers and fisherfolk in Galilee, Lake Gennesaret could simply be "the sea." Two analogies can be applied. In his *Meteorologica*, Aristotle mentions shrinking rivers that have no outlet to the sea: "In Greece this natural phenomenon is rarely seen. But there is a lake beneath the Caucasus, which the inhabitants call a sea: for this is fed by many great rivers, and having no obvious outlet runs out beneath the earth in the district of the Coraxi and comes up somewhere about the so-called deeps of Pontus, an immeasurably deep point in the [Black] Sea" (1.13.351a).

Possibly, Aristotle means the Caspian Sea. In any case, what for him is a λίμνη represents a θάλασσα for the inhabitants themselves. A similar distinction between the language of the inhabitants and that of an author writing from a broader perspective can be found with regard to the Dead Sea. For most ancient authors it was a "lake," a λίμνη or *lacus*.[110]

The designation "ocean" occurs only here and there, as in Pompeius Trogus (end of the first century B.C.E.), together with the word "lake" "In ea regione latus lacus est, qui propter magnitudinem aquae et immobilitatem Mortuum Mare dicitur" (quoted in Justin *Epitome* 3.6 = *GLAJJ* 1.336).[111] This "dicitur" probably conceals the inhabitants of Judea, who had always called the Dead Sea *yam*,[112] as the "desert sea," or "Sea of the Arabah" (Deut 3:17; 4:49; Josh 3:16; 2 Kgs 14:25); the "Salt Sea" (Gen 14:3; Num 34:3, 12); or the "eastern sea" (Joel 2:20; Ezek 47:18; Zech 14:8). Since for the Jews the east was "ahead," the Dead Sea, as the "sea ahead" (eastern sea), could be distinguished from the Mediterranean, the "sea behind" (western sea). In one instance, "yam" without any other attribute could mean the Dead Sea: "They came and told Jehoshaphat, 'A great multitude is coming against you from Edom, from beyond the sea' " (2 Chr 20:2). Thus the designation "sea" given to the salty desert lake in the

---

110. Cf. Aristotle *Meteorologica* 2.3.359a (*GLAJJ* 1:7); Hieronymus of Cardia (*GLAJJ* 1:19); Diodorus Siculus *Bibl. Hist.* 2.48.6 (*GLAJJ* 1:173); 19.98 (*GLAJJ* 1:176); Strabo *Geogr.* 16.2.34 (*GLAJJ* 1.294); Vitruvius *De Architectura* 8.3.8 (*GLAJJ* 1:346); Seneca *Quaest. Nat.* 3.25.5 (*GLAJJ* 1:432); Pliny the Elder *Nat. Hist.* 7.65 (*GLAJJ* 1:482–83); 5.71 (*GLAJJ* 1:469); Claudius Ptolemaeus *Geography* 5.15.2 (*GLAJJ* 2:167); Alexander of Aphrodisias *In Arist. Meteor.* 2.359a (*GLAJJ* 2:336); Solinus *Collectanea Rerum Memorabilium* 1.56 (*GLAJJ* 2:417).

111. This is the oldest occurrence of the name "Dead Sea," which was probably derived from the Hebrew name, "Desert Sea." Josephus possibly is already presupposing this name when he describes the Sea of Asphalt as "salt and barren" (ἄγονος) in *Bell.* 4.456. Hebrew *araba* also means "sterile."

112. Cf. V. Burr, *Nostrum mare*, 89.

Jordan Valley is probably of local origin. Beginning in the second century C.E., however, this name spread beyond Palestine and throughout the ancient world.

Thus we arrive at the following conclusion: the word "sea" is applied to an inland lake by those in the immediate area surrounding it. From a perspective of greater distance, it is called a "lake."

A possible objection arises: the spread of the name "Dead Sea" in the ancient world from the beginning of our era, even outside Palestine. This "exception" proves the rule. The ancient authors who applied the words *mare* or θάλασσα to the "Dead Sea" normally add some reservations. Pompeius Trogus calls it a "lacus" and gives the name "Mortuum Mare" only as information he has received (*GLAJJ* 1.336). Tacitus calls it a "lacus," but adds: "Lacus immenso ambitu, specie maris" (*Hist.* 5.6.2 = *GLAJJ* 2:20). Pausanius uses a similar expression: he first speaks of a lake (λίμνη) and adds, in a relative clause, that this lake is called the "Dead Sea" (θάλασσα; *Descriptio Graeciae.* 5.7.4–5 = *GLAJJ* 2:194). Aelius Aristides was in Scythopolis when he heard about this lake (λίμνη) "which some now call a sea" (*Oratio* 36.82.88 = *GLAJJ* 2:218–19). Galen speaks of a lake with two names: some call it the "Dead Sea," others "Lake Asphaltitis." For him, it is a lake; once he even calls it the "Dead Lake" (*De simplicium Medicamentorum Temperamentis ac Facultatibus* 4.20 = *GLAJJ* 2:316).[113] Similarly, Dio Chrysostom, who evidently knows the name "Dead Sea," alters it to "the Dead Water" (τὸ νεκρόν ὕδωρ; quoted in Synesius *Vita Dionis* 2.317 = *GLAJJ* 1:539). In all these places it is clear that for ancient authors the "Dead Sea" is really a lake. They explain the unusual expression either through the size and sluggishness of the lake (e.g., Pompeius Trogus) or by its sterility (e.g., Olympiodorus *In Aristotelis Meteora Commentaria* = *GLAJJ* 2:680–81).[114] The salt content of its water really does make the "Dead Sea" similar to the open ocean. But when, nevertheless, outside Palestine this relatively large lake is still called a "sea" only with reservations, how much more is this true of the little freshwater Lake of Galilee that we read of in the Gospels.

Thus, when the three Markan miracle stories (as well as the rest of Mark's Gospel) speak of the "sea" when they mean the Lake of Galilee, we can conclude that these stories were formed in the proximity of that lake. Their tellers live in a world in which the great sea is a faraway phenomenon. From this we can understand why Luke consistently changes the designation: where Mark writes of a θάλασσα, Luke writes λίμνη (Lk 8:22, 23, 33). He is looking at Palestine from a greater distance. Acts shows that he knows the broader Mediterranean world.

---

113. At another place in the same work, Galen explains the idea of a "dead sea" (τὴν νεκρὰν ὀνομαζομένην θάλασσαν) with the words ἔστι δ᾽ αὐτὴ λίμνη τις (9.2.10 = *GLAJJ* 2:324).

114. Olympiodorus (sixth century C.E.) is one of the few ancient writers to speak of the "Dead Sea" without offering clear reservations about it. Another is Eusebius (*Onom.* 16.2). But in *Onom.* 100.4, he uses the biblical name θάλασσα ἡ ἁλυκή and adds: ἡ καλουμένα νεκρὰ καὶ ἀσφαλτῖτις.

Are there other indicators of place in the three miracle stories that might confirm our hypothesis about their local character? In particular, the exorcism by the lake (Mk 5:1-20) contains rather specific information about the place and its surroundings, but also an obvious geographical mistake. Gerasa is placed close to the Lake of Galilee, although the city actually lies about fifty kilometers from the lake. In its present form, the story seems to identify the "land of the Gerasenes" (5:1) with the "Decapolis" (5:20). As a matter of fact, Gerasa experienced a sudden expansion in the second half of the first century C.E.[115] At that time the quadratic city plan, still visible today, was laid down with its central axis and gate. It is possible that the city enjoyed some years as capital of the Decapolis.

Despite the geographical error, the story fits well within the tensions between the Decapolis and its Jewish neighbors. The first people who told the story must have been well acquainted with the situation.

The Decapolis was a Roman creation.[116] When Pompey incorporated Syria in the Roman Empire in 63 B.C.E., he liberated the Hellenistic cities east of the Jordan from Jewish rule (*Ant.* 14.74–76). No wonder that most of the cities of the Decapolis saw the appearance of the Roman legions as the decisive moment in their history, the date from which they reckoned time. Abila, Dium, Gadara, Gerasa, Canatha, Pella, Philadelphia, and Hippos all had a Pompeian era. Even in the first century C.E. the Roman legions remained the guarantors of their independence, not least of all against their Jewish neighbors and former rulers. The tensions exploded in 44 C.E. in violent clashes between the Philadelphians and the Jews over a village, a conflict that was quashed by the Roman procurator Fadus (*Ant.* 20.2). In 66 C.E., in the wake of a bloodbath visited on the Jewish population in Caesarea, the territory of the Decapolis was laid waste: "The news of the disaster at Caesarea infuriated the whole nation; and parties of Jews sacked the Syrian villages and the neighboring cities, Philadelphia, Heshbon and its district, Gerasa, Pella, and Scythopolis. Next they fell upon Gadara, Hippos, and Gaulanitis, destroying or setting fire to all in their path" (*Bell.* 2.458–59). Here, too, Roman legions had to restore peace.

These kinds of tensions between the gentile inhabitants of the Decap-

---

115. Cf. C. H. Kraeling, ed., *Gerasa*, 27–69. Kraeling emphasizes that "the real change in its character and life begins approximately with the second half of the first century" (p. 35). At that time the city experienced "a definite upturn." "The most important token of and element in Gerasa's transformation in the second half of the first century is its new, ambitious city plan" (p. 40). Between 22 and 76 C.E., the hippodamic city plan was adopted: "the city would hardly have ventured upon an expansion program of such magnitude as that implied in the new plan until some wealth and the possibility of continued prosperity were in evidence" (p. 41).

116. On the history of the Decapolis, cf. H. Bietenhard, "Die syrische Dekapolis"; Schürer, *History of the Jewish People* 2:85ff., esp. 125ff.

olis and the Jews furnish the perspective for Mk 5:1ff.: a Jewish exorcist comes into the neighboring district. There he meets a possessed man ruled by a "legion" of unclean spirits and living in unclean places: in the tombs. Probably he represents the Gentiles as such, since the unclean spirits enter the swine, which Jews regarded as disgusting.[117] A herd of swine was unimaginable except in a gentile region. At the same time, the religious contrast between Jews and Gentiles symbolizes the political aspect of the conflict: the demon reveals itself as "legion."[118] It represents a whole army. Its most urgent petition is to be allowed to remain in the land—exactly what the Roman occupying force wanted. It is driven into the sea, perhaps because that was supposed to be the entrance to the underworld, but certainly also because the desire to chase a whole legion into the sea could be expressed in this guise. The connection of the demon legion with swine could have been suggested by the Roman legions themselves. The tenth legion Fretensis had been stationed in Syria since 6 C.E., had taken part in the Jewish war and the siege of Jerusalem, and was subsequently stationed in Judea. On their standards and seals they had, among other things, the image of a boar.[119] Wherever the tenth legion was known, the story of the exorcism at the lake must have awakened associations with the Roman occupation, and in the Syrio-Palestinian region it would have had more overtones and undertones than anywhere else. That is the place where it probably was told.

A second feature of this story may also indicate a local connection: the Gerasenes ask Jesus "to leave their neighborhood" (5:17). In other words, Jesus is being gently expelled from the country. He is to leave the city's territory. In view of the damage he has caused, that is understandable. But any exorcist capable of attacking a "legion" would probably have been undesirable for other reasons, since someone who had destroyed a legion of demons could rouse opinion against other legions, inasmuch as people in the Decapolis were well informed about Jewish resistance to Rome: one of the leaders of the Jewish revolt, Simon Bar Gioras (= son of the prose-lyte) may have come from Gerasa (*Bell.* 4.503). It was vitally important for

---

117. Cf. F. Annen, *Heil für die Heiden,* 162, on the "swine" in Mk 5:1ff.

118. T. Reinach ("Mon Nom est Légion") was the first to detect the political undertones of this story. He saw in the possessed man a symbol of the Jewish people thus marked by the Romans. The swine are found in the Roman military standards, and their fate is a veiled aggressive desire directed against the oppressor. When I suggested such an interpretation in *Urchristliche Wundergeschichten,* 252–53, I had not yet seen Reinach's essay. Annen (*Heil für die Heiden,* 170–71, 184) also recognized this political motif, without making it the principal motif of the story.

119. Cf. W. Liebenam, "Feldzeichen." On Roman military standards we find the eagle, wolf, minotaur, horse, and boar. The boar was on the standards of the Legio I Italica, XX Valeria-Victrix, II Adiuntrix, and X Fretensis (see col. 2157).

Gerasa and all the Hellenistic cities of Palestine to keep their distance from the Jewish rebellion against Rome. This stance was strengthened by anti-Jewish attitudes. At the beginning of the Jewish war there were violent attacks on Jewish minorities in many cities. There were murders and pogroms in Scythopolis, Ascalon, Ptolemais, Tyre, Hippos, and Gadara. Gerasa was an exception: "The people of Gerasa not only abstained from maltreating the Jews who remained with them, but escorted to the frontiers any who chose to emigrate" (*Bell.* 2.480). This banishment under escort is similar to the "gentle" banishment of Jesus in Mk 5:17. I do not mean to imply that Mk 5:17 was composed under the influence of the events of 66 C.E. The relatively "humane" treatment of the Jewish minority could be connected with a structural situation that had already existed in the past: Gerasa had the right of asylum. As Theon, son of Demetrios, boasted in donating a large sum of money for building a temple ca. 69 or 70 C.E., anyone who fled to "Zeus Phyxios" received special protection.[120] At a later date, the city appears as "Gerasa hiera et asylo[s] et autonomos."[121] There was a tradition here of sheltering people in flight and those who begged protection. The people distanced themselves from the rebellious spirit of the surrounding region, but they did so in humane fashion. Could there be a trace of this in Mk 5:1ff.? It is not certain, but we may say that what we hear about the Decapolis in Mk 5:1ff. corresponds well with what sparse information we have about this area.

We can no longer determine precisely where this story circulated, although its conclusion indicates that it had spread within the Decapolis. It could just as well have been told among the Jewish population of Galilee, since its pride in the superiority of the "Most High God" (5:7) before whom the foreign demons bow down (5:6) represents a Jewish perspective, and the distaste for unclean places and animals found in the story could easily occur among people who, with neighborly antipathy, credited their fellows "on the opposite bank" with everything that was unclean and disgusting. In any case, the story must have been a common popular tradition about Jesus, the exorcist, because it has no specifically Christian features.

To summarize our reflections on the miracle stories: their tradition history corresponds to that "boundary-spanning character" formed by their internal structure. Again and again, in these stories, the limits of human ability, human finitude and futility are surpassed. Socially and locally they would seem already to have overcome "boundaries." They

---

120. Gerasa, inscriptions 5 and 6. Cf. Kraeling, ed., *Gerasa*, 375–78.
121. Gerasa, inscription 30, ca. 130 C.E., in Kraeling, ed., *Gerasa*, 390–91.

crossed social boundaries, inasmuch as they quickly began to be told beyond the circle of Jesus' associates. They became folk traditions; in fact, some of them probably circulated as popular traditions from the beginning. They also crossed the bounds of locality: it is probable that they quickly began to be told in neighboring regions of Palestine, even if their original ties to Galilean-Jewish territory are unmistakable. The author of Mark reintegrated this "free" miracle tradition into the Gospel. In his story about Jesus' journey he shows that the principal actor in the miracle stories can only be correctly understood when one follows his way, even to the cross.

Thus we arrive at the following conclusion: the decisive elements of the sayings of Jesus were handed down by the disciples, while part of the narrative tradition—those miracle stories that have a somewhat secular flavor—was drawn from popular tales. Apophthegms lie somewhere between these two genres. By whom were they handed down?

CONDITIONS FOR THE TRANSMISSION
OF APOPHTHEGMS

New Testament apophthegms[122] are brief stories, the point of which is, in each case, a saying of Jesus. The situation described gives the saying, as critique, apology, or confirmation of a previous statement, an "excess of meaning" that the unframed saying would not have.[123] Although apo-

---

122. Fundamentally, there are two available concepts to designate this genre: "apophthegm" (Bultmann, *Die Geschichte der synoptischen Tradition*, 8ff.) and "chreia" (Berger, "Hellenistische Gattungen," 1092ff.; idem, *Formgeschichte des Neuen Testaments*, 82ff.). Each emphasizes a different aspect of the same genre: "apophthegm" stresses the relationship to a concrete person who made the "statement." This personal connection differentiates the apophthegm from general statements or "gnomae." "Chreia," on the other hand, stresses the situational context of the saying: it is a question of the "application" ($\chi\rho\epsilon\iota\alpha$) of a general statement to a particular case. The concept of "apophthegms" also covers those cases in which the situational context of a saying is less important. Of the 24 "apophthegms" of Aristotle in *Diog. Laert.* 5.17–21, seven have no situational context. On the other hand, "chreia" can also include those cases in which the point is closely related to a surprising action. If, in the Jesus tradition, we consider the connection with the person of Jesus to be constitutive, the concept of "apophthegm" is more suitable; but if we think primarily of the parenetical "use" of the saying, "chreia" is preferable. I have chosen "apophthegm" because it has the additional advantage of being a familiar concept in exegetical usage. "Paradigm," the concept suggested by Dibelius (*Formgeschichte*, 34ff.), is associated with his "preaching theory." To use it would be to anticipate a functional designation of the genre that is still subject to debate. The concept of "apophthegm," on the contrary, covers an undisputed descriptive characteristic of the genre.

123. R. C. Tannehill ("Types and Function of Apophthegms") has suggested systematizing this relationship of "stimulus" and "response": correction, commendation, quest, objection, inquiry.

phthegms are thus part of the narrative tradition,[124] they are clearly distinct from miracle stories. As a rule, they contain no place names. The narrative introduction seldom has a corresponding ending (as in Mk 8:13; 10:16). Only by way of exception do we hear anything about the reactions of Jesus' interlocutors and hearers (as in Mk 10:22; 12:17, 34, 37). Usually, a saying of Jesus forms the conclusion. Even when the two genres overlap—as we see in those miracle stories that are counted among the "apophthegms" or "paradigms" (e.g., Mk 2:1-12)—it is reasonable to suppose that the two genres reflect different conditions of transmission. The following comparison focuses on three questions. Who transmitted the apophthegms? For what purpose were they handed down? In what locality were they formed or transmitted?

Who Transmitted the Apophthegms?

While miracle stories contain indications of their tradents in "circulation notices," there are no similar notes in the apophthegms. Nowhere is it indicated that Jesus' interlocutors disseminate his teaching. But something must be known about it because people expect Jesus, as a teacher, to take a position on a problem (cf. Mk 12:14, 19, 32). Witnesses are called up against Jesus, and they think they already know something about his teaching (14:55-59). They use his prophecy about the temple against him, but their witness is regarded as false. A saying of Jesus that was circulating outside the circle of Jesus' adherents is here rejected by Mark as inauthentic, even though its kernel could go back to Jesus. By contrast, Jesus' reputation as a miracle-worker, which was circulating among the people, is confirmed within Mark's Gospel, even though Jesus was opposed to this kind of miracle tradition.

However, there is one direct statement about the transmission of an apophthegm. At the end of the story of the anointing at Bethany, Jesus says, "Truly I tell you, wherever the good news is proclaimed in the whole world, what she has done will be told in remembrance of her" (Mk 14:9). It is debatable whether the woman's story is thus to be understood as a part of the good news, or whether it is merely attached to the good news, but it is clear that the proclamation and transmission of this story belong together. It is reasonable to conclude that the preachers of the gospel are also the tradents of this apophthegm, and of other apophthegms as well.[125]

---

124. But Bultmann (*Die Geschichte der synoptischen Tradition*, 8ff.) included them within the "sayings tradition," because he finds that often the unit begins with a saying that is only secondarily given a frame. Today, generally speaking, we are more inclined to define a genre by means of synchronic textual structures than on the basis of its diachronic prehistory.

125. J. Jeremias ("Markus 14,9"; rev. in idem, *Abba* [Göttingen, 1966], 115–20) interprets Mk 14:9 eschatologically: angels will retell the woman's deed at the last judgment in order

The social roles depicted in the apophthegms give a further (analytical) indication of possible transmitters. Jesus' opponents are scribes (Mk 2:16; 7:1ff.; 12:28ff.; cf. 2:6ff.) or Pharisees and Sadducees, whose arguments reveal them as persons well versed in the Scriptures (Mk 10:2ff.; 10:17ff.; 12:18ff.) or who are confronted with "scribal arguments" (Mk 2:25-26). Conversely, Jesus is addressed as "teacher" (Mk 10:17, 20; 10:35; 12:14, 19, 32). Clearly, the confrontation depicted in the apophthegms is a contest between the "learned," that is, between persons exercising a special role that not everyone can perform. In the miracle stories, by contrast, Jesus is in contact with all sorts of persons. It is a logical supposition that, unlike the miracle stories, the apophthegms were not common popular traditions, but should be attributed to people who had special roles, namely, those who preached and taught in Christianity's earliest days.

A comparative inference lends support to this supposition: early Christian apophthegms are one among many variants of the ancient genre of *chreiai,* or *apophthegmata.* Certainly, they have some special characteristics in contrast to the brief, polished *chreiai*—a somewhat more elaborate narrative introduction and expansion into dialogue—but there are analogies to these "peculiarities" in other ancient traditions.[126] *Chreiai* and apophthegms were cultivated in the schools of rhetoric. They were part of the standard repertoire of the orator, a role characterized by professional competence with words.[127]

Unfortunately, we have few examples of concrete ways in which synoptic apophthegms were used. The single survivor confirms our previous suppositions: it is in an early Christian homily, the *Second Letter of Clement:*

> For when someone asked the Lord when [the rule of God]
> was going to come, he said: "When the two shall be one,
> and the outside like the inside, and the male with the female,
> neither male nor female."
>
> (*2 Clem.* 12:2)

Thus apophthegms are probably not popular stories, but community traditions. Within the community they would not have been handed on by just

---

that God may graciously remember her. It is certain, however, that Mark himself understands the saying in terms of the mission, as shown by the iterative sense of ὅπου ἐάν. This would also have been the interpretation of the pre-Markan tradition, since in the provenance of Mark's tradition, εὐαγγέλιον means the message proclaimed on earth.

126. The *chreiai* and apophthegms collected by Lucian (*Demonax* 12ff.) are formally closer to the synoptic apophthegms to the extent that they often contain a rather extensive narrative introduction and a brief dialogue. But the whole work reveals illuminating analogies to the Gospels. Cf. H. Cancik, "Bios und Logos."

127. Fables and *chreiai* were part of the "progymnasmata," exercises in paraphrasing and elaborating prescribed themes (cf. H. Gärtner, "Progymnasmata"). Quintilian therefore treats them in *Inst.* 1.9.1; 2.14.1; 10.5.11f.

anyone, but by teachers, preachers, missionaries, and itinerant charismatics. Therefore, their social radius of circulation would have been more "limited" than that of the miracle stories. Further reflections point in the same direction.

> It is characteristic of the synoptic apophthegms that the questioners are groups or representatives of groups. As a rule, Jesus' interlocutors, unless they are particular disciples, lack individual names. Individual disciples are mentioned by name when they are called by Jesus (Mk 1:16ff.). John (Mk 9:38-41) and Peter (Mk 10:28ff.; Mt 18:21ff.) ask questions in the name of all, or are themselves questioned as representatives of the disciples (Mt 17:24ff.). The sons of Zebedee (Mk 10:35-40) appear individually, as do Mary and Martha (Lk 10:38ff.). All those named are among Jesus' closest associates. But in the miracle stories the disciples appear almost exclusively as a collective. Sometimes, when they are mentioned by name (Mk 1:29-30, 5:37; Mt 14:28ff.), these can be proved to be additions to the text.[128] But other people who come to Jesus seeking help are occasionally named (Mk 5:22; 10:46). Can we interpret this by saying that in the miracle stories the disciples are seen from outside as a collective? From an external perspective, they appear as a unit. The apophthegms take an internal perspective: here the various groups in the external world are regarded collectively from the viewpoint of Jesus' closest associates, that is, "from the outside."

What Was the Function of Apophthegms?

The ancient analogies show that apophthegms often have a critical aspect. In these pointed sayings, common conventions, convictions, and weaknesses are called into question. It was therefore a form well adapted to the Cynic tradition. The sayings of Diogenes gathered in *Diogenes Laertius* 6 are classics of the genre, as are those in Lucian of Samosata's collection of anecdotes about the Cynic philosopher Demonax. The Jesus tradition, because of its critical nature, could easily be assimilated to this form.[129]

Against the background of this common characteristic, we wish to point to a special accent in the Jesus tradition. Whereas, in the anecdotes about

---

128. In Mk 1:29 the disciples who have already been called (1:16-20) are mentioned again in order to establish a context extending beyond the pericope. In Mk 5:37 the same group appears (cf. 9:2; 13:3; 14:33). Matthew 14:28ff. is an addition to the walking on the water that is found only in Matthew. In Jn 6:5ff. the named disciples, Philip and Andrew, are unknown to the synoptic parallel, but they appear elsewhere in John (cf. 12:22). The disciples appear collectively in Mk 4:38; 5:31; 6:35ff., 45ff.; 8:1ff.; 9:14ff.; 10:46.

129. Tannehill ("Types and Functions of Apophthegms," 1826) correctly emphasizes that apophthegms express "value conflicts." Berger also touches this point: "Since the previous history of chreiai is primarily to be traced to the field of Cynic thought, they are by nature endowed with a critical tone. For the Cynics stood for a revolution of values. But it is precisely this characteristic that makes chreiai/apophthegms appropriate for Jesus' message" ("Hellenistische Gattungen," 1106).

Diogenes, the interlocutors often are either anonymous or are well-known individuals such as Alexander the Great, in the synoptic tradition we primarily find stereotypic groups as partners in the discussion: scribes, Pharisees, Sadducees, and Herodians. What is accomplished is less a stance against convictions common to the whole society than an opposition to other groups within one particular social unit. Jesus also speaks here not as an individual "wise person," but as representative of a group, when, for example, he defends the behavior of the disciples (Mk 2:18; 2:23; 7:2). In other words, in the synoptic apophthegms one group affirms its own convictions and behavior by differentiating itself from other surrounding groups. The Gospel apophthegms define social identity. In this they are clearly different from miracle stories because the fears, values, and hopes expressed in the latter transcend the boundaries of any particular group—everyone can identify with them. When demarcations are important in these stories, they are barriers to Gentiles, which are broken down (Mt 8:5-13; Mk 5:1-20; 7:24-30). Demarcations toward other groups within the nation itself are found only in the miracle stories that have apophthegmatic character, that is, those Dibelius counted among the paradigms (Mk 2:1-12; 3:1-6; Lk 13:10-17; 14:2-6). To summarize all this in a simplifying formula, we could say that apophthegms tend to have a socially demarcating function, while miracle stories tend toward social transcendence.[130]

Because social identity constantly must be redefined, stories with a socially demarcating function can be used again and again, even outside their original context. Originally, the apophthegms served to differentiate one group within Judaism from other groups. Even in Mark's Gospel we can observe a tendency to use them to distinguish Christian groups from Judaism as a whole. Thus, a secondary function appears as an overlay to their primary intention.[131]

In the series of apophthegms (or miracle stories with strongly apophthegmatic character) in Mk 2:1—3:6, the contrast between Jesus and his opponents is raised to the level of insuperable enmity. At the end of the series, the evangelist adds the note: "The Pharisees went out and immediately conspired with the Herodians against him, how to destroy him" (3:6).

---

130. On the socially transcendent function of miracle stories, see Theissen, *Urchristliche Wundergeschichten*, esp. 251ff.

131. We may be able to detect this overlay even in the typical interlocutors of Jesus in Mark's Gospel: Mark mentions the "scribes" (21 times) more often than the "Pharisees" (12 times). "Scribes" can be found outside Palestine as well (especially in Rome; cf. H. J. Leon, *Jews of Ancient Rome*, 183–86 and inscriptions 7, 18, 67, 99, etc. on pp. 265ff.). "Pharisees" cannot be found outside Palestine. In the "scribes," Mark draws a line between his own group and Diaspora Judaism as he knew it. So Lührmann, *Markusevangelium*, 50–51; cf. idem, "Die Pharisäer und die Schriftgelehrten im Markusevangelium."

This deadly enmity does not result from the scenes that have preceded it; it is only in the context of Mark's Gospel as a whole that it constitutes a link between the conflict stories and the Passion.[132]

The intensification of opposition is accompanied by generalization. The discussion about what is "clean" and "unclean" takes place in confrontation with Pharisees. But the evangelist inserts a parenesis into the dialogue that clearly indicates that he is talking about Judaism as a whole: "For the Pharisees, *and all the Jews*, do not eat unless they thoroughly wash their hands, thus observing the tradition of the elders" (Mk 7:3, emphasis mine). The custom of hand-washing probably was not yet general practice at the time of Jesus.[133] What we have here is an anachronistic generalization.

It is only in the Markan context that the apophthegms first acquire this function of forging a distance from Judaism. Outside this context, their original function of establishing an identity within Judaism is still clearly recognizable. In this connection, we can distinguish two groups of apophthegms: the short apophthegms in Mk 2:1—3:6 and the longer conflict stories in chapter 12. In the first group there is always a "christological argument," the appeal to Jesus' authority as "Son of man" (Mk 2:10), as "physician" (2:17), and as "bridegroom" (2:19). In the content, reasons are given for certain norms by which Jesus' adherents are distinguished from other Jews: greater liberality in table-fellowship (2:15ff.), in questions of fasting (2:18ff.), and in Sabbath practices (2:23ff.)—in other words, in those areas that were experienced in daily life as barriers separating Jews and Gentiles. It is interesting that Jesus' personal authority is established by reference to ordinary logic and experience: doctors visit the sick; in the same way, Jesus turns toward sinners. No one can fast at a wedding, and thus in Jesus' presence the customs of fasting can be ignored. The Sabbath was made for the sake of human beings, from the time of creation; thus, the "Son of man" is also master of the Sabbath. Jesus' charismatic authority does not appear here as a "higher claim" backed by a complete Christology.[134]

The second group of conflict stories, on the other hand, contains an

---

132. E. Stegemann ("Von Kritik zur Feindschaft") has accurately located this "tradition of conflicts between Jesus' early adherents and their Jewish brethren raised to the level of enmity" (p. 54) in the process of separation between Judaism and Christianity after 70 C.E.

133. The cultic prescriptions for purity probably became important in daily life only after the temple was destroyed and the household table acquired some of the attributes of the altar. Then it became necessary to approach it in a condition of ritual purity. On rabbinic prescriptions for hand-washing, cf. Billerbeck, *Kommentar* 1:695ff.

134. H.-W. Kuhn (*Ältere Sammlungen im Markusevangelium*, 53–98, esp. 80ff.) concludes from the "christological *logia*" in Mk 2:1—3:6 that the apophthegms are addressed to Christians who are already convinced of Jesus' authority. Thus the conflict is not so much with Judaism outside the community, but with a Jewish Christianity within it. However, we must

expressly "theocentric argument": God is superior to Caesar. Unstated, but understood, is the point that if the emperor is to receive the denarius because the money belongs to him, how much more must everything be given back to God, who is Creator and owner of the world (12:17). The resurrection of the dead is not explained by Jesus' resurrection, but in terms of faith in the God of Israel: because God is the God of Abraham, Isaac, and Jacob, God is a God of those who have died (12:26-27). Decisive for human behavior are the commandments of this God, all of which are summarized in the twofold love commandment: in the *sh^ema* and in the command to love one's neighbor. In this, Jesus and a scribe are in agreement (12:28-34). The pericope on divorce also has a "theocentric" structure of argument: because God placed man and woman together at the beginning, no human being may separate them (10:9).

The self-identification of Christian groups that is expressed in the apophthegms accomplishes both their location within and their distinction from Judaism. The conflict stories with theocentric arguments formulate convictions that these groups have in common with parts of Judaism or with all Jews. The apophthegms with "christological" arguments focus on norms in which Christians differ from the majority of other Jewish groups. In the course of tradition the distinguishing function becomes intensified, so that in Mark it is dominant. The following conclusion is important for us: traditions that have a distinguishing function toward the outside cannot be handed on by those who are excluded by them. Here we obviously are dealing with traditions that were passed along within the Christian communities.[135]

Where Were the Apophthegms Handed On?

In contrast to the miracle stories, the apophthegms contain no indications of place.[136] Sometimes we can tell from the content that teller and audi-

---

also consider that the personal charismatic claim of Jesus in Mk 2:1—3:6 is often rendered plausible in terms of common experiences. With such arguments, one could address people outside the community. Still, external problems are usually reflected in problems within a group as well.

135. Mark's Gospel has developed a special literary form for conflicts and problems within the community: Jesus' public preaching is followed by private teaching. Both Jesus' major speeches are in this form. The parable discourse in Mk 4:10ff. concerns the development of the church, and the apocalypse in Mk 13:3ff. deals with its fate at the end of time. Mark 7:17-23 discusses the question of food restrictions, an acute problem in the communities (cf. Gal 2:11-14). Mark 9:28-29 warns against the overestimation of charismatic gifts in serious cases of demonic possession. We find such warnings about the overvaluing of charisms also in 1 Cor 12–14. Mark 9:33ff. admonishes against hierarchical claims, another notorious intracommunity problem (cf. 3 John). Mark 10:10-12 takes a position on the disputed question of divorce (cf. 1 Cor 7:10ff.).

136. Cf. Bultmann, *Die Geschichte der synoptischen Tradition*, 67–69. Many place indications

ence assign them to a particular place, for example, the calling of disciples at the "sea" (Mk 1:16-20; 2:13-14). What we have said about the miracle stories at the "sea" is also true for these brief call narratives: they were formulated in a region remote from the great ocean. The banquet with the tax collectors can also be located indirectly. In the Markan context it takes place in or near Capernaum.[137] In this region, a tax booth can only have been a border station;[138] in fact, from the time of the division of the Herodian kingdom in 4 B.C.E., a frontier ran between Capernaum and Bethsaida. It continued in existence until 39 C.E.[139] and then vanished. After 39 C.E., Agrippa I united the regions of Galilee east and west of the Jordan (*Ant.* 18.252; *Bell.* 2.183), and they remained united even after his death in 44 C.E.; at that time Claudius sent Cuspius Fadus to Palestine, not only as procurator of Judea and Samaria, but "of Judea and of the whole kingdom" (*Ant.* 19.363). He deliberately rejected the incorporation of the kingdom within the province of Syria. A later division of the two parts of the region was only temporary. In 53 C.E., Claudius gave Agrippa II the former tetrarchies of Philip and Lysanias (*Ant.* 20.138), so that the Jordan again formed the boundary. However, in the following year Nero, after ascending to the throne, bestowed parts of Galilee and Perea on Agrippa II (*Ant.* 20.159; *Bell.* 2.252), with the result that Agrippa united the tetrarchy of Philip with eastern Galilee under one rule. This situation continued until the king's death in the 90s. That means that from the year 39

---

are contained only implicitly in the material, e.g., the "lake" in the stories of the calling of disciples in Mk 1:16-20, the "tax booth" in Mk 2:14, or the temple in Mk 12:41-44. The same is true of Jerusalem in Lk 13:1-5, Galilee in Lk 13:31-33, and Samaria in Lk 9:51-56. The only places mentioned explicitly are "Bethany" in Mk 14:3-9 and Jericho in Lk 19:1-10, two apophthegms that are also notable for their use of concrete personal names: Simon the leper and the chief tax collector Zacchaeus. (The localized apophthegms cited by Bultmann, on p. 68 [Mk 2:1ff.; Mt 8:5ff.; Mk 7:24ff.] are, in my opinion, clearly miracle stories. The latter are quite frequently given a local designation.)

137. The location of the tax booth in Capernaum is only evident from the broader Markan context (Mk 2:1). A location "by the sea" (2:13) might instead have been part of the original pericope. The *Gospel of the Ebionites* locates the tax booth quite clearly in the neighborhood of Capernaum (cf. E. Hennecke, *Neutestamentliche Apokryphen* 1:102). The considerations on the call of Levi and the banquet with tax collectors sketched previously presume that the tradition knew the tax station to have been north of Lake Gennesaret, in the locality where Jesus' activity was centered.

138. "Tax [or toll] collectors" were those who farmed excises (market and weight duties) or taxes (manufacturing, household, and use taxes). Cf. H. Merkel, "τελώνης," *EWNT* 3:836. It is thus not a question of frontier duties. But it is evident from Mk 2:13-14 that the tax booth is depicted as being on the road, and outside the town; cf. ἐξῆλθεν in Mk 2:13. The one telling the story very probably thought of road taxes and frontier duties.

139. The borders remained in place even after the death of Philip the tetrarch in 34 C.E. because the emperor Tiberius added the province of Syria to his territory, but continued to treat it as a separate governmental unit that was required to send a tribute separate from that of Syria (*Ant.* 18.108).

C.E. there was de facto no longer a boundary at the Jordan and thus no need to maintain a toll station in this region in a little town like Capernaum.[140] Stories about tax collectors and toll stations in this region on the northern shore of the Lake of Galilee must have been formed before 39 by storytellers who were acquainted with the local situation.

A familiarity with circumstances of which the reader is not fully aware is evident also in the pericope about the "widow's mite" (Mk 12:41-44). "The treasury" (τὸ γαζοφυλάκιον) is mentioned here without further explanation (vv. 41, 43). According to Josephus, there were any number of treasury chambers in the forecourt of the temple (*Bell.* 5.200). Nevertheless, Josephus can also speak once, without further elaboration, of "the treasury": after King Agrippa I, by a stroke of luck, was transformed from a prisoner under Tiberius to a king under Gaius, he hung a golden chain, which Gaius had given him as a memorial of his captivity, "within the sacred precincts, over the treasure-chamber [ὑπὲρ τὸ γαζοφυλάκιον]" (*Ant.* 19.294).[141] I do not think it is important for our particular subject to know exactly where this treasury was located. What is important is to note that a Jew such as Josephus, who was familiar with the temple, could speak of "*the* treasury" without further explanation. It is easy to suppose that the expression "the treasury" was coined by people who knew the situation of the place.

Rudolph Bultmann locates a good many of the apophthegms within the original Palestinian community, basing his judgment on their formal kinship to rabbinic conflict dialogues and anecdotes.[142] But this is difficult to prove.[143] The synoptic apophthegms are, from a form-critical point of view, as closely related to those in the Greek tradition as to rabbinic conflict dialogues and anecdotes. Since no form-critical analysis of the apophthegms is possible here, I will offer only a few indications. First, some apophthegms can be located in Galilee in the first century C.E. I will mention three examples.

---

140. Here again I am making an assumption that I regard as plausible: old customs boundaries could, of course, be maintained for the collection of internal taxes, even if they no longer coincided with political boundaries. But the few toll collectors we can locate are found at border stations: in Jericho (Lk 19:1ff.), Caesarea (*Bell.* 2.287, 292) and on the northern shore of the Lake of Galilee (Mk 2:13-14).

141. I am grateful to S. Köchler-Maslo and R. D. Maslo for calling my attention to this passage in Josephus.

142. Cf. Bultmann, *Die Geschichte der synoptischen Tradition*, 49–50, 57–58, 60ff.

143. G. G. Porton ("Pronouncement Story in Tannaitic Literature") examines the rabbinic parallels cited by Bultmann and concludes that there are closer analogies to the synoptic apophthegms in the apophthegms of Greek philosophers and politicians. This seems to me to undervalue the rabbinic parallels somewhat: only there do we find the use of scriptural citations, and it is only these parallels that bring us into immediate historical proximity to the beginnings of early Christianity.

Diogenes Laertius records an apophthegm from *The Wreath*, by Justus of Tiberias, a contemporary of Josephus.[144] It stems from the trial of Socrates:

> "In the course of the trial, Plato mounted the platform and began: "Though I am the youngest, men of Athens, of all who ever rose to address you"— whereupon the judges shouted out: "Get down! Get down!" (*Diog. Laert.* 2.41)

An anecdote about R. Eliezer ben Hyrcanos (ca. 90 C.E.) is often read as an encounter with Jewish Christians.[145] I introduce it here because it is a Galilean witness from the second half of the first century to an apophthegm like those in the Jesus tradition:

> Once I was walking up the main street of Sepphoris when there came toward me a man named Jacob of Kefar Sekaniah who told me something in the name of So-and-so [i.e., Jesus the Nazarene], which pleased me, namely, "It is written in your Torah, 'Thou shalt not bring the hire of a harlot or the price of a dog into the house of the Lord thy God for any vow' (Deut 23:18). What is to be done with them?" I told him that they were prohibited [for every use]. He said to me, "They are prohibited as an offering, but is it permissible to destroy them?" I retorted, "In that case, what is to be done with them?" He said to me, "Let bath-houses and privies be made with them." I exclaimed, "You have said an excellent thing," and the law [not to listen to the words of a *min*] escaped my memory at the time. When he saw that I acknowledged his words, he added, "Thus said So-and-so: From filth they came and on filth they should be expended; as it is said: For the hire of a harlot hath she gathered them and unto the hire of a harlot they shall return (Mic 1:7). Let them be spent on privies for the public," and the thought pleased me. (*b. Abod. Zar.* 16a; cf. *t. Hull.* 2.24; *Eccl. Rab.* 1:1, 8)

As in many of the synoptic apophthegms, two scriptural passages are played off against one another (cf. Mk 7:1ff.; 10:2ff.). We need not suppose this to be an apocryphal Jesus tradition. It would be just as easy to conclude a Galilean milieu in which this kind of free dealing with the Scriptures was possible, and in which synoptic conflict dialogues were also formed and handed on. The same is true, mutatis mutandis, for a tradition about the miracle-working Rabbi Hanina ben Dosa (ca. 70), who lived in the Galilean city of Arab, about ten kilometers north of Nazareth.[146]

---

144. On Justus of Tiberias, see Schürer, *History of Jewish People*, 34–37. Josephus expressly attributes a Greek education to him (*Vita* 40).

145. See the thorough analysis of the tradition in J. Maier, *Jesus von Nazareth*, 144–81. According to him, the explicit reference to "Jeshu han-nosri" is almost surely secondary. It is uncertain whether the James who appears in the story was a Jewish Christian. In any case, he was a "heretic."

146. G. Vermes (*Jesus the Jew*, 72ff.) sees Jesus as inhabiting a charismatic Galilean milieu that we find also surrounding Hanina ben Dosa.

> It is said of Rabbi Hanina ben Dosa that, as he was standing and praying, a poisonous snake bit him, but he did not interrupt his prayer. His disciples went and found the snake lying dead before its hole. They said: woe to the person whom the snake bites; woe to the snake that bites Ben Dosa! (*t. Ber.* 3.20; cf. *y. Ber.* 9a; *b. Ber.* 33a)

It cannot be denied that apophthegms and conflict dialogues could occur in first-century Galilee. Hellenistic Greek influences are also possible in this region. Therefore, a form similar to Hellenistic apophthegms is no evidence against a Palestinian origin of the synoptic apophthegms.

Additionally, in the synoptic apophthegms it is seldom a single, quick-witted wise person who questions social conventions (although this type is not totally lacking). Instead, the apophthegms formulate group norms in conflict with those of other groups. In this formal trait, they are similar to the rabbinic dialogues. But in the latter, the opposing schools appear as equal partners in the dialogue. They receive equal formal treatment, as in the typical scheme: "The school of Hillel said to the school of Shammai. . . . The school of Shammai replied . . ." (see, e.g., *b. Git.* 90a). But in the Jesus tradition, Jesus receives more formal emphasis. There is an asymmetry between the questioners and Jesus. In this, the apophthegms about him are closer to many Hellenistic analogies. But these also share unmistakably in a "culture of controversy"[147] that we may presume existed in first-century Palestine.

Thus we affirm the results of our investigation of the "small units" in the Jesus tradition. Where we can more closely define their origins in terms of locality and date, we find that they come from Palestine or Galilee. The beginnings of the sayings and narrative tradition are to be sought in the places where Jesus worked. Two possible groups can be detected that were bearers of the tradition: on the one hand, Jesus' disciples, who preserved his words (including their narrative context) because they founded their lives as disciples on those words; on the other hand, the people who wanted to hear marvelous stories about his miraculous deeds, just as they wanted to hear about the Baptizer's death. The two groups are not mutually exclusive. Jesus' disciples and followers would have transmitted both sayings and miracle stories. But the spread of the miracle stories beyond the circle of Jesus' followers was more rapid than the propagation of his words.

---

147. This phrase is from D. Dischon, *Culture of Controversy in Israel,* a book known to me only indirectly by way of a seminar paper by M. Jacobs (1987).

PART II

SOCIAL CONTEXT AND POLITICAL HISTORY IN THE LARGE UNITS OF THE SYNOPTIC TRADITION

In addition to the "small units," there are "large units" in the synoptic Gospels, including the infancy narratives, the Passion story, and the great apocalyptic discourse in Mark 13. These large units contain a number of parts in the form of pericopes, but they are not compilations of small units. Instead, the composition preceded the subunits, even if it has been secondarily expanded by the addition of other pericopes.

In larger units we cannot speak of synoptic genres. The texts are unique. There is no analogy to the Passion narrative in all of ancient literature. Elements of Hellenistic acts of the martyrs and Jewish tales of martyrdom have been melded into something quite new. Amazing stories about the birth of a great person existed in antiquity in many variations. Nevertheless, we cannot view the infancy narratives in Matthew and Luke as examples of the same genre. They do not have the typical structure of miracle stories, parables, or apophthegms. The synoptic apocalypse is also a unique text. Although there are parallels to many of its individual motifs, it is common in apocalyptic literature for a mediator of revelation, not a "contemporary," to foretell the future.

All the major units are marked by Old Testament quotations, allusions, or motifs. The Passion narrative is pervaded by the sorrow of the psalms of lament. The synoptic apocalypse paints the future in the bleak colors of the Book of Daniel. Matthew's infancy narrative is shaped around reflective citations, and the first chapters of Luke are full of hymns written in Old Testament language. The large units point toward a milieu in which the Scriptures were familiar. This closeness to the Scriptures suggests that a written tradition is more likely to underlie the large units than the small ones.

The large units are thus distinguished from the small by greater complexity, individuality, and "literary" character. In them, the movement from oral tradition to the Gospels is already underway. Precisely for this reason, it is important for a history of the synoptic tradition that we give a more exact account of their historical context as revealed by indications of time and place.

3

The Great Eschatological Discourse and the Threat to the Jerusalem Temple in 40 C.E.

In Mark's Gospel, "narrated time" extends from Jesus' baptism to his Passion. In only a few places is this narrative interrupted by forward or backward glances: in Mk 6:14-29 by a retrospective account of the death of the Baptizer, which took place before the mission of the disciples in Mk 6:7-13; and in Mark 4 and 13 by references to the time after Jesus' death. In the parable discourse, Jesus describes the beginning and internal perils of the church (4:13-32), and in the apocalyptic discourse he speaks of external threats to the community: wars, catastrophes, and persecutions. If the historical background of a synoptic text is ever evident, it must be in these two "secret instructions to the disciples." This is especially true in the case of Mark 13. There is a consensus among exegetes that in this discourse historical experiences have been reworked in the framework of a convinced apocalypticism.[1]

By general agreement, the discourse reflects crisis conditions. Three types of interpretation may be distinguished, although they sometimes appear in combination.

1. Many exegetes take persecution of Christians to be the background for Mark 13. In that case, vv. 9-13 are central. L. Schottroff supposes a persecution at the time of Vespasian (68–79 C.E.) in the eastern part of the Roman Empire.[2] It would have been brought on by an early Christian messianism, regarded as politically dangerous by the rulers and rejected in Mark's Gospel. This would

---

1. For an evaluation of the immense literature on Mark 13, see G. R. Beasley-Murray, *Jesus and the Future.* For the period 1954–67, there is a summary in R. Pesch, *Naherwartungen,* 19–47. On more recent research, see E. Brandenburger, *Markus 13,* 21–42.

2. L. Schottroff, "Die Gegenwart." N. Walter offers good reasons for a date after the destruction of the temple in "Tempelzerstörung und synoptische Apokalypse." In my opinion, this analysis of the situation is plausible on the redactional level, but it does not exclude the search for an earlier context for the traditions incorporated in Mark 13.

explain the warnings against false prophets and false messiahs. The destruction of the temple is presupposed. On the other hand, M. Hengel sees the discourse in terms of Nero's persecution of Christians (ca. 64 C.E. in Rome).[3] According to him, Mark's Gospel was written ca. 68 C.E. in Rome, when memory of the persecution was still vivid. Mark 13:12 would reflect the action against the Christians described by Tacitus: "First, then, the confessed members of the sect were arrested; next, on their disclosures, vast numbers were convicted, not so much on the count of arson as for hatred of the human race" (*Ann.* 15.44). Mark 13:12 would presume that Christians had delivered their Christian "brothers and sisters" up to death, Mk 13:13 that they were hated by everyone. Mark's Gospel would have been written after Nero's death, when civil wars and rebellions in Germany and Judea and the approaching destruction of the temple at Jerusalem had reawakened apocalyptic expectations. Bo Reicke dates the persecutions of Christians in vv. 9-13 even further back: they are identical with the persecution of the Jerusalem community reported in Acts.[4]

2. The flight of the early community from Jerusalem is often regarded as the experience behind these verses, whether it is supposed that Mark 13 is a call to a future flight or that the text refers to this flight as already in the past. The motif of flight in 13:14 here becomes the interpretative key. In fact, we find in Eusebius (*Eccl. Hs.* 3.5.2–3) a report that, because of an oracle, the Jerusalem community moved to Pella, east of the Jordan, immediately before the Jewish war. Since a persecution of the Jerusalem community had broken out shortly before—in the year 62 the high priest Ananus had James, the brother of the Lord, and other unknown persons (i.e., Jewish Christians) executed (Jos. *Ant.* 20.200–201)—this feature also fits well in the presumed situation. The conclusion is either that Mark's Gospel itself is to be interpreted as a call to the exodus from Jerusalem[5] or that Mark 13 is adapting a tradition identical with the oracle mentioned by Eusebius.[6] The tradition of an exodus to Pella has

---

3. M. Hengel, "Entstehungszeit," 1–45. There are two arguments that, I think, stand in the way of this fascinating interpretation. First, in the literary composition of Mark, the wars in 13:6-8 are mentioned before the persecutions in 13:9-13, but in historical reality the persecutions (ca. 64 C.E.) preceded the wars (66–70). It is true that Mark seems to think of both as occurring simultaneously. But while with the wars "the end is still to come" (v. 7), the persecutions last "to the end" (v. 13). The evangelist thus indicates a temporal sequence in the sense that, even when the wars are over, the persecutions continue. Second, a local-historical consideration may be added to this chronological argument: the governors and kings mentioned in 13:9 make us think of the East. Kings were found especially in the eastern parts of the empire (cf. D. Braund, *Rome and the Friendly King*). Governors had judicial powers only in the provinces, not in Rome.

4. B. Reicke, "Synoptic Prophecies on the Destruction of Jerusalem," 121–34, esp. 131ff.

5. W. Marxsen, *Der Evangelist Markus*, 112ff. Marxsen later retreated from his intelligent hypothesis.

6. H. J. Schoeps, "Ebionitische Apokalyptik im Neuen Testament"; R. Pesch, *Das Markusevangelium* 2:195–96. But in *Naherwartungen* (207ff.) Pesch had supported the pamphlet hypothesis: the tradition adapted in Mark 13 stemmed from the Caligula crisis, but was revived and "misused" in the Markan community circa 70 C.E.

been repeatedly attacked as unhistorical,[7] but it can scarcely be doubted that there was an emigration of refugees during the Jewish war.

3. Both of these types of interpretation are connected by the presumption that the threat to the temple by the "desolating sacrilege" stands at the center of Mark 13. Frequently, this is regarded as a prophecy inserted after the fact: the temple has already been destroyed (e.g., D. Lührmann).[8] But now and then someone regards it as a genuine prophecy: the threatened fate has not yet occurred, but lies like a shadow over the land. Two situations would make this possible. F. Hahn thinks that the tradition adapted in Mark 13 belongs to the first phase of the Jewish war, when the fighting was still concentrated entirely in Galilee. The addressees would thus far only have "heard" of these wars (13:7). They now fearfully await the southward advance of the troops and the danger to the temple, where they will "see" the abominable sacrilege (13:14). In that case, the synoptic apocalypse would have been written ca. 67–69 in Judea.[9] G. Hölscher, on the other hand, refers the situation to the threatened profanation of the temple in the year 40 C.E., when the emperor Gaius Caligula proposed to set up his own statue there. At that time the Syrian legate, Petronius, had already advanced with his troops as far as Ptolemais, in order to bring the statue to Jerusalem by force, if necessary. Only Caligula's sudden death on 24 January 41 preserved the land from catastrophe.[10]

---

7. Thus G. Lüdemann, "Successors of Pre-70 Jerusalem Christianity." According to Lüdemann, the tradition about the flight to Pella was a foundational etiology of the Christian community at that place. In that case, the tradition about the flight could be historical, and only the connection with Pella secondary—it is well attested that in the war years members of the upper classes left Palestine (*Bell.* 2.556). Johanan ben Zakkai is also supposed to have succeeded in fleeing Jerusalem during the siege (*Aboth R. Nat.* 4). Theon, son of Demetrius, who appears on an inscription in Gerasa from about 70 as a petitioner for asylum, could also have been a refugee from Palestine (cf. C. H. Kraeling, *Gerasa*, 376–77, inscription 6). The early Jerusalem community had a motive for flight: the rebellion brought the high priest Ananus into power (*Bell.* 2.563), the same man who had persecuted the community four years previously (*Ant.* 20.200–201).

8. D. Lührmann, *Markusevangelium*, 222. In this interpretation, the *"desolating* sacrilege" is referred to the desolation of the temple, which was sacked by the Roman army. On the plethora of interpretations, cf. G. R. Beasley-Murray, *Commentary on Mark 13*, 59–72.

9. F. Hahn, "Die Rede von der Parusie." This fascinating interpretation is in tension with the fact that the war in Jerusalem began with the destruction of a cohort (*Bell.* 2.449–56). There were struggles between the rebellious factions (*Bell.* 2.442–48) and a futile attempt by Cestius Gallus, the legate of Syria, to conquer Jerusalem with his legion. This early phase of the war ended in a fiasco for the Romans (*Bell.* 2.499ff.; 527ff.). "Those in Judea" (Mk 13:14) had thus experienced the war in person from the beginning and had not merely "heard" of it from a distance. But Hahn's investigation has formulated a criterion for every analysis of the situation: Was there a place, or a situation, in which people had only heard of wars, but were immediately threatened by a "desolating sacrilege"?

10. G. Hölscher ("Der Ursprung der Apokalypse Mk 13") gave this thesis its classic form, but was not the first to propose it. Starting with the text of Matthew, F. Spitta (*Die Offenbarung des Johannes*, 493–96) had first referred the synoptic apocalypse to the Caligula crisis (p. 496), without giving reasons for his thesis. A critique of this hypothesis is found in P. Bilde, "Afspejler Mark." Bilde admits only for the isolated verses 7, 14, and 18 the possibility that

DISSONANCES BETWEEN
TEXT AND SITUATION IN MARK 13

Opinions about the historical experiences behind Mark 13 are widely divergent. An inference from the text to a situation underlying it is only possible through a threefold process of division because the text contains a mixture of tradition and redaction, past and present, and experience and thematic arrangement. Each of these divisions will be carefully considered.

1. Although Mark 13 is often interpreted as a text that has been carefully composed by the evangelist, its use of traditional material is unmistakable. There are tensions between the framing of Jesus' words and the discourse itself. In 13:5 and 13:37, Jesus addresses "hearers," in accord with the situation as it is depicted, but in 13:14 the addressees are "readers." First he demands of these readers that they correctly understand the mysterious figure of the βδέλυγμα τῆς ἐρημώσεως,[11] then tells the people of Judea to flee to the mountains. The call for understanding and the warning to flee are in the third person, the first in the singular and the second in the plural. Both appeals belong together: the "desolating sacrilege" is not rightly understood until it is seen as a reason for flight.

The interpretation of this appeal for understanding is a subject of controversy. Is the evangelist demanding that readers of Daniel take note of the "abomination that desolates" (Dan 12:11, etc.) so that all will realize that the ancient prophecy is being fulfilled? At any rate, that is how the author of Matthew understood him. The latter mentions Daniel specifically and locates the desolating sacrilege in the temple, "in the holy place" (Mt 24:15). But if Mark wanted to say that, why does he not refer more specifically to the Old Testament (as in Mk 1:2; 7:6-7; 11:17, and elsewhere)? Furthermore, there is nothing in Daniel about flight, and yet this fleeing is the necessary consequence, when one correctly understands the appearance of the "desolating sacrilege"! A reference to Daniel would only confuse the readers of Mk 13:14. The only thing that is certain is that the appeal for understanding in Mk 13:14 refers to the figure of the "desolating sacrilege" in the text itself. There are comparable appeals in Rev 13:9, 18; 17:9.

A second possibility would be that the evangelist is thinking of his own

---

they refer to the situation in the year 40. But insofar as they are read in their context, they cannot refer to that year. Here again, we have an important criterion for situation analysis: not only individual elements in a text, but also their combination and ordering within the text as a whole must fit the supposed situation.

11. For interpretation of this appeal to the readers for understanding, cf. Beasley-Murray, *Commentary on Mark 13*, 57; Pesch, *Naherwartungen*, 144–45.

Gospel and calling on those who read it aloud to give the community assembly a correct interpretation of the "desolating sacrilege."[12] But νοείτω does not mean διερμηνευέτω (1 Cor 14:27). A demand for understanding is not necessarily a call to interpret something for others. Besides, in an invitation to interpret Mark's Gospel we would expect a formula calling for attention, such as we find in Mk 4:9: "Let anyone with ears to hear listen!" Although Mark's Gospel exists in written form, it was meant to be read aloud (and thus to be heard). Appeals to listeners such as that in Mk 4:9 are found also in Rev 2:7, 11, 17 and elsewhere, and refer to written letters to the seven churches. What the writer has in mind is that the letters will be read aloud to the congregations.

Therefore, the third possibility is the most probable: that the appeal for understanding is directed to individual readers. The one who reads is identical with the one who understands and must draw the correct conclusions for himself or herself. Although he or she is addressed as an individual reader, the call to flight is for all those who live "in Judea." This presupposes that the text will also be read by other individuals, one by one—in short, that it circulated as a leaflet. The author of Mark could not have written that. He is not thinking of private readers, but of "all" (13:37). However, all this can be explained, without violence to the text, if Mk 13:14 refers to a written source that was not meant for public circulation, but that used mysterious symbols as a signal for flight and was intended to be unintelligible to outsiders.

In addition to this tension between oral and written communication in the discourse and its frame, there is a problem of content. The question is about the destruction of the temple—"when will this be?"—and about the sign that "all these things are about to be accomplished." And yet the answer makes no clear reference to the temple. We can even recognize a certain contradiction in the fact that the question concerns an event that is interpreted in Mark as the fulfillment of prophecy and the accomplishment of divine judgment (cf. Mk 12:9), while the answer talks about an "abomination" or "sacrilege." The key word βδέλυγμα (sacrilege) is usually connected with idolatry in the Old Testament. It means an impious human action, and in no case an act of God. This makes it difficult to refer the "desolating sacrilege" to the destruction of the temple.[13] When the author of Luke does so (Lk 21:20ff.), he omits the difficult word βδέλυγμα and speaks merely of the "desolation" of Jerusalem. His reinterpretation of the

---

12. So J. Wellhausen, *Das Evangelium Marci*, 103, referring to C. Weizsäcker.

13. Lührmann (*Markusevangelium*, 222) identifies the "desolating sacrilege" with the "destruction of the city and the Temple." This destruction could not, then, be referred to a just divine judgment. In my opinion, it could only refer to a wicked act in connection with

passage in terms of the destruction of the temple and the conquest of Jerusalem involves such extensive changes in the Markan text that it is difficult to suppose that ancient readers would have taken Mark's text as it stands to refer to the temple's fall. But the frame of the eschatological discourse inquires about the destruction of the temple. If Mk 13:14ff. also refers to this, there has been a shift between the frame and the discourse. Mark 13:14ff. might possibly have been applied secondarily to the destruction of the temple, but the original composition of the passage could scarcely have referred to that event.[14]

That a tradition has been adapted in Mark 13 is, in my opinion, rather certain. *What* belongs to the tradition remains unclear. We can discern a two-part structure:[15] the "beginning of the birthpangs" (13:8) is followed by "those days" (13:19, 24), in which there will again be great "suffering" (13:19); the Parousia (the coming of the Son of man) will ensue only "after that suffering" (13:24). Mark's *Vorlage* would thus have included, at a minimum:[16] the beginning of the birthpangs (13:7-8); the suffering (13:14-20); the Parousia (13:24-27). But that is only a minimum. Other parts of the discourse could have been part of the source, for example,

---

that destruction. It relates to a crime on the part of either the defenders or the besiegers. The crime of the defenders could be the choice of a new high priest by the Zealots (*Bell.* 4.155–56). This is the opinion of S. Sowers, "Circumstances and Recollection of the Pella Flight." Looking for the outrage on the besieging side, some have interpreted the "desolating sacrilege" as the appearance of the Roman army under Cestius Gallus on Mount Skopos on 17 November 66 (thus J. J. Gunther, "Fate of the Jerusalem Church"); or, like W. Schmithals (*Das Evangelium nach Markus*, 575), as pagan sacrifices before the Roman standards within the burning temple (*Bell.* 6.316). These interpretations all presume a *vaticinium ex eventu*. Those who suppose this to be a genuine prophecy think mainly of the antichrist as the "desolating sacrilege." This is, in particular, the opinion of Hengel, "Entstehungszeit," 29ff., 38ff. For a review of the earlier history of interpretation, see Beasley-Murray, *Commentary on Mark 13*, 59–72.

14. The author of Mark could have seen the prophecy of the destruction of the temple as being fulfilled in the wars mentioned in 13:7-8. In that case, the first question in 13:5, about the time of the temple's fall, would have been answered in 13:7-8, and the second question, about the "signs" of the final days, in 13:14.

15. This division into "last days" before the end and the end time itself has an analogy in Qumran. (This was pointed out by H.-W. Kuhn.) In 1QpHab 7.1–2 we read of the "last generation"; in 7.12 we read of the "last days," for which the prophet has received a revelation. This is distinguished from the "completion of the time" (1QpHab 7.2). The author of Mark, however, would have developed this twofold division into a threefold one: the present is already the "beginning of the birthpangs," but it is not followed simply by the end; instead, there is a historical future (13:14-23) that human beings must still endure before the cosmic Parousia, which is determined solely by the action of God and of the Son of man (13:24-27). According to H. Conzelmann ("Geschichte und Eschaton nach Mc 13"), that is the point of the Markan redaction.

16. It would make no sense to list all suggested divisions of the text. I will refer merely to the careful discussion in Brandenburger, *Markus 13*, 21–42.

13:5-6, 12-13, 21-23.[17] The relegation of verses 9-13 to a secondary level is widespread: here we find sayings about persecution that could come from an independent tradition. The author of Matthew includes them in his mission discourse (Mt 10:17-22), and thus treats them as an independent unit. But for the moment we can leave open the precise definition of the *Vorlage* for Mark 13. It may be that analysis of the situation will provide us with an additional criterion for determining its extent: whatever fits the reconstructed situation of the text could have originated within it. The following rule of method is to be applied: the fewer the parts of the text that under no circumstances fit the supposed situation and that must be excluded, the better! We can never be completely sure that they did not, in fact, form part of the supposed source text.

2. A second shift between text and situation occurs when the text, at a certain point, passes from "prophesied past time" to the real future. Only those parts of the text that refer to events that have already occurred, are happening in present time, or are clearly about to happen must fit the supposed situation. But where in Mark 13 (or in its source text) is the transition from fictional to real future?

We should begin with the parallel introductory phrases ὅταν δὲ ἀκούσητε (v. 7) and ὅταν δὲ ἴδητε (v. 14). First there is a report of events about which the addressees have already "heard." These are the "beginning of the birthpangs." On the other hand, they will "see" the decisive events of the end time, even the terrible thing represented by the "desolating sacrilege," as well as the saving appearance of the Son of man from heaven (13:26). I think there is every evidence that the author of the tradition behind Mark 13 stood between these two parts. What is prophesied in 13:14 is that author's immediate future.[18] The following arguments support this conclusion.

The two-part structure implies a contrast between the events mentioned in vv. 5-8 and those after verse 14: the first events belong to the "beginning of the birthpangs," but are "not yet the end." This is something that can only be determined after the fact. Only in retrospect, after the military catastrophes in verses 7-8, is it possible to say that they did not bring on the end. But such a conclusion is only meaningful if the addressees had, at one point, seen the wars and catastrophes of vv. 7-8 as the end, and if that

---

17. R. Bultmann (*Die Geschichte der synoptischen Tradition,* 129) adds 13:12, 21–22 to the previously mentioned minimum. Hahn ("Die Rede von der Parusie," 240ff.) includes 13:9b, 11-12, 21-22 in the traditional material. I find that especially persuasive for verses 21-22. Brandenburger (*Markus 13,* 21ff.), however, insists that these verses should be omitted.

18. So Wellhausen, *Das Evangelium Marci,* 103; E. Klostermann, *Das Markusevangelium,* 135; E. Schweizer, *Evangelium nach Markus,* 157; W. Grundmann, *Das Evangelium nach Markus,* 266–67; and others.

point of view is now being corrected. An expectation is aroused in readers of the little apocalypse: if these events were "not yet the end," then it must be coming in the things that follow. Thus, they will expect the end after the renewed beginning in 13:14ff.

In fact, the events in 13:14ff. have features that are only imaginable in things that really lie in the future. Thus, it is not yet certain at what time of year the great suffering will begin. Otherwise it would not make sense to tell people to pray that it should not come in the winter (v. 18). It is still unknown whether the false prophets and messiahs will be able to lead the elect astray before the Parousia (vv. 21-22). Although the false teachings in v. 5 "will" lead many astray—which means, in retrospect, that they *have* already seduced many—the apocalypticist in vv. 21-22 reserves judgment: the false prophets and messiahs do signs and wonders, in order to lead the elect astray, "if possible" (v. 22).

In addition, the events following v. 14 have a cosmic dimension. They surpass all the suffering that has occurred since the beginning of creation[19] and threaten all life on earth: "And if the Lord had not cut short those days, no one would be saved" (13:20). We almost expect a new deluge. Probably it is not merely wars that are meant, because they have already been mentioned in 13:7-8. What follows after 13:14ff. must exceed even that horror.

Finally, it should be pointed out that the text encourages a specific behavior. After the occurrence of a particular event, the addressees are to flee to the mountains. It is improbable that a flight that has already occurred is being concealed here in the form of *vaticinia ex eventu*. In that case, we would tend to expect a prophecy formulated in the future tense: "But when the desolating sacrilege stands where it should not stand, those in Judea *will* flee to the mountains."

It is another question where the author of Mark is positioned. Theoretically, those things that are still in the future as far as the tradition is concerned are already past for him. His standpoint could have shifted to the time between 13:23 and 13:24. However, I do not find the arguments advanced for this position to be persuasive.

---

19. Cf. Dan 12:1: "There shall be a time of anguish, such as has never occurred since nations first came into existence." This expression was taken up at the beginning of the first century C.E. in *As. Mos.* 8:1: "And there shall come upon them . . . retribution and wrath, such as has not befallen them from the beginning until that time." In both cases the expression is used to announce future events. D. Lührmann ("Markus 14,55-64," 467–68) concludes from the statement in Mk 13:19, which goes beyond that in Dan 12:1, that the prophesied suffering has not yet happened "and will no longer occur." Mark is thinking of an inner-historical suffering, after which there will still be historical time. But the statement says only that suffering of this magnitude is the last. No other will follow.

a. The statement "But be alert; I have already told you everything" (13:23) sounds as if the author wished to say that the events that have happened in the meantime cannot upset the readers because Jesus has already predicted them. E. Brandenburger supports this interpretation with similar statements in apocalyptic literature that he thinks have a retrospective character.[20] But expressions like "I have already told you this" occur in *T. Levi* 19:1, *As. Mos.* 11:1, and *2 Bar.* 84:1 after events that, from the perspective of the apocalypticist, are part of the real future. *Testament of Levi* 19 follows the promise of Levi's reception of the eschatological priesthood and kingship in *T. Levi* 18; *As. Mos.* 11:1 follows the prophecy of the coming of the reign of God and the end of Satan in chapter 10; *2 Baruch* 84 is preceded by a description of the eschatological overturning of all values at the judgment. A form-critical examination of Mk 13:23 therefore does not permit the conclusion that everything before it has already happened.

b. It is sometimes concluded from Mk 13:20 that the suffering is already past: "And if the Lord had not cut short those days, no one would be saved; but for the sake of the elect, whom he chose, he has cut short those days." Ἐκολόβωσεν is in the aorist, which Schottroff considers a reason for placing the author's standpoint immediately before the Parousia.[21] But the aorist could simply express the idea that God has already decided to shorten the days.[22] Matthew first retains the aorist, but then places the second ἐκολόβωσεν in the future: κολοβωθήσονται (Mt 24:22); in other words, he understands the aorist as having a future meaning. Probably Mark understands it the same way. The "shortening of the days" is a traditional apocalyptic *topos*. Originally, it was grounded on a concrete experience: the solar calendar of 364 days in the astronomical book in *1 Enoch* 72–82 is one and one-fourth days shorter than the real year, but was regarded in many apocalyptic circles as the only real calendar, even if it was not followed on earth. If the seasonal changes on earth coincide with the "false" earthly calendar—even though, according to the "real" calendar in heaven, they should have happened sooner—there is only one explanation: God has shortened the real time in heaven so that the real time on earth could catch up with it. That is just what is presumed in *1 Enoch* 80:2-3: "But in the days of the sinners the years will become shorter, and their seed will be late on their land and on their fields." In this context, the idea that at the end of the ages the "speed of time" would

---

20. Brandenburger, *Markus 13*, 75–87, esp. 78 and n. 166.
21. Schottroff, "Die Gegenwart," 708.
22. Wellhausen writes, "The past tense ἐκολόβωσεν instead of the future is explained by the fact that God has already made the decision" (*Das Evangelium Marci*, 104).

change had become more persuasive. In *1 Enoch* 80:2 this happens in such a way that everything occurs later than expected. The delay is a punishment for human sin. But in most instances the shortening of the days has a positive meaning. The longed-for salvation will come sooner than expected, despite all the delays (*2 Bar.* 20:2; 83:1; *Barn.* 4:3; 2 Esdr 2:13). These "positive" texts all relate to future events, and this also seems to be the case in Mk 13:20.[23]

c. A third argument for a transition from fictional to real future between Mk 13:23 and 13:24 is the repeated warning against false prophets, which, like an *inclusio*, frames the prophecy of the events before the Parousia (Mk 13:5-6; 13:21-22). The false prophets mentioned in 13:5-6 are certain to have been historical. Is the author also referring to known events in 13:21-22? Probably not, since the false teachings in Mk 13:5 have their effect in words. Their claim, "I am he," would also be possible among Christian prophets who preached Jesus' words in the first person. The false prophets and pseudo-messiahs in vv. 21-22, however, work signs and wonders. This is clearly an intensification.

Therefore, the author of Mark probably locates himself, in harmony with the tradition he has received, between verses 13 and 14. The last statement before the appearance of the "desolating sacrilege" points in the same direction: "But the one who endures *to the end* will be saved" (13:13). It seems likely that, after these words, the author really does speak about the end, especially since we encounter statements similar to Mk 13:13 in connection with eschatological events (cf. *2 Bar.* 70:9; 2 Esdr 7:27-28). Matthew also moves at this point from fictional to real prophecy. He adds pointedly: καὶ τότε ἥξει τὸ τέλος (cf. Mt 24:14). Luke can only (re)interpret the text in terms of events that have already occurred by making fundamental changes and completely reshaping the saying about enduring *to the end*. The key word "end" is missing in his text (cf. Lk 21:19).

3. A third shift between text and situation is necessitated by the genre. Mark 13 is an apocalyptic prophecy. The notion of the necessity of historical events, expressed in 13:7 in the words δεῖ γενέσθαι, is apocalyptic. But not everything in the text belongs to the apocalyptic genre. For example, we find a concrete appeal to flee to the mountains (13:14). This does not

---

23. Thus also 1 Cor 7:29: "the appointed time has grown short" can be understood in light of this apocalyptic *topos*. So J. Weiss, *Der erste Korintherbrief*, 197. But *3 Bar.* 9:7, where God, out of wrath, shortens the days of the moon, is not a true parallel. On the origins of the *topos* of the shortening of the days from false calendrical calculations, cf. K. G. Kuhn, "Zum Essenischen Kalender"; idem, "Der gegenwärtige stand der Erforschung der in Palästina neu gefundenen hebräischen Handschriften. 5: Der essenische Kalender," *ThLZ* 85 (1960): 654–58.

say what has to happen, but how people should behave in a particular situation. Not everything is fixed in the divine plan. Consequently, we can call this apocalyptic prophecy. It relies heavily on given motifs and *topoi*. The dependence on the apocalypse in Daniel is especially striking.[24] The phrase "this must take place" (v. 7) comes from Dan 2:28, and the "desolating sacrilege" (v. 14) from Dan 12:11 (cf. 9:27; 11:31). A "great suffering" is prophesied in Dan 12:1. Above all, the appearance of the Son of man with the clouds is a reprise of Daniel's vision of the Son of man (Dan 7:13-14). Thus, the author interprets present and future in the light of existing tradition. For that reason we can never be sure whether tradition is being recalled or whether a real situation is reflected in the text. The fact that reality is visible behind the *topoi* can only be shown if we can see that the choice, combination, and modification of traditional *topoi* in Mark 13 can be explained on the basis of a particular situation.

Ordinarily, the prophecy of "war, earthquake and famine" in 13:8 is regarded as a recitation of apocalyptic *topoi*, but it is often overlooked that these are only a small fragment of the repertoire of apocalyptic horrors.[25] In *2 Bar.* 70:6-10 the series includes death in war, death in anguish, destruction by one's own people, the war of the people against the rulers, earthquake, fire, and famine. *Second Baruch* 27:1-15 offers a numbered list of terrors: unrest, assassinations of the mighty, the death of many, destruction by the sword, famine and drought, earthquakes and cracking of the earth, spectres and demons, fire from heaven, havoc and oppression, wickedness and impurity, and chaos caused by the mixture of all these evils. The *Apocalypse of Abraham* counts ten plagues (30:3-5): distress through want, burning cities, animal plagues, famine, destruction of the mighty by earthquake and sword, hail and snow, attacks by wild beasts, famine and pestilence, sword and flight, and thunder and earthquakes. The series of apocalyptic miseries in *Jub.* 23:13 and Revelation 8–12 and 15–16 are impressive. Most similar to Mk 13:7-8 is 2 Esdr 9:3. There the signs of the end are "earthquakes, tumult of peoples, intrigues of nations, wavering of leaders, confusion of princes." In 2 Esdr 13:31 there are wars: "city against city, place against place, people against people, and kingdom against kingdom." But here again the terrors do not correspond to those in Mk 13:7-8

---

24. See the careful investigation of all the references to and echoes of biblical prophecy in L. Hartmann, *Prophecy Interpreted*.

25. On apocalyptic calamities, see P. Volz, *Die Eschatologie der jüdischen Gemeinde*, 152ff. Nor can the Old Testament triad of sword, hunger, and pestilence (found in various orders in Jer 14:12; 21:7; 38:2; Ezek 5:12; cf. 14:21) explain Mk 13:7-8, because pestilence is missing here and is only added in Lk 21:11. Schweizer (*Evangelium nach Markus*, 151) has a different interpretation.

because Mark lacks any emphasis on "princes" and 2 Esdras does not prophesy famine.

If we run through the contemporary apocalyptic scenery, the catastrophes mentioned in Mk 13:7-8 seem comparatively realistic. Luke's changes are interesting. He excises the section Mk 13:7-8 (= Lk 21:10-11) from the series of events that precede the end: the persecution mentioned there takes place, in Luke's time scheme, "before" those events (cf. Lk 21:12). Probably Luke has in mind the Jewish war, which Jesus already anticipates in verses 10-11. But the miseries described in Mark do not suffice for Luke's description of this historical event. He goes beyond the Markan text to speak of "dreadful portents and great signs from heaven" (Lk 21:11). Does this not imply that the much "simpler" collection of terrors in Mark really does refer to concrete experiences? We note also the reserve of the Markan formulations: he does not write of a universal, catastrophic earthquake, but of σεισμοὶ κατὰ τόπους, regional earthquakes.[26]

If there is a concrete situation behind those *topoi* that are undoubtedly present, it would have to have the following characteristics: wars between kingdoms and nations, regional earthquakes, and famines (perhaps also false teachers). As "the beginning of the birthpangs," these are already in the past. They were interpreted as the beginning of the end, but that has proved to be an error. The audience has not experienced these wars and calamities directly, but has "heard" of them. Therefore we must look for wars that (1) were in the recent past at the time of writing, (2) had not occurred in the same place where the text was written, but (3) had succeeded in creating such powerful existential emotion in the addressees that some of them saw those events as the prelude to the end of the world. It would have to be a situation in which the following events were foreseen in the immediate future: a mysterious "desolating sacrilege" will appear in a place where it should never "stand." This place is close to the addressees because they will be able to "see" the desolating sacrilege there. Its appearance heralds a terrible time for the inhabitants of Judea, and therefore they must flee. The flight could happen in winter—in other words, winter is approaching.

In what follows we will take up once more the old thesis that there are many similarities between the crisis year 40 C.E. and the apocalyptic prophecy in Mark 13 that are more than coincidental. The tradition adapted in Mark 13 could have been recorded in that year. Since it looks back to

---

26. It would be possible to point to the "motio locorum" in 2 Esdr 9:3. But in context this "shaking of places" could also refer to political unrest, although in that case one would expect the word "motus" ("uprising," "commotion," "unrest").

events that have already taken place, we need to consider the period between about 35 and 41. In the following section, we will sketch the history of Palestine in this period, without, for the moment, bringing Mark 13 into the picture.

EVENTS IN PALESTINE IN THE YEARS 35–41 C.E.

The period from 35 to 42 C.E. covers the terms of office of L. Vitellius (35–39? C.E.) and P. Petronius (39–42 C.E.) as legates of Syria. Both intervened frequently in the affairs of Palestine.

When Vitellius was sent to Syria in the year 35,[27] he was assigned the task of curbing the activities of the Parthian king Artabanos, who had just taken possession of Armenia. At first he was successful. He installed two royal pretenders favored by Rome, making Mithridates king of Armenia and Tiridates king of Parthia. Artabanos took flight, but later succeeded in regaining his kingdom. After the death of Tiberius, and thanks to the diplomatic skills of Vitellius, a peace was concluded at a bridge over the Euphrates, where Herod Antipas played host to the treaty partners (*Ant.* 18.101ff.).[28] Thus, war and conflict with the Parthians overshadowed the years 35–37.

At the same time, a war broke out in Palestine between Herod Antipas and Aretas IV, king of the Nabateans.[29] There had been enmity between the two princes since the Herodian had divorced his first wife, a Nabatean princess. In 35–36 there came a favorable moment for the Nabateans to proceed against Antipas because the Romans were occupied with the Parthians. Antipas's brother, the tetrarch Philip, had died in 34 C.E, and the Nabateans had claims on his territory. Now they hoped to be able to make them good through military force. In 36, Herod Antipas suffered a smashing defeat, and Vitellius, at Tiberius's orders, had to move against the Nabateans.

Simultaneously, there were signs of increasing religious unrest in Palestine. In the year 36 C.E. (i.e., during the Nabatean conflict) a prophet

---

27. See T. Mayer Maly, "Vitellius." Tacitus reports extensively on the Parthian war in *Ann.* 6.35–37, 41–44. The Romans in this instance allowed the war to be conducted on their behalf, but did not intervene militarily.

28. Josephus (*Ant.* 18.101ff.) dates this agreement within the reign of Tiberius, but according to Suetonius (*Cal.* 14) it took place in that of Gaius Caligula (cf. also Suetonius *Vitell.* 2; Dio Cassius 59.27). On the problem of dating, cf. E. Schürer (*History of the Jewish People* 1:351), who considers the later date more likely.

29. Cf. Josephus *Ant.* 18.111–12 and the discussion of the Herodian–Nabatean conflict in chap. 2. In the course of the war, the Nabateans may have reached Damascus and endangered Paul while he was there. Cf. G. W. Bowersock, *Roman Arabia*, 67–69.

arose in Samaria.[30] He led a horde of people up Mount Gerizim, promising to uncover there the lost vessels of the temple. Pilate intervened, and a bloodbath resulted. The captured leaders were executed. Samaritan complaints about Pilate's actions led to his being deposed by Vitellius. Pilate had to return to Rome, where he arrived after the death of Tiberius (*Ant.* 18.85–89).

Also at this time, there was evidence of heightened religious sensitivity in Judea. When Vitellius advanced with his army against the Nabateans in 37 C.E., Jewish leaders implored him not to desecrate the Holy Land with the standards of his legions. In response to this request, Vitellius went to Jerusalem without his army, in company with Herod Antipas, and celebrated Passover there on 20 April 37.[31] On his fourth day in the city he received the news of Tiberius's death on 17 March 37 (cf. *Ant.* 18.120ff.). It is possible that he had already been in Jerusalem; in any case, it was during a stay in the city that he returned the high priestly vestments, which previously the Romans had only released on feast days, to the Jews (*Ant.* 18.90–95; cf. 15.405). We can sense at this period the same intent among Jews and Samaritans: to take control of their own cultic life by getting possession of or rediscovering the necessary vessels and vestments.

EXCURSUS

The chronology and number of Vitellius's visits to Jerusalem are disputed.[32] Josephus mentions three incidents: according to *Ant.* 15.405, Vitellius wrote to Tiberius at the people's request, asking that he might again place the high priest's vestments under Jewish control; *Ant.* 18.90–95 reports that, at a Passover feast, he agreed to the return of the garments, remitted some taxes, and removed the high priest Caiaphas, appointing Jonathan in his place; and according to *Ant.* 18.120–26 he went to Jerusalem for a feast (not further described) during preparations for the Nabatean campaign, agreed not to let his legions cross the Holy Land, and removed the high priest Jonathan.

1. The three reports in the *Antiquities* cannot be harmonized. *Antiquities* 15.405 says that the high priest's vestments were handed over because of an order from Tiberius, but according to *Ant.* 18.90ff. it was the result of Vitellius's own decision. In *Ant.* 20.11–14, Josephus quotes a later order from the emperor Claudius to the procurator Cuspius Fadus, in which, referring to a decision

---

30. On this Samaritan prophet, see J.-P. Lémonon, *Pilate*, 231–39; M. F. Collins, "Hidden Vessels in Samaritan Traditions."

31. On this dating, see U. Holzmeister, "Wann war Pilatus Prokurator von Judaea?" 229.

32. Lémonon (*Pilate*, 242–45) and H. Schwier (*Tempel und Tempelzerstörung*, 109–14) argue for three visits to Jerusalem. E. M. Smallwood ("Date of the Dismissal of Pontius Pilatus," 17–19) supposes two visits. Cf. idem, *Jews under Roman Rule*, 171–73. However, W. Otto ("Herodes," cols. 185–87) holds for a single visit, as does Mayer Maly ("Vitellius," col. 1735).

by Vitellius, he directs that the high priest's vestments be handed over (*Ant.* 20.12). Had there already been a directive from Tiberius, Claudius would certainly have referred to it, apart from the fact that the procurator Fadus would scarcely have dared to take possession of the high-priestly vestments in defiance of an imperial order. It is thus possible that *Ant.* 15.405 attributes to Tiberius an imperial decree that was actually written by Claudius (*Ant.* 20.11–14). In that case it would not be absolutely necessary, on the basis of *Ant.* 15.405, to suppose that Vitellius visited Jerusalem twice, once to receive and transmit the people's request for the return of the vestments, and a second time to hand them over in accordance with the emperor's reply.

2. The rapid installation and deposition of the high priest Jonathan is confirmed by *Ant.* 19.314, where Jonathan states that he has worn the high priest's vestments only once. Must his appointment and dismissal be assigned to two separate visits? According to *Ant.* 18.95, Jonathan was installed after Vitellius had handed over the vestments. The delivery of the vestments occurred, as Josephus emphasizes, "seven days before each festival" (*Ant.* 18.94). Afterward (ταῦτα πράξας), Caiaphas was replaced by Jonathan, so that the latter was able to function as high priest at the same feast. According to *Ant.* 18.123, Vitellius deposed this same Jonathan during a three-day visit to Jerusalem, after Vitellius himself had offered sacrifice at a festival, probably after the high point of the feast. Is it absolutely unthinkable that Jonathan was installed before a feast and removed immediately after it? We need not suppose any dramatic political circumstances. According to *Ant.* 19.314, Jonathan says, "God has adjudged me in no way worthy of the high priesthood." This could cover a mistake in the ritual, a bad omen, or something else that made a rapid transfer of the high-priestly office desirable.

3. Another reason to suppose that the two reports of Vitellius's visits to Jerusalem in *Ant.* 18.90–95 and 18.120–25 could refer to the same events is that, in the first passage (concerning a visit in 37 C.E.), Josephus is referring back to things that had happened earlier—that is, the conflict with the Parthians in 35–36 C.E.—although he writes as though they had followed the first visit. The trip to Jerusalem after the treaty with the Parthians could fall within the same time period as the visit after Pilate's removal. In terms of absolute chronology, also, the two trips must have been close together. The first took place after the deposition of Pilate, who hurried to Rome, but did not arrive until after the death of Tiberius on 17 March 37 (*Ant.* 18.89). But during the (supposed) second visit, the news of Tiberius's death reaches Vitellius in the course of a feast at Jerusalem, and from there is brought to the other provinces (*Leg. Gai.* 231, 288). The change of rulers would have been reported as quickly as possible to the commander of one of the largest armies, the legate of Syria. If we consider that express messengers covered up to 150 kilometers a day, the news of Tiberius's death would more likely have reached Jerusalem during the Passover feast, five weeks after March 17, than during the feast of Pentecost, fifteen weeks later. In that case, the "feast" at the second visit would be identical with that of the first visit. It is possible that there had been another visit earlier, but it

seems fairly certain that Vitellius's last visit to Jerusalem was at Passover in the year 37. Josephus relates details of it in *Ant.* 18.90–95 and 18.120–125.

The change of rulers in Rome also shifted political weights in Palestine. Agrippa I was made king of the former tetrarchy of Philip and of Abilene. His ascendancy led to tensions with Herod Antipas, the tetrarch of Galilee. When the latter also sought to be made king at Rome in the year 39, he was instead deposed by Gaius Caligula after being denounced by Agrippa I. In the same year, Vitellius was recalled. He returned in mortal fear to Rome (Dio Cassius 59.27.4) and rescued himself only by a servile submission to Gaius, being the first to prostrate himself before him.[33]

Vitellius's successor was Petronius, whose name is associated in particular with the great Caligula crisis of 39-40. After Jews in Jamnia had pulled down a large altar to the emperor, he was ordered to use military force to transform the temple at Jerusalem into a sanctuary of Zeus Epiphanes Gaius. His slow execution of the order gained him time for negotiations with the Jewish aristocracy, and he even allowed himself to be persuaded to make a formal request for the withdrawal of the order. Meanwhile, through the intervention of Agrippa I at Rome, Gaius had agreed to change his decree. He commanded that the execution of the order be stopped, but Petronius, because of his disobedience, was to take his own life. The emperor's murder on 24 January 41 ended the conflict.

We are relatively well informed about the Caligula crisis, both by Josephus (*Bell.* 2.184–203; *Ant.* 18.256–309) and by Philo (*Leg. Gai.* 197–337).[34] The sources are not unbiased,[35] and they contradict themselves. Yet

---

33. Tacitus (*Ann.* 6.32) also says that Vitellius "through dread of G. Caesar" had transformed himself from a capable provincial governor to a servile flatterer. We do not know why Vitellius feared for his life. Was he afraid of falling out of favor along with Herod Antipas, with whom he was, despite certain tensions, closely associated? Antipas was deposed in the same year in which Vitellius was (probably) recalled from Syria.

34. P. Bilde presents a thorough analysis of the sources and their biases in *Josefus som historieskriver*, which is concerned primarily with the Caligula crisis in the year 40 C.E. Josephus's report is often preferred to that of Philo, although Philo was a contemporary and eyewitness, while Josephus clearly employs novelistic motifs in the *Antiquities* (cf. the miraculous rain in *Ant.* 18.285ff. and the banquet at which a request is granted in *Ant.* 18.289ff.). Bilde had previously described some of his theses in "The Roman Emperor Gaius (Caligula)'s Attempt to Erect His Statue." For a critical evaluation of Bilde's work, see N. Hyldahl, "Josefus som historieskriver."

35. Philo's *Legatio ad Gaium* is not so much a work of history as a tract "de mortibus persecutorum," intended to show that human hubris brings divine punishment. Philo was a contemporary writing shortly after the events, but was personally involved in the conflict: we have to consider that, as leader of the Jewish delegation to Rome, he did not want to place himself in an unfavorable light. Josephus first wrote of these events in the 70s. For him, Petronius is the model of an exemplary Roman official. Philo, as an eyewitness, may well be the better source for the events at Rome; for the events in Palestine, Josephus had access to good information. Both sources agree in their tendency to depict the peaceful intentions of the Jews. They both write as apologists for an oppressed minority.

together they offer a vivid picture of the events.[36] We may collate the most important differences in a synopsis (Table 3) and then discuss them individually.[37]

Causes and Occasion of the Conflict

All the sources agree that the emperor's self-deification was the fundamental cause of the conflict. Historically speaking, that is not quite accurate. From Philo we learn of a concrete occasion, namely, that Jews in Jamnia had torn down a newly erected imperial altar. The procurator at that place, Herennius Capito,[38] sent an exaggerated report of this to Rome. Under the influence of anti-Jewish advisors, the emperor responded with an order to the legate of Syria forcibly to erect an imperial statue in the Jerusalem Temple (*Leg. Gai.* 200–207). Philo minimizes the Jewish part in the creation of the conflict. For him, the erection of an altar in Jamnia constitutes a pagan provocation offered to the Jews, and its destruction is their reaction to an impious encroachment. Josephus is silent about the conflict at Jamnia. Instead, he connects Gaius's proceeding with the failure of the delegation of Alexandrian Jews under Philo (*Ant.* 18.261–62). Understandably enough, we do not find this version in Philo's account. If he had presented his appearance in Rome as the cause of the emperor's action against the Jerusalem Temple, it would not have said a great deal for his diplomatic gifts. But he, too, is aware that events in Rome played a role, as is evident by his making the anti-Jewish advisors from Ascalon and

---

36. Among modern historical depictions we may mention, in addition to the detailed monograph by Bilde, *Josefus som historieskriver,* J.P.V.D. Balsdon, *The Emperor Gaius,* 135–40; Smallwood, *Jews under Roman Rule,* 174–80; Schürer, *History of the Jewish People* 1:394–98.

37. The Caligula crisis also left traces in rabbinic sources. In *b. Sota* 33a we hear of a Bath Qol: "Next, Simon the Just heard a resounding voice crying from the holy of holies: the adoration of idols, which the enemy wished to bring into the Temple, has been removed. At that time Gaius Caligula was destroyed and his orders were cancelled. They wrote down the hour, and it was exactly the same. This was spoken in Aramaic." On this, see P. Winter, "Simeon der Gerechte und Gaius Caligula." This probably represents a confusion of the well-known high priest Simon the Just (cf. Sir 50:1ff.) with the Simon Cantheras mentioned in *Ant.* 19.297, 313, who was appointed high priest by Agrippa I circa 41, perhaps as early as 40. Among Roman historians, Tacitus mentions the Caligula conflict in Palestine twice (*Hist.* 5.9.2; *Ann.* 12.54.1).

38. Jamnia, originally under Herodian control, had passed to the Roman imperial family through inheritance and was governed by an imperial procurator. C. Herennius Capito is attested in inscriptions (cf. E. M. Smallwood, ed., *Philonis Alexandrini,* 261). If we consider that there were imperial temples in Caesarea and Sebaste and that these were tolerated by the Jews, we can appreciate that the destruction of an altar of Caesar, erected on the emperor's own territory, would encounter no sympathy at all on the part of the Romans. The Jews, on the other hand, would have regarded Jamnia as traditional Jewish land that must remain free of pagan symbols and cults. Just before this they had managed to persuade a Roman legate, Vitellius, not to enter Jewish territory with his legions because of the pagan symbols they bore with them (cf. *Ant.* 18.121–22).

TABLE 3
Sources for the Caligula Crisis

Philo Legatio ad Gaium 197–337	Josephus Bellum Judaicum 2.184–203	Josephus Antiquities 18.256–309
1. Causes and Occasion of the Conflict		
A. The emperor's self-apotheosis. B. Destruction of an imperial altar. C. Anti-Jewish imperial advisors.	A. The emperor's self-apotheosis.	A. The emperor's self-apotheosis. B. Anger over the Jewish embassy from Alexandria headed by Philo.
2. The Order to Petronius for the Desecration of the Temple		
Petronius, already governor of Syria, with half the army of the Euphrates (two legions), is to bring one statue to Jerusalem. Petronius has doubts from the beginning.	The governor of Syria is to move on Jerusalem with three legions and statues. If there is resistance, the opponents should be killed and the people enslaved. There are rumors of war.	Petronius is sent to Syria as successor to Vitellius, in order, with the help of two legions, to bring one statue to Jerusalem.
3. The First Negotiations in Phoenicia		
Petronius has a statue made in Phoenicia, in order to gain time.		Petronius moves to Ptolemais for the winter, planning to begin the war in the spring. He informs Gaius about the status of his preparations. Gaius gives a friendly response.
Petronius first talks with Jewish spiritual and political leaders in Phoenicia (or Antioch?). The Jewish people, including women and	The Jewish People, including women and	The Jewish people demonstrate, emphasiz-

TABLE 3 (continued)
Sources for the Caligula Crisis

Philo *Legatio ad Gaium* *197–337*	*Josephus* *Bellum Judaicum* *2.184–203*	*Josephus* *Antiquities* *18.256–309*
children, demonstrate in Phoenicia. Consultations with Petronius's staff lead to a letter to Gaius requesting delay. The harvest (in the spring!) serves as an excuse to wait longer. Gaius sends a neutral response.	children, demonstrate on the plain of Ptolemais (192). Their protest is summarily depicted.	ing their loyalty to the emperor and their own willingness to suffer in defense of their religion.

4. The Second Negotiations in Tiberias

	Petronius calls together the people and their leaders at Tiberias. A. He negotiates with the people, who emphasize their loyalty and their readiness to suffer. B. Negotiations are continued separately with the leaders and the people.	Petronius, with his friends and attendants, hastens to Tiberias. A. Demonstrations take place there, lasting forty days, during which the sowing is neglected (autumn!). B. Negotiations with the Herodian royal house and the aristocracy lead to conciliatory moves by Petronius. The threats of an agricultural strike, resulting failure of tax revenues, and the increase of banditry are effective. After Petronius's intervention a miraculous rainfall occurs, ending a long drought.
	Neglect of the sowing for fifty days during the negotiations (in the autumn: October/ November) gives Petronius cause for conciliation.	

(continued)

TABLE 3 (continued)
Sources for the Caligula Crisis

Philo *Legatio ad Gaium* *197–337*	*Josephus* *Bellum Judaicum* *2.184–203*	*Josephus* *Antiquities* *18.256–309*
	Petronius returns with his army to Antioch and from there writes to the emperor, asking the withdrawal of the order.	Petronius writes to Gaius, asking that the order be withdrawn.

5. Agrippa's Intervention in Rome

Agrippa, suspecting nothing, comes to Gaius in Rome, learns from him of the threatened desecration, and faints. From his sickbed, he writes a long petition to Gaius.		At a banquet, Agrippa succeeds in winning a concession from Gaius, after the emperor has offered to grant him a request.

6. The End of the Conflict

Gaius withdraws his order conditionally: Petronius is to take no further steps. The imperial cult is to be permitted outside Jerusalem. Gaius plans to make a journey to Jerusalem and bring the statue there in person. (Philo promises to continue his report in the form of a palinode, which will probably describe the punishment of the transgressor.)	Gaius writes to Petronius, condemning him to suicide, but the letter reaches Petronius twenty-seven days after the news of the death of Gaius.	Gaius condemns Petronius to suicide, but the letter containing this order is preceded by news of the death of Gaius.

Egypt partly responsible for Gaius's attitude. Both sources together thus point toward the fundamental historical causes: tensions between Jews and non-Jews in Egypt (emphasized by Josephus) and in Palestine (emphasized by Philo). Both of these discordant situations manifested themselves at the same time: the destruction of the imperial altar in Jamnia happened not long after conflicts in Alexandria brought about by the erection of imperial images in the synagogues there (*Flacc.* 41ff.).[39] Suddenly, in several places, the Jews saw the status quo being called into question. They could have had the impression that their religion was faced with a fundamental challenge, first from the pagan world at large, and then from the emperor's policies. On the other side, the parallel appearance of Jewish protests in Alexandria and Palestine could have been interpreted by the Romans as a "concentrated action" against the emperor.[40] They certainly had neither understanding nor sympathy for the destruction of an imperial altar on the emperor's own property in Jamnia. Must it not have seemed to them as if some Jews wanted to eliminate the basis for traditional Roman tolerance of the Jewish religion?[41] Finally, if we consider that the Romans acted on the basis of an exaggerated report from the procurator, Herennius Capito, the principled character of their reaction—the assault on the Jewish sanctuary—is more readily understood. At any rate, it was a bad political decision. Had it not been for Gaius Caligula's propensity to self-deification, the Roman reaction might have exhibited more wisdom and calm. But Gaius's self-apotheosis was, contrary to the Jewish sources, not the cause of the conflict; it was merely a factor in the sharpening of the clash. It made an already existing conflict insoluble and could, as a result, have come to be regarded in the minds of those involved as the principal issue.

---

39. The unrest in Alexandria can be dated to the year 38 C.E. (Schürer, *History of the Jewish People* 1:391 n. 161), the conflict at Jamnia to the year 39 or the winter of 39–40. Both were rooted in local tensions between Jews and non-Jews, with which the emperor had nothing to do. However, his inclination to self-deification could be used by the Jews' opponents as a means to secure the withdrawal of the traditional *protectio romana* from the Jews and to compromise them in the eyes of their protectors, since they did not perform the usual cultic rites of fidelity.

40. Cf. Smallwood, *Philonis Alexandrini*, 264. Gaius received the news of the destruction of the altar in Jamnia soon after he learned of the resistance of the Alexandrian Jews to the erection of imperial images in their synagogues. "Either episode alone might have been regarded as merely a disturbance of the peace. But the two occurring within perhaps eighteen months of each other looked like organized disloyalty, and this probably accounted for the severity of the punishment which Gaius decided to impose on Palestine."

41. Bilde (*Josefus som historieskriver,* 69–70) shows that Gaius's reaction was by no means that of an irresponsible despot. Rather, it was caused by a "rational Roman interpretation of the Jews' action [i.e., the destruction of the altar in Jamnia] as a breach of political loyalty to Rome and of the basis for the traditional Roman policy of tolerance toward the Jewish people" (p. 70).

Gaius Caligula's Order

According to Philo and Josephus *Bell.* 2.184ff., the order was sent to the legate Petronius, who had been governing in Syria since 39 C.E. But according to *Ant.* 18.261, Petronius was sent from Rome to Syria bearing the order to desecrate the temple.[42] In that case, his conversion from command-bearer to command-resister seems even more remarkable. Josephus stylized his report in the *Antiquities* in that direction.[43] In fact, he presumes there as well that Petronius was already in Syria; in rescinding the decree Gaius writes to him that he should dismiss the army and gives his attention to the matters for which he had "originally" sent him (*Ant.* 18.301). Thus, Petronius "originally" had another assignment in Syria, before he received the orders to violate the temple. There is another discrepancy regarding the number of legions. According to *Bell.* 2.186, Petronius entered Palestine with three legions. In *Ant.* 18.262 that is corrected: here he moves south with only two legions. This agrees with Philo, who speaks of half of the army of the Euphrates, which consisted of four legions (*Leg. Gai.* 207). This is an astonishing force. When Cestius Gallus moved on Judea in 66 C.E. to contain the incipient Jewish uprising, he took only one legion with him. The size of the army in 39–40 shows that a major war was expected. Josephus mentions "rumors of war" (*Bell.* 2.187). According to Tacitus, there really was an armed uprising (*Hist.* 5.9.2). The Jewish authors, in contrast, emphasize the "pacifist character" of the Jewish resistance. Is Tacitus writing under the influence of the Jewish war? Or is he reproducing the estimate of the situation on which the Romans were proceeding? After all, Philo emphasizes that Herennius Capito had "immeasurably exaggerated the situation" in his report to Gaius (*Leg. Gai.* 202). Did the exaggeration consist in Capito's having seen the destruction of the imperial altar as a signal for war, or even an initial military action? That would certainly be understandable.[44]

The First Negotiations in Phoenicia

The critical difference between Philo and Josephus is that Philo knows only of negotiations in Phoenicia and says nothing about subsequent dis-

---

42. Bilde (ibid., 71–72) thinks that Petronius really did leave Rome for Syria bearing the order to violate the temple, and that he was originally in agreement with this assignment. On this point, his fundamental preference for Josephus's report over that of Philo is not very persuasive. Bilde overlooks *Ant.* 18.301 (see above).

43. In *Ant.* 18.277, Petronius distances himself much more clearly from Gaius's order than he does in *Bell.* 2.201, speaking of the "mad orders of Gaius."

44. In the Jewish war also, the cessation of sacrifices for the emperor was the signal for revolt (*Bell.* 2.415). Furthermore, at the time of the revolt of the Maccabees, the destruction

cussions in Tiberias. While the statue is being prepared in Sidon (*Leg. Gai.* 222), Petronius calls together the spiritual and secular Jewish leaders and tells them of Gaius's order.[45] Only after this are there mass demonstrations on the plain of Phoenicia against the Romans' plan (*Leg. Gai.* 225–26). The result of the negotiation is a temporizing letter from Petronius to Gaius, in which the Syrian legate makes clear that the people could stage a protest by ravaging their fields and burning the grain (*Leg. Gai.* 249). This would mean that the scene takes place shortly before harvest (ca. May of 40 C.E.). The fact that Petronius sees danger to the fruit harvest does not mean that Philo is thinking of autumn because firing or cutting down the trees could also destroy the fruit harvest in the spring.[46] The emperor is enraged by this letter from Petronius, but writes a reply compelling him to carry out the order (*Leg. Gai.* 259–60). Philo adds, however, that Gaius hid his rage "waiting for an opportunity." Does he know of a second letter from Gaius, in which he condemned Petronius to suicide? It is understandable that Philo says nothing about it, since his report breaks off in the summer of 40 C.E. We do not have the promised continuation. While Philo thus places his whole emphasis on the first negotiations in Phoenicia, in Josephus the accent shifts to the second set of discussions in Tiberias. He knows nothing of a first, temporizing letter following the Jewish protests, but he seems to have some knowledge of a letter from Phoenicia in the winter of 39–40 or the spring of 40, in which Petronius reports on the progress of his preparations and to which Gaius sends a cordial reply (*Ant.* 18.262). Both authors thus know of two letters from Petronius to Gaius, and two answering letters!

---

of a pagan altar in Modein signaled the beginning of the uprising (1 Macc 2:25). In fact, Philo also anticipates war: in *Leg. Gai.* 209–17 he depicts Petronius as reflecting on the threat of armed conflict. In his supposition that the war was already in progress, Tacitus could be indirectly dependent on Herennius Capito's report, which, according to *Leg. Gai.* 202, is supposed to have been "highly exaggerated."

45. Josephus knows nothing of these original discussions with the Jewish aristocracy. In his account, the crucial negotiations with them take place only after there have been popular demonstrations. They lead to an initial, partial victory (*Ant.* 18.273ff.). In this way, Josephus emphasizes the importance of the aristocracy—that is, of his own class—in all Jewish questions. For Philo, on the other hand, the decisions are made at Rome, where he himself was in 39–40 C.E. It is disputed whether Philo locates the first negotiations in Antioch or in Phoenicia (cf. Smallwood, *Philonis Alexandrini,* 273). Philo first says that Petronius assembled the artists of Phoenicia to give them material for the statue. Here he is probably in Phoenicia. When he subsequently summons the Jewish aristocracy, he must be in the same place (*Leg. Gai.* 222). In *Leg. Gai.* 225 he is also in Phoenicia, and nothing has been said about a change of place.

46. Bilde (*Josefus som historieskriver,* 114), however, sees an insuperable contradiction in *Leg. Gai.* 249. According to *Spec. Leg.* 4.208–9, the grain and fruit harvests do not coincide. Bilde locates the negotiations at the time of the fruit harvest.

The Second Negotiations in Tiberias

Only Josephus reports a second set of negotiations in Tiberias. While he, in contrast to Philo, has said nothing about the Jewish aristocracy in connection with the protests in Phoenicia, they now appear in an active role. Members of the Herodian royal house—that is, the government in Tiberias—take part in the discussions. The popular protests continue. It is the time for sowing, and the people neglect their agricultural labors for forty or fifty days.[47] We can conclude from this that we are now late in the year 40, at the time of the winter sowing, which took place shortly before the rainy months of October and November. If we combine the reports of Philo and Josephus, the most probable conclusion is that there were negotiations in two different places and at two different times: first in Phoenicia in May, then in Tiberias in October. The shadow of threatened disaster had hung over the land for at least half a year, and the whole sequence of events would have extended over more than a year. The Jamnia conflict had been in 39–40. In that winter, Petronius moved his residence to Phoenicia, where he gained time while he waited for the preparation of the statue. The demonstrations in Phoenicia can be dated to May of 40, the negotiations at Tiberias to October of that year. However, some think that such a long period of idleness for the Roman legions is improbable and therefore assign all the negotiations either to the spring or to the fall of 40.[48] In any case, according to Josephus it is primarily the negotiations in Tiberias that lead to Petronius's spectacular step of asking that the order be rescinded. Gaius answers his letter with an order to commit suicide.

---

47. Hyldahl ("Josefus som historieskriver," 63–64) points out that 40–41 was a Sabbath year, in which, theoretically, no agricultural work was done. But it is not clear to what extent the Sabbath year was really observed. It is certain that, if it was a Sabbath year, those who wanted to put pressure on the Romans by refusing to work the land would have had a good argument, namely, that it was God's own will that there be no sowing this year.

48. The "long chronology" adopted here corresponds to that in Schürer, *History of the Jewish People* 1:397 n. 180. We obtain a short chronology if we identify the two negotiations (and the two letters from Petronius to Gaius). In that case, we could place both either in the spring (with Philo) or in the fall (with Josephus). In the first case, the events could have begun with the outburst at Jamnia in the winter of 39–40. So E. M. Smallwood, "The Chronology of Gaius' Attempt to Desecrate the Temple," *Latomus* 16 (1957): 3–17; idem, *Jews under Roman Rule,* 174–80, esp. nn. 114–15. If the negotiations were in the fall, the events have to be telescoped still more: they would all have taken place in the years 40–41. So J.P.V.D. Balsdon, "Notes Concerning the Principate of Gaius," esp. 19–24; Bilde, *Josefus som historieskriver,* 106–17. One principal argument for a short chronology is *Ant.* 18.269, according to which Petronius "hastened" (ἠπείγετο) from the first negotiations in Phoenicia to Tiberias. But according to the long chronology, some months would have had to intervene between the two negotiations. Could Petronius have been idle so long? I think his "haste" has been overemphasized. First, according to *Ant.* 18.262 the legate Petronius, sent from Rome, "hastened" (ἠπείγετο) to Syria to carry out Gaius's orders, but the report continues by saying that he first entered winter quarters with his legions and put off the war until spring. His "haste" here refers to a period of several months. Philo is accurate in crediting

King Agrippa's Intervention at Rome

In the two extended reports, crucial significance is assigned to the intervention of Agrippa I in Rome. In detail, the descriptions vary sharply from one another. According to Philo, Agrippa comes to Rome knowing nothing of the crisis, after Gaius has already replied to Petronius's first, temporizing letter. He receives the terrible news from Gaius himself, falls down senseless, and has to be carried home (*Leg. Gai.* 261ff.). It is unbelievable that Agrippa would have received his first information about the threatened desecration of the temple from Gaius. The Jewish envoys from Alexandria already knew about it. Every Jew in Rome would have known that a catastrophe for the temple was brewing. Would Agrippa have spoken with Gaius before he had had any contact with the Jews in Rome? Philo needs this dramatic scene to illustrate the monstrosity of the threatened desecration of the temple, something that for Jews was simply unbearable. Agrippa suffers a physical collapse. From his sickbed he directs a long petition to Gaius, beseeching him to retract his order to Petronius. This letter would contain the arguments that were assembled at the time to dissuade Gaius. Whether it was really written or not is of secondary importance.

According to Philo, Agrippa was the crucial spokesperson for Jewish concerns. It is all the more remarkable that Josephus does not mention him at all in his first account. In *Bell.* 2.184ff. we hear nothing of any activity on the part of the Herodian royal house, either in Palestine or in Rome. Petronius is here the dominant figure. In the *Antiquities* it is quite different. There, Agrippa gives a glittering banquet, is granted a wish, and asks that the temple be preserved as a Jewish sanctuary (*Ant.* 18.289ff.). At about the same time the Herodian royal family is busy in Tiberias and influences Petronius to adopt its arguments (*Ant.* 18.273ff.). When his letter with its diplomatically worded "refusal to obey" arrives in Rome (*Ant.* 18.302ff.), Agrippa has already persuaded Gaius to change his mind; in other words, in this account, the major credit for saving the temple falls on Agrippa and the Herodians. This shift in Agrippa's favor (which, according to Philo, has a historical kernel of truth) could have resulted from Josephus's contacts with the Herodian family in Rome. They would certainly have emphasized their own services to the temple, and Josephus would have valued their favor.

Petronius with a type of delaying tactic. Second, in the parallel report in *Bell.* 2.192–93, nothing is said about "haste." Here Petronius comes from Ptolemais to Galilee (προελθών). But in the *Antiquities* we notice the implicit conviction that everything must have taken place in the course of a single year. Starting with this idea, Josephus had to telescope the events severely and make the legate "hasten."

The End of the Conflict

The conflict came to a close with the murder of Gaius on 24 January 41. According to Josephus, the messenger with this news overtook the other messenger who was carrying Petronius's death sentence. This could be a novelistic motif. It is true that Petronius's life was in danger. But before his death Gaius had already rescinded his order, although he did so only half-heartedly, so that anxiety about a repetition of the events remained acute. This we learn from Tacitus (*Ann.* 12.54.1). Unfortunately, there is a gap in the text at the crucial point, but the missing part can be supplied from *Hist.* 5.9.2.[49] The added portion is in brackets:

> The like moderation, however, was not shown by his brother, surnamed Felix; who for a while past had held the governorship of Judaea, and considered that with such influences behind him all malefactions would be venial. The Jews, it is true, had given signs of disaffection in the rioting prompted [by the demand of Gaius Caesar for an effigy of himself in the Temple; and though] the news of his murder had made compliance needless, the fear remained that some emperor might issue an identical mandate. (*Ann.* 12.54.1)

It is clear from the text that at the time of the procurator Felix (ca. 52–60 C.E.) there was still a lively fear among the Jews that the temple could be violated. The general expression "quis principum"—any one of the emperors might revive Gaius's plan—refers to a number of emperors, at least Claudius and Nero and probably others of Gaius's successors. The reports of Josephus and Philo confirm, in different ways, that these fears were justified. According to Josephus, Gaius only retracted his order out of affection for Agrippa and not because of critical consideration; in fact, he had commanded that if the statue was already in the temple it should remain there (*Ant.* 18.301). According to Philo, the retraction of the order was connected with an express command that the imperial cult was to be tolerated outside Jerusalem—something Philo rightly saw as the seed of revolts and civil wars (*Leg. Gai.* 333–35). Besides this, Gaius had a new, colossal statue made at Rome, which he himself intended to bring to the temple during a visit to the Orient (*Leg. Gai.* 337–38). So the conflict had a twofold end: first through an ambiguous retraction of the order by Gaius and then through his murder.

The figure of Petronius is worthy of note. As commander of the Syrian army he was one of the most powerful officials of the Roman Empire. His *cursus honorum* included the consulate (in 19 C.E.) and six years as proconsul in the province of Asia (ca. 29–35 C.E.). Would a member of the

---

49. For this conjecture, see E. Koestermann, *Cornelius Tacitus*, 200–201.

imperial power elite really have committed civil disobedience out of inner conviction? Gaius cannot imagine such a thing. He thinks Petronius must have been bribed by the Jews (*Ant.* 18.304). According to Philo (*Leg. Gai.* 232) the demonstrating Jews in fact offer all their property to avert the desecration of the temple. That could be understood as attempted bribery.[50] But for the Jewish authors he is practically a God-fearer: "Indeed it appears that he himself had some rudiments of Jewish philosophy and religion." The idea of civil disobedience was suggested to him by God (*Leg. Gai.* 245). Philo, like Josephus, depicts him in such an idealistic fashion that we must question whether, for them, the legend had obscured the reality.[51] But the legend must have been rooted in reality: under the consulate of Petronius, a humane law for the benefit of slaves was enacted, bearing his name.[52] In addition, there are analogous cases in which clever provincial governors evaded imperial orders. For example, Gaius had commanded that the famous Zeus of Phidias be transported from Olympia to Rome, but the proconsul for Asia, Memmius Regulus, argued successfully that the statue would be destroyed in transit. Not only that, but divine omens spoke against the transfer. He, too, risked death, according to Josephus, but was rescued by Gaius's murder (*Ant.* 19.8–10).

THE CALIGULA CRISIS AND THE INTERPRETATION OF THE SYNOPTIC APOCALYPSE

An interpretation of the synoptic apocalypse in the context of the Caligula crisis cannot expect to find data from those events, as we have sketched their course, reflected in the text. It is just as important, however, to achieve some understanding of the way those events were interpreted, because events do not affect human actions directly, but only by being experienced and interpreted. The categories in which the interpretation and experiencing take place are socially conditioned. They are part of the common tradition. Thus, the same events are perceived by different groups from different perspectives. In Mark 13, we are looking into the intellectual and spiritual world of a small group within Judaism, in which a limited perspective is to be expected from the start. The addressees are

---

50. Balsdon (*The Emperor Gaius*, 138) considers it possible that Petronius was bribed.

51. Thus, esp., Bilde, *Josefus som historieskriver,* 73–80. For him, Philo's Petronius is "the product of bias."

52. Cf. R. Hanslick, "Petronius." The law bearing his name, the *lex Iunia Petroniana* (*Dig.* 40.1.24), provides that if the votes were even in a hearing on the question whether a person were slave or free, the decision must be for freedom. The *lex de servis*, too (*Dig.* 48.8.11.2), by which slaves could not be assigned to combat with beasts without a judicial order, can probably be traced to him.

simple people who cultivate their own fields (Mk 13:15-16). In this text they do not perceive events in their political context, but as signs of the longed-for end of the world. It would be unrealistic to expect of them the kind of comprehensive awareness of political background and connections that we find in upper-class authors such as Philo and Josephus. And yet it is unmistakably true that the events depicted by Philo and Josephus have left their traces in Mark 13. They are still clearly visible, even when they have, perhaps deliberately, been "blurred." It could be that the author and audience knew more than they said. There were reasons enough to express oneself carefully in a tense political situation![53]

In our search for traces of these events, we will go through the text bit by bit. The crucial question will be whether we find correspondences to Mk 13:7-8, 14-16 in the situation in the late 30s, since these verses are almost universally assigned to tradition. But we will also seek correspondences in the other parts of the text, since it is possible that they also belong to the source text.

The Beginning of the Birthpangs (Mk 13:6-8)

Jesus' discourse speaks first of false teachers who will come in his name and whose teaching is characterized by the phrase ἐγώ εἰμι (Mk 13:6). This could refer to early Christian prophets, who uttered "I sayings" of Jesus in the belief that the exalted Lord was speaking through them. Celsus caricatured such prophets in the second century. They say: "I am God or the Son of God or the divine Spirit. I have come because the end of the world is approaching" (Origen *Contra Celsum* 7.9). Montanist prophets spoke in the same style: "I am the Father and I am the Son and I am the Paraclete."[54] There probably were prophets of this type from the

---

53. E. Haenchen (*Der Weg Jesu,* 443ff.) thinks that the author of Mark consciously chose a cryptic language for political reasons. The author expects a general persecution of Christians. If the Christians ("those in Judea") are forced to participate in the imperial cult ("desolating sacrilege"), they should flee from their homes. But the presumed political situation is improbable circa 70 C.E. because the imperial cult had only a limited function in proceedings against Christians, serving as a test of loyalty after their arrest, but not as the cause or object of their being arrested. Persecutions were, at first, limited to certain localities. Still, the notion of encrypting for political reasons is plausible.

54. It is disputed whether or not the figures mentioned in Origen *Contra Cels.* 7.9 are Christian prophets. H. Lietzmann *(An die Korinther,* 68–69) favors this interpretation; H. Weinel *(Die Wirkungen des Geistes und der Geister,* 90–91) opposes it. I think the similarity to Montanist prophecy is in favor of their being Christians (cf. the fragments in E. Hennecke and W. Schneemelcher, *Neutestamentliche Apokryphen* 2:486–87), as are the trinitarian formula, the references to glossolalia, and the eschatology that is presupposed. In addition, the "I am" sayings in John's Gospel could point to similar spirit-inspired speakers in early Christianity.

very first years of Christianity, who could have interpreted the wars and catastrophes described in the text as the beginning of the end time.[55]

It is less likely that this refers to "messianic figures" outside Christianity. There were some at this time. In the year 36 a Samaritan prophet led a crowd up Mount Gerizim to find the lost vessels of the temple (*Ant.* 18.85ff.). At about the same time, Simon Magus may have been working in Samaria, but that is not certain: Justin (*Apology* 1.26) dates him in the time of the emperor Claudius (41–52 C.E.).[56] The story of Philip and Simon in Acts 8 in any case points to earlier contacts between him and the Christians.

Verse 5 is not crucial for the question about the background of events behind the tradition adapted in Mark 13. It is possible that the author of Mark composed this introduction, looking back to the multitude of false teachers and prophets.[57] It is more important to identify the wars mentioned in verses 7-8: "When you hear of wars and rumors of wars, do not be alarmed; this must take place, but the end is still to come. For nation will rise against nation, and kingdom against kingdom."

All the characteristics contained in this text could apply to the Nabatean war of 36–37.[58] In that war, "nation [arose] against nation"—Jews against Nabateans. It was a struggle of one "polis" against another. Both nations had monarchical governments: it is true that Herod Antipas only bore the title of "tetrarch," but among his Aramaic-speaking people he was called "king" (cf. Mk 6:14).[59] Josephus calls the tetrarchy of Lysanias βασιλεία (*Bell.* 2.215, 247; cf., in contrast, *Ant.* 18.237; 20.138). The decisive point is that the Nabatean war fits other criteria as well. On the basis of Mk 13:14

---

55. É. Trocmé gives a quite different interpretation in *La formation de l'Évangile selon Marc*, 164–65. According to him, Mk 13:5-6 is a polemic against the leadership group in the Jerusalem community surrounding James, the brother of the Lord, who had assumed for himself the role of the Davidic messiah.

56. Justin dates Simon Magus's work at Rome to the time of Claudius, but presumes a previous period of activity in Samaria, where, according to Justin, Simon Magus had an especially large group of adherents. It is thus possible that the "historical Simon" appeared in Samaria in the late 30s.

57. Circa 40–70 C.E., many prophets and "false teachers" appeared in Palestine: Theudas (ca. 44–48; *Ant.* 20.97–99; Acts 5:36); under the procurator Felix (ca. 52–60), an anonymous prophet (*Ant.* 20.167–68; *Bell.* 2.259) and an Egyptian (*Ant.* 20.168–72; *Bell.* 2.261–63; cf. Acts 21:38); under Festus, a prophet (60–62 C.E.). On these, see P. W. Barnett, "Jewish Sign Prophets A.D. 40–70."

58. The first to suggest a relationship between Mk 13:7 and the Nabatean war was A. Piganiol ("Observations sur la date de l'apokalypse synoptique") though he did not give a thorough reasoning for his idea.

59. Josephus calls the Nabatean prince Aretas IV "king" (*Ant.* 16.298; 18.109). Aretas III (84–72 B.C.E.) had coins minted at Damascus with the legend "Basileos Aretou Philhellenos" (cf. R. Wenning, *Die Nabatäer,* 25).

we can locate the apocalyptic prophecy in Judea, but the Nabatean war was fought between the rulers of Galilee and Perea and the king of the Nabateans, while the prefectures of Judea and Samaria lay outside the struggle. Those who lived in Jerusalem or in Judea would have "heard" of this war (Mk 13:7). At the same time, it was the sort of struggle that would have had an existential impact: the people interpreted Antipas's defeat as punishment for the execution of the Baptizer (*Ant.* 18.116–19). For Christians and followers of the Baptizer the defeat also implied that, if God had visibly punished the Baptizer's execution, the latter's message was affirmed. Central to this preaching was the message of approaching judgment. This, too, must be true. God was in the process of accomplishing what had been announced: the end must be near. When a prophet appeared at the same moment in Samaria and awakened hope for a new age of grace, this only reinforced the impression. It was a time filled with prophetic expectation.

A modest detail in the text may be clarified by the situation at that time. In Mk 13:7 "wars and rumors of wars" are mentioned, in that order, although rumors of war normally precede the wars themselves—unless ἀκούσητε . . . ἀκοάς is a *figura etymologica* meaning nothing more than "they will hear of wars." In fact, the events took place as follows: after the defeat of their client prince, Antipas, the Romans could not remain inactive. The Syrian legate, Vitellius, was therefore commissioned to intervene with two legions. He marched from Antioch to Ptolemais, left his troops there, and traveled to Jerusalem, probably to prepare for his campaign. There he received the news of the death of Tiberius (*Ant.* 18.124) and so broke off his preparations. Thus, in the years 36–37 there was, first, a real war between Antipas and Aretas, and then the threat of a second and greater war involving the Romans. Rumors of war followed wars!

It could be objected that Mk 13:7 speaks of "wars" in the plural. But here again the situation corresponds to the text: at the same time as the Nabatean war there were wars between pretenders to the Parthian throne, with the Romans in the background (cf. Tacitus *Ann.* 6.31–37). Simultaneously, the Romans installed a client king in Armenia.

The synoptic apocalypse also reports "earthquakes in various places" and "famines." "For nation will rise against nation, and kingdom against kingdom; there will be earthquakes in various places; there will be famines" (Mk 13:8). Can these events also be related to the situation of the period? Vitellius spent Passover of the year 37 in Jerusalem. In that year, the 15th of Nisan fell on April 20.[60] Four days later he received the news of the death of the emperor Tiberius, who died on 15 March 37. At just this

---

60. For this date, see Holzmeister, "Wann war Pilatus Prokurator von Judaea?" 229.

time, Jerusalem must have received news of an earthquake that shook Antioch and parts of Syria on 9 April 37, which is reported by the Antiochene chronicler Malalas.[61] Cancellation of the campaign against the Nabateans was natural in this situation: the one who had ordered it was dead, and the Parthians could have taken advantage of the favorable moment, with half the troops tied up in the southern part of the province and the capital city damaged by an earthquake. It is understandable that Vitellius returned to Antioch as soon as possible.

Of the three apocalyptic calamities—wars, earthquakes, and famines— only the famines cannot directly be shown to have happened at that time. But there are indications of some difficulty with the food supply. Vitellius, in preparing for his campaign against the Nabateans, understood the need to keep the countryside quiet. The Jewish aristocracy took advantage of this favorable situation to obtain certain concessions, including the removal of all taxes on agricultural products (*Ant.* 18.90). The occasion could have been an acute problem in obtaining food. Herod I had previously abolished taxes during poor harvests (*Ant.* 15.365). But beyond that, famines are the natural sequel to wars, and Palestine had to prepare to feed two legions. We can be fairly certain that there was anxiety about hard times.

The events mentioned in the synoptic apocalypse as "the beginning of the birthpangs"—wars, earthquakes, and famines—can thus be related to the years 36–37.[62] At that time, the impression could have arisen among

---

61. Malalas *World Chronicle* (ed. Dindorf) 243.10; cf. Schenk v. Stauffenberg, *Römische Kaisergeschichte bei Malalas X*, 243, 10.

62. As an alternative, and rightly, exegetes have discussed relating the wars, earthquakes, and famines to the great crisis of 66–70, most persuasively Hengel, "Entstehungszeit," 34ff. But I think the modifications of apocalyptic *topoi* in Mk 13:7-8 fit the years 36–37 better than the years 66–70. First, the wars of the years 66–70 are described thus by Tacitus: "Four emperors fell by the sword; there were three civil wars, more foreign wars and often both at the same time" (*Hist.* 1.2). The characteristic conflicts of 68–69 between various "princes" and aspirants to their thrones find no echo in Mk 13:7-8, although catastrophes among the "powerful" are certainly part of the repertoire of apocalyptic horrors (cf. 2 Esdr 9:3; *2 Bar.* 27:3; 70:7; *Apoc. Abr.* 30:6). Second, in Mk 13:7-8, the earthquakes are synchronized with the wars. But the major earthquakes reported in the later period were all either before or after the Jewish war: in Laodicea in Phrygia, 60 C.E. (Tacitus *Ann.* 14.27), as well as in Achaia and Macedonia (Seneca *Quaest. Nat.* 7.28.2). In 62–63 Pompeii and Herculaneum were destroyed for the first time by an earthquake (Tacitus *Ann.* 15.22.2). For the time after the destruction of the temple, we note an earthquake in Salamis and Pophos (*Sib. Or.* 4.128–29), probably in the year 77 C.E.; in 79 C.E., the great eruption of Vesuvius that destroyed Pompeii occurred. Only minor earthquakes are reported in 68 C.E.: one was in Maruccia on the east coast of Italy (Pliny *Nat. Hist.* 2.199). There were also two prodigies: an earthquake during Nero's flight, just before his death (Dio Cassius 63.28.1) and one during Galba's march into Rome (Suetonius *Galba* 18.1). Cf. A. Hermann, "Erdbeben." It is especially important to note that earthquakes are not part of the general idea of catastrophe; otherwise Tacitus would have

eschatologically conscious Jewish groups (including Christians) that the end of the world was at hand. How often do so many things happen in such a short time: wars with Parthians and Nabateans, the death of an emperor, earthquake, God's visible intervention on behalf of a prophet who had announced the impending end? In the perspective of world history it may have been a rather quiet year. But people who are living in eager anticipation of the end of the world can easily detect the beginning of the end in minor crisis phenomena. That is why the synoptic apocalypse warns that "the end is still to come" (13:7). Both the Nabatean and the Parthian wars ended quickly. But history went on. They had been mistaken.

I think that Mk 13:9-13 must have been inserted into this context at a later time. These are persecution logia that have independent variants in the tradition: for 13:9, see Lk 12:11-12; for 13:11, see Lk 21:15; and for 13:12, see Mt 10:34-35 and Lk 12:53. These logia are linked by key words (cf. παραδιδόναι in 13:9, 11, 12). Matthew includes them in the mission discourse (10:17-22). The author of Mark has placed them in his "apocalyptic travel plan" at exactly the point at which we find his own present time, that is, a time of persecution and of missionary activity (13:10). Therefore, this section is of crucial importance for determining the situation in which Mark's Gospel was written, and we must return to the discussion of it later. Still, we cannot exclude the possibility that parts of 13:9-13 belong to the traditional material. This is repeatedly suggested, in particular, for v. 12. What could the synoptic apocalypse have been thinking of in this case? Persecutions are the background of this verse, and we know of persecutions of the Hellenist community at Jerusalem in the 30s. After the stoning of Stephen, they were driven out of the city (Acts 6:1—8:3). Acts connects Paul with this persecution, but he had probably acted against Christians in other places, for the communities in Judea did not know him (Gal 1:22-23; cf. Gal 1:13; Phil 3:6; 1 Cor 15:9). He is connected, instead, with the community at Damascus (Acts 9:1ff.), where in 36-37 he himself was persecuted and had to flee quickly (2 Cor 11:32-33; Acts 9:24-25).

In Mark 13:12, the traditional *topos* of the collapse of the family is tied to these persecutions: Christians were denounced by members of their own families. It is interesting that we encounter a quite different variant of this *topos*[63] in Philo's report of the crisis year 40. The crowd demonstrating before Petronius

---

included them among the impressive collection of crisis phenomena in the introduction to his *Histories* (1.2). Third, as far as famine is concerned, the siege of Jerusalem involved the most terrible starvation among the besieged (*Bell.* 6.193ff.).

63. The *topos* itself is traditional: cf. Mt 7:6; *1 Enoch* 56:7; 90:6-7; *Apoc. Esdr.* 3:12-13. We find it in many variations. It is applied to friends in 2 Esdr 5:9; 6:24; to the relationship between the generations in *Jub.* 23:19; and in general to hatred of people for one another in *2 Bar.* 70:3. It has a long prehistory and is already found in the myth of the plague god Ira in Babylon: cf. H. Gressmann, *Altorientalische Texte zum Alten Testament*, 228.

swear that they are prepared, if necessary, to slaughter one another: "our selves will conduct the sacrifices, priests of a noble order: wives will be brought to the altar by wife-slayers, brothers and sisters by fratricides, boys and girls in the innocence of their years by child-murderers" (*Leg. Gai.* 234). In such an atmosphere the *topos* of family collapse could gain a new lease on life, even when it means something other than a collective suicide carried out by family members against one another. But we should again emphasize that, although it is not impossible to find events of the years 30–40 worked into Mk 13:9-13, especially 13:12, still it could very well be true that the author of Mark inserted this section into the source text in view of the events of his own time.

The "Desolating Sacrilege"

The puzzling phrase "desolating sacrilege" takes up a key expression from the religious persecution under Antiochus IV in 168–167 B.C.E. "Now on the fifteenth day of Chislev, in the one hundred forty-fifth year, [the king] erected a desolating sacrilege on the altar of burnt offering. They also built altars in the surrounding towns of Judah, and offered incense at the doors of the houses and in the streets" (1 Macc 1:54-55).

"Desolating sacrilege" is a literal translation of Hebrew *shiqquz m^eshomem* (Dan 9:27; 11:31; 12:11), a bowdlerization of the name of the principal pagan god, Baal Shamaim or "Olympian Zeus," to whom the temple was dedicated in 168 (cf. 2 Macc 6:2).[64] Concretely, the "desolating sacrilege" refers to the transformation of the traditional altar of immolation before the temple into a pagan altar, on which swine may have been sacrificed (according to Jos. *Ant.* 12.253).[65] The author of Mk 13:14 must have something similar to this "desolating sacrilege" in mind. But what is it?

This "desolating sacrilege" can be satisfactorily explained on the basis of the events of the years 39–40. The conflict between Gaius Caligula and the Jews must have recalled the religious struggles under Antiochus IV Epiphanes. This is true regarding both the originating cause of the conflict—the destruction of a pagan altar in Jamnia—and its climax in the threatened desecration of the temple. To work out the analogies in detail, we should quote Philo's report of the conflict at Jamnia:

Jamneia, one of the most populous cities of Judaea, is inhabited by a mixture of people, the majority being Jews with some others of alien races,

---

64. Cf. E. Nestle, "Zu Daniel," 248.
65. From 1 Macc 1:54, 59; 6:7, we can conclude that the "desolating sacrilege" stood on the altar. According to 1 Macc 4:43, the cleansing of the altar involved removing the defiled stones. E. Bickermann (*Der Gott der Makkabäer,* 105–9) gives a religious-historical explanation for this proceeding. He states that Syro-Phoenician religion worshiped deities in the form of stones and altars that were often erected on a separate base: "the altar for whole burnt offerings before the Temple became the podium for a fetish" (p. 108).

intruders for mischief from the dwellers in adjacent countries. These people
being new settlers have made themselves a pest and a nuisance to those who
are in a sense indigenous by perpetually subverting some part of the institutions of the Jews. Hearing from travellers visiting them how earnestly Gaius
was pressing his deification and the extreme hostility which he felt towards
the whole Jewish race, they thought that a fit opportunity of attacking them
had fallen in their way. Accordingly they erected an extemporized altar of
the commonest material with the clay moulded into bricks, merely as a plan
to injure their neighbours, for they knew that they would not allow their
customs to be subverted, as indeed it turned out. For, when they saw it and
felt it intolerable that the sanctity which truly belongs to the Holy Land
should be destroyed, they met together and pulled it down. (Philo *Leg. Gai.*
200–202)

The parallels with the events that created the Maccabean revolt have
received too little notice heretofore. At that time also, pagan altars were
raised in Jewish territory. Judas Maccabeus began the uprising by destroying one of these altars, in Modein, in accord with the law for altars in Deut
7:5-6 and 12:2-3 (1 Macc 2:25). The Jews of Jamnia probably had his
example in mind when they destroyed the pagan (imperial?) altar, because
Modein is only 35 kilometers from Jamnia. In that area the memory of the
uprising would not have faded so quickly.[66]

Recollections of the religious persecution under Antiochus IV were
alive in the general population. In the *Assumption of Moses,* a renewed
persecution along the same lines is predicted:

And there shall come upon them [a second] retribution and wrath, such as
has not befallen them from the beginning until that time, when he will stir
up against them the king of the kings of the earth, a man who rules with
great power, who will crucify those who confess their circumcision. And
those who deny it he will torture and put in chains and imprison. And their
wives will be given to the gods among the Gentiles, and their young sons will
be operated on by the doctors to look as though they had not been circumcised. And others among them will suffer punishment by torture and fire
and sword; and they will be forced to carry round their idols publicly, pol-
luted things, just like the shrines that house them. And in the same way they

---

66. The annual Feast of Dedication (Hanukkah; cf. Jn 10:22; *Ant.* 12.325) kept alive
memories of the Maccabean revolt. According to 2 Macc 10:5, the day of the purification of
the temple fell exactly on the day on which it had been profaned by the pagans—on the 25th
of Chislev, when the desolating sacrilege had been erected. The Feast of Dedication was
celebrated in memory of the evil times just past: "They celebrated it for eight days with
rejoicing, in the manner of the festival of booths, remembering how not long before, during
the festival of booths, they had been wandering in the mountains and caves like wild animals" (2 Macc 10:6). Thanks to the Feast of Dedication, every Jew, whether educated in the
law or not, knew (1) what the "desolating sacrilege" was, and (2) that it had already, once
before, been the occasion for fleeing to the mountains.

will be forced by those who torture them to enter their inmost sanctuary and forced with goads to blaspheme and insult the Name, and, as if that were not enough, the laws as well by having a pig upon the altar. (*As. Mos.* 8:1-5)

The *Assumption of Moses* can be dated between 4 B.C.E. and 30 C.E.: Herod's death is presupposed, but at the time of writing the reigns of his sons have been shorter than his thirty-four-year rule (cf. *As. Mos.* 6:6-7).[67] Thus, in the decades before the Caligula crisis there was expectation of a religious persecution on the model of the conflict under Antiochus Epiphanes. It is revealing that a "desolating sacrilege" in the temple plays no part in these speculations, even though the temple will not remain untouched in the expected religious persecutions: it is predicted that Jews will be forced to enter the Holy of Holies. They are to blaspheme the law and the cult! Thus, when the "desolating sacrilege" reappears in later texts, as we find it in the Synoptics, it is likely that concrete events have caused people to revive just this "key expression" out of memories of the earlier persecution. The reference to the "desolating sacrilege" in the synoptic apocalypse, then, is certainly not the reproduction of a preformed *topos*, but the reflection of experience, namely, of Gaius's threatened desecration of the temple.

When Gaius Caligula learned of the destruction of the altar in Jamnia, he ordered that his statue be erected in the temple at Jerusalem as a punishment. Petronius marched with two legions to Ptolemais and, to gain time, had the statue prepared at Sidon with extreme care (*Leg. Gai.* 222).[68] At the same time, he attempted through negotiations to avoid a military clash. Mark 13:14ff. could have been composed in this situation: "But when you see the desolating sacrilege set up where it ought not to be (let the reader understand), then those in Judea must flee to the mountains." The following arguments favor this interpretation.

1. "Sacrilege" (βδέλυγμα) is often connected with idolatrous practices.[69] The word refers to an action against God, and in no sense a punishment from God! The statue being made in Phoenicia was a sacrilege ("abomination" in other translations) for Jews because it was intended to transform cultic worship in Jerusalem into idolatry.

2. The expression "desolating sacrilege" is a cipher to be decoded, as the address to the readers indicates. It is thus legitimate to regard the

---

67. Cf. E. Brandenburger, *Himmelfahrt Moses*, 60.

68. Most of the sources refer to a statue (*Leg. Gai.* 220; *Ant.* 18.261). But in *Bell.* 2.185ff., Josephus speaks of "statues." Perhaps, in *Bellum Judaicum*, he is influenced by the notion that the emperor's image was usually placed next to that of the goddess Roma, as in Caesarea (*Bell.* 1.414) and elsewhere (Suetonius *Aug.* 52).

69. Cf. W. Foerster, "βδελύσσομαι."

expression as a *terminus technicus* meant to remind us of some particular thing. The only thing that fits is the establishment of the cult of Zeus Olympios in 168–167 B.C.E. The Jamnia conflict shows that the traditions of the Maccabean revolt were still alive. Anyone who knew the Scriptures could learn from 1 Macc 1:54 that what was meant was the establishment of a pagan cult in the temple, and from Dan 12:11 that such a "desolating sacrilege" was also threatened in the end time! But even apart from that kind of knowledge, the "desolating sacrilege" could become the slogan of a pious group.

3. The synoptic apocalypse refers to the "desolating sacrilege" as if it were a person, using the participle ἑστηκότα instead of the grammatically correct neuter ἑστηκώς. (This is like saying in English, "the thing *who* stands where it should not stand.") The *constructio ad sensum* leads us to suspect that the "desolating sacrilege" represents a person. The emperor's statue is both: as lifeless matter, it is neuter (a βδέλυγμα), but as the image of the emperor it is a person. In addition, the participle "standing" is ideally chosen to represent a statue.[70]

4. Finally, the importance attached to the location of the statue is significant. What is objectionable is not its existence: every Jew knew that there were many statues of the emperor outside the Holy Land. Anyone could admire the statue of Augustus as "Zeus Olympios" in the temple of Augustus at Caesarea (*Bell.* 1.414). It was not scandalous that Petronius was having a statue of the emperor made in Sidon. What was so objectionable was its intended location: Jerusalem and Judea. Thus, the sign for eschatological flight is the location of the "desolating sacrilege" in a place where it should not stand.[71]

If the "desolating sacrilege" refers to the statue that is to be erected in the temple, then everything after verse 14 is talking about the near future.

---

70. Cf. Gaius Caligula's order in *Ant.* 18.261: ἱστᾶν αὐτοῦ ἀνδριάντα ἐν τῷ ναῷ τοῦ θεοῦ (cf. 18.264). But see esp. the formulation of the retraction of the order: νῦν οὖν εἰ μὲν φθάνεις τὸν ἀνδριάντα ἑστακώς, ἑστάτω (*Ant.* 18.301). Here we have the same expression as in Mk 13:14! In addition to ἱστάναι, Philo and Josephus use other verbs for the "erection" of a statue.

71. This very location of the "desolating sacrilege" in the temple has been used as an objection against the dating of the synoptic apocalypse suggested here. Is it not too late to flee, when the statue is already in the temple? Cf. Bilde, "Afspejler Mark 13," 118–19. But even if it were impossible for the Jerusalemites to flee, those "in Judea"—that is, the Jews and Christians living in the countryside—could still take flight. Contemporaries did not merely regard the erection of the statue in the temple as blasphemy, its mere transportation through Jewish territory was a provocation. For this very reason, Vitellius had agreed not to lead his legions through the Jewish land (cf. *Ant.* 18.121). The destruction of the imperial altar in Jamnia shows that any kind of pagan cult in the land counted as sacrilege, not merely that in Jerusalem. According to *Bell.* 2.195, the Jews negotiating with Petronius in Tiberias expressly emphasize that the law against setting up an image of God or of human beings applies "not only in their sanctuary but even in any unconsecrated spot throughout the country."

The call for flight would be a genuine appeal, not a *vaticinium ex eventu.* Therefore, the fact that we have no record of groups of people actually fleeing to the mountains in the year 40 would not furnish an argument against the suggested dating of the synoptic apocalypse. What has to be established historically is not flight, but the readiness to flee. That is not difficult, because the demonstrating Jews say, according to Philo: "We are evacuating our cities, withdrawing from our houses and lands; our furniture and money and cherished possessions and all the other spoil we will willingly make over" (*Leg. Gai.* 232). In *Ant.* 18.274, the Jewish authorities point to the danger that neglect of agriculture will lead to an increase of banditry, since the desperate people will no longer be able to pay their taxes. But banditry usually means that people have left their houses and farms. Because we thus have clear evidence of people's readiness to leave their ancestral homes and possessions, either as a demonstration or to become "robbers" and thus escape the grasp of the tax collectors, we can presume that other groups were also prepared to leave house and home in anticipation of the Parousia of the Son of man.

The composition of the synoptic apocalypse would thus be dated to the year 40 C.E. We can limit the date even further: it would be in that period when the erection of one or several statues of the emperor in the temple was threatened. Even though Philo and Josephus differ in their chronology of events, they still indicate a dating of the negotiations either in the spring (Philo) or in the fall (Josephus). Whether the threatened desecration of the temple was generally known at harvest time in May (Philo) or at the time of sowing in October–November (Josephus), in either case the winter was inexorably approaching. Thus, the plea that the flight not occur in winter is understandable because it is especially difficult to secure food at that time of year.

We can also specify the place of composition more accurately. Those who are directly addressed in the second person must be in a position to "see" the statue in the place where it is destined to stand. They can only be Jerusalemites. Those "in Judea" are then spoken of in the third person plural. They need not be identical with those in Jerusalem, but could be Judeans living in the countryside. However, it could also be that the Jerusalemites are included; they, too, are Judeans. In any case, the change of number shows that not all those addressed must see the statue standing in its place in order to take flight. It cannot be objected against this location that it would be unthinkable to call on people living in Judea to flee to the mountains, since they are already living there.[72] The flight of

---

72. As does Bilde, "Afspejler Mark 13," 118.

the Maccabees from the hill country of Shefela is also described in 1 Macc 2:28 (cf. *Bell.* 1.36) as a flight "to the hills." In 1 Macc 9:40 those fleeing are even in the highlands of Madaba; still, the text speaks of their flight "to the mountains" (cf. *Bell.* 2.504; *Ant.* 14.418). The call to flee to the mountains refers to a retreat into uninhabited mountainous country, the kind of place that was always the refuge of rebels, from David to Bar-Kochba. Hence, the motif of flight to the mountains, the caves, and the wilderness is found in many parts of Jewish literature.[73]

Dating the synoptic apocalypse to the Caligula crisis of the year 40 C.E. makes it possible to compare the reaction to the threatened desecration of the temple depicted in it with other forms of response. Four such responses can be observed among the Jews.

1. There are impressive nonviolent demonstrations. The people rush to Petronius and declare that they prefer to let themselves be cut down without resistance rather than agree to the abolition of their religion, that is, to the violation of monotheism and the law against images (*Leg. Gai.* 229ff.; *Ant.* 18.261–72; *Bell.* 2.192–98).[74] There was a tradition of this kind of demonstrative nonviolence. The same strategy had already succeeded against Pilate some time between 26 and 29 C.E., when he attempted to bring images of the emperor to Jerusalem (*Bell.* 2.169ff.; *Ant.* 18.55). Since Pilate had given in at that time, the demonstrators could hope to achieve their aims again this time.

2. Next, there is a "farmworkers' strike," or at least the threat of one. The farmers refuse to sow their fields (*Ant.* 18.272–74). This was in part a natural consequence of the demonstrations, since no one can demonstrate and work the fields at the same time. But partly it represents an additional type of warning, because it included a threat to destroy the harvest if necessary (*Leg. Gai.* 249), probably in order to create supply difficulties for the army. The aristocracy also warns of an increase of banditry, since those who are not farming cannot pay their taxes and must often leave house and home to join the "bandits" (*Ant.* 18.274). It is possible that this "agricultural strike" could have taken advantage of the Jewish tradition of the sabbatical year in which the fields remain fallow— 40–41 would have been such a Sabbath year.[75] But it is possible that it was also a distant Palestinian variant of the anachoristic custom that is attested

---

73. *1 Enoch* 96:2; *As. Mos.* 9:6-7; *Ps. Sol.* 17:17; cf. Heb 11:38; Rev 12:6.

74. The threats vary from readiness to let themselves be slaughtered by the Romans without resistance (*Bell.* 2.197) to infliction of collective suicide on one another (*Leg. Gai.* 234–35).

75. J. Jeremias, "Sabbathjahr und neutestamentliche Chronologie." Hyldahl ("Josefus som historiesriver," 62ff.) sees the so-called "farmworkers' strike" as a consequence of the sabbatical year.

in Egypt, whereby workers in some places left their fields and returned to work only after having fulfilled certain specific conditions.[76]

3. If the aristocrats referred to "bandits" in their discussions with the Syrian legate, they were thinking of armed resistance. Philo and Josephus are silent on this point, but Tacitus reports warlike maneuvers: "Under Tiberius all was quiet. Then, when Caligula ordered the Jews to set up his statue in their temple, they chose rather to resort to arms, but the emperor's death put an end to their uprising" (*Hist.* 5.9). Among these resistance fighters, no doubt, the tradition of the religious wars of liberation, so vivid at the time of the Maccabean revolt, lived on.

4. On a higher level, of course, the first reactions were diplomatic in character. Petronius dealt with the "magnates of the Jews, priests and magistrates" (*Leg. Gai.* 222). The Herodian princes were also brought in: in Tiberias, the brother of King Agrippa, Aristobulus, appealed to Petronius (*Ant.* 18.273); in Rome, King Agrippa himself intervened. Both these interventions were successful, but it was only the murder of Gaius Caligula on 24 January 41 that finally ended the danger to the sanctuary.

The synoptic apocalypse acquaints us with a fifth type of reaction to the crisis. The groups addressed here have not yet left house and land. They are not among those who went to Ptolemais and Tiberias to protest Gaius's plans. But they are also prepared in principle to leave their work and their fields when, as appears likely, the situation becomes more acute. This is important for the assessment of their attitude, because they are ordered with prophetic authority to behave in a way that will, in its objective consequences, serve to support the agricultural strike that was about to take place in Palestine. What they are not ordered to do is to engage in armed resistance. This idea was also in the air. There was no doubt at all that there would be a bloody war if Gaius did not retract his plan. The Judeans addressed in Mark 13, however, are to flee to the mountain wilderness to await the appearance of the Son of man. In so doing, they will also continue traditional patterns of resistance; during the Maccabean revolt we hear of a group that withdrew into desert caves and allowed itself to be slaughtered on the Sabbath without offering resistance (1 Macc 2:29-38).

It has often been supposed that the prophecy redacted in Mark 13 has no specifically Christian character and was originally a Jewish prophecy from the year 40 C.E. that was later adopted by Christians;[77] however, it is unnecessary to think so. In the year 40, the paths of Jews and Christians

---

76. Cf. W. Schmidt, "Der Einfluss der Anachorese."
77. This is the opinion of Hölscher, "Der Ursprung der Apokalypse Mk 13," 196.

had not yet separated. Mark 13 shows us a Christianity that was still completely within Judaism. These Christians wanted to be Jews who believed in Jesus as the Messiah and the Son of man who was to return. Of course, they distinguished themselves from other Jewish groups, as Mark 13 also shows. We find nothing here about readiness to defend the temple by violence, either against others or against oneself. Instead, there is the dream of an "evasive" solution: removing oneself from the point of crisis. Fear of the emperor Gaius Caligula, who blasphemously makes himself out to be God, is countered with hope in the "human one" who comes from heaven to save his own. We hear nothing of a judgment on the impious. The dreams of revenge characteristic of apocalyptic fantasy are missing. Identification with the visible temple is clearly less strong than among other groups, which is understandable because Jesus' saying about the destruction of the temple—or rather, its replacement by another temple—was current among Christians. Christians had already gotten into trouble because of that prophecy. Stephen had been stoned for it (cf. Acts 6:14ff.). We can guess what a difficult situation ensued for these Christians after the surprising rescue of the temple. The aggressions aroused among the people against the Romans in the crisis year 40 could only be expressed in a muted manner against the rulers of the land, especially since a leading Roman official had evaded the command to desecrate the temple. It was all the more likely that the pent-up tensions would be vented on a group of outsiders who had dissociated themselves from the temple and circulated ambiguous sayings about its destruction. When Agrippa I received authority over Judea and Samaria after the crisis, there really was a persecution of Christians, which this time did not strike the more radical Hellenistic wing (as in Acts 6:8—8:3), but the center of the first community: James, the son of Zebedee, was executed, and Peter only narrowly escaped death (Acts 12:2-3). The account in Acts reveals that Agrippa's actions against the Christians found a positive response among his people. Anyone who maintained a reserved attitude toward the temple, in the face of God's obvious intervention on its behalf, could get into a fatal situation. It is possible that the Caligula crisis of the year 40 C.E. led to a first step toward the separation of Jews and Christians. In the years 40–50 the gentile mission was accepted, and with it Christianity began to grow beyond the limits of Judaism.

But the synoptic apocalypse is a document from a time when Christians were a small group within Judaism. It can help us better understand Jewish and Christian apocalyptic. In particular, it reveals itself as an apocalyptic of opposition—the opposition of subordinate groups to world powers and world empires. This is true of all the apocalyptic books in the canon, from Daniel to Revelation, and it is true also of Mark 13. This apocalyptic opposition stands in a close historical and functional correspondence to other forms of political resistance. Without religious legitimation there could have been no resistance at that time—no peaceful demonstrations, no agricultural strike, no diplomatic pressure, but also no threat of war. It was only the recognition that, in case of conflict, the Jewish people would place their fidelity to God above their loyalty to the emperor that caused the Roman state to hesitate in carrying out its intentions.

In addition to this functional correspondence, there is also a more essential connection between apocalyptic and political resistance in the biblical apocalypses: the universal catastrophe that they presuppose has not yet occurred, but what it implies continues in force, in an altered form, namely, that these calamities will take place if the human being is elevated to the place of God—or, more precisely, when the state and its leaders place themselves in God's stead. Then the state itself will be the "desolating sacrilege." Its power of destruction has reached monstrous proportions today. But it is not certain whether there is still an official who, like Petronius, will refuse to obey and will sabotage the orders she or he has received. Petronius was a pagan. But Philo acknowledges that he must have had some rudiments of Jewish philosophy and religion (*Leg. Gai.* 245), and Josephus puts words in his mouth that remind us of Jesus— that he is prepared to give his life for many: ἑτοίμως ἐπιδώσω τὴν ἐμαυτὸν ψυχήν (*Bell.* 2.201).

The importance of a study of Mark 13 for the history of the synoptic tradition should never be underestimated. If the traditions behind Mark 13 can be traced to a situation in the year 40 C.E. that can be precisely located, both in space and time, then, because of chance circumstances, some thirty years of the prehistory of a Markan text become visible to us. We can conclude that as early as ten years after Jesus' death, traditions circulating in his name were taking on new forms within Judea. The apocalyptic prophecy behind Mark 13 presumes the sayings about the future Son of man and inserts them in a new situation, abandoning the forms of the "small units" of synoptic tradition. This is a longer text with a complex structure. Probably it existed in written form, which means that we have to acknowledge an early transition from oral to written tradition. Inevitably, we must ask ourselves whether that can also be established for other parts of the synoptic tradition. Were there also "large units" in the narrative tradition that were composed (and written down) some time before the canonical Gospels? The most likely unit to have been so treated was the Passion narrative, which is the subject of the next chapter.

4

A Major Narrative Unit
(the Passion Story)
and the Jerusalem Community
in the Years 40–50 C.E.

The story of the Passion forms a "large unit" within the narrative tradition. In it, partial, smaller units, or pericopes, are woven together in such a way that it is hard to imagine them in isolation. They presuppose the pericopes that precede them and prepare for those that follow. Often there are references forward and backward, beyond the pericopes immediately before and after: for example, the identification of the betrayer and the prediction of the disciples' flight and of Peter's denial (Mk 14:17-21, 26-31) point beyond the Gethsemane pericope to Jesus' arrest and the subsequent flight and denial described in Mk 14:43-54, 66-71. In the other direction, the mocking of Jesus by Roman soldiers (15:19-32) echoes earlier scenes in the Sanhedrin and before Pilate. This tight interweaving of the pericopes is generally recognized. What is disputed is whether they are the creation of the author of Mark[1] or whether they belong to the tradition, and how extensive that tradition is.[2]

In my opinion, in Mark we can discern behind the text as we now have it a connected narrative that presupposes a certain chronology. According to Mark, Jesus died on the day of Passover, but the tradition supposes it

---

1. Classic form criticism deliberately exempted the Passion story from the decomposition of the synoptic material into "small units." Cf. K. L. Schmidt, *Der Rahmen der Geschichte Jesu,* 303–6. In the late 1960s the first dissent was expressed by J. Schreiber (*Die Markuspassion*), who chose to regard the Passion story in a "consistent redaction-historical manner" as a composition of the author of Mark. E. Linnemann (*Studien zur Passionsgeschichte*), using the tools of tradition criticism, concluded that the author of Mark had only fragments of tradition at his disposal and created the connected story himself. E. Güttgemanns (*Offene Fragen,* esp. 226ff.) regarded the prehistory of a text (especially its oral tradition), for reasons drawn from the principles of linguistics, as unrecoverable. This turn to a view of the Passion story as a coherent text composed by Mark is upheld and systematically described in W. H. Kelber, ed., *The Passion in Mark,* esp. 14ff., 153–59.

2. An overview of the problem is given by G. Schneider, "Das Problem einer vorkanonischen Passionserzählung," *BZ* 16 (1972): 222–44; and J. Ernst, "Die Passionserzählung des Markus."

was the preparation day before Passover: in 14:1-2 the Sanhedrin decides to kill Jesus before the feast in order to prevent unrest among the people on the day of the feast.[3] This fits with the circumstance that in 15:21 Simon of Cyrene is coming in from the fields, which can be understood to mean he was coming from his work. It would be hard to imagine any author's using a formulation so subject to misunderstanding in an account that describes events on the day of Passover, since no work was done on that day. Moreover, in 15:42 Jesus' burial is said to be on the "preparation day," but a relative clause is added to make it the preparation day for the Sabbath. Originally, it was probably the preparation day for the Passover (cf. Jn 19:42). The motive for removing Jesus from the cross and burying him before sundown would probably have been to have this work done before the beginning of the feast day, which would not make sense if it were already the day of Passover. Finally, the "trial" before the Sanhedrin presupposes that this was not a feast day, since no judicial proceedings could be held on that day. It would have been a breach of the legal code that the narrator could scarcely have ignored, because the point of the narrative is to represent the proceeding against Jesus as an unfair trial with contradictory witnesses and a verdict decided in advance by the high priests.

The chronology that thus emerges behind Mark's Gospel corresponds exactly with that of John. There, Jesus dies on the preparation day before the Passover. In the burial scene we find the same key phrase, "day of preparation," as in Mk 15:42, but here as the day before the feast (Jn 19:42). Because John's Gospel is in no way dependent on the Synoptics— in the sense that it does not use them as literary sources—but at most has modified its own traditions under the influence of the Synoptic Gospels[4] (although this is by no means certain), it is quite probable that Mark and John both presuppose an older account of the Passion, in which Jesus died on the day before Passover.

The chronology of this precanonical Passion account is in accord with a consistent narrative motif that appears in a number of its pericopes. If Jesus is to be executed before the feast, everything has to move swiftly.

---

3. Thus M. Dibelius, *Formgeschichte,* 181; D. Lührmann, *Markusevangelium,* 229. Objections have been raised to this interpretation. First, Mark wanted to make a deliberate contrast between divine acts and human plans; thus 14:1-2 are redactional. So L. Schenke, *Studien zur Passionsgeschichte des Markus,* 49. But there is no stress placed on the notion that by divine decree Jesus lives a day longer than his opponents desired. Schenke retracted this opinion in his *Der gekreuzigte Christus,* 127 n. 35. Second, W. Schmithals, *Das Evangelium nach Markus,* 588) reads ἐν τῇ ἑορτῇ in a local sense as "at the festival gathering." But the temporal sense is also there: the introduction in 14:1 contains two references to time. And the "cunning" demanded of Judas the betrayer did not consist merely in seeing that Jesus was arrested away from the feast-day crowds, but also that it be done "at the opportune time" (Mk 14:11).

4. This is the thesis of A. Dauer, *Die Passionsgeschichte im Johannesevangelium.*

According to Mk 14:11 it is the task of the betrayer to deliver Jesus up "opportunely" (εὐκαίρως). The identification of this betrayer at the last supper illuminates the abrupt shift from table fellowship to enmity: one who is still eating with Jesus from the same dish is going to betray him immediately afterward (14:20). The prediction of Peter's denial emphasizes that Peter will deny his Lord in the very same night (14:30). The Sanhedrin's decision is made "as soon as it was morning" (15:1). Crucifixion and death also follow quickly. Jesus is crucified at the third hour, about 9 A.M. (15:25); in the sixth hour, at noon, darkness comes (15:33); and at the ninth hour, about 3 P.M., he dies (15:34). Other victims of crucifixion suffered longer before dying.[5] Thus Pilate is right to be astonished when he hears that Jesus is "already" dead (15:44). We notice this about the whole story: everything happens with terrible speed, too fast for the disciples. Only Jesus saw it all coming.

In light of the chronology, then, we can demonstrate the existence of tensions between tradition and redaction, agreements with the Johannine Passion account, and a consistent narrative motif. All this points to a precanonical Passion story, but it tells us nothing about its extent.

The account could have begun at Mk 14:1-2.[6] Starting at the corresponding decision to put Jesus to death in Jn 11:47-53, John's Gospel has a remarkable number of pericopes in the same sequence as Mark, even though large pieces of text (including the farewell discourses) are inserted in the sequence and other pericopes, such as the cleansing of the temple, are displaced. One factor favoring a Passion story beginning with Mk 14:1 could be that all the Synoptics have a break at this point. The time of Jesus' preaching concludes with the great apocalyptic discourse, and now his time of suffering begins.

Besides this "synoptic form" of the Passion story, we could also imagine a short form beginning with Jesus' arrest.[7] In that case, the Passion story would encompass exactly those things that appear in the Passion sum-

---

5. Josephus (*Vita* 420) tells how, on returning from Tekoa to Jerusalem, he found three of his acquaintances among many crucified men and begged Titus to pardon them. They were taken down from their crosses, and one survived. If we add together the time of his journey, the length of the discussion, and everything else, the crucified men must have suffered on the cross quite a long time. For all questions relating to crucifixion, see H.-W. Kuhn, "Die Kreuzesstrafe während der frühen Kaiserzeit."

6. So Dibelius, *Formgeschichte*, 181ff.; Lührmann, *Markusevangelium*, 227ff.

7. R. Bultmann (*Die Geschichte der synoptischen Tradition*, 301–2) presumes this kind of "historical account" beginning with the arrest of Jesus. Schenke (*Der gekreuzigte Christus*) reconstructs an account beginning with the Gethsemane pericope. It is notable that Judas is introduced in Mk 14:43 as "one of the Twelve," almost as if he were unknown, although he had just been presented to readers in the same way in 14:10-11. But that is not a certain indication, since the "sons of Zebedee" are also introduced several times in Mark (1:19; 3:17; 10:35), signs, in each case, of separate traditions.

maries: betrayal, condemnation, execution, and resurrection (cf. especially Mk 10:33-34).[8] The Johannine account also makes a new beginning with Jesus' arrest (Jn 18:1ff.). Here Jesus' teaching concludes with the great farewell discourses.

We could just as easily imagine a much more extensive long form.[9] Because the synoptic pericopes parallel the Johannine order more than coincidentally from about Jn 11:47 onward, the precanonical Passion account could have begun with the entry into Jerusalem. In that case, it would have had a unitary bridge stretching from the acclamation of Jesus as "king" to his execution as "king of the Jews."

The fact is that we do not know the exact dimensions of the Passion story, and the course of its development is equally opaque to us.[10] It is possible that the first version was a connected account of the crucifixion, which was then expanded into the "short form" of the Passion story and subsequently to the long form. But it is also possible that there was a long account at an early date, and that this account was revised with additions—or perhaps there were two long versions that were blended into a single account.[11]

The following investigations of clues to locality and dates in the Passion story are planned in such a way as to take into account our lack of knowledge of the story's scope and internal layers. We will inquire about the characterization of persons within the Passion story. People are often described in such a way that the implicit hearer needs previous knowledge in order to identify them and their roles correctly. These kinds of "indica-

---

8. J. Jeremias (*Abendmahlsworte*, 88–89) refers especially to the Passion predictions as "Passion summaries" to support the idea of a pre-Markan Passion story. This argument is still valid if we take the Passion predictions to be Markan redaction. Just as the redactional miracle summaries refer to Mark's received miracle tradition, redactional Passion summaries could presume a received Passion tradition. The fact that these Passion summaries do not begin where the Passion story in Mark begins (in 14:1ff.) could favor the idea that we are dealing with a traditional body of material not dependent on Mark. On the other hand, 14:1ff. begins with the necessary steps toward that "handing over" with which the Passion summaries begin.

9. So T. A. Mohr, *Markus- und Johannespassion*. R. Pesch (*Das Markusevangelium* 2:1ff.) went still further, postulating a Passion story reaching back to the messianic confession in Mk 8:27ff., which Mark, as a conservative redactor, had taken over without any major alterations.

10. Jeremias (*Abendmahlsworte*, 83–90) supposes a development from the brief kerygma in 1 Cor 15:3b-5 to a short account beginning with the arrest, which was then expanded into the long account. G. Schneider (*Die Passion nach den drei älteren Evangelien* [Munich, 1973] 25ff.) thinks that the account of the crucifixion is the kernel of the tradition, which was then expanded backward to the point of Jesus' arrest.

11. For example, Schenke (*Der gekreuzigte Christus*, 141ff.) and D. Dormeyer (*Die Passion Jesu*) suppose a pre-Markan stage of redaction. W. Schenk (*Passionsbericht*) posits a Passion account written in the historical present and an apocalyptic Passion tradition, which are worked together in Mk 11:1ff.

tions of familiarity" point to a relative proximity to the persons described, or to traditions about them.

As to the unknown scope of the Passion account, it would be interesting to learn whether these indications of familiarity are more frequent in certain parts of the Passion story and missing in other parts. Regarding the internal layering of the story, indications of familiarity in a secondary layer would be just as significant as in the primary text—if they could be dated to a later addition, the primary text would have to be older. But even if we were to doubt the existence of a pre-Markan Passion story altogether, the following inquiries would be useful, either for the assessment of individual traditions or for the historical placement of their redaction.

The impulse to search for indications of familiarity comes from an idea of R. Pesch. He deduced from the fact that "the high priest" in Mk 14:47ff. is not named that the Passion story must have been composed at a time when the high priest Caiaphas (18–37 C.E.) was still in office. Only at the time of his successor would it have been necessary to distinguish the high priests by name.[12] Even though this suggestion has not often been taken up, it should be reason enough to make a systematic study of the description of persons in the Passion story.[13] Only then will we be able to judge what these characterizations can tell us about the traditionists, the addressees, and the origins of the Passion account. We may distinguish three groups of persons:

1. Officials such as Pilate and "the high priest";
2. Persons described
   a. by family connections (Mk 15:21, 40, 47; 16:1)
   b. by place of origin (15:21, 43)
   c. by association with a group (14:43, 67; 15:7);
3. Anonymous persons, such as the one who drew a sword (14:47) and the young man who ran away (14:51).

---

12. According to Pesch (*Das Markusevangelium* 2:21), this fact "indicates (almost conclusively) that Caiaphas was still high priest when the pre-Markan Passion story was first composed and narrated. Caiaphas was in office from 18–37 C.E. It follows that the terminus ante quem of the creation of the pre-Markan Passion story is the year 37 C.E. He illustrates this with a modern analogy: "If I talk about the 'chancellor of the republic,' or the 'president,' my hearers will normally think of the current incumbent. If I want to talk about a previous incumbent, I will add his or her name." But the exodus story speaks of Pharaoh without giving his name, although it was not composed during the reign of the oppressive Pharaoh in the story! If the readers of a narrative can clearly locate it in time by means of other temporal indications, people can appear in it without mention of their names. It is always implied that this is the emperor, pope, and so forth of that time.

13. What follows is the product of a seminar on "cultural context research" and is indebted to some suggestions in a paper by Ute Kinder, "Datierungsindizien für eine vormk Passionstradition."

Even this brief summary suggests the question, Are particular motives discernible in the fact that different people are described differently?

OFFICIALS IN THE PASSION STORY

In Mark, it is striking that Pilate is mentioned by name but not by official title, while the high priest is designated by his office and not by name. We might overlook this fact had Matthew and Luke not corrected their Markan text. At the first mention of the high priest, Matthew adds the name "Caiaphas" (Mt 26:3, 57), and when Pilate first appears, he mentions his office: ἡγεμών (Mt 27:2). Luke has already introduced these persons in a "synchronization" at 3:1-2: the Baptizer appears in the time of Pontius Pilate (ἡγεμονεύοντος Ποντίου Πιλάτου τῆς ᾽Ιουδαίας) and in that of the high priests Annas and Caiaphas. Thus, the two major evangelists correctly introduce the officeholders and speak of them in a way that is accessible to an uninformed reader. Only Mark presupposes a certain familiarity with the persons and events of the story. Can we still discern what it is that he presumes?

Readers of Mark's Passion story know from the preceding Gospel account that there are "high priests" (in the plural) who, together with the scribes and elders, are responsible for Jesus' rejection (cf. 8:31; 10:33; 11:18, 27, etc.). When, beginning with 14:47, the text speaks without further preparation of "the high priest" (singular), readers apparently know that one among the group of high priests stands out as representative of the Jewish community as a whole. Neither the author nor the readers have any need for explanation of the relationship between high priests (plural) and high priest (singular).[14]

Previous knowledge of Pilate is also expected: readers of Mark must know that Jesus, in traveling from Galilee to Jerusalem, has moved from the territory of a Herodian prince (Mk 6:14ff.) to that of Pilate. They are also supposed to know that Pilate is the Roman prefect. None of this is explained.[15]

---

14. The two parallel authors treat the problem more elegantly. According to Lk 3:1 there are two high priests in office, "Annas and Caiaphas," and the trial is accordingly held before the high priests (plural). Luke speaks of "the high priest" in the singular only in mentioning the "slave of the high priest" or the "high priest's house" (Lk 22:50, 54). In Matthew one could suppose that the high priests assembled in the house of their colleague, Caiaphas (Mt 26:3, 57), who appears as "master of the house," so to speak. But the parallel authors also have the problem of switching between "the high priest" and "the high priests."

15. The audience would have known that the prefect was called "Pontius Pilate," but we learn Pilate's praenomen only from Lk 3:1 and 1 Tim 6:13. It is a later addition in the text tradition of Mt 27:2.

Why is one person characterized only by his office, the other only by name? If "Pilate" is a familiar name to the readers, why should they not know "Caiaphas" as well? The following interpretation seems probable: as regards Jewish institutions, the proceeding against Jesus is attributed to the "office," independently of its concrete incumbent, while with respect to Roman institutions, the actual person receives the blame. This emphasizes that Roman prefects are not against Jesus (and Christianity) qua institution; however, in the conflict between Jews and Christians, the discords are connected directly to the institution. Apologetic motives may lurk in the background: it would not be helpful to emphasize tensions between Jesus and the powerful Romans, but it would be less dangerous to depict him in conflict with Jews.[16] The causal connections expressed unconsciously in the description of officials could, however, be founded on concrete experience. Within Palestine, in the period after the death of Jesus, we hear mainly about conflicts with Jewish officials. The martyrdoms that are recorded either are attributable, as in the case of Stephen, to a quasi-legal popular proceeding (Acts 7:54ff.)[17] or fall, like the execution of James, son of Zebedee, within the reign of Agrippa I (41–44 C.E.) or in a vacancy in the office of procurator, which occurred in the year 62 C.E., at which time James, the brother of the Lord, was executed (*Ant.* 20.200–201). Thus, persecutions always occur when there is no representative of Roman authority in the country.[18] In fact, the Romans even appear as a protective force in one instance: they rescue Paul from a plot by his countrymen (Acts 23:12ff.). If the Passion account was formed in Palestine, which is suggested by the existence of these indications of familiarity, it could reflect the structure of the life-situation there. Contrary to historical reality, the Sanhedrin receives a greater share of the "blame" because that reflects the experiences of the years that followed.

There could be still another reason for the anonymity of the high priest. His name was certainly known among Christians; it is impossible that Matthew, Luke, and John would have identified him with the same person, independently of one another. They are repeating traditional

---

16. S.G.F. Brandon (*Trial of Jesus of Nazareth*) interprets the whole Gospel of Mark as an apologetic work by Roman Christians to distance themselves from Judaism, in order that they may not be subjected to the hatred of Jews that was current in the period after 70 C.E.

17. The sanctions against real and supposed blasphemers of the temple were a form of Jewish community court proceeding that was regarded as legal and was tolerated by the Romans. The temple was a kind of "legal enclave" within the Roman prefecture of Judea. H. Schwier gives an extensive documentation in *Ideologische und theologische Faktoren*, 61–65.

18. These martyrdoms have been intensively discussed in connection with the question about the authority of the Sanhedrin to pass death sentences. Let me mention as examples of summary descriptions O. Betz, "Probleme des Prozesses Jesu"; A. Strobel, *Stunde*, esp. 21ff.; and the brief sketch by Lührmann in *Markusevangelium*, 251–52.

knowledge. Therefore, we must suppose that there was deliberate silence about him in the oldest Passion account. And there is a probable reason for this, namely, the fact that the house of Annas and Caiaphas was an important power factor in Jerusalem and Judea in the period before the fall of the temple.[19] When Caiaphas was deposed, together with Pilate, in 36–37 C.E., the office of high priest remained in his family. Vitellius, the Syrian legate, first replaced him with his brother-in-law, Jonathan, son of Ananus (*Ant.* 18.95), but shortly thereafter deposed Jonathan and installed his brother Theophilus (*Ant.* 18.123). The same Jonathan was offered the high priesthood again under Agrippa I, but declined in favor of his brother Matthias (*Ant.* 19.316). He later played an important role under Cumanus (ca. 50–52 C.E.): together with other Jewish leaders, he was sent as a prisoner to Rome (*Bell.* 2.243) and was released at the behest of Agrippa II (*Ant.* 20.136–37). The procurator Felix (55/60–62) had him killed, which is understandable only if this action rid him of an influential aristocrat (*Bell.* 2.256; *Ant.* 20.163). The great power of his house is clear from the fact that his son Ananus was high priest for a few months in the year 62, and during that time acted ruthlessly against the Christians, with the result that he lost his office due to the protests of those devoted to the law (*Ant.* 20.200–201). Ananus experienced a comeback in the first phase of the Jewish war, leading the uprising, but fell victim to radical factions (*Bell.* 4.314–25). It is significant that the last legal high priest of the sanctuary, Matthias, was a grandson of Annas (*Ant.* 19.316). Altogether, we know of eight high priests from the house of Annas in the period from 6 to 66 C.E. (Fig. 5).

Thus, between 30 and 70 C.E. there was no time when Caiaphas and his family were not powerful. This was especially true of the 30s and 40s, when they supplied the high priests, and in the 50s and 60s, when they exercised considerable political influence. Their Sadducean mentality is attested by *Ant.* 20.199 and can be inferred from Acts 4:1ff. Their enmity toward the new Jewish sect of "Christians" is apparent in their proceedings against Jesus, the apostles, and the brother of the Lord (*Ant.* 20.200–201). In the rabbinic literature they are represented as powerful and wealthy (*b. Pesah.* 57a; *t. Men.* 13:8) and are criticized (*m. Ker.* 1:7ff.).[20] Traditions circulating in their sphere of influence were well advised not to mention their names in a negative context.

It was quite different in the case of Pilate. He lost his office in 37 C.E. because of complaints by the Samaritans. Philo (*Leg. Gai.* 302) attests that

---

19. On the high priests, see E. Schürer, *History of the Jewish People* 2:227–36.
20. Cf. J. Guttmann, "Ananos."

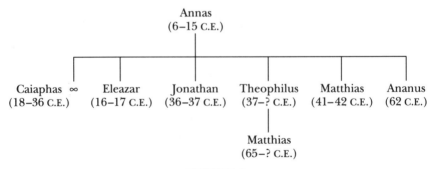

FIGURE 5
High priests from the house of Annas and Caiaphas 6–66 C.E.

his "image" was poor in the 40s.[21] He speaks of "the briberies, the insults, the robberies, the outrages and wanton injuries, the executions without trial constantly repeated, the ceaseless and supremely grievous cruelty" of which Pilate was accused. Josephus also writes of him mainly in negative terms, mentioning a series of conflicts that could have been avoided by a more judicious conduct of office (*Ant.* 18.55ff.). There was no reason not to mention Pilate by name in placing blame for Jesus' execution on him. Josephus, a resident of Jerusalem, attests that in that city he was the subject of more negative tradition than many other prefects and procurators.

PERSONS DESCRIBED IN THE PASSION STORY

While the two officials appear in the Passion story only by name or office, we find there a series of other persons mentioned by name and briefly described in terms of their family relationships, place of origin, association with a group, or function. This is all the more noticeable because Mark's Gospel contains comparatively few persons who are both named and described. In studying Table 4, it should be kept in mind that chapters 1–13 of Mark are related to the Passion story in a ratio of about 5:1.

---

21. In the first instance, Philo is only a witness to the fact that Pilate had a bad image in Alexandria. But his description of Pilate is found in Agrippa's long petition to Gaius. If this rests on an authentic text (so, most recently, J.-P. Lémonon, *Pilate*, 208–9), Pilate's bad reputation would also be attested in Palestine. Still, Agrippa I's petition primarily represents Philo's point of view.

TABLE 4
Persons Mentioned by Name with Additional Description

Characterized by	*In Mark 1–13*	*In Mark 14–16*
Family	Andrew, brother of Simon (1:16). John and James, sons of Zebedee (1:19; 3:17; 10:35). Levi, son of Alpheus (2:14). James, Joses, Judas, and Simon, as brothers of Jesus (6:3). Bartimaeus, son of Timaeus (10:46).	Simon, father of Alexander and Rufus (15:21). Mary, mother of James the younger and of Joses (15:40; cf. 15:47; 16:1).
Place of origin	Jesus from Nazareth (1:9) or of Nazareth (1:24). Judas Iscariot (?)[22] (3:19).	Jesus of Nazareth, or the man from Nazareth (14:67; 16:6). Judas Iscariot (?) (14:10). Peter as Galilean (14:70). Simon of Cyrene (15:21). Mary Magdalene (15:40, 47; 16:1). Joseph of Arimathea (15:43).

(continued)

---

22. Judas Iscariot could be interpreted as "man from Kerioth" (cf. Josh 15:25). Other interpretations connect the word with Latin *sicarius* ("bandit") or derive it from *sheqarya* ("liar"). See the summary of the arguments in M. Limbeck, "Ἰσκαριώθ." He firmly favors the last interpretation. In that case, Mark's Gospel would not have a single mention of anyone's place of origin outside the Passion account, except for "Jesus of Nazareth," and the special quality of the Passion tradition would emerge even more clearly.

TABLE 4 (continued)
Persons Mentioned by Name with Additional Description

Characterized by	In Mark 1–13	In Mark 14–16
Group and Function	John the Baptizer (cf. 1:4; 6:14). Simon the Cananean[23] (3:18). Jairus, the head of the synagogue (5:22).	Judas, one of the Twelve (14:10; 14:43). Peter, "one of them" (14:70). Barabbas, one of the "rebels" (15:7).

1. Notice, regarding the people described by their family connections, that both Simon and the second Mary in 15:40 are not identified as usual, through their fathers, but through their sons.[24] This generally happens only when the sons are better known or more important to the community in which the story is being told than is their father. Thus, for example, Josephus speaks of the Alexandrian alabarch, Alexander, as the father of Tiberius (*Bell.* 5.205), because this Tiberius Alexander, later procurator of Judea (44–46 C.E.), prefect of Egypt (ca. 68 C.E.) and military advisor to Titus, was a far more important figure for readers of the *Bellum Judaicum*. Mark 15:21 and 15:40 should be regarded in the same light, especially since other indications point in the same direction.

Simon of Cyrene would be adequately described by mention of his place of origin, Cyrene (cf. Mk 1:9; 15:40, 43). The addition of the two sons is not necessary to identify him. Matthew and Luke omit them. They have no function in the narrative. The only plausible motive for mentioning their names at this point would be that they are known to the tradi-

---

23. "Simon the Kananaios [Καναναῖος]" is a literal rendering of Hebrew "the fervent," "the zealot" (cf. Lk 6:15; Acts 1:13; *Gospel of the Ebionites*, frag. 1 = Epiphanius *Adv. Haer.* 30.13.2–3). "Cananean," as a description of his place of origin, would be Χαναναῖος (cf. Mt 15:22). See the discussion in M. Hengel, *Die Zeloten*, 72–73. Of course it is not impossible that the author of Mark himself understood "Kananaios" as referring to the place of origin.

24. Identification through the father was the norm in the whole ancient world; cf. H. Rix, "Personennamen." It is also dominant in the Old Testament; cf. L. Köhler, "Archäologisches, Nr. 18," 20–36, esp. 22–24. Only rarely is a father identified by his children.

tionists of the Passion story. That they were members of the Christian community is a probable surmise, but cannot be proved.[25]

In the case of the second Mary, the readers must also bring previous knowledge of her, because the text permits six different translations:

1. καὶ Μαρία ἡ ᾽Ιακώβου τοῦ μικροῦ καὶ ᾽Ιωσῆτος μήτηρ = a woman named "Mary."

   a. Mary, (the wife)   of James the younger and   the mother of Joses
   b. Mary, the mother   of James the younger and   the mother of Joses
   c. Mary, (the daughter)   of James the younger and   the mother of Joses.

2. καὶ Μαρία ἡ ᾽Ιακώβου τοῦ μικροῦ καὶ ᾽Ιωσῆτος μήτηρ = two women, both called Mary, or the second being unnamed.

   a. Mary, (the wife)   of James the younger and   (Mary?) the mother of Joses
   b. Mary, the mother   of James the younger and   (Mary?) the mother of Joses
   c. Mary, (the daughter)   of James the younger and   (Mary?) the mother of Joses.

Not all the translations are equally probable. "Mary, the mother of James the younger and of Joses" (1b) has the advantage of being intelligible without speculative additions. Besides, it corresponds to the view of the author of Matthew, who knows only two Marys: Mary Magdalene and the "other Mary" (Mt 27:61; 28:1).[26] But what is important for us is that the family relationships of Mary were transparent to the traditionists and audi-

---

25. Cf. Dibelius, *Formgeschichte*, 183; idem, "Das historische Problem," 61; Schneider, *Die Passion*, 112. The three personal names in Mk 15:21 have been exploited as place indications, both for Jerusalem and for Rome. Thus Schenke *(Der gekreuzigte Christus*, 91–92) thinks that Simon belonged to Stephen's group, which, according to Acts 6:9, had contact with Diaspora Jews from Cyrene. The early Hellenistic community would have introduced their representative, Simon, in a secondary redaction of the Passion tradition, not least as a polemic jab at the disciples (i.e., the Hebrews in Acts 6:1ff.), who had decamped and were not present at the crucifixion. We should mention at least in passing that a burial chamber in the Kidron Valley dating from the first century contains an inscription for "Alexander, the son of Simon," who may have come from Cyrene; cf. N. Avigad, "Depository of Inscribed Ossuaries in the Kidron Valley." The name "Rufus" has been taken as a clue to the Roman community, since Paul greets someone by that name in Rom 16:13; cf. V. Taylor, *Mark*, 588; E. Lohse, *Die Geschichte des Leidens und Sterbens Jesu Christi*, 92. It is by no means certain that Simon was a member of the community. He is introduced as "a passerby . . . Simon of Cyrene," not as a known figure. By contrast, the names Alexander and Rufus refer to well-known persons. They are not explained.

26. Among others, L. Schottroff ("Maria Magdalena und die Frauen am Grabe Jesu," 8) and Pesch *(Das Markusevangelium* 2:505–7) argue for a total of four women in Mk 15:40 (mainly in the sense of translation 2b above). The critical point for our discussion is that the names as given are so subject to misunderstanding that they presume existing knowledge that enables the readers to identify the persons intended.

ence of the story. They must have known which of the six possible relationships was accurate. We may add a second observation: the distinguishing characterization of James as "the younger" presumes that the audience knows several people with the same name.[27] There are four disciples of Jesus with this name in Mark's Gospel alone. Besides James the younger, we find there the son of Zebedee (Mk 3:17), the brother of the Lord (Mk 6:3), and the son of Alphaeus (Mk 3:18). Two of them are closely connected with the Jerusalem community: James the son of Zebedee was beheaded in Jerusalem between 41 and 44 C.E. (Acts 12:2; cf. Mk 10:35ff.). James the brother of the Lord was the dominant figure in the early community at Jerusalem from the 40s onward and was stoned to death there in 62 C.E. It would have been particularly necessary in Jerusalem to distinguish a "James the younger" (or "the less") from other "older" (or "greater") bearers of that name in the period circa 30–65 C.E.[28]

Let us add a third observation: like Simon of Cyrene, the second Mary mentioned in 15:40 is described in terms of her sons (at least Joses). Once more, the sons are better known to the group of traditionists than are the parents. Again we are returned to the time of the generation after Jesus' appearance, that is, the period between about 40 and 70 C.E. We need to keep in mind that in the Johannine tradition one of the Mary-figures has become the mother of Jesus (Jn 19:25-26). The generation of the sons of these women is still the generation of Jesus and James, the brother of the Lord, who survived Jesus by about thirty years.

---

27. When there is similarity of names in early Christianity, we observe a tendency to distinguish by the use of a nickname. "Simon" is called Simon Peter, and there are Simon the Cananean (Mk 3:18), Simon of Cyrene (Mk 15:21), Simon the leper (Mk 14:3), Simon the tanner (Acts 9:43), and Simon Magus (Acts 8:9). One "Judas" is distinguished from another by the nicknames Iscariot (Mk 3:19) or Barsabbas (Acts 15:22), or by being called "the son of James" (Lk 6:16).

28. The author of Mark leaves open the question of the relationship between "Mary of James the younger and the mother of Joses" (15:40) and the mother of Jesus in Mk 6:3, although in 6:3 a James and Joses are also mentioned in the same order. Since the evangelist made no conscious comparison, he must have taken the names in both places from his tradition, without identifying them. That does not exclude the possibility that the pre-Markan tradition referred to the same Mary. In Jn 19:25-26 we encounter a tradition according to which the mother of Jesus was present at the cross. If we spin out this line of thought, we could conclude that James, the brother of the Lord (Mk 6:3), must be identical with James the younger (15:40). It was especially necessary to distinguish him as the "younger" or "less" from an older or greater James up to the death of James, the son of Zebedee, who had an important place in the original community because he was arrested along with Peter as one of its representatives (Acts 12:1ff.). That would mean that the expression "James the younger" belongs to the time before 44 C.E. Later, James himself was a great figure, for whose sake the *Gospel of Thomas* (*Logion* 12) says that heaven and earth were created. Since the precondition for this reflection—namely, the identity of the Mary in Mk 15:40 with the mother of Jesus—is not certain, it must remain only a vague possibility that cannot be introduced as an argument.

2. The persons identified by their place of origin are also revealing. They are more numerous in the Passion account than the names characterized by their familial relations. What can we learn from them?

First, a trivial item: names relating to place of origin were not created in those same places. Jesus was not called "the Nazarene" in Nazareth, and Joseph was not known in his home town as "Joseph of Arimathea."[29] Thus, the traditionists of the Passion stories are not to be sought in Nazareth, Magdala, or Arimathea (and certainly not in Cyrene). But that is no more informative than the fact that Peter was suspected as a "Galilean" (14:70), because that categorization is made by a Jerusalem maidservant and says nothing about the perspective of the narrator.

A second observation takes us somewhat further. The mention of places of origin presumes that the places named have a differentiating character for the traditionists and the audience—that is, they must be recognizable as alternatives to other place names that are approximately as well known. Towns such as Nazareth, Magdala, and Arimathea are on about the same level as far as their degree of recognition is concerned: outside Palestine there would not be a soul who would have the faintest idea where they were. In these three place-names—and perhaps also in Kerioth, if Ish-Kerioth is to be interpreted as "man from Kerioth"—we encounter a limited Palestinian local perspective. On the other hand, for people who inhabited this limited horizon, a name such as "Cyrene" must have had a distinguishing character—that is, it would appear as an alternative to other provinces or regions, just as Cyrene is encountered in Acts 6:9 in contrast to Alexandria, Cilicia, and Asia. Here we meet a transregional perspective. The combination of local and extraregional horizons would be readily imaginable in a major Palestinian city, and especially in Jerusalem, where Jews from Cyrene are expressly mentioned (Acts 6:9).

A comparison with the statements of origin in Josephus's *Bellum Judaicum* is interesting. As a rule, in that book the father is mentioned for identification, and the place of origin appears only in exceptional cases. There is Syllaeus the Arab (*Bell.* 1.574), Antipater the Samaritan (*Bell.* 1.592), Judas the Galilean (*Bell.* 2.433; cf. 2.118), Niger the Perean (*Bell.* 2.520; 2.566), and Silas the Babylonian (*Bell.* 2.520; 3.11). In the cases of Judas and Niger, Josephus emphasizes specifically that they were called "the Galilean" and "the Perean" respectively—that is, their nicknames were commonly known attributes (*Bell.* 2.433; 2.520). In his book, which was intended for a broad, Greek-speaking group of readers, Josephus thus

---

29. An illuminating example is the founder of the fourth Jewish sect, Judas, in Josephus's work. In *Ant.* 18.4 he is called a "Gaulanite," in 18.23 a "Galilean." "Gaulanite" could have been his nickname in Galilee, and "Galilean" his epithet in Judea (cf. *Ant.* 5.37).

mentions, for the most part, large areas such as Samaria, Galilee, or Perea to identify persons because he can expect his readers to have sufficient knowledge to distinguish them. The two exceptions (*Bell.* 3.233; 5.474) confirm the rule, for in these cases the obscure town of Ruma or Garis is supplemented by a mention of Galilee.[30] The only concrete place mentioned without explanation is the world-renowned city of "Babylon." In the Passion account, the local perspective is clearly more limited than that of Josephus.[31]

Finally, let me briefly indicate a third consideration: the identification of persons was made in the ancient world by mentioning their fathers. This was as true in Palestine and Greece as in Rome. For that very reason it is remarkable that in the Passion account, while more people are identified than elsewhere in the synoptic tradition, none of them is identified through his or her father. Behind this fact lies a concrete historical process. The father's name is important in the place where the father and family are known. But the first Christian community gathered in Jerusalem was made up of people who, at least in part, had moved there from other places. In their case, the place of origin was more significant than the name of the father. If we include the fact that the first Christians often joined the followers of Jesus after making a radical break with their parents and leaving the family home (cf. Mt 8:20-21), it is plausible that fathers became less important as points of identification. People were identified by their fathers in the larger society, but not in the Christian community, for the community is the *familia dei*, which replaces the earthly family.

From the names that are mentioned, we can in any case learn one thing about the community behind the Passion account: it included people who had come to Palestine from the Diaspora. A community composed in that fashion—of Palestinians from Galilee and Hellenists from the Diaspora—is attested at the beginning of Christianity in Jerusalem. Everything points to the fact that the Jerusalem community is to be regarded as the point of origin for the Passion traditions.

3. Three of the persons named in the Passion account are described in

---

30. Josephus speaks of "Netiras and Philip, also Galileans, from the village of Ruma" (*Bell.* 3.233). Here Josephus supplements the unknown village "Ruma" (present Rumah) with the known region of "Galilee." In *Bell.* 5.474, Garis is located for the readers with the aid of the phrase "a town in Galilee."

31. A glance at the *Antiquities* confirms this impression. Josephus speaks of Berosus the Chaldean (*Ant.* 1.93); Hieronymus the Egyptian (1.94); Nicolas of Damascus (1.94); Herodotus of Halicarnassus (8.260); Strabo of Cappadocia (14.104); Judas the Gaulanite, from the city of Gamala (18.4); and Judas the Galilean (18.23). All these are designations of place of origin that would be intelligible to a reader outside Palestine. Judas is the only exception.

terms of their association with some group. Judas is introduced twice as εἷς τῶν δώδεκα (Mk 14:10, 43), underscoring the point that one of Jesus' most intimate circle of disciples had betrayed him. This repetition need not necessarily point to an old Passion account that mentioned Judas for the first time at 14:43,[32] especially since the familiar nickname "Iscariot" (3:19; 14:10) is missing.[33]

More revealing is the assignment of Peter to the group of disciples. A maidservant identifies him as a follower of Jesus of Nazareth. She has seen him with Jesus. Peter denies it twice. Then other bystanders address him as a follower of Jesus, this time on the basis of the general observation "you are a Galilean" (14:70). It is simply presumed that Galileans are easily identifiable, through either their clothes or their manner of speech.[34] Peter had spoken in the meantime, so it is quite logical for Matthew to have the high priest's slave say explicitly: "your accent betrays you" (Mt 26:73). The narrating community behind the Markan Passion account felt no need of explanation at this point. Was it because they were acquainted with this situation?[35] That is at least a possible explanation, the plausibility of which is, however, weakened by the fact that Luke gives no more explanation of Peter's being recognizably a Galilean than does Mark (cf. Lk 22:59).

The most interesting figure among the three who are described in

---

32. Jeremias *(Abendmahlsworte,* 89) offers the following three arguments for the old Passion account's having begun with Jesus' arrest: (1) the agreement with the Passion summaries; (2) the introduction of Judas as an unknown person, with a parallel (independent of Mark?) in Lk 22:47; and (3) the neutral description of the "disciples" as bystanders. G. Schneider ("Die Verhaftung Jesu") also sees in Mk 14:43ff. the beginning of an old Passion story, but regards the description of Judas as redactional (cf. p. 196). It is meant to emphasize the monstrousness of the betrayal by a member of the closest circle of disciples. But it is not clear why a Passion account beginning with Jesus' arrest would not also have included the preparations for the arrest (Mk 14:1-2, 10-11) and other parts of Mark 14: the announcement of the betrayer, the flight of the disciples, and Peter's denial.

33. Some manuscripts (A, K, Θ, 565, 1241, 1424) insert the name "Iscariot." The more complete description of the betrayer here is certainly no sign of the introduction of an otherwise unknown Judas!

34. On the different language patterns in Galilee and Jerusalem, see C. Rabin, *Hebrew and Aramaic in the First Century,* 1007–39. "While we may assume that in Jerusalem and Judaea mishnaic Hebrew was still the ruling language, and Aramaic took the second place, the situation must have been reversed in areas such as the coastal plain and Galilee. There Aramaic, and possibly Greek, were the dominant languages spoken by people from all classes, while Hebrew mainly functioned as a literary language" (p. 1036).

35. According to Schneider *(Die Passion,* 72–79) and Schenke *(Der gekreuzigte Christus,* 21–22), this bit of tradition (which they think was handed down in isolation) reflects the situation of the Jerusalem community, whose members were in danger of being denounced to the authorities. Weak-kneed and apostatized Christians were given Peter's example as a warning to repent. Was the fact that the community contained a good many Galileans a factor here? According to J. Gnilka *(Evangelium nach Markus* 2:291), the identification of Peter as a Galilean even "suggests that the tradition should be located in Jerusalem."

terms of a group is Barabbas. There are several remarkable things about the way he is presented.

First, he is introduced as ὁ λεγόμενος Βαραββᾶς, as if he had already been mentioned somewhere. But previously there had only been a reference to the common custom of a Passover amnesty. So should we translate "The (prisoner) named (to be released in accord with this amnesty) was Barabbas . . ."?[36] But the people's petition for the release of a prisoner is introduced only at a later point (15:8), and the nomination is left open. That is why Pilate can present two prisoners from whom to choose. It is more likely that the narrators presume that everyone knows who the "one called Barabbas" is. Matthew writes in this vein, saying that it is a question of "a notorious prisoner, called Barabbas" (Mt 27:16). What Matthew explicitly states, from his narrative distance, Mark naively presumes, namely, that Barabbas is well known. Is this not an indication of familiarity that betrays a remarkable closeness to the events?[37]

Second, Barabbas is not expressly described as a rebel. The literal reading is that he was "in prison with [μετά] the rebels," so that the narrative may have regarded him as innocent. The preposition μετά can mean that someone is thought to be part of a group but really does not belong to it. Thus, in Lk 22:37, Jesus is "counted among the lawless" (μετὰ ἀνόμων), and in Lk 24:5 he is thought to be "among the dead" (μετὰ τῶν νεκρῶν), but in reality he is innocent and alive. However, μετά can also indicate an objectively real adherence to a group. Thus, Peter belongs "with" Jesus, μετὰ τοῦ Ναζαρηνοῦ (Mk 14:67). Luke was the first to create a clear picture in this regard. For him, Barabbas "had been put in prison for an insurrection that had taken place in the city, and for murder" (Lk 23:19).

---

36. The dysfunctional λεγόμενος can be interpreted in three ways: (1) Barabbas was known at the time (cf. Mt 27:16); (2) Barabbas was the prisoner who had been designated for release (so Pesch, *Das Markusevangelium* 2:463); (3) the word "Jesus," in the original text, has been omitted (cf. Mt 27:16 Θ f¹ 700). This Jesus is distinguished from Jesus of Nazareth by the nickname "Barabbas." Klostermann (*Das Markusevangelium*, 220) thinks there was originally an additional "Jesus" also in Mk 15:7.

37. The Barabbas pericope is often regarded as unhistorical. Two partly conflicting arguments are adduced. First, an amnesty on feast days or at Passover (Jn 18:39) cannot be documented (cf. P. Winter, *On the Trial of Jesus*, 94). In that case, we must explain how the narrator's fantasy came to create this custom. The second argument closes this gap: the Barabbas pericope was created secondarily, on the basis of common customs of release of prisoners at festivals in the ancient world, to relieve the Romans of blame. The most recent author to advance this argument is R. L. Merritt, "Jesus Barabbas and the Paschal Pardon," 57–68. Defenders of the pericope's historicity also suggest two partly conflicting arguments in its favor. Supposing that there was no general Passover amnesty, it is possible that the tradition has generalized the unique case of Barabbas to a common institution. So Gnilka, *Evangelium nach Markus* 2:300–301, 304. Or the assumption that there was no Passover amnesty is disputed: it could be that a Jewish custom was adopted by the Romans out of respect for provincial legal traditions. This is the position of Strobel, *Stunde*, esp. 120–21.

By contrast, the Markan version could possibly be understood to say that Barabbas was innocent, or at least that he was not implicated in murder. In that case, the people's petition for his release would be understandable.[38]

Finally, the text speaks quite simply of "*the* rebels," who were taken prisoner during "*the* insurrection." The repetition of the definite article suggests to the readers that they should know what is meant. Matthew omits reference to the insurrection. Luke alters it skillfully: Barabbas has been arrested because of a certain insurrection that had taken place in the city (διὰ στάσιν τινὰ; Lk 23:19). The third evangelist thus takes over the role of the narrator who acquaints us with unknown events. Mark possesses a similar narrative competence, as the introduction of the Jordan (1:5), Gethsemane (14:32), and Golgotha (15:22) shows. But here his text calmly presumes knowledge that would not have been available to readers only a short time later. The text must have been composed at a time when no one would have been likely to confuse the rebellion it refers to with any other. There were a number of clashes under Pilate. Josephus even calls one of them, the conflict over the aqueduct, an "uprising" (στάσις; *Ant.* 18.62) or "uproar" (ταραχή; *Bell.* 2.175). The struggle over images and the Samaritan conflict fall under the designation θορυβεῖν or θόρυβος (cf. *Ant.* 18.58, 85–87). In Lk 13:1ff. we hear about an otherwise unknown conflict with pilgrims. In short, there was a lot of unrest, and yet the narrative community of the Passion account felt itself adequately informed by a reference to "the insurrection." We can only suppose that the text was composed before the next great uprising; after that, the author would have "historicized" the account by distinguishing the previous "stasis" from the more recent one. The next unrest coupled with bloody clashes that struck Jerusalem was the appearance of Theudas under Cuspius Fadus (44–45 C.E.; cf. Acts 5:36; *Ant.* 20.97–98). Is it possible that the story of Barabbas is older than that?[39]

---

38. Pesch (*Das Markusevangelium* 2:463) points to this possibility. If there is another tradition visible in Mk 15:6ff., according to which Barabbas was a fellow prisoner who was not guilty of murder, there would be no apologetic motive in this account intending to blame "the Jews" instead of Pilate. Even now it is only the high priests who are active in the Barabbas pericope, and not, as usual, the scribes and elders as well. The high priests are Jesus' real opponents: even here there is no evidence of a general accusation against the Jews. Compare the version in Jn 18:38-40, where it is not the high priests, but "the Jews" who ask Barabbas's release. Here there is no longer a distinction made between the high priests and the people.

39. Lührmann (*Markusevangelium*, 256) thinks otherwise. He sees in the mention of "the stasis" an anachronism on the part of the author of Mark, for whom "the insurrection" is identical with the Jewish war. The different phases of the resistance between the time of Jesus and 66–70 C.E. have become a single event from his point of view. That can be true of the Markan redaction, but it does not exclude the possibility that Mark took over an earlier text.

The investigation to this point has thus drawn together a number of indications of familiarity within the Markan Passion account that point to its having been shaped in the generation following Jesus' activity, and probably in Jerusalem. But we have not yet examined all the persons in the Passion story. Two figures that may be crucial to our inquiry are still missing.

ANONYMOUS PERSONS IN THE PASSION STORY

In the tradition about Jesus' arrest, two anonymous persons appear almost simultaneously: a "bystander," who cuts off the ear of the "slave of the high priest" with his sword (Mk 14:47), and an anonymous young man who evades arrest by running away (Mk 14:51-52). Both are introduced with τις, and the one who draws his sword is even described as εἷς δέ τις τῶν παρεστηκότων, as if Mark wanted to say "someone or other among those who stood near." Εἷς with the genitive is the usual formula in Mark's Gospel for introducing an anonymous person, while τις occurs otherwise only in Mk 11:3 and 15:36.[40]

The relationship of these two people to Jesus within the narrative is a matter of debate. Are they meant to be followers of Jesus? Are they people who are there by accident? Or is the man with the sword one of the "police" who hits the wrong person? We must admit that the unprejudiced reader thinks of people who are with Jesus. But is the correction of such innocence by some exegetes completely unjustified?[41]

The story speaks of Jesus' arrest by a "crowd" who come with swords and clubs to seize him. The bailiffs have swords. Therefore, when in the course of the scuffle someone draws a sword, could it not be one of these bailiffs, whose sword strikes the wrong man? Can we attribute the use of force to the adherents of the preacher of nonviolence? The problem is, however, that the first Christians certainly did not understand the text in that way. For Luke, the man with the sword is one of the οἱ περὶ αὐτόν, thus one of the disciples (Lk 22:49). In Matthew, also, he is "one of those with Jesus." John 18:10-11 even identifies him with Peter. The tradition always regards him as a disciple, and it is all the more striking that in

---

40. Εἷς + genitive in Mk 5:22; 6:15; 8:28; 9:17, 42; 12:28; 13:1; 14:20. The plural τινες is rather common.

41. Schenke (*Die gekreuzigte Christus*, 118–20) and Pesch (*Das Markusevangelium* 2:400) argue particularly for an explanation of the man with the sword as one of the arresting party. It is true that the disciples in the arrest scene are not clearly identified as such. But when it says that "they all fled," the reader will obviously think of the disciples, even if they are not expressly called "disciples."

Mark's Gospel this sword-wielder is not clearly identified with Jesus. His relationship to Jesus remains obscured—or is it deliberately designed to remain so?

The same is true of the much-discussed young man in 14:51. He is following Jesus, with the others: συνηκολούθει αὐτῷ. In Mk 5:37, the verb συνακολουθεῖν refers to the innermost group of disciples, but that cannot be the intention in the report of Jesus' arrest because immediately before this it was stated that "all of them deserted him and fled." It is only after the flight of "all" the disciples that we hear of the "young man" running away after the failed attempt to seize him. Thus, it remains obscure here again whether he is a follower of Jesus who narrowly escapes arrest by running away, or whether he does not belong to the more intimate circle of disciples at all. Again we can ask whether his relationship to Jesus is meant to remain shadowy.

Three kinds of interpretation may be distinguished within the exegetical speculations about this young man:

1. The disciple in Mk 14:51 is a *witness* to the events. He is mentioned in the narrative in order to establish the credibility of these happenings.[42] It can be objected that Jesus' arrest and the flight of the disciples are two facts that need no witnesses because all the disciples were present. Besides, the witnessing function of the young man would be more convincing if we knew his name, as in the cases of Simon of Cyrene and his sons in 15:21.

2. The young man's flight in Mk 14:51-52 could be included as a *fulfillment of Scripture*. Amos speaks of the "stout of heart" who will flee away naked on the day of the Lord (Amos 2:16).[43] But the "stout of heart" (plural) are something different from a young man (singular); moreover, at this point the Septuagint speaks of someone who is "persecuted," which is not in Mk 14:51; and finally, Amos has otherwise left few traces on the Passion account (although we should note Mk 15:33). The interpretation of Mk 14:51 as Joseph typology is still less probable.[44] Joseph left his robe behind in the hands of Potiphar's wife, but that was for very different reasons (cf. Gen 39:12).

3. The symbolic interpretation of the young man appears in two variants. In one, his flight is seen as a *symbol* of the rescue of Jesus out of the hand of his oppressors, from whom he is saved through his

---

42. Cf. Dibelius, "Das historische Problem," 60–61; Taylor, *Mark*, 561–62. Zahn (*Einleitung in das Neue Testament*, 250) wishes to identify this young man with the evangelist himself.
43. So A. Loisy, *L'évangile selon Marc*, 425; Klostermann, *Das Markusevangelium*, 153.
44. So H. Waetjen, "Ending of Mark."

resurrection. In this case, all manner of latent connections between the young man in Mk 14:51 and the one at the empty tomb are suggested.[45] The Markan context indicates rather the contrary interpretation, whereby his flight is not a symbol of rescue, but of failure and the disciples' lack of understanding.[46] But in that case, why is he not more clearly described as a disciple?

It remains an open question what the narrative function of these two anonymous persons may have been. Are they really only witnesses, types, or symbols? Or are they included for a very simple reason? It was indisputable that one of Jesus' inner circle had betrayed him, and equally indisputable that all the disciples had fled. The reasons for this had to be made credible in the community. Would it not have been a relief to be able to say that at least one person had tried to rescue Jesus by force (14:47)? Was the image of Jesus' total abandonment not at least a little less depressing if an attempt was made to arrest someone else along with him? The key word κρατεῖν is found both in Mk 14:46 and in 14:51.

But why the anonymity of these two disciples of Jesus? Why the lack of clarity about their relationship to him? We cannot simply gloss over this anonymity, because the point of the whole pericope is that Jesus is pointed out by a betrayer. Even the dark night and the out-of-the-way place offer him no protection. Jesus loses his "anonymity," but two people close to him remain anonymous. When we consider that, in the Passion tradition, other people are quite often described in some detail, these two anonymous persons are all the more striking.

It seems to me that the narrative motive for this anonymity is not hard to guess: both of them run afoul of the "police." The one who draws his sword commits no minor offense when he cuts off someone's ear. Had the blow fallen only slightly awry, he could have wounded the man in the head or throat. This blow with a sword is violence with possibly mortal consequences. The anonymous young man has also offered resistance. In the struggle, his clothes are torn off, so that he has to run away naked. Both these people were in danger in the aftermath. As long as the high priest's slave was alive (and as long as the scar from the sword cut was visible) it would have been inopportune to mention their names; it would not even have been wise to identify them as members of the early Christian community. Their anonymity is for their protection, and the obscur-

---

45. So A. Vanhoye, "La fuite du jeune homme."
46. So H. Fleddermann, "Flight of a Naked Young Man."

ing of their positive relationship to Jesus is a strategy of caution.[47] Both the teller and the hearers know more about these two people. Only they could tell us who they were, whether Peter was the one with the sword, whether both are the same person,[48] and whether reference was made to them in order to make the story of Jesus' end more credible. All that will have to remain closed to us.

John's Gospel shows that the idea of protective anonymity was not remote from the minds of those who narrated the Passion stories. There, the sword-wielder is identified as Peter, and the high priest's wounded slave as Malchus (Jn 18:10). This identification enables the Fourth Gospel to offer a motive for Peter's denial that makes sense within the narrative: Peter denies Jesus for the third time when he is questioned by one of the high priest's slaves who is a relative of Malchus. This person asks him specifically about the scene at Jesus' arrest: "Did I not see you in the garden with him?" (Jn 18:26). It is by no means necessary to accept the Johannine version as historical or closer to the original. What is crucial is that even ancient traditionists and narrators were aware that the man with the sword would have been in danger had his identity been revealed.

We can cite two instances from the contemporary literature in which we may suspect the use of protective anonymity. Justin, in his second *Apology*, tells the story of a respectable Christian woman who had divorced her husband because she disapproved of his "dissolute life," whereupon her husband had denounced her as a Christian. She was able to obtain a delay of her trial from the emperor, but this did not prevent her Christian teacher from being sentenced to death, and with him two other Christians who had protested the sentence (*Apology* 2.2). It is striking that we learn the names of two of these martyrs, Ptolemaeus and Lucius, but the principal figure remains anonymous. Justin is writing at Rome, and the woman is still alive. It would certainly have been easy for anyone to learn her name, but tact and caution led Justin to conceal it.[49] The second example comes from Josephus and is not quite so illuminating. When, during the siege of Jerusalem, Josephus discovered three of his relatives among a

---

47. J. M. Lagrange (*Évangile selon Saint Jean*, 458) had already attributed the anonymity of the man with the sword to caution, "car l'administration romaine goûtait peu ce recours à l'epée." C. H. Dodd's opinion is similar: "It was not politic to let him be represented as a man of violence" (*Historical Tradition in the Fourth Gospel*, 80). We must, however, distinguish the hypothesis of anonymity for the sake of protection from the opinion that it was Peter who wielded the sword.

48. So M. Goguel, *Das Leben Jesu*, 339–40.

49. If we can identify this teacher, Ptolemy, with the author of the letter to Flora (Epiphanius, *Adv. Haer.* 33.3–7), the woman could have been called Flora. Ptolemy's letter includes divorce among its topics. On this, see P. Lampe, *Die stadtrömischen Christen*, 200–203.

group of crucified men, he begged Titus to spare their lives. They were taken down from their crosses, and one survived. Josephus mentions no names (*Vita* 420). It would not have been a good idea to broadcast the name of someone who had at one time been sentenced to death by the Romans. Both cases concern people who had gotten into trouble with the Roman state. Certainly, the motives for anonymity are different in the two cases, but in both instances silence serves the interests of those concerned.

To return to the arrest of Jesus, it could be objected to the considerations detailed here that we are presuming what first needs to be proved, namely, that the narrative corresponds in its essential details to the historical events. But even if Mk 14:47 and 14:51-52 represent legendary additions—which I do not believe—that would not change much. An endangered minority would not wish to attract unnecessary suspicion to itself through its stories. An invented follower of Jesus who threatened the life of another with a blow of his sword would be as much of a problem for the community as a real swordsman. Anyone who associates with people who, in the eyes of the authorities, have committed "criminal actions" is helpless to avoid suspicion. The fact that Jesus was executed as a result of a Roman legal process was already a burden to the young community. For that reason, I think that the story of the one who drew a sword and the fleeing young man are no more invented than is the crucifixion of Jesus.

The question of the literary origins of Mk 14:43-52 is a separate problem. The story of Jesus' arrest does not seem to be homogeneous.[50] We could simply eliminate the two "problematic" episodes—what remains would be an apophthegm that presumes a larger narrative context, but could be told as a separate unit (perhaps Mk 14:43-46, with vv. 48-49 containing the point of the apophthegm). It is possible that such a version once existed. There was certainly motive enough to leave out the two damaging episodes. But it is likely that from the very beginning people told various stories about Jesus' arrest, either in a form that represented the opponents as cunning and deceitful (in which case the story could end with a saying of Jesus criticizing the clandestine character of their actions), or in a form that told of the unsuccessful resistance of some of Jesus' followers.

If we are correct in our hypothesis of protective anonymity, the location of the Passion tradition would be unmistakable. Only in Jerusalem was

---

50. Linnemann (*Studien zur Passionsgeschichte*, 42ff.) went farthest in the decomposition of the pericope. She distinguishes three traditions: (1) a biographical apophthegm in Mk 14:43, 48-49; (2) a betrayal narrative in vv. 44-46; and (3) fragments of an arrest narrative telling of the disciples' resistance in vv. 47, 50, 51-52. Schneider ("Die Verhaftung Jesu," 188–89) criticizes her analysis, but arrives de facto at an extensive dissoluton of the tradition into an originally isolated narrative (14:43-46) that was later expanded by addition.

there reason to draw a cloak of anonymity over followers of Jesus who had endangered themselves by their actions. The date could also be pinpointed: parts of the Passion account would have to have been composed within the generation of the eyewitnesses and their contemporaries, that is, somewhere between 30 and 60 C.E.

REFLECTIONS ON THE SITUATION IN WHICH THE PASSION STORY WAS COMPOSED

None of the verses we have studied is assigned to the same layer by all the literary critics; they do not even agree on assigning them to a "relatively older" or "relatively newer" layer. But even so, our results are relevant because, if indications of locality and familiarity appear in a secondary layer, the primary layer must be still older. Thus, for example, from the texts in Table 5, L. Schenke assigns only Mk 14:47 and 14:55ff. to the original; Mk 15:7 and 15:21 are thought to be secondary. The consequence, in his analysis, is that even at the time when the Passion account was being revised, "the insurrection" and the name "Barabbas" must have been as familiar to the tellers and hearers as "Simon of Cyrene" and his two sons.

Another result is still more important: the indications of locality and familiarity begin with the arrest of Jesus. This accords with the supposition that an older account existed, beginning at the latest with Jesus' arrest (R. Bultmann, J. Jeremias, Schenke). On the basis of the indications of date we have discussed, it could have been composed in Jerusalem, in the generation just after Jesus. The question is whether we can still further limit the situation of its composition, at least tentatively. Taking for granted that narratives are marked by the conditions under which their narrating community lives, we wish to develop the hypothesis that the choice, shaping, and stylizing of traditions into a connected Passion account was especially feasible in the 40s.[51]

1. The narrating community behind the Markan Passion tradition is convinced that the Sanhedrin can pass sentences of death (Mk 14:64).

---

51. The dating and localization of an original Passion tradition in the first generation of the Jerusalem community (ca. 40–70) is independent of this hypothesis; however, the limitation of the situation of composition to the 40s is not independent of the assignment of the Passion story to the Jerusalem community. It is not a question of a new hypothesis. In fact, the Passion account is often unquestioningly dated to the 30s. Cf. Schenke, who writes, "The composition of the Passion account in the Jerusalem community seems unquestionable" (*Der gekreuzigte Christus,* 140). He traces the secondary editing to the group around Stephen (p. 143)—perhaps even before they were driven out of the city in the 30s! Pesch (*Das Markusevangelium* 2:20–22) also wishes to date the oldest Passion story in the 30s.

TABLE 5

Indications of locality and familiarity	Taylor[52]	Schenk[53]	Schenke[54]	Dormeyer[55]
Mk 14:47—the anony-mous sword-wielder	P2	P1*	P	sec.
Mk 14:51-52—the flee-ing young man	P2*	red.	P	
Mk 14:55-56—the high priest (sg.)	P1	P1/P2	P*	sec.*
Mk 14:70—Galileans recognizable	P2	P1	iso.	red.
Mk 15:7—the insurrection is known	P2	iso.	sec.	P

52. Taylor (Mark, 654–64) distinguishes a Source A, which the evangelist found at Rome and which he filled in with segments, often complete in themselves, from Source B. The sections from B are distinguished by their many Semitisms and are traceable to Peter's reminiscences. He gives a summary of his analysis on p. 658, and a tentative reconstruction of Source A on pp. 660–62. For purposes of comparison, in the table above we will equate A with P1 and B with P2.

53. Schenk (Passionsbericht, 272–73) gives a summary of his literary analysis. He distin-guishes a source in the historical present (P1 above) beginning with the entry into Jerusa-lem; a second, apocalyptic Passion tradition (P2 above); and isolated individual traditions ("iso." above).

54. Schenke (Der gekreuzigte Christus, 135–37) gives his reconstruction of the original form of the Passion story. It began (adding Mk 14:1a) with the Gethsemane story. He traces a very early secondary level to the Hellenistic community in Jerusalem. Here, anti-Jewish accents appear more strongly. There are also redactional notes by the author of Mark.

55. See Dormeyer, Die Passion Jesu, 297–301, for a summary of his analysis. A set of acts of the martyrs, already a complex document (T = P above) has been revised by way of a secondary redactional layer utilizing dialogue (Rs = "sec." above) and a separate, parenetic contemporary application by the author of Mark (Rmk = "red." above).

TABLE 5 (continued)

Indications of locality and familiarity	Taylor	Schenk	Schenke	Dormeyer
Mk 15:40— Simon of Cyrene and his sons	P1	P1	sec.	P
Mk 15:40— the women under the cross	red.	red.	red.	P

Key:

P	=	precanonical Passion story, to the extent that this is seen as a unit and not divided into versions P1 and P2.
P1/P2	=	two versions of a precanonical Passion story (here no unitary original is posited).
sec.	=	secondary parts that have entered the precanonical Passion story before the Markan redaction.
red.	=	redactional parts that are traceable to the author of Mark.
iso.	=	isolated individual units that were handed down independently as small units and then secondarily (or redactionally) introduced.

This is contrary to historical reality:[56] the power to impose capital punishment belonged to the Roman prefect (*Bell.* 2.117). Jewish courts were not allowed to execute anyone (Jn 18:31), since authority in criminal cases had been taken from them (*p. Sanh.* 1:18a, 24b). The much-discussed evidence to the contrary points to exceptional instances that are explained by factors of "space" and "time." On the one hand, the Romans recognized the temple as a limited "judicial realm," so that any foreigner who

---

56. It is well known that H. Lietzmann ("Der Prozess Jesu") firmly maintained the contrary, i.e., that the Sanhedrin at Jerusalem had full authority to impose capital punishment. Had Jesus been condemned by them, he would have to have been stoned to death. But since he was subjected to a Roman form of capital punishment—crucifixion—the description of Jesus' "trial" must be largely unhistorical. Strobel (*Stunde*, esp. 21–45) disputes Lietzmann at length. There is a short summary of the view I consider correct in Lührmann, *Markusevangelium*, 251–52.

entered the sanctuary (*Bell.* 6.124ff.; *Ant.* 15.417; Acts 21:28)[57] or anyone who entered the Holy of Holies as high priest more than once a year (*Leg. Gai.* 306–7) was subject to death without a Roman judgment. Probably there were some Jewish groups that would have been glad to extend this sacral enclave in order to be able to react sharply to every kind of transgression against or critique of the temple. Stephen, with his criticisms of the temple, may have fallen victim to that kind of view of the law, which, however, could only be carried out through lynching (Acts 7:54-60). On the other hand, we have evidence of death sentences passed at times when the Romans' direct control of the country was interrupted. King Agrippa I had James, the son of Zebedee, killed during the years 41–44 C.E., when he was temporarily ruler of all Palestine. The high priest Ananus took advantage of a short vacancy between the procurators Festus and Albinus in 62 C.E. to condemn James, the brother of the Lord, and other Jews (or Jewish Christians?) to death (*Ant.* 20.200–201). He was criticized, among other reasons, for having summoned the Sanhedrin for this purpose without the assent of King Agrippa II.[58] We may conclude from this that where there was a Jewish king, some groups understood the law to mean that the Sanhedrin could be called to hear a capital case. It is possible that others may have offered more extensive criticisms of Ananus's proceedings.[59]

Thus, in the period that interests us (ca. 30 C.E.), the Sanhedrin had no power in capital cases. There was no Jewish king with limited authority in Jerusalem, as there would be in 62 C.E. It is true that Jesus' criticisms of the temple touched an area in which the Sanhedrin had more authority than elsewhere, but the narrators of Mk 14:55ff. are convinced that Jesus' attitude to the temple was not a valid reason for his condemnation. According to Mk 14:56-59, the attempt to construct a charge on the basis of Jesus' prophecy against the temple was a failure. The Passion account confirms indirectly that the Sanhedrin did not play the critical role and that Jesus was executed by the Romans. The Roman punishment by crucifixion is the best proof of this. Tacitus, in his remarks about the Christians,

---

57. This is confirmed by two inscriptions in the temple court, discovered in 1871 and 1935. Cf. A. Deissmann, *Licht vom Osten*, 63; E. J. Bickermann, "Warning Inscriptions of Herod's Temple."

58. Protesting Jews informed the new procurator "that Ananus had no authority to convene the Sanhedrin [καθίσαι συνέδριον] without his consent [χωρὶς τῆς ἐκείνου γνώμης]" (*Ant.* 20.202). Syntactically speaking, "his consent" should really refer to King Agrippa II, who, according to *Ant.* 20.216, really could convene the Sanhedrin (καθίσαντα συνέδριον). Strobel (*Stunde*, 33–34) is correct on this point.

59. That there were further criticisms could be deduced from the πρῶτον in *Ant.* 20.201. Those protesting to Agrippa say that "Ananus had not even been correct in his first step [i.e., the calling of the Sanhedrin]," or: "this was not the first time that Ananus had acted unjustly." Cf. Josephus, *Ant.* (LCL) 9.496–97.

leaves no doubt about who was responsible for the death sentence: "per procuratorem Pontium Pilatum supplicio affectus erat" (Tacitus *Ann.* 15.44.3). Consequently, the Sanhedrin cannot have condemned Jesus to death; they could only accuse him before the prefect. A wide variety of traditions, including those of Luke, the Johannine Passion account, and the *Testimonium Flavianum* (*Ant.* 18.64)[60] agree on this. Therefore, when Mk 14:64 says that "all of them condemned him as deserving death," the statement cannot correspond to the historical reality.

Probably, the tellers of the story projected their own circumstances back into the time of Jesus. The idea that a Jewish court could pass death sentences against religious dissidents could have arisen no earlier than the reign of Agrippa I (41–44 C.E.). We hear previously of measures taken by the Sanhedrin against the first Christians (Acts 4:1ff.; 5:17ff.), but not of death sentences. The stoning of Stephen was not the result of any regular legal process. But under Agrippa I the conditions could have existed in which accounts of the Passion of Jesus could exaggerate the role of the Jewish court beyond historical reality; at that time there were legal actions against leading Christians: James, the son of Zebedee, was executed by King Agrippa I, and Peter was imprisoned, although he managed to escape (Acts 12:1ff.).

However, we should emphasize that we do not know whether the Sanhedrin was involved in the condemnation of James. We hear only that his execution pleased "the Jews" (Acts 12:3). It is possible that the Sanhedrin cooperated; in the year 62 the groups protesting the deeds of Ananus the high priest presuppose that the Sanhedrin could have acted with the permission of King Agrippa II. In their eyes, the two authorities acting together—a Jewish king, with oversight of temple affairs, and the Sanhedrin—would have had the right to try James, the brother of the Lord, although that does not include *eo ipso* the right to pass a sentence of death. The cooperation of the two authorities, which they seem to postulate, could have been modeled on the time of Agrippa I. Still, the fact remains that we hear nothing directly about the Sanhedrin proceeding against Christians in the years 41–44. All that is certain is that, in the brief reign of Agrippa I, Jewish authorities could act in their own right against Christians and could pass and execute death sentences—and that this actually happened in those years. The motif of Jesus' condemnation by

---

60. The *Testimonium Flavianum*, of course, can only be introduced as a source if it is not a Christian interpolation. The statements that Jesus had won over many Greeks and that Pilate was the one principally responsible for his condemnation do not appear to come from Christian tradition. It is quite obvious that *Ant.* 18.63–64, if not written by a Christian, has been redacted by one.

the Sanhedrin could have entered the Passion account in light of those circumstances. In that case, we would have a terminus a quo for the pre-Markan Passion story. The terminus ante quem would be 62 C.E., since nowhere in the Passion account is the summoning of the Sanhedrin for Jesus' "trial" criticized as something that overstepped their competence. The critique around which public discussions revolved in the 60s, after the execution of James, the brother of the Lord, is not reflected in the Passion account.

2. For the community that shaped the tradition of Jesus' "trial" before the Sanhedrin, his prophecy about the temple must have been an additional problem, because they distance themselves from that traditional saying of Jesus. Although its authenticity seems probable to us, it is treated in Mk 14:57-58 as false testimony. Mark confirms that it was circulating in several versions: the witnesses contradict themselves by asserting that Jesus said, "I will destroy this temple that is made with hands, and in three days I will build another, not made with hands" (Mk 14:58). It seems to me that this kind of detachment from the temple prophecy would be hard to imagine in the years after 70 C.E. If Jesus was accused on that basis, his judges would have been proved wrong by the destruction of the temple, and Jesus would have been vindicated by the fulfillment of his prophecy. After 70 there were good reasons to identify with the temple prophecy. The detachment from Jesus' saying about the temple, apparent in Mk 14:55ff., thus points us to an earlier time. The author of Mark could include it, however, because for him Jesus' words in Mk 13:2 were the "authentic prophecy."[61] There the destruction of the temple is not attributed to Jesus, and nothing is said about a miraculous rebuilding. Mark 13:2 thus corresponds to the historical events of the year 70 C.E. Thus, for historical-critical exegesis, in contrast to the author of Mark, it is Mk 14:58 that is more likely to be the authentic version of Jesus' saying, while Mk 13:2 represents its adaptation to the events that have unfolded in the meantime.

We know of one instance in which the temple prophecy has become a burden to the early Christians. According to Acts 6:14, Stephen is accused by false witnesses of having said, "This Jesus of Nazareth will destroy this place and will change the customs that Moses handed on to us." As in Mk 14:58, the destruction of the temple is here attributed to Jesus himself; the difference is that now no new temple is promised, but rather a change in the Mosaic laws. This change replaces the "new temple." The withdrawal

---

61. The motives behind the Markan redaction have been accurately analyzed by Lührmann in "Markus 14, 55-64." Therefore, the temple prophecy in Mk 14:55ff. is not a redactional insertion by the author of Mark.

from Jesus' temple prophecy as reported in Mk 14:55ff. would be understandable as a consequence of the first persecutions of Christians in the 30s, and after the Caligula crisis in 40–41 it must have become a real question of survival for Christians in Jerusalem. In those years the temple was miraculously saved by the direct action of God—the sudden death of the tyrant. This put every criticism of the temple in the worst light. God stood behind the temple in its physical reality. In this situation it would be understandable if Christians insisted that Jesus never wanted to change the temple in any fundamental way, and that such reports were only malicious gossip.

3. Jesus' confession before the Sanhedrin points also to the period after Easter. It not only combines the three most important christological titles of majesty—Christ, Son of God, and Son of man (Mk 14:62-63)—but its condemnation as "blasphemy" presumes the Christian belief that the crucified one has been exalted to the right hand of God. The claim to be the Messiah was not in itself a blasphemy, but the claim that someone who had been executed on the cross was the Messiah certainly was.[62] The stoning of Stephen sheds light on this situation: after he says that he sees the heavens opened and the Son of man standing at the right hand of God, he is seized by the furious throng and stoned outside the city (Acts 7:56ff.). Faith in the Son of man has by this time become a shibboleth, but also a consolation in persecution. This faith has a similar function in the Lukan beatitude of the persecuted (Lk 6:22), in the Parousia promise in Mt 10:23, and in the healing of the blind man in Jn 9:35ff.[63] But in the traditions behind Mark 13, too, the Son of man appears as the savior of his own in their time of greatest danger (Mk 13:26-27), and the narrative of Jesus' "trial" unmistakably reveals parallel motifs to this apocalyptic prophecy from the year 40.[64] Here also, changes regarding the temple are con-

---

62. Lietzmann ("Der Prozess Jesu," 256) correctly argues that a post-Easter situation like that in Acts 7:55ff. is the background: "Jesus, blameless up to this point, can still hope to sit at the right hand of God as the future Messiah. The judges may regard that as foolishness, but not as punishable blasphemy. But Stephen sees Jesus, after his execution, at God's right hand: now the situation is utterly changed." Those who insist that Jesus was tried by the Sanhedrin have to presuppose a totally different accusation: that of false prophecy and leading the people astray, as in Deuteronomy 13 and 18. So Betz, "Probleme des Prozesses Jesu," 565–647; Strobel, *Stunde*, 81ff.

63. W. Bousset (*Kyrios Christos*, 18) already noted that the Son of man title is found several times in situations of persecution and has its *Sitz im Leben* there: "The confession of the Son of man became the shibboleth that separated the disciples of Jesus from the Jewish synagogue."

64. Lührmann ("Markus 14, 55-64," 467ff.) has, in my opinion, accurately described these motif parallels. But are they only at the redactional level? If both Mark 13 and the Passion account come from the Jerusalem community, the relationship of the two texts could just as well be accounted for by their historical origins.

nected with the appearance of the Son of man. For this reason also it seems evident that Mk 14:55ff. more likely originated in the years 40–44 than at any other time.

4. The image of Peter in the Passion tradition would also fit well in this period. Peter's denial appears there as a contrast to Jesus' confession before the Sanhedrin: Jesus is executed, while Peter escapes. The prophecy of the denial (Mk 14:29-31), the admonition to watchfulness directed to Peter in Gethsemane (Mk 14:37), and Peter's failure (14:54, 66-72) show how much emphasis the Passion tradition gives to this one disciple. In the years 41–44 there was almost a "doublet" of the story of Peter in the Passion tradition. James, the son of Zebedee, was executed (Acts 12:2), and Peter was arrested, but he managed to escape by some means or other. Again he fled: "he left and went to another place" (Acts 12:17). This time Peter is contrasted, not with Jesus, but with James, the son of Zebedee. This is not to say that he denied his Christian faith under Agrippa or that the story of his failure is a reflection of his later behavior.[65] The point is simply that it was especially appropriate in the circumstances of those years to create a Passion tradition in which the role of Peter appeared in this ambivalent light. This is true, mutatis mutandis, for all the disciples. It is characteristic that not they, but "Alexander" and "Rufus," together with women from Galilee, represent the (later) Christian community. On the basis of these names, we may suspect that people in the community behind the Passion tradition knew that the Christian community contained Hellenistic Jews from the Diaspora and Christians from Palestine, which was true of the Jerusalem community. The consciousness of having sympathizers in the surrounding Jewish community also fits this group: Joseph of Arimathea is described as someone who was waiting for the "reign of God." He need not have been a member of the Christian community. He represents an environment in which, as within the community, eschatological expectations were current.

5. The relationship to other groups that appears in the Passion account also fits the situation of the 40s. The story of Barabbas would have been of lively interest to a community that sensed that, if it came to a choice, most people would be more likely to side with the rebellious elements in the country than with them. Rebel groups of that sort were active during the Caligula crisis. In the struggle for the national sanctuary, they were in harmony with the whole population. Even if they are mentioned only by Tacitus (*Ann.* 12.54.1) we can feel secure in presuming that they existed,

---

65. G. Klein ("Die Verleugnung des Petrus") proposes the thesis that Peter's threefold denial reflects a threefold change in his position within the post-Easter community. That is somewhat exaggerated. The threefold repetition of a motif is part of the art of storytelling.

because they were successfully attacked in the 40s by Cuspius Fadus (44–45 C.E.) and Tiberius Alexander (46–48 C.E.) (*Ant.* 20.5, 97, 102). Only at the time of Cumanus (50–52 C.E.) can we be sure that high-priestly groups conspired with them. At that time the high priest Jonathan, with other Jewish leaders, was sent as a prisoner to Rome (*Bell.* 2.243). His brother Ananus, who cooperated with the rebels during the Jewish war, revealed himself in 62 C.E. as a dedicated enemy of the Christians. The "coalition" that appeared during the war could have been in the making beforehand, since a process of cooptation of the rebels for the purposes of the Jewish aristocracy was already visible when those aristocrats, at the time of the Caligula crisis, threatened an increase of banditry should the temple be desecrated (*Ant.* 18.274).

6. A final observation relates to the metaphor of the cup in the Gethsemane story. Jesus asks his Father to "remove this cup from me" (Mk 14:36). We find the same metaphor in the dialogue with the sons of Zebedee, when Jesus asks them: "Are you able to drink the cup that I drink, or be baptized with the baptism that I am baptized with?" (Mk 10:38). In both places the metaphor is connected to a violent death, whether it refers only to the fact of death or to death as a result of God's wrathful punishment.[66] In both places it refers to Jesus' death, if not exclusively, and in both places we find the same disciples: the sons of Zebedee, with Peter, are the three most intimate disciples, who are supposed to watch with Jesus in Gethsemane. Mark 10:35-45 presupposes James's martyrdom.[67] This occurred, according to Acts 12:2, during the reign of Agrippa I. We can leave open the question whether his brother John died with him, or whether the death of James led people to expect that John would also suffer a martyr's death because it was said that both of them had asked Jesus that they might share his fate. The latter seems to me to be more likely. In any case, James and Peter were persecuted under Agrippa I, and they were members of the group that was with Jesus in Gethsemane. James's execution was interpreted with the aid of the "cup metaphor." All this points to a proximity, in the development of the tradition, between the Gethsemane story and the dialogue with the sons of Zebedee: it would have been the same groups that, in the 40s, interpreted the death of Christian martyrs as "drinking a cup" and who narrated the story of Jesus' fear of death in Gethsemane in such a way as to make it a model for every Christian facing death.

Thus we arrive at the conclusion that there was almost certainly a con-

---

66. On the cup metaphor, see R. Feldmeier, *Krisis*, 176–85. He argues strongly for the second interpretation.

67. On this problem, see E. Schwartz, "Über den Tod," 48ff.

nected Passion tradition. It can be detected beginning with Mk 14:1ff., and with Jesus' arrest it is more clearly evident. Indications of locality and familiarity undergird the supposition that it was composed in Jerusalem in the first generation after Jesus' death, ca. 30–60 C.E. Probably we can limit the phase in which this Passion tradition underwent its critical shaping still more: it could well have been composed in light of the persecutions that occurred during Agrippa I's reign (41–44 C.E.). Those were years when the Passion tradition's narrating community lived in fear. At that time, it is understandable if the names of its inner circle were given the protection of anonymity in order that no negative consequences should ensue from their conflicts with the authorities. In this period, the community could recognize its own fate in that of Jesus. It needed that memory in order to come to terms with its own conflicts with the world outside. The roots of this memory are in the events themselves, but they have a present function. The life-situation of the oldest Passion tradition is that of a threatened minority whose confession of Jesus (Mk 14:62-63) constantly brings it into danger of denial and failure. The Passion account is a conflict parenesis in the form of a narrative of remembered events.

Now that we have analyzed two "large units" drawn from the sayings and narrative traditions, we can draw some general conclusions for a history of the synoptic tradition. As early as the middle of the first century—by 40 C.E.—the move had already been made from small to large units. This step occurred in Jerusalem and Judea. While we can trace the origins of the tradition of small units to Galilee, the second stage of synoptic tradition history is connected with a shift in location, and at the same time with a change of its *Sitz im Leben*. While the small units are traditions handed down by the disciples and/or popular tradition (and community traditions are hard to discern in this group), a new life-situation emerges clearly in the investigation of the large units studied: the apocalyptic prophecy behind Mark 13 is addressed to Christians living in one place, and the Passion account is written from the perspective of the Jerusalem community. In these local communities, the Jesus tradition is shaped by a theological reflection that saturates it with Old Testament citations and references. Despite the differences between Mark 13 and the Passion account, they are related by their "scribal character"—in other words, the readers and hearers understand these texts better if they are acquainted with the Book of Daniel and the psalms of suffering. This closeness to "sacred Scripture" and the extent of the large units permit the supposition that both these units were composed in written form—an assumption that is expressly confirmed, in the case of Mark 13, by the appeal for interpretation in v. 14. A second feature common to both these large units relates to the historical situation in which they were created. Both reflect a situation of conflict: the apocalyptic prophecy, arising in the Caligula crisis, shows a conflict between Judaism and the Roman state in which Christians have their part; the Passion story, on the other hand, reflects heightened tensions between Christians and their Jewish milieu in the wake of that crisis.

This brings us to a larger question: If the Jesus traditions began to be written down in the form of large units even before 40 C.E., are there indications that other parts of the Jesus tradition were committed to writing after the middle of the first century? Now and again we suspect such "older collections" of small units behind the oldest Gospel. These could be connected oral traditions. Only the Sayings Source (Q), which we can reconstruct on the basis of the agreements between material in Matthew and Luke against Mark, can really be proved. At a central point in Q we find a "large unit," the temptation story, in which a number of complete scenes have been composed into a complex whole. Like the synoptic apocalypse and the Passion account, this story has a clearly scribal character: it breathes Old Testament citations. We could have discussed it among the "large units." However, because it is closely associated with the composition of the Sayings Source and can illuminate the progress from large and small units to the synoptic structuring genres, it will be analyzed and interpreted in connection with Q.

PART III

SOCIAL CONTEXT AND
POLITICAL HISTORY
IN THE STRUCTURING GENRES
OF THE SYNOPTIC TRADITION

5

The Sayings Source:
Palestine-Centered Perspectives
at the Middle of the First Century

The redaction of the Sayings Source is difficult to detect, and even more difficult to locate in time and place.[1] The individual sayings of Jesus are for the most part thought to be traditional material that was not yet shaped before Q was written down. Redactional additions and commentary cannot be definitively separated from traditional elements. Only the choice, combination, and composition of the Jesus traditions can be regarded with certainty as redaction.[2]

Regarding the *choice* of Jesus traditions we can know very little, since we do not know the extent of the traditions from which the choice was made. A definite redactional decision to include a tradition is only discernible where traditional material within the Sayings Source differs from other material in form or content. Thus, the three scenes of the Temptation story form a dramatic dialogue between mythical persons, and as such are unique within Q. The story of the centurion from Capernaum is also unique. The redactor of the Sayings Source knows of many more stories about Jesus' miracles (cf. Lk 7:21Q; 10:13Q) but includes only this one healing.

The *combination* of different traditions in Q is clearly discernible.[3] Individual sayings tell us very little about the redaction of Q, since they can always be traditional; however, out of their joining together in the Sayings

---

1. In what follows, we will posit a written Sayings Source Q, probably in Greek. On this point, see J. S. Kloppenborg, "Literary Genre."
2. On the methodological problems in researching the redaction of Q, see the very clear remarks of J. S. Kloppenborg, "Tradition and Redaction."
3. An interpretation of the combination of different themes can be made without separating tradition and redaction (except for the fact that the combination of themes is regarded in itself as redactional). H. E. Tödt, *Der Menschensohn in der synoptischen Überlieferung*, and P. Hoffmann, *Studien zur Theologie der Logienquelle*, are based on this method. I consider it an advantage of these studies that they succeed without excluding redactional elements. They are thus free of arbitrary analyses of different layers.

Source we can reconstruct a combined image of a historical world that very likely underlies the composition of Q. This picture must fit the circumstances of the redaction, even if the individual sayings of which it is composed are not traceable to those particular circumstances. The words of Jesus were traditions that were of the greatest contemporary relevance for the authors and addressees of Q. Within the framework of Q, they speak directly to the contemporary situation. There are only the rudiments of a narrative structure that would place them at a historical remove. The combined picture that results from their joining in Q emerges from two questions that can be answered independently of any analysis of various layers within the document:

1. What themes appear repeatedly in Q in different contexts? These themes must have been important in the historical world of Q.
2. What divergent themes are combined in Q? That association must have had its counterpart in the real situation.

It is quite unlikely that, at every time and place in the first century, people could have spoken at the same time of "Israel," "Gentiles," and "Pharisees" exactly as Q does.

Observations regarding *composition*—that is, the order in which the material is arranged in Q—sometimes offer us a confirmation of or additional security in our analyses. Redactional interest is discernible in the composition of the beginning and end of the Sayings Source.[4] The beginning of a writing always shapes the readers' further expectations. Here it must be made clear what the author or redactor of a document has in mind. Of course, we must emphasize our limitations: we do not know for certain what was at the beginning and end of Q. We can only say approximately what may have been found near the beginning and near the end. A conscious composition is also visible in the combination of groups of sayings related to one another in form or content. When the redactor puts together or reproduces a series of woes against the Pharisees and inserts in them a powerful polemic against "this generation" (Lk 11:49-51Q), the resulting image of the Pharisees must have been important to him.[5]

---

4. The investigation of the beginning and end of the Sayings Source is for A. Polag (*Christologie*, 15–17) the beginning point for his analysis of its "late redaction." He believes he can identify two additional layers—which, in my opinion, overestimates our powers of discernment. We must be clear about the fact that Q itself is the result of a deduction, a "construct" that we possess only in the Gospels in revised form.

5. The redaction-critical evaluation of this "insertion" in the woes by D. Lührmann (*Redaktion*, 24–48) is, in my opinion, correct.

Three further groups of criteria for discerning the redaction in Q seem to me more problematic:

1. These include literary-critical observations about contradictions and fissures on the basis of which individual sentences are judged redactional. Even if we could show that a sentence or a saying is secondary in its present context, which is already difficult enough, that still does not prove that it was first created or put in its present location by the redactor.[6]

2. Criteria of tradition history by which older Jewish-Christian material is distinguished from newer, hellenistically colored traditions are also problematic.[7] We can expect to find traditions with a Hellenistic stamp in Palestine at a very early date because there was a Hellenistic community quite soon after Easter. Besides, all of Palestine had been under Hellenistic influence for over a century.

3. Form-critical criteria for the distinction of layers are also, in my opinion, unpersuasive. That the Sayings Source was first a book with a "wisdom" character, at a second stage incorporated prophetic sayings, and then finally developed into a "bios" of Jesus by integrating narrative traditions cannot, I think, be verified.[8] Thus, in the double saying in Mt 12:41-42Q, Jesus is compared with both Jonah and Solomon. He is both a prophet and a wisdom teacher. It is precisely this coupling of both aspects that is typical of Q (and probably of the historical Jesus).

Therefore, in drawing conclusions about the redaction of Q, we will limit ourselves to observations on the choice, combination, and composition of the traditional material.

In a first section, the "frame" of Q will be studied, that is, the formation of the beginning and end of this document. In a second section we will sketch a picture of the various groups in Q, in order to delimit the historical circumstances in which this image (and the constellation of these various groups) would have been plausible.

---

6. Lührmann (*Redaktion*, 62ff., 91) identifies only two sentences as redactional additions by the Q editor: the comparison with the fate of Sodom in Lk 10:12Q and the likening of the sign of Jonah with the Son of man in Lk 11:30Q. Polag (*Christologie*, 16–17) thinks he can identify many more "additions" in the late redaction: Lk 7:2-10; 7:27 (= Mal 3:1); 7:28 (the saying about the "greater one"); 10:21-22 and 10:23-24 (the cry of joy and blessing of the eyewitnesses); 12:10 (blasphemy against the Spirit); 12:49-53 (ἦλθον sayings).

7. R. Bultmann, (*Die Geschichte der synoptischen Tradition*, 354) applies this criterion, with the result that only the Temptation story, the "centurion of Capernaum," and the saying about the revealer in Lk 10:21-22 (in part) are Hellenistically colored. The major effort of S. Schulz, *Q*, consists in ascribing the major part of *Q*, on the basis of more elaborate criteria, to a newer, Hellenistic layer. For a critique, see Kloppenborg, "Tradition and Redaction," 39–45; P. Hoffmann, review of *Q: Die Spruchquelle der Evangelisten*, by S. Schulz, *BZ* 19 (1975): 104–15.

8. This distinction of three layers (within the framework of a developing concept of genre) is very cleverly worked out in Kloppenborg, "Literary Genre," 410ff.

THE FRAME OF THE SAYINGS SOURCE:
THE TEMPTATION OF JESUS AND
THE SELF-APOTHEOSIS OF GAIUS CALIGULA

The Sayings Source begins with the appearance of the Baptizer and the Temptation story and ends with apocalyptic sayings. The preaching of judgment stands at the beginning and at the end. But the beginning has a special function: it is supposed to legitimate the collected sayings of Jesus that follow by identifying their speaker, Jesus, as the "more powerful" one the Baptizer had proclaimed was to come (Mt 3:11Q). Jesus shows in the Temptation story that he really is this "more powerful" one. This story depicts a "qualifying test":[9] Jesus fulfills, in exemplary fashion, the will of God that was revealed in the Torah and will remain obligatory and inviolate until the end of the world (Lk 16:17Q). He overcomes Satan. This makes it clear why the redactor of the Sayings Source has provided a narrative introduction so different from the formal character of the other sayings and speeches. He shows by this that, in the words of Jesus, God's will is authentically interpreted. The one who was foretold by the prophets and who can disarm Satan with the words of Scripture must be speaking in the name of God. These considerations invite us to regard the whole Temptation story as a statement by the last redactor of the sayings collection.[10] In its present form, it was composed all at one time; in fact, it could have been a written composition from the beginning.[11] The literal agreement of Matthew and Luke shows that those two authors knew this story only in the versions of Q and Mark and were not aware of any variant traditions that could have influenced their own retelling.

The three scenes in the Temptation story were conceived as a single whole, but from the standpoint of tradition history they are different. The scenes in the desert and in the temple could be developed from motifs that are also present in the Markan version: the former, because the subject of hunger was already implicit in Jesus' sojourn in the desert; the latter, because Mk 1:12-13 also speaks of ministering angels.[12] The tempta-

---

9. This accurate description was introduced by D. Zeller, "Die Versuchungen Jesu in der Logienquelle," 63–64.

10. The Temptation story is generally regarded as one of the latest parts of the Sayings Source. This was already the opinion of Bultmann (*Die Geschichte der synoptischen Tradition*, 354). I believe that Kloppenborg ("Literary Genre," 387ff.) connects it correctly with the redaction of Q.

11. U. Luz is correct when he says that the Q version was conceived as a single whole (*Matthäus*, 160). This commentary gives a good overview of the present state of research. So also J. Gnilka, *Das Matthäusevangelium*, 82–93; H. Schürmann, *Das Lukasevangelium*, 204–20.

12. Q's version of the Temptation story is usually regarded as a developed form of a narrative that had evolved from a short story similar to Mk 1:12-13. So Schürmann (*Das Lukasevangelium*, 208) and others. The contrary position is represented by Schulz (*Q*, 182):

tion on the mountain is the only one of the three that has no point of contact at all within the tradition. It is notable for other special features: in the desert and temple scenes, Jesus is tempted by Satan through invocation of his status as "Son of God." The word-for-word repetition of the conditional clause in Lk 4:3 and 4:9 and the strict parallels in construction are not accidental. These are comparable temptations. Each time, Satan approaches with apparently positive expectations. He wants Jesus to demonstrate the miraculous powers already at his disposal, either as his own or as the gift of another. After Jesus (in Matthew's ordering of the scenes) has exposed Satan's "pious requests" as tempting God, Satan drops his mask.[13] His interest is not in revealing Jesus' majesty, but in gaining his submission; yet he tempts him with the opposite of submission: power. He promises Jesus a new status as ruler of all earthly kingdoms—without reference to his already present status as "Son of God." And he places conditions. The temptation on the mountain, which originally was probably at the end, as in Matthew's version,[14] may represent the point of the Temptation story in Q. It should therefore also reveal the intent of the Q redaction, if we connect the Temptation story with the redaction.

The temptation on the mountain combines three elements: (1) a prostration (*proskynesis*) before the ruler of the world, who (2) has the power to bestow kingdoms; to worship this ruler is (3) a direct offense against the worship of the one and only God. All three motifs appear united, in this historical period, for the first time and most clearly in the person of

---

Mark has radically abbreviated the Temptation story because it contains a polemic against any interpretation of Jesus as a miracle worker, and in Mark it is Jesus' wonder-working that is presented as a vital witness for the gospel preaching. But this motive for shortening would have no purpose in the case of the temptation on the mountain, and there is no trace of this part of the story in Mark's Gospel. Instead, this particular temptation would fit very well as a stage on the road followed by the Son of God to the cross, as depicted in Mark. But the two other scenes do not contravene his intention either. In fact, the tradition about Jesus' refusing to give a sign appears in Mk 8:11-12.

13. So M. Dibelius, *Formgeschichte*, 274 n. 2. He explains the difference between the first two temptations and the last by saying "that in the third act the devil drops his pretence of interest in Jesus' success and openly offers a pact." But it is less a question of a pact than of submission—which, of course, every pact with the devil is by its very nature.

14. Matthew's order makes more sense in and of itself. In the second temptation, the tempter hides behind "God's word" by using a scriptural citation to appeal for trust in God; only then does he drop his mask and demand open idolatry. It is quite unlikely that, after that, he can still be a persuasive tempter, especially behind a feigned piety. Furthermore, the local horizon expands from temptation to temptation: from the desert to the holy city, and then to the whole world. The decisive faith in the one and only God stands emphatically at the conclusion. Luke's order is less reasonable in itself, but is understandable in Luke's whole scheme, since the sequence "desert, mountain, Jerusalem" reflects Jesus' journey from beginning to end. The Lukan note in 4:13, "he departed from him until an opportune time," also links beginning and end. For discussion of this point, see Schürmann, *Das Lukasevangelium*, 218. He argues for the originality of the Lukan version.

Gaius Caligula, while parts of them are evident later in the autocratic rulers Nero and Domitian. In what follows we will develop the hypothesis that the narrative of the temptation on the mountain was composed in light of such absolutist rulers, and that in its first version in Q it was probably formulated in the context of the conflict between the emperor Gaius Caligula and Jewish monotheism in the year 40 C.E. It would then appear that the background of experience behind this event in a mythical world was a real event in this world, which is not to say that the Temptation story describes this earthly event. What is intended is the description of a mythical occurrence. But the model for this occurrence comes from the real world. It is easy to suppose that the mythical narrative deals with the problems and conflicts associated with its earthly model in the real world. In short, the prostration before the mythical "ruler of this world" is a socio-mythic parallel to prostration before an earthly ruler. In order to confirm this thesis, we must reconstruct the background of experience for each of the motifs in the Temptation story: prostration, the conferral of power, and conflict with monotheism.

Prostration

Prostration, or *proskynesis*, is an ancient component of Persian court ceremonial.[15] The Greeks rejected it as barbaric. Alexander introduced it into his court ceremonies, but encountered sharp resistance from his own people. In Rome, too, for a long time it was found only in submission scenes involving barbarians. The first evidence is a victory monument of Sulla's,[16] which he erected before the capitol in 91 B.C.E. It shows the handing over of the Numidian king Jugurtha by Bocchus, king of Mauretania: both kings are kneeling before Sulla. It is typical that this monument was destroyed by Sulla's opponents in 85 B.C.E., because it was rightly regarded as a symbol of his absolutist claims and rejected as such. The *proskynesis* remained in Rome the symbol of the hated monarchy. When Mark Antony knelt to offer Caesar the diadem, it was interpreted as an attempt to seize monarchical power and led to Caesar's murder.[17] From the time of Augustus we have only representations of the prostration of barbarians. What is striking in these cases is that coins showing the pros-

---

15. On *proskynesis*, see J. Horst, *Proskynein*. There is a basic study by A. Alföldi, *Repräsentation*, esp. 11–16, 46–65. For pictorial representations of *proskynesis*, see esp. H. Gabelmann, *Audienz- und Tribunalszenen*. W. Fauth ("Proskynese") gives a brief summary.

16. See the treatment of this monument in Gabelmann, *Audienz- und Tribunalszenen*, 111–13. Only some fragments of the base have survived, but there is a coin (ca. 56 C.E.) that depicts the scene. Cf. Table 22, 1, no. 33; see also E. A. Sydenham, *Coinage of the Roman Republic*, 145, no. 879, Table 24.

17. Cf. Cicero *Phil.* 2.86; Alföldi, *Repräsentation*, 51, 54.

tration of a barbarian do not display the image of Augustus, who would thereby have been likened to a god;[18] on the other hand, coins with Augustus's image show a barbarian standing, not kneeling.[19] The Augustus cup from Boscoreale[20] is the first object that shows both in a single scene: here a barbarian is kneeling before Augustus, who is represented on the reverse of the goblet in a group of Roman gods. But it is possible that this goblet dates from the time of Claudius. The prostration of a Roman before Augustus is mentioned only in a very special situation: during a triumphal procession, Tiberius descended from his chariot and threw himself at the knees of his stepfather in order to offer him the victory over the Germans (Suetonius *Tib.* 20). But in general, prostration as a gesture of homage was avoided by Augustus and Tiberius because it betrayed monarchical ambitions.

Things were different under Gaius Caligula. He introduced prostration in his court ceremonial in the most ostentatious way. It was a familiar gesture in the eastern parts of the empire, and among the Jews as well; in fact, the former Syrian legate Vitellius was the first to prostrate himself before Gaius Caligula:[21]

> He had also a wonderful gift for flattery and was the first to begin to worship Gaius Caesar [Caligula] as a god; for on his return from Syria he did not presume to approach the emperor except with veiled head, turning himself about and then prostrating himself. (Suetonius *Vitell.* 2)

It is interesting that Suetonius connects deification closely with prostration. It is not the statements of Gaius himself that are regarded as the beginning of his self-apotheosis, but the gesture of homage offered by others who fell on their knees before him. Vitellius probably learned the gesture in the East; his special service as legate of Syria consisted in his having, by his diplomatic skills, not only induced the Parthian king Artabanus "to hold a conference with him, but even to do obeisance to the standards of the legion" (Suetonius *Vitell.* 2). Can we imagine this homage

---

18. Parthians are depicted as kneeling at the return of the Roman standards, but they are not kneeling before anyone; cf. *BMC* 1, Table 1, 7–9; Table 2, 11–12.

19. Cf. *BMC* 1, Table 12, 13–14; Gabelmann, *Audienz- und Tribunalszenen*, 121–24.

20. See Gabelmann, *Audienz- und Tribunalszenen*, 127–31, Table 13, 1–2.

21. See also Tacitus *Ann.* 6.32, where prostration is not mentioned *expressis verbis*. In reading these contemptuous stories about Vitellius we should keep in mind that, as the father of the later emperor, he was subject to the same scorn as his son. Dio Cassius reports that he begged Gaius for his life in fear and trembling: "he fell at the emperor's feet with tears and lamentations, all the while calling him many divine names and paying him worship [θειάσας αὐτὸν πολλά καὶ προσκυνήσας]; and at last he vowed that if he were allowed to live he would offer sacrifice to him" (59.27.4–6). Prostration as a supplicating gesture was already customary, as was the address to Gaius as a god; cf. Alföldi, *Repräsentation*, 50. But the vow to sacrifice was unusual.

as a prostration? In terms of the symbolic language of Parthian culture, it is to be expected.[22] On coins minted under Augustus, Parthians who surrendered field standards were depicted as kneeling (*BMC* 1, Table 1, 7–9; Table 2, 11–12), although the emperor is not shown on the same side of the coin. Homage to Roman field standards was probably performed with the same symbolic gesture. But if Artabanus had reverenced the standards by kneeling before them after his parley with Vitellius, the fact could have been known in Palestine, because the tetrarch Herod Antipas had played an important role at those negotiations (*Ant.* 18.101–2) and Vitellius visited Jerusalem with him a short time late (*Ant.* 18.122).

The Jews at Alexandria also were well aware of the new custom at the imperial court. Philo writes with some pride of his people:

> For all others, men, women, cities, nations, countries, regions of the earth, I might almost say the whole inhabited world, groaning though they were at what was happening, flattered him all the same and magnified him out of all proportion and augmented his vanity. Some too even introduced into Italy the barbarian practice of prostrating themselves [τὴν προσκύνησιν], a degradation of the high tradition of Roman freedom. One nation only standing apart, the nation of the Jews, was suspected of intending opposition, since it was accustomed to accept death as willingly as if it were immortality, to save them from submitting to the destruction of any of their ancestral traditions, even the smallest. (Philo *Leg. Gai.* 116–17)

This is a significant statement, because it stands at an important place in the *Legatio*. There, Gaius's self-apotheosis is first illustrated by his inclination to compare himself to the Greek demigods Dionysus, Heracles, and the Dioscuri (78ff.); then follows an inflation of his claim, so that he identifies himself with the Olympian gods Hermes, Apollo, and Ares (93ff.). But the high point of his madness is his action against the Jews, because here he offends against the one and only God (114ff.). Only at this point is prostration mentioned. The readiness of the Jews to undergo martyrdom is connected with the self-deification that becomes fully evident in this action.

Philo plays skillfully on the irritation that the new form of homage had aroused in the proud Roman aristocracy. Senators were even required to prostrate themselves before Gaius's empty chair in the capitol (Dio Cassius 59.24.4). Beyond this, individual members of the senatorial aristocracy

---

22. We can deduce this from an analogous case: when the Armenian king Tiridates sacrificed to Nero's images in 63 C.E. in a similar situation, he prostrated himself before them (Dio Cassius 62.23.3). When, some thirty years earlier, Artabanus sacrificed to the images of Augustus and Gaius (Dio Cassius 59.27.3), he would probably have prostrated himself also.

were subjected to deep personal humiliation. Seneca expresses his disgust
in the following words:

> Gaius Caesar granted life to Pompeius Pennus, that is, if failure to take it
> away is granting it; then, when Pompeius after his acquittal was expressing
> his thanks, Caesar extended his left foot to be kissed. Those who excuse the
> action, and say that it was not meant to be insolent, declare that he wanted
> to display his gilded—no, his golden—slipper studded with pearls. Yes, pre-
> cisely—what insult to the consular if he kissed gold and pearls, since other-
> wise he could have found no spot on Caesar's person that would be less
> defiling to kiss? But this creature, born for the express purpose of changing
> the manners of a free state into a servitude like Persia's, thought it was not
> enough if a senator, an old man, a man who had held the highest public
> offices, bent the knee and prostrated himself before him in full sight of the
> nobles, just as the conquered prostrate themselves before their conquerors;
> he found a way of thrusting Liberty down even lower than the knee! (Seneca
> *De Benef.* 2.12.1–2)

Seneca speaks here for that group who despised prostration as the hybrid
claim of an autocratic ruler, and who nevertheless were forced to perform
it themselves. There are also indications in Philo that he and the delegation of Alexandrian Jews he led had to prostrate themselves before Gaius.
He says of his second audience with the emperor:

> When we were brought into his presence the moment we saw him we bowed
> our heads to the ground with all respect and timidity [μετ' αἰδοῦς καὶ
> εὐλαβείας τῆς ἁπάσης νεύοντες εἰς τοὔδαφος] and saluted him addressing
> him as Emperor Augustus. The mildness and kindness with which he replied
> to our greeting was such that we gave up not only our case but our lives for
> lost! In a sneering, snarling way he said, "Are you the god-haters who do not
> believe me to be a god, a god acknowledged among all the other nations but
> not to be named by you?" And stretching out his hands towards heaven he
> gave utterance to an invocatory address which it was a sin even to listen to,
> much more to reproduce in the actual words. (Philo *Leg. Gai.* 352–53)

The text is formulated in such a way that one need not necessarily imagine a prostration: the wording could also mean a deep bow. But it can
scarcely have been in Philo's interest to emphasize that he and the other
four delegates knelt before Gaius. That could have compromised him. On
the other hand, prostration is attested in a number of places for the years
39–40 in the reign of Gaius,[23] so that this Jewish delegation, in its precari-

---

23. The difficulty of proving that prostration was a regular part of court ceremony is
rooted in the fact that the attested cases all point to special situations, when the prostration
can always be interpreted as a gesture of supplication; this is true both of Vitellius (Dio
Cassius 59.27.4–6) and Pompeius Pennus (Seneca *De Benef.* 2.12.1–2). Similarly, Domitius
Afer successfully petitioned Gaius for his life in the senate, "and finally he threw himself on

ous situation, would scarcely have been able to appear before Gaius without respecting this aspect of court ceremonial. Thus, we must suppose with E. M. Smallwood that the Jewish delegates also prostrated themselves before Gaius.[24] Here the demand had really become a diabolical temptation. In itself it was a normal act for petitioners and those seeking protection to kneel. Great crowds of Jews knelt before Pontius Pilate to stop him from desecrating the holy city with imperial images (*Bell.* 2.171, 174).[25] But no one would have thought, in that case, that they were thereby attributing divine character to the Roman prefect. Gaius, on the other hand, connected prostration with his claim to divine honors. In the audience scene described by Philo he openly ridicules Jewish reverence for God and speaks the name of Yahweh in blasphemous fashion: this seems to be the interpretation we must place on Philo's report. Here we really do see the emerging alternative that is crucial in the Temptation story: the choice between worship of God and worship of idols.

In deliberate contrast to Gaius Caligula, his successor Claudius forbade prostration (Dio Cassius 60.5.4). It is then attested again in the reigns of Nero and Domitian, that is, before those young emperors whose absolutist claims to power ruptured the traditional conception of the *res publica.*

Nero also allowed himself to be addressed as a god in his lifetime, by the Parthian king Tiridates (Dio Cassius 63.5.2), and Domitian claimed the title "dominus et deus" for himself. But only under Gaius Caligula was the latent conflict of such claims with Jewish monotheism manifest. His attempt to transform the Jerusalem Temple into a sanctuary of the imperial cult had to be experienced as a direct attack on the worship of the one and only God.

Conferral of Power

The Satan of the Temptation story boasts that he has power over all the kingdoms of the earth. This is especially emphasized in the Lukan version.

---

the ground and lying there prostrate played the suppliant to his accuser" (Dio Cassius 59.19.5). Another time, people in Gaius's immediate surroundings fell down before him when the suspicious emperor accused them of concealed hatred for him (Dio Cassius 59.25.8, in Patricius's version). Still, some general observations are indicative, including Philo's note about Gaius's introduction of a new and barbaric custom (*Leg. Gai.* 116–17), or Dio's statement that "to most of the senators, even, he merely extended his hand or foot for προσκυνεῖν" (Dio Cassius 59.27.1). It is true that only the *supplicatio* of Vitellius is offered as an example. But that is an instance in which it was done by a senator. If his prostration is particularly emphasized, it will have been the rule for all the other *ordines.* The best proof that prostration had become part of normal court ceremony is its prohibition by Claudius: καὶ προσαπηγόρευσε μήτε προσκυνεῖν τινα αὐτόν (Dio Cassius 60.5.4).

24. E. M. Smallwood, *Philonis Alexandrini,* 209–11, 318. The Jewish delegates could have called on the example of Naaman the Syrian to justify their prostration (cf. 2 Kings 5:18).

25. Compare also the kneeling supplication of the Jewish throng before Petronius (*Ant.* 18.271–72).

After he has shown Jesus all the kingdoms of the world (οἰκουμένη; Matthew has κόσμος), he says to him: "To you I will give *their glory* and all this authority; *for it has been given over to me, and I give it to anyone I please.* If you, then, will worship me, *it will all be yours* (Lk 4:6-7). The italicized portions are lacking in Matthew. Luke emphasizes, on the one hand, the *ecumene*—that is, the inhabited world—that for him is largely identical with the Roman Empire (cf. especially Lk 2:1; Acts 17:6). On the other hand, he states explicitly what is only implicit in the Matthean version: the ruler of the world has the power to confer authority. Perhaps Matthew omitted this part because for him Jesus already has all power in heaven *and on earth* (Mt 28:18). But could it be that Luke also emphasizes these features that hint at the Roman emperor, against the background of figures such as Nero and Domitian?[26]

However, the original Temptation story in Q probably was already shaped by such experiences. The notion of a ruler who possessed power over the "kingdoms" of the earth and could bestow them at will on others could easily have suggested Gaius Caligula in particular.[27] During his short reign he established six kings in the East. The first of these was the Jewish king Agrippa I, whom he released from prison soon after he began to rule. Agrippa had encouraged Gaius's aspirations to the imperial throne even during Tiberius's lifetime, and this had lost him the favor of Tiberius. Now, "as compensation" he received the tetrarchies of Lysanias and Philip (*Ant.* 18.237). In inscriptions, Agrippa proudly calls himself μέγας βασιλεύς (*OGIS* 1:419). He did in fact rule a number of kingdoms, especially after he inherited the territories of Herod Antipas in 39 C.E. and, beginning in the year 41, reigned over the whole kingdom that had once belonged to Herod I.

Another Herodian prince was less fortunate. Agrippa's uncle, Herod Antipas, at the urging of his wife Herodias, made a bid for the royal title in the year 39. But Agrippa I denounced him, with the result that he was deposed and banished to Gaul (*Ant.* 18.240–56). Both the surprising success of Agrippa I and the misfortune of Antipas made clear to all Palestine who it was that had the power to bestow kingdoms and to take them away.

We hear of still other client kings established by Gaius: he made Antio-

---

26. Thus R. Morgenthaler, "Roma—Sedes Satanae." He indicates correctly that in Luke's text "the second temptation is about the Roman Empire" (p. 292), but considers the corresponding features in Lk 4:6 to be Lukan redaction. Yet the demonizing of the Roman Empire hinted at here is contrary to the tendency we find otherwise in Luke, to underplay conflicts between early Christian groups and the Roman state. For this reason, Schürmann, (*Das Lukasevangelium*, 211) considers Lk 4:6 to be traditional.

27. This idea had already occurred to Augustus: "From my hand did the nations of the Parthians and Medes receive their kings" (*Res Gestae* 33; cf. 27).

chus IV king of Commagene and Cilicia (Dio Cassius 59.8.2); Soemus he placed over Iturea (59.12.2); and three sons of Antonia Tryphaena were made kings of Armenia Minor, Thrace, and the kingdom of Pontus and the Bosporus (59.12.2). People in Palestine were also well informed about these and other rulers, because Agrippa I invited no less than five Roman client kings to Tiberias between the years 41 and 44 C.E.: Antiochus of Commagene, Sampsigeramus of Emesa, Cotys of Armenia Minor, Polemo of Pontus, and Herod of Chalcis (*Ant.* 19.338–42).[28] The Syrian legate Marsus was so suspicious of this meeting that he sent the kings home as soon as he heard of it. This demonstrated once again, in a very public manner, who in the Roman Empire could give orders to kings.

Did kings prostrate themselves at their investiture? Dio Cassius describes a festive ceremony at which Gaius appointed four kings at one time. Gaius sat on the rostra in the Forum, with consuls at his left and right and silk awnings forming a canopy over the whole (Dio Cassius 59.12.2). But we read nothing about a prostration. Still, there are many traditions about client kings who knelt before Roman authorities as signs of their subordination. For example, Prusias, king of Bithynia, appeared before the senate in 167 B.C.E. in the garments of a freedman. He fell down and kissed the threshold of the senate house, hailing those assembled as his "savior-gods." Polybius condemns this servile behavior as unworthy of a king (Polybius 30.18.5; cf. Livy 45.44.20).

We may also recall Sulla's monument from the year 91 B.C.E., showing two kneeling client kings: one as a prisoner who was soon to be throttled during the triumphal procession, the other as a true vassal. Under Pompey a similar scene was repeated: King Tigranes prostrated himself before him (Dio Cassius 36.52.3).

From the first century C.E., we have witnesses to the prostration of King Tiridates of Armenia before Nero. In 63 he knelt and laid down his crown before Nero's image (Dio Cassius 62.23.3). After a magnificently planned procession of homage through Syria, Asia Minor, and Illyria, he came to Rome to receive his kingdom from the hand of Nero. At that moment, he and his whole company prostrated themselves. An outcry arose from the crowd of onlookers, and after a confused pause, Tiridates addressed Nero as a god. In his answer, Nero explained the meaning of the ceremony: it was to demonstrate his power to take away and to bestow kingdoms (ὅτι καὶ ἀφαιρεῖσθαι βασιλείας καὶ δωρεῖσθαι δύναμαι; Dio Cassius 63.5.3). The irritation aroused by the prostration shows that it was still something extraordinary in Rome, even if it represented an old tradition in the East.

---

28. On these client kings, see E. Schürer, *History of the Jewish People* 1.448–51 n. 34.

Only under Gaius Caligula had it become identified at Rome as the symbol of a tyrannical ruler, and it retained its negative associations with the tyrant.

On the basis of all this evidence, it seems likely to me that it was possible, in Palestine, to imagine the investiture of a king in connection with a prostration. It is thus a secondary question whether the bestowal of the kingdom on Agrippa I was actually accompanied by a prostration.[29] In any case, Agrippa had acquired the reputation at Rome of encouraging the absolutist tendencies of Gaius. Dio Cassius calls him and Antiochus of Commagene "teachers of tyrants" (τυραννοδιδασκάλους; Dio Cassius 59.24.1) and, after mentioning their negative influence on Gaius, briefly alludes to the humiliating prostration of all the senators before Gaius's empty chair in the capitol: τὸν τοῦ Γαίου δίφρον τὸν ἐν τῷ ναῷ κείμενον προσεκύνησαν (59.24.4). Josephus makes clear that Agrippa I also emphasized the symbols of his royal power in Palestine, and that it was precisely that which excited the envy of his sister Herodias (*Ant.* 18.241). We can therefore suppose that this prince expected oriental court behavior from other people and practiced it himself before his emperor.[30]

The Conflict with Jewish Monotheism

The two motifs discussed so far—prostration and conferral of power— would fit any Roman emperor with absolutist tendencies, but conflict with Jewish monotheism is attested only for Gaius Caligula. He was the only emperor who attempted to have himself worshiped in the temple at Jerusalem in place of the biblical God. It was only he who demanded of Jews the worship that belonged to Yahweh alone. The Temptation story quite

---

29. K. Matthiae and E. Schönert-Geiss (*Münzen aus der urchristlichen Umwelt*, 41–42, 78) interpret (with some reservations) a temple scene on one of Agrippa I's coins (= Y. Meshorer, *Jewish Coins*, no. 89) as representing the coronation of Agrippa I by Claudius. They identify the kneeling figure with Agrippa I, but this interpretation is not certain. It could also be a sacrificial scene. The coronation of Agrippa I could be depicted on another coin (Meshorer, *Jewish Coins*, no. 93), on which Agrippa I (?) is shown standing between two figures. Independently of this, however, we can suppose that the people of Palestine might have interpreted the kneeling figure on the first-mentioned coin as the Jewish prince, since the legend reads "Agrippa, the Friend of Caesar, the Great King."

30. It is evident from the Gospels how routine prostration before a king as a gesture of homage was in the East. In Matthew, the wise men from the East do homage to the new king by kneeling before him (Mt 2:11). The soldiers of the cohort mock Jesus in Mark by kneeling in homage (Mk 15:19; cf. Mt 27:29). This prostration is missing in John, and Luke omits the whole scene. It is only plausible in the East and shows that the soldiers of the cohort were oriental mercenaries, not Roman soldiers. Senators and free Roman citizens rejected prostration: "The most that could be depicted in this connection is revealed by a scene on Trajan's column (no. 75, xliv) in which a Roman soldier makes a deep bow before the seated emperor, in order to kiss his hand in gratitude for a gift of money" (Gabelmann, *Audienz- und Tribunalszenen*, 103).

clearly revolves around this kind of alternative. Prostration before the diabolical "ruler of the world" is identical with refusal to worship the one and only God. The scene was probably drawn deliberately on the model of a prostration before a blasphemous ruler. The importance within this text of the gesture of kneeling in homage is evident from the way the demand made of Jesus is worded: "if you will fall down and worship me" (Mt 4:9). Luke expresses the same thing in a more veiled fashion: Jesus is to worship "before" Satan. In the scriptural citation with which Jesus rejects this demand, we again find the key word *proskynein*, but that word is neither in the Hebrew text nor in most of the Septuagint manuscripts, whose reading in Deut 6:13 and 10:20 is: κύριον τὸν θεόν σου φοβηθήσῃ καὶ αὐτῷ λατρεύσεις. This reading would not permit any reference within the text to a prostration.[31]

However, Codex Alexandrinus (fifth century C.E.) has at this point the reading that is also in Mt 4:10 and Lk 4:8: κύριον τὸν θεόν σου προσκυνήσεις καὶ αὐτῷ μόνῳ λατρεύσεις. In Deut 6:13, A's reading of προσκυνήσεις is supported by another minuscule (82, from the twelfth century) and by a number of early Christian authors: Justin, Clement of Alexandria, Origen, Cyril, and Chrysostom. In Deut 10:20 the witness for this reading is weaker: προσκυνήσεις in Codex Alexandrinus is supported only by Cyril. But the attestation of μόνῳ in both places is much broader.

This finding allows the possibility that the Christian scribe of Codex Alexandrinus was consciously or unconsciously influenced by the Temptation story when copying Deut 6:13 and 10:20. This seems probable when we compare the Hebrew text. There we find יָרֵא ("fear"), which most manuscripts correctly translate with φοβηθήσῃ. יָרֵא is not translated by προσκυνεῖν anywhere in the Septuagint[32] except in our two texts: Deut 6:13 and 10:20 (and here only in Codex Alexandrinus and one minuscule). Did the tellers of the Temptation story bend the quotation ad hoc

---

31. The conviction that Q was composed in a "consciously LXX milieu" (so K. Stendahl, *School of St. Matthew,* 150) rests especially on the Temptation story. The only citations that offer proof of this are those in which agreement with the Septuagint (LXX) wording means disagreement with the Masoretic text (MT). Three passages are relevant. First, in Mt 4:4, ἀλλ᾽ ἐπὶ παντὶ ῥήματι ἐκπορευομένῳ διὰ στόματος θεοῦ, the MT lacks an equivalent for ῥήματι. But only Matthew includes this part of Deut 8:3, and he could have added it to the text before him. Where Matthew and Luke agree, they both agree with LXX and MT. Second, Mt 4:7 and Lk 4:12 agree with the LXX in recording the admonition "Do not put the Lord your God to the test" in the singular, while MT has the plural. But the context permits only the singular. Third, Mt 4:10/Lk 4:8 (see above) is by no means "marked by typical Septuagint variations" (so Schulz, *Q,* 185), but is a variant reading within the LXX tradition. Here again we may have an adaptation to the action in the Temptation story that is determined by the context (so Schürmann, *Das Lukasevangelium,* 212 n. 184). It is thus possible, but not certain, that the Temptation story (and so Q) was influenced by the LXX.

32. Cf. E. Hatch and H. A. Redpath, *Concordance to the Septuagint* 2:1297–98.

for their own purposes? They were certainly not afraid of that kind of "manipulation" of the biblical text, because in the second temptation they also have Satan quote the Bible incorrectly. He omits a phrase that would not fit the situation:

> He will command his angels concerning you
> *to guard you in all your ways.*
> On their hands they will bear you up,
> so that you will not dash your foot against a stone.
>
> (Ps 91:11-12)

The italicized line is missing. Satan is not interested in talking about protection "[on] your ways," but about confidence in leaping from the pinnacle of the temple. Anyone who could leave out a whole phrase at this point was also capable of making a free translation of the Old Testament text in the third temptation. But the willful variation from the Old Testament text as given can be explained by the fact that the narrators wanted to hear in the text a condemnation of "prostration" before the "ruler of this world"!

There is another possible explanation for the variation from the Old Testament text in Mt 4:10 and Lk 4:8.[33] In its content, the commandment Jesus quotes against Satan corresponds entirely to the *sh^ema*, the confession of the one and only God that is to be spoken daily by every Jew. The question is whether there was a variant of the *sh^ema* that matches the text of Mt 4:10 and Lk 4:8. In fact, Justin cites the *sh^ema* in such a form: "Thou shalt worship [προσκυνήσεις] the Lord thy God and him only [μόνῳ] shalt thou serve with all thy heart and all thy strength, the Lord who made thee" (*Apology* 1.16.7). Was a form like this already in circulation in the first century C.E.? Or is Justin also writing under the influence of the Temptation story? In *Dial.* 125.4, Justin quotes the beginning of the "first commandment" cited above, and quite clearly he is drawing on the first part of the Temptation story.

We can leave open the question whether the Temptation story has adapted the Old Testament text ad hoc to the historical situation as we have surmised it, or whether it was following a traditional monotheistic confessional formula in the variations it makes in the Old Testament verses. In any case, it is clear that the prostration before Satan that is demanded is a denial of monotheism.

All this makes it probable that the model for Satan in the Temptation story was the emperor Gaius Caligula. In principle, Nero (54–68) and Domitian (81–96) would also be candidates. But the latter must be elimi-

---

33. Cf. Polag, *Christologie*, 148; Gnilka, *Das Matthäusevangelium*, 91.

nated as an inspiration for the Temptation story in Q for chronological reasons, although he could have influenced the Matthean and Lukan versions. Nero is a real possibility. But only in the case of Gaius Caligula do we find the sharp conflict between self-apotheosis and Jewish monotheism; only with him do we find the bestowal of a kingdom on a Jewish ruler in Palestine. Only at his court did prostration as a new custom arouse so much attention, both in Rome and among the Jews in the East. We would have, in that case, a terminus a quo for the Temptation story in Q. To the extent that we view the Temptation story in close connection with the redaction of the whole of the Sayings Source, we would at the same time have a point from which to date Q as a whole. Of course, the crucial question will be whether we can also find bases for fixing a terminus ad quem.

But first we should apply our observations on the temporal context of the Temptation story to the interpretations that have been advanced by scholars. All three of the basic types of interpretation—salvation-historical, christological, and parenetic—have, I believe, illuminated important aspects of this story.[34]

1. The salvation-historical interpretation[35] sees a reference running through the whole story to Israel's temptations in the desert. Jesus stands in the place of Israel and experiences anew Israel's temptations. It is certainly correct that the Temptation story focuses on Israel; it climaxes in Israel's fundamental confession of the one and only God and upholds it against all temptations and dangers. The Christian groups behind this story consider themselves unconditionally obligated to the Torah (cf. Lk 16:17Q). They unite with all Jews in their confession of God. To fall away from this confession is the greatest of all temptations, which Jesus has withstood in an exemplary manner.[36]

---

34. Surveys of interpretation may be found in H. Mahnke, *Versuchungsgeschichte*; Luz, *Matthäus*, 160–62; Gnilka, *Das Matthäusevangelium*, 84–85; Kloppenborg, "Literary Genre," 318–20.

35. The salvation-historical interpretation is most developed in J. Dupont, *Die Versuchungen Jesu in der Wüste*. The Old Testament *typoi* behind it include the miracle of the manna in Exodus 16, the water miracle at Massa in Exodus 17, and the worship of strange gods in Exodus 23 and 34. But the manna came down from heaven, while in the Temptation story earthly stones are to be turned into bread!

36. According to B. Gerhardsson (*Testing of God's Son*), the Temptation story is modeled on the *sh⁽e⁾ma* as interpreted by the rabbis. Loving God "with the whole heart" is opposed to the natural needs of eating and drinking; "with the whole soul" means readiness to stake one's life; "with all one's strength" refers to wealth. I agree that there is a reference to the *sh⁽e⁾ma*, but not necessarily with this interpretation.

2. The christological interpretation[37] sees the Temptation story as a struggle over the correct understanding of the Messiah, either as determined by faith in miracles (as in the first two temptations) or by hope in a political messiah who will assume power over the world (as in the last temptation).[38] If the emphasis lies on the third temptation, we would have to agree in principle with a "political" interpretation, except to say that here it is no Zealot ideal of the messiah that is being rejected, but a religiously inflated absolutist claim to power (a point on which those behind this text would have agreed with the Zealots). The problem is not the ordinary imperial cult that was widespread in all the provinces, but the extraordinary claims of absolutist rulers such as Gaius Caligula. The confession of Jesus as Son of God is incompatible with such claims.

3. The Temptation story as a whole has "parenetic" intent.[39] Like Jesus, his adherents must confess the one and only God without compromise and reject competing religious claims as satanic temptation. In the context of the whole Temptation story this means that nothing in the world—the promise of food, security, or power—is worth a single step away from the monotheistic confession. In the Caligula crisis of the year 40, this point of view was put to a very real test among Jews and Christians in Syro-Palestine.

The more one is convinced of the connections between the Caligula crisis and the Temptation story in Q, the more one will be inclined to bring the Temptation story (and Q) into proximity with the events of the year 40. Therefore, let me emphasize once more that memories of experiences under Caligula could have been revived in light of the actions of

---

37. Mahnke (*Versuchungsgeschichte*, 51–152, 190–94) sees here a rejection of the understanding of Jesus as a prophet like Moses, the eschatological high priest and messianic king. W. Stegemann ("Die Versuchung Jesu"), referring only to Matthew's Gospel, sees the meaning of the Temptation in the fact that Jesus' end on the cross was "transparent" from the beginning "as the expression of Jesus' unique relationship to God."

38. So esp. P. Hoffmann, "Die Versuchungsgeschichte in der Logienquelle." But the freedom movement preached the same monotheistic pathos as the Temptation story: since God alone is Lord, no one should pay taxes to the emperor (*Bell.* 2.118). They determined "neither to serve the Romans nor any other save God, for[God] alone [μόνος] is [humanity's] true and righteous Lord" (*Bell* 7.323).

39. The most prominent representatives of this type of interpretation are L. Schottroff and W. Stegemann, *Jesus von Nazareth*, 72–76. Schottroff sees in the third temptation the rejection of rebellious groups' illusionary dreams of power. But she cautions: "In view of the role that world power played in the political ideology of the *imperium Romanum*, one may not eliminate the anti-Roman aspect of the third temptation. Zealot and similar aspirations to power *and* Roman ideology are addressed in the same way" (p. 75). This point of view is heightened in the interpretation I am presenting here, except that the Zealot attempt at world power need not be regarded as a temptation for Christians. The temptation, rather, is the denial of God in face of world power.

later absolutist rulers such as Nero. Only when we have some points by which to fix a terminus ad quem can we exclude the possibility of a much later dating.

If the Temptation story as introduction to the sayings of Jesus gives us indications of a terminus a quo, the same is true of the conclusion of Jesus' words in Q. Here we find a series of apocalyptic sayings from which we can gather something about the future expectations of the Sayings Source. According to this, the Parousia of the Son of man will come quite suddenly, when all is at peace. It is comparable to the flood in the time of Noah: "They were eating and drinking, and marrying and being given in marriage" (Lk 17:27). In a parallel comparison with the time before the destruction of Sodom, the normal routines of peacetime are still more vividly depicted: "They were eating and drinking, buying and selling, planting and building" (Lk 17:28). No one expects the end. Instead, when the Son of man comes some will be grinding grain, while others will be sleeping (Lk 17:34-35). Nothing is said about wars and catastrophes preceding the end. The mood is more like that in 1 Thessalonians, written in 52 C.E.: "When they say, 'There is peace and security,' then sudden destruction will come upon them" (1 Thess 5:3). How differently the Gospels (Matthew 13 par.), written after the Jewish war, speak about the time before the end!

That in Q we are still in the time before the Jewish war is evident also from other statements about the future. Thus Lk 13:34-35 and Mt 23:37-39 contain a saying against the temple[40] that threatens its abandonment rather than its destruction: "See, your house is left to you [desolate]. And I tell you, you will not see me until the time comes when you say, 'Blessed is the one who comes in the name of the Lord' " (Lk 13:35; Mt 23:38-39). The passive ἀφίεται is to be interpreted as *passivum divinum*: God will forsake the temple. The time of God's absence is limited; when the one who is to come in the name of the Lord appears, God will be present again. The idea of God's leaving the temple is not foreign to Jewish thought. It is part of the message of Ezekiel, and during the Jewish war the thought arose once more, probably a revival of existing fears and apprehension.[41] But what happened in the year 70 C.E. was more than a "forsak-

---

40. O. H. Steck (*Israel*, 40–58) sees in this prophecy a piece of Jewish tradition. But even if it originated outside early Christian circles, it must have been adopted by them as their own tradition, so that in any case we must find a way to understand it as part of Christian tradition, even if it is not only that.

41. According to *Bell*. 6.299, a voice was heard in the temple by night: "We are departing hence." Tacitus confirms this tradition: "et audita major humana vox excedere deos" *(Hist.* 5.13).

ing" of the temple. A threat against the temple composed after 70 would have spoken more plainly of its destruction.

J. Wellhausen's late dating of the Sayings Source was based primarily on two arguments.[42]
    1. A comparison between the content of the tradition in Q and the same tradition in Mark's Gospel often shows that Q's version is more recent. But there are contrary examples. R. Laufen's systematic comparison of all the double traditions showed that in most cases Mark's is the later version.[43]
    2. Matthew 23:34-36 and Lk 11:49-51 presuppose the murder of Zechariah, the son of Barachiah or Baruch, in the year 67–68 C.E., as reported by Josephus (*Bell.* 4.335–43). However, O. H. Steck has shown, I think persuasively, that this is true only of the Matthean version, and not for that of Luke, which is identical on the whole with Q.[44]

THE SOCIAL ENVIRONMENT OF
THE SAYINGS SOURCE

By general consensus, the Sayings Source originated between 40 and 70 C.E. In what follows I will attempt to fix the period more closely. Methodologically speaking, our starting point is the depiction of three social groups and figures in Q: "Israel," "Gentiles," and "Pharisees." The decisive question will be whether a historical situation can be recognized in which the constellation of these social groups and figures that is assumed in Q is, in fact, possible—in contrast to other situations in which it would be improbable or impossible. We need to keep in mind that the texts give us no direct picture of the social environment of the Sayings Source; all we have is an interpretation of it based on a number of traditions.

Israel

The theological focus of the Sayings Source is Israel. At the beginning, and again at the end, there is a preaching of judgment directed at Israel. John the Baptizer attacks a false sense of security based on collective descent from Abraham. Salvation is only for individuals who repent. This individualizing message of judgment also marks the little "sayings apocalypse" at the end of Q. The judge separates the good from the bad and severs the most intimate social ties: two will be sleeping in one bed, but only one will be "taken"; two will be grinding at one mill, but only one will

---

42. J. Wellhausen, *Einleitung*, 64–79, 118–23, 157–76.
43. R. Laufen, *Die Doppelüberlieferungen der Logienquelle*. In a total of nine instances, Q has the older version four times, Mark twice. In three cases it is partly Mark and partly Q that is closest to the older version (p. 385).
44. Steck, *Israel*, 26–33.

be saved (Lk 17:34-35Q). This preaching of judgment is so sharp and inexorable in Q that some exegetes think the Sayings Source did not expect Israel's conversion.[45] And yet, the individualized preaching of judgment is aimed at Israel. This is evident in the case of the Baptizer: only Jews can be told not to rely on their descent from Abraham! But this address to Israel is also emphasized at the end of Q. The sayings apocalypse is followed by the promise to the Twelve that they will join the Son of man in "judging" the twelve tribes of Israel (Mt 19:28-29; Lk 22:28-30).[46] Although the preaching of judgment sees the whole "generation" in danger, it calls to conversion in order that individuals may be saved in the coming catastrophe, as were Noah and Lot in their day. Behind Q is a renewal movement within Judaism that, with prophetic radicalism, demands the conversion of every individual in Israel.[47] In this way it continues the message of the Baptizer and of Jesus.

We know of a movement in the history of early Christianity that believed it was sent to Israel. This mission to Israel was represented at the apostolic council by Peter, who is counterposed at that point to the gentile missionaries Paul and Barnabas. The following indications point to connections between the Sayings Source and this Israel mission, which did not originate at the apostolic council.

1. Peter is closely identified with the "Twelve." In lists of the Twelve, he is always the first one named (Mk 3:16-19 par.). Paul also knows him in this connection (1 Cor 15:5). Two of the Twelve, Peter and John, appear as dialogue partners of the Antiochene delegation, along with James, the brother of the Lord, as representative of the Jerusalem community. These same "Twelve" are associated with Israel at a crucial point in the Sayings Source—near the end. The fact that they will judge Israel in the end time can mean either that they will carry out the final judgment on the people or that they will reign over Israel in the end (Mt 19:28-29).

---

45. Thus esp. Lührmann, on Lk 11:49-51Q: "This proclamation of judgment no longer anticipates a conversion of Israel; all that remains is its condemnation" (*Redaktion*, 47). This is also the opinion of Kloppenborg ("Literary Genre," chap. 4, esp. pp. 200–204).

46. It is not certain that Mt 19:28-29Q was the end of Q. E. Bammel ("Das Ende von Q") sees this saying as a testamentary decree with which Q came to a close. The whole sayings collection would thus have received the character of a testament. In any case, this Q logion contains a message of salvation for Israel: the twelve tribes will return from the Dispersion. Their being "judged" does not imply a judgment of vengeance and destruction. The nearest analogy is *Ps. Sol.* 17:26, 29, where the messiah judges a sanctified people from which all evil has been removed.

47. Thus also Steck: "The sayings source itself could be a collection of logia for the instruction of these preachers to Israel, from which they could extract their message to Israel, words to followers and words for themselves, but also woes and words of judgment for the stiff-necked" (*Israel*, 288).

2. The Israel mission is faithful to the law. It concedes the admission of an uncircumcised man into one of the new gentile Christian communities, but not without resistance (Gal 2:3-4). Peter believes that he himself is sent to "the circumcision." When he is later prepared to eat with gentile Christians at Antioch (Gal 2:11-12), that does not mean that he transgressed Jewish food regulations. The Sayings Source is also faithful to the law. This is clear not only from the Temptation story at the beginning, but also from the saying about the indissolubility of the law (Lk 16:17Q). All the Jesus traditions that indicate a "liberal" attitude toward the Torah are missing from Q. We find no word that relativizes the Sabbath norms or the food laws. The tithe is taken for granted (Lk 11:42Q) and the demand for purity is not criticized—instead, it is extended from the outside of the vessel to its contents. It is more important that the contents are not contaminated by greed and wickedness (Lk 11:39Q).[48]

3. The apostolic council results in a mutual limitation of the missions to Israel and to the Gentiles, based on geographical and ethnic criteria and on the content of the message. The traditionists of the Sayings Source feel themselves sent to Israel. They expect that at the end people (Jews and Gentiles?) from all four corners of the world will enter the reign of God (Mt 8:11-12Q). They accept the incorporation of individual Gentiles at present, by way of exception (Mt 8:1ff.). But if Mt 10:5-6 and 10:23 are, literarily or historically, part of the Sayings Source, this would indicate that they restricted their active mission to Israel, as agreed upon at the apostolic council.

> The two Israel sayings in Matthew's special material can be related only secondarily to the situation of Q. It is not at all certain that they were in Q, but even so they are important for an assessment of the document. Either they entered the Sayings Source at a second level, before Matthew incorporated it in his Gospel—in which case their acceptance must have occurred in a situation in which a restriction of the mission to Israel was a reasonable option, which would mean that Q was older than that situation—or else they were sayings handed down independently of Q. In that case, we need to consider that the three Israel sayings (Mt 10:5-6; 10:23; 19:28-29) are connected both in content and in the history of their transmission. The Sayings Source, addressed to Israel, would have in these Israel sayings a "parallel," only one part of which was accepted into the Sayings Source. If we look for a historical location for the three Israel sayings, we arrive at the ambience of the apostolic council; there the restriction to Israel demanded in Mt 10:5-6 and 10:23 is made programmatic for some

---

48. Schulz (*Q*, 244-45) correctly emphasizes Q's faithfulness to the Torah. See also idem, " 'Die Gottesherrschaft is nahe herbeigekommen.' "

Christians. However, in view of the uncertainty surrounding the literary and historical relationship to Q of the two sayings in Mt 10:5-6 and 10:23, we must make our decisions independently of them.

Therefore we must ask, When would we be most likely to find a mission to Israel, faithful to the law and, at least ideally, connected with the "Twelve"? At the latest, in the mid-50s we find missionaries from Palestine in Paul's mission territory, some of them arguing for the circumcision of gentile men and thrusting the communities into sharp conflict. These Jewish-Christian missionaries crossed not only the boundaries that had been established at the apostolic council, but also boundaries that were implicitly—and perhaps explicitly—laid down in Q. It follows that Q must have existed before that time.

We may even have a witness for the existence of Q traditions in the 40s, namely, Paul. It is striking that in his reflections on the mission to Israel in Romans 11 he refers to *topoi* that reveal some contact with ideas present in Q.

1. As in Q, the Deuteronomic picture of the persecution of prophets is extended by Paul into the present time: as Elijah was persecuted, so are the apostles (Rom 11:1ff.). The correlation of the *topos* of persecution of prophets is even closer between Q and 1 Thess 2:14-16.

2. The idea that Gentiles will make Israel "jealous" for the faith (Rom 11:11) has an analogy in those exemplary Gentiles in Q who shame Israel by their faith and their readiness for conversion: the centurion of Capernaum, the Ninevites, and the queen of the South.

3. The expectation of a pilgrimage of nations to Zion is the basis not only for the *logion* Mt 8:11-12Q, but also for Paul's hope that at the end of the ages "the full number of the Gentiles [will have] come in" (Rom 11:25).

4. Paul hopes that Christ, at his return, will effect a reconciliation with all Israel, even if it rejects the gospel now (Rom 11:26). Similarly, Q promises that those who now reject the message will greet Jesus at the Parousia with "Blessed is he who comes in the name of the Lord" (Lk 13:35Q).

Nowhere here do we find a direct quotation. Paul makes independent use of these *topoi*. It is probable that at the apostolic council he had argued against the Israel mission's interpretation of itself. Ten years later he refers back to ideas that he encountered at that time, in order to create a solid place for the Israel mission in his own theological universe. None of this gives us any secure data, but the question arises whether Q, for example, could have originated in the climate of the apostolic council, when the Israel mission had to interpret itself clearly in its confrontation with the newly created gentile mission. In order to pursue this question we need to clarify the image of the Gentiles in Q.

The Gentiles

Q's attitude toward "the Gentiles" is ambivalent. In two places we find a clear line of demarcation: "If you greet only your brothers and sisters, what more are you doing than others? Do not even the Gentiles do the same?" (Mt 5:47). Luke substitutes the vaguer word "sinners," which can also mean Gentiles, at this point (cf. Gal 2:15). The second instance speaks of care about eating, drinking, and apparel and concludes: "It is the Gentiles who strive for all these things" (Mt 6:32Q). The things attributed to Gentiles in both these verses are normal behavior: elementary social communication and the satisfaction of basic material needs. The addressees are supposed to elevate themselves above this "normal life." They are to develop a way of life that goes beyond all this. Here we have the voice of a tiny minority with an almost elitist way of thinking, which wants to distinguish itself in a positive way from the Gentiles. That makes the places where Gentiles are mentioned as examples of the right attitude all the more urgent: Tyre and Sidon would have repented long ago if they had seen the miracles Jesus performed in Galilee (Mt 11:20-22Q). The Ninevites and the queen of the South, in contrast to "this generation," listened to God's prophets and God's wisdom—for they were impressed by Jonah and Solomon (Mt 12:41-42Q). It is interesting that in these two sayings the hearers of the message are presented with "Gentiles" as examples, but in the places where we detect an aristocratic elevation beyond the "normal life" of the Gentiles, it is Jesus' disciples, the bearers of the message, who are addressed. Nevertheless, it is difficult to evaluate these sayings as indicators of the "social world" of Q, since they belong to the tradition.

For that same reason it is also difficult to give an unambiguous answer to the question whether Q already presumes a gentile mission. D. Lührmann presents three arguments in favor of this hypothesis.[49]

a. The judgment sayings indicate a very fundamental conflict with Israel. In them it is not only a question of conversion and awakening, "but simply of judgment."[50] But the prophet Jesus, son of Ananias, who appeared in Jerusalem in the years 62–70, also preached only destruction, and he addressed himself solely to Jews (cf. *Bell.* 6.300–309).

b. The mission discourse begins in Q with a promise to the Gentiles: "The harvest is plentiful, but the laborers are few; therefore ask the Lord of the harvest to send out laborers into his harvest" (Mt 9:37-38Q). But the harvest image does not imply any reference to the Gentiles. The Baptizer uses the same image, with his characteristic sharpness, but he addresses himself to Jews (Mt

---

49. Cf. Lührmann, *Redaktion*, 86–88.
50. Ibid., 88.

3:12). Matthew has applied the saying to the Israel mission; in his Gospel it introduces instructions for missionary activity restricted to Israel.

c. The positive descriptions of Gentiles are the most important argument: the centurion from Capernaum (Mt 8:5-13), and the people of Tyre and Sidon ripe for conversion (Mt 11:20-24Q). But these examples could also be interpreted as reproaches to the addressees, who are thereby called to repentance. Anyone who has these examples in mind is at least spiritually prepared to accept the gentile mission, even if he or she does not actively pursue it in person.[51]

In any case, the inclusion of the story of the centurion of Capernaum may well be traceable to a conscious act of redaction. Q knows of other miracles of Jesus—there are summary references to them at least in Mt 11:5Q and 11:20Q. But only one miracle story is included, even though, from a formal point of view, it does not fit in with the material collected in the Sayings Source. Does this positive portrayal of a gentile centurion not contradict the idea that effects of the Caligula crisis are still perceptible in Q? Could anyone see in the Roman state a satanic temptation to apostasy, and still represent a gentile centurion, possibly a representative of that state, as a a model of faith?

First, let us examine the function of this miracle story in Q. The Temptation story attests Jesus' authority and so legitimates all his words. The centurion, as a hearer of Jesus' words, also witnesses to Jesus' authority. In other words, in the Temptation story the author of the Sayings Source (who, in the final analysis, is Jesus) is present in the story; through the centurion, the readers are also incorporated in it. This vignette underscores the power of Jesus' words by relating them to the system of command and obedience in which the centurion himself is located. Jesus' words have greater authority than military orders: that is the centurion's message.

Can we imagine this kind of positive portrayal of a gentile centurion in the historical context of the time? Certainly! In the Caligula crisis it was the Roman army itself that appeared as a factor in maintaining balance. Its commander, the Syrian legate Petronius, avoided executing the emperor's orders and thus prevented war from breaking out. Jewish sources speak of him with great admiration. Philo as much as calls him a "God-fearer" (*Leg. Gai.* 245). This very Petronius refers, in his negotiations with the demonstrating Jews, to his orders: "War will be made on you by him who sent me, not by me; for I too, like you, am under orders [καὶ γὰρ

---

51. This is the thesis of P. D. Meyer, "Gentile Mission in Q." The most thorough discussion of the question of a gentile mission in Q is in U. Wegner, *Der Hauptmann von Kafarnaum*, 296–334, in which arguments against a gentile mission prevail.

αὐτός, ὥσπερ ὑμεῖς, ἐπιτάσσομαι]" (*Bell.* 2.195). This is similar to the attitude of the centurion of Capernaum: "For I also am a man under authority [καὶ γὰρ ἐγὼ ἄνθρωπός εἰμι ὑπὸ ἐξουσίαν]" (Mt 8:9). Obviously, these words are not an echo of Petronius's statement. Josephus is simply attributing to him the same "professional ethics" that are articulated by the centurion in the Sayings Source. The analogy extends still farther: Petronius acknowledges that the Jews are also under orders that they cannot evade. God's law is to be respected above that of the emperor, and he too (according to Josephus) eventually sets God's commandment above the emperor's orders. In the same way, the centurion acknowledges the superiority of Jesus' word.

Let me reemphasize that the story of the centurion of Capernaum is not a reflection of the people's experiences with the Syrian legate Petronius. The story already existed in the tradition. But its incorporation in a collection of sayings dating from the time after 40 C.E. is understandable if we know that gentile officers could also have a positive image. Some of them behaved in exemplary fashion, and that had become clear especially in the Caligula crisis.

Pharisees

Except for "this generation," the Pharisees are the only group subjected to an obvious polemic in Q. The individual sayings against them are traditional, but their collection into a "chain" of accusations betrays a redactional interest, especially since some of them had their "addressees" added only at a later point. The "Pharisees" as addressees are missing in Mt 23:6 (contra Lk 11:43), as well as in Lk 11:44, 47 (contra Mt 23:27, 29-30).

It is possible that Q distinguishes two overlapping groups: the "Pharisees" (Lk 11:39-44) and the "lawyers" (νομικόι; Lk 11:46-52).[52] This differentiation of the addressees corresponds to differences in the content of the polemic. The Pharisees are criticized for their dubious practice of religion. They are addressed in terms of themes that are characteristic of them, concerning ritual purity and tithing (Lk 11:39; 11:42Q). In two of the sayings against the lawyers, on the other hand, the misuse of "teach-

---

52. Matthew has erased this distinction in his characteristic united front of "scribes and Pharisees." Luke has more probably retained the original differentiation. Or did Luke deliberately change and extend the group of those addressed in the second half of the "woes"? In favor of this could be the fact that νομικός appears six times in his Gospel. But outside the woes (three examples) it is clearly redactional only in Lk 7:30, while in Lk 10:25 (= Mt 22:35) it is just as obviously traditional. Luke 14:3 is hard to judge. In my opinion, the following consideration is decisive: had Luke been the first to introduce a distinction between Pharisees and "lawyers," one would expect that he would retain this distinction in the closing redactional note (11:53). Instead, he speaks there of "scribes and Pharisees" and thus varies the distinction between "Pharisees" and "lawyers" that was given in the Sayings Source.

ing" is criticized: laying burdens on others and the abuse of the "key of knowledge" to lock away the truth (Lk 11:46, 52). This would correspond to the situation before the Jewish war: not all the scribes were Pharisees at that time, and not all Pharisees were scribes.[53]

The collection of woes against Pharisees and lawyers could have existed already, but a particular redactional interest is visible in the insertion of a saying into the chain of woes that (1) is directed to a more general audience and (2) raises the critique to an extreme level by charging the addressees with a share of responsibility for the death of the prophets (Lk 11:49-51).[54] There is more at stake here than pious practices or the misuse of the social role of the teacher.

In Luke, the saying stands between two woes. Since the parallel in Matthew has clearly been edited, the Lukan version should be closer to Q:[55]

> Therefore also the Wisdom of God said,
> "I will send them prophets and apostles,
> some of whom they will kill and persecute,"
> so that this generation may be charged
> with the blood of all the prophets
> shed since the foundation of the world,
> from the blood of Abel to the blood of Zechariah,
> who perished between the altar and the sanctuary.
> Yes, I tell you,
> it will be charged against this generation.
>
> (Lk 11:49-51)

The saying refers to the Old Testament prophets, beginning with Abel—who surprisingly appears here among the prophets—and extending to the last prophet named in the Bible, Zechariah, who according to 2 Chr 24:20-22 was stoned to death in the temple. The idea that this is the prophet who is meant seems to presume an unusual degree of familiarity with the Bible. What lay person knows that Zechariah is the last prophet in the canon to be killed? The exactitude on this point does not accord very well with the much less precise inclusion of Abel among the prophets. Still, the saying can be satisfactorily explained. The lawyers attacked in Lk 11:47-48 have themselves given thought to the persecution of prophets in earlier

---

53. "Pharisees" were members of societies in which lay people and scribes practiced extraordinary devotion. "Scribes" exercised a social role that was not restricted to Pharisees. There were also Sadducean scribes. The insertion of the reproach of killing the prophets in the woes against the "lawyers" is consistent—it was not the lay Pharisees, but only the Pharisaic (and Sadducean) scribes who could conduct legal proceedings against "prophets" and Christians.

54. The suggestion that this "insertion" is an indication of redactional work was first made by Lührmann, *Redaktion*, 43–48.

55. The best analysis of this saying is Steck, *Israel*, 26–33, 50–53, 282–83.

days. They contrast the times in which the prophets were persecuted with the present, when their tombs are reverenced. We can expect of them that, in reviewing the epoch of the persecutions, they would be able to point out with scribal exactness the last of the murdered prophets. They could even have created a popular notion that the prophets were killed up to the time of Zechariah, but that that was no longer the case. They could look back to those evil times with smug satisfaction. The judgment speech in Lk 11:49-51 obliterates this distance between past and present. The addressees could not claim moral superiority over the bad old days, for the past evils have caught up with them.

The original saying does not accuse the present audience of killing prophets. Instead, it presumes that everyone knows that the murder of prophets is a thing of the past. But in the context of the Sayings Source, Christian prophets are included in the concept. Here, Jesus' sayings begin with the beatitudes (Lk 6:20-23Q), which draw an analogy between present-day Christians and the prophets of old: happy are those who are persecuted, "for that is what their ancestors did to the prophets" (Lk 6:23Q). The woes against the Pharisees are followed in Q by sayings that presuppose a situation of persecution: an admonition not to fear those who can kill the body (Lk 12:4-5Q), the saying about acknowledging and denying the Son of man (Lk 12:8-9Q), and the promise that the Holy Spirit will personally undertake the defense of the Christians (Lk 12:11-12Q). Later, the murder of prophets is again addressed directly:

> Jerusalem, Jerusalem,
> the city that kills the prophets
> and stones those who are sent to it!
> (Lk 13:34Q)

Here there is no time limit set on the killing of prophets; instead, a concrete place is mentioned as the center of their persecution: Jerusalem. The reference is unmistakable. Every reader of the Sayings Source must have thought, at this point, of Jesus and other figures in early Christianity who had lost their lives in Jerusalem.

Our preliminary conclusion is that the Sayings Source, by a combination and composition of a variety of traditions, has connected the "Pharisees" and "lawyers" with the persecution of contemporary Christian prophets. This can offer us an important time reference for the dating of Q, because not every situation between circa 40 and 70 C.E. was apt for the development of this kind of image of Pharisees and scribes on the part of Christians. It cannot be deduced from the Passion traditions, where the Pharisees are never explicitly referred to as Jesus' enemies. In those traditions, the Sanhedrin and the Roman governor are responsible for Jesus' execution. Of course, there were Pharisees in the Sanhedrin. But that makes it all the more astonishing that they are not specially mentioned. On the contrary, when one of them emerges from obscurity, he is described as a secret sympathizer with Jesus, such as the Pharisee Nicodemus in the Johannine tradition (Jn 3:1ff.; 7:50ff.; 19:39ff.) and Joseph of Arimathea in the synoptic tradition. The latter is not actually called a Pharisee, but as someone "who was . . . waiting expectantly for the kingdom of God" (Mk 15:43); he did not belong to the Sadducees, who denied any eschatological expectations. Thus, if we encounter the notion, both in the Sayings Source and in Mk 3:6, that the Pharisees persecuted Jesus (and were enemies to the Christians), it cannot be a reaction to Jesus' execution. Here later experiences have penetrated the image of the Pharisees.

In seeking a situation between circa 30 and 70 C.E. in which this image of the Pharisees might have originated, we can eliminate the whole decade of the 60s. At that time we find the Pharisees, and other scribes who insisted on fidelity to the law, siding with the Christians in a grave conflict. The Sadducean high priest Ananus had taken advantage of a temporary vacancy in the office of procurator to proceed against the Christians on his own initiative:

> He convened the judges of the Sanhedrin and brought before them a man named James, the brother of Jesus who was called the Christ, and certain others. He accused them of having transgressed the law and delivered them up to be stoned. Those of the inhabitants of the city who were considered the most fair-minded and who were strict in observance of the law [καὶ περὶ τοὺς νόμους ἀκριβεῖς] were offended at this. They therefore secretly sent to King Agrippa urging him, for Ananus had not even been correct in his first step [or: for this was not the first time that Ananus had acted unjustly], to order him to desist from any further such actions. (*Ant.* 20.200-201)

The people being praised here for their fairness and fidelity to the law are Pharisees. This emerges not only from their conflict with the Sadducean high priest. Josephus also characterizes the Pharisees elsewhere in terms of their ἀκρίβεια in interpreting the Law (*Bell.* 2.162) and their practice of it (*Vita* 191). The same word is applied to the scribes Judas and Matthias (*Bell.* 1.648), Simon (*Ant.* 19.332), and the Galilean Eleazar (*Ant.* 20.43), all of whom probably belonged to the Pharisee movement. Therefore, those who protested against the execution of James and other Christians were Pharisees, and the purpose of their protest was to prevent similar high-handed proceedings by the aristocracy against the Christians, or other groups, in the future. They were successful: the Sadducean high priest was deposed. All that happened in the year 62 C.E.

We have evidence of the Sadducees and Pharisees holding different attitudes toward the Christians at a still earlier period. When Paul was arrested in the late 50s at Jerusalem and brought before the Sanhedrin, there was a clash between representatives of the two movements. In Luke's version, the Pharisees say, "We find nothing wrong with this man" (Acts 23:9). The Lukan account could be historical to the extent that the positive attitude of the Pharisees toward the Christians that became evident in 62 had already been in the making beforehand. Thus, Christian and non-Christian sources agree that at the end of the 50s or the beginning of the 60s the attitudes of the two great scribal movements toward the Christians were divided. Therefore, the negative image of the Pharisees as persecutors must have been formed earlier, that is, ca. 30–55 C.E. Paul states as early as 1 Thessalonians (ca. 52 C.E.) that there were persecutions in Judea. Interestingly enough, he explains them in light of the same scheme of interpretation that we have already encountered in the Sayings Source—that is, he refers to the Deuteronomic tradition of the killing of the prophets (1 Thess 2:14-16). Is he writing out of the same background experiences as the redactors of the Sayings Source?

In any case, we have abundant evidence of persecutions in the 30s and 40s. Paul mentions them (Gal 1:13, 23; 1 Thess 2:14-16). We read in Acts of the stoning of Stephen in the 30s (7:54-60) and, in the 40s, of the killing of James, the son of Zebedee, with the sword (12:2). The parties to the conflict, in the case of Stephen, are representatives of the Hellenistic Jewish community (among whom was Saul; Acts 7:58); in the case of James, it is King Agrippa I, whose actions against the Christians pleased "the Jews." What interests us is the question whether Pharisees were directly or indirectly involved in these persecutions. Could the image of the Pharisees as persecutors, which has had such an impact on the Sayings Source in its present state of composition, have arisen at that time?

One Pharisee has testified to his part in the persecution of Christians—namely, Paul. He was active in the early 30s. For the persecution under Agrippa I between 41 and 44 C.E. we have to rely on indirect references. Josephus regarded Agrippa I as an indulgent ruler who gladly forgave his opponents, "for he considered mildness a more royal trait than passion" (*Ant.* 19.334). Then why did he move against the Christians? And what part did the Pharisees play?[56]

Agrippa I began his reign over all Palestine in 41 C.E. at a difficult moment. After the unexpected end of the Caligula crisis, some of the Jews who had been encouraged by their success appear to have lost all moderation. In Alexandria they took up arms and attacked their opponents (*Ant.*

---

56. On Agrippa, cf. Schürer, *History of the Jewish People* 1:442–54. He calls the reign of Agrippa I "golden days again for Pharisaism" (p. 446).

19.278). In Palestine, unrest was threatened after the desecration of a synagogue in Dor (cf. 19.300–311). Agrippa acted wisely. On arriving in Jerusalem he made a great ceremony of offering thanksgiving sacrifices, "omitting none of the ritual enjoined by our law [οὐδὲν τῶν κατὰ νόμον παραλιπών]" (19.293). At the same time he softened moods by remitting some taxes (19.299). He was no legalist; he was the first Jewish prince to permit himself to be depicted on coins. There were even statues of his daughters (19.357). It is understandable that he had difficulties with scrupulous people. Simon, one of their scribes, denounced him at a public meeting and asserted that he ought to be excluded from the temple (19.332). This Simon is described as ἐξακριβάζειν δοκῶν τὰ νόμιμα— probably meaning that he was a Pharisee. Agrippa succeeded in winning him over to his side and thus gained the allegiance of the law-observing factions by acceding to their demands. Josephus says of the king that "he scrupulously observed the traditions of his people. He neglected no rite of purification, and no day passed for him without the prescribed sacrifice" (19.331). Only by a demonstrative adherence to the law could he establish a stable rule in a country that had been set aflame by the Caligula crisis.

The Christians probably had gotten into a difficult situation on account of the Caligula crisis. It was known that they maintained a certain aloofness from the temple. According to Acts 6:14 it was his criticisms of the temple and Torah that caused Stephen to be stoned. But now God had visibly repulsed all the temple's critics. The death of Gaius Caligula showed what awaited anyone who acted against the temple. People were excited, and just as that agitation led to violence by some Jews in Alexandria against their gentile fellow citizens, so in Palestine it brought persecution on a minority within Judaism. It must at the very least have been tempting for Agrippa I to divert the pent-up tensions onto this group of Christians, and by the same act to demonstrate his scrupulous observance of the law. It is possible that in doing this he was influenced by the groups that, like Simon the scribe, were agitating for the sacredness of the temple.

The image of the Pharisees we find in Q thus fits best in the period after 40 C.E. By the end of the 50s it would no longer have been plausible. Within the space of twenty years there must have been an important shift in the relationship between Palestinian Jewish Christians and the Pharisees. Probably this rapprochement was due to James, the brother of the Lord,[57] who became the leading figure among the Jerusalem Christians in the 40s. But another factor may well have been changes in the relationship of the Pharisees and Sadducees that are no longer obvious to us.

---

57. For an assessment of James, the brother of the Lord, see the recent work of W. Pratscher, *Der Herrenbruder Jakobus*; and M. Hengel, "Jakobus der Herrenbruder."

We may now summarize our results. The indications of time that we have collected from within the Sayings Source point to a dating in the 40s as most probable. Traces of the Caligula crisis can still be detected in the Temptation story. At that time there may well have been a mission concentrated in Israel, but possibly drawing a line between itself and an incipient gentile mission. Gentile officers can be viewed in a positive light, because they had played a crucial role in overcoming the Caligula crisis. But in particular, the image of the Pharisees as persecutors is more plausible in this context than in later situations.

If Palestinian history has marked Q to such a large extent, the document itself must have originated in Palestine. Wherever the individual logia in Q reveal a local perspective we can, without doing violence to them, read them as the expressions of a Palestine-centered point of view. The places that appear in the Temptation story are all in Palestine, or at least can be imagined there: a rocky desert, the temple, a mountain from which one can view several kingdoms. It was really possible in the 40s to see two kingdoms from the top of Mount Hermon: that of Chalcis in the north and that of Agrippa in the south. Of course, the mythical mountain of temptation is not Hermon, but mythical mountains have their models in the world of real experience, to which the temple also belongs. It is taken for granted that everyone knows what the "pinnacle" of the temple is, even though modern scholarship has still not been able to identify it with absolute certainty.[58] However, we can do without a more precise location, because what are collected in the Sayings Source are primarily the traditions of itinerant charismatics—traditions that are not tied to a particular local community.

This suggested location of the Sayings Source in time and place makes it possible for us to discern the historical motive behind the collecting of these sayings of Jesus. Pride in the overcoming of the Caligula crisis, viewed as a great satanic temptation, imbues this document. While the synoptic apocalypse and the Passion account, which also originated in the middle of the first century, tend more to react to crisis and conflict and to depict the Christians in their suffering, the Sayings Source contains the plan for an active, ethical way of life that takes radical demands seriously. Among these are readiness for suffering and conflict. But the lack of a Passion account at the end of the document and its anticipation of the final judgment show that its focus is the realization of Jesus' commands as the authentic formulation of the will of God and the responsibility of human beings before their judge for the way they have lived their discipleship.

---

58. Cf. N. Hyldahl, "Die Versuchung auf der Zinne des Tempels."

While the events succeeding the Caligula crisis led the local community at Jerusalem into difficulties and brought additional pressure on them, that same crisis had encouraged other Christians to a disciplined life of discipleship. That crisis had shown that unconditional fidelity to the will of God has its promise and can be practiced even in hopeless situations and in the face of the world's pressures.

The Sayings Source thus belongs, in its thought and in its timing, to the second phase of the creation of the synoptic tradition, when, in the middle of the first century, the first parts of the Jesus tradition were committed to writing in Palestine. The composition of the Gospels themselves represents a third phase in the history of the synoptic tradition. It begins outside Palestine and is marked by both its nearness to and its distance from the Jewish war of 66–74 C.E. It will be the subject of the last chapter of this book.

6

The Gospels and Their Provenance

The Jesus traditions became historically powerful when they were shaped into the new form called "gospel," an early Christian variant of the ancient "biography"[1] devised by the author of Mark. Matthew and Luke further developed the form by incorporating material from the Sayings Source. The situation in which the Jesus traditions were written down as Gospels had changed greatly from the time when the Sayings Source was recorded. Thus, the latter probably was written in Palestine, while the Gospels originated at varying distances from that land. Our purpose here is to investigate whether their relationship to Palestine can be better clarified. The Sayings Source was composed between 40 and 55 C.E., against the background of a "Temptation" that had been successfully resisted. All the Gospels, however, have the Jewish war of 66–70 C.E. already behind them. Our question will be how the growing distance from that war has influenced the shape of the Gospels. The Sayings Source is close to the culture of the itinerant charismatics, but in the Gospels we detect an orientation to a different way of life. This makes it appropriate to ask whether Jesus traditions have been adapted in the Gospels to fit the needs of resident local communities. In what follows, we will investigate the locating, dating, and *Sitz im Leben* of the Gospels. In doing so, we will give most of our attention to the oldest Gospel and somewhat less to its further development by Matthew and Luke.

---

1. Classic form criticism emphatically differentiated the Gospels from ancient biographies; cf. K. L. Schmidt, "Die Stellung der Evangelien." However, they are now being reevaluated as a special variant of the ancient form; see, e.g., A. Dihle, "Die Evangelien und die griechische Biographie," an essay that relates the Gospels to the biographical tradition, but distinguishes them as descriptions of a unique event in which the Old Testament promises are fulfilled. K. Berger (*Formgeschichte des Neuen Testament,* 352ff.) goes still further in including the Gospels within the genre of "biography." His polemic against A. Dihle rests, in my opinion, on a misunderstanding.

PROXIMITY TO AND DISTANCE FROM PALESTINE
IN THE GOSPELS AND THE QUESTION
OF THEIR LOCATION

Despite intense efforts, the location of Mark's Gospel remains unclear. Some, on the basis of an ancient church tradition witnessed by Irenaeus, place it in Rome (*Adv. Haeres.* 3.1.1 = Eusebius *Eccl. Hs.* 5.8.2–4).[2] Others, on general historical grounds, locate it in Syria; it seems natural to think that the oldest Gospel was written in the land where Hellenistic Christianity originated, especially since that form of Christianity was the home of Gospels written in Greek.[3]

It is important to note that the earliest form of ancient church tradition about Mark's Gospel is neutral on the question of "Syria or Rome." We learn from Papias (Eusebius *Eccl. Hs.* 3.39.14–15) only that Mark wrote the Gospel on the basis of oral traditions received from Peter, but not when and where this occurred. Irenaeus could have deduced those points from Papias's account.[4] Most of our reports about Mark himself point more to the East: in Acts, he is in Palestine (12:12) and Syria (12:25; 13:5; 15:37); in the Pauline letters he is in Asia Minor (Philem 24; Col 4:10; 2 Tim 4:11). In both branches of the tradition, Mark is connected with Barnabas (cf. Acts 12:25; Col 4:10), which favors the identity of those two persons.

---

2. Irenaeus does not say explicitly that Mark's Gospel originated in Rome, but it seems to me that he presumes it: "Matthew among the Hebrews issued a writing of the gospel in their own tongue, while Peter and Paul were preaching the gospel at Rome and founding the Church. After their decease Mark, the disciple and interpreter of Peter, handed down to us in writing what Peter had preached" (*Adv. Haeres.* 3.1.1). The oldest unambiguous localization of Mark's Gospel in Italy is in the anti-Marcionite gospel prologues (text in K. Aland, *Synopsis Quattuor Evangeliorum* [Stuttgart, 1964], 532) and in Clement of Alexandria (= Eusebius *Eccl. Hs.* 6.14.5–7). At present this traditional location is supported with historical-critical arguments in an especially impressive fashion by M. Hengel ("Entstehungszeit," 1–45).

3. The alternative to a Roman origin of Mark's Gospel is the entire East: so W. G. Kümmel, *Einleitung in das Neue Testament*, 70. But most scholars limit its origins to Syria. D. Lührmann writes: "[Mark] and his readers may have lived anywhere around Palestine, fairly close or more distant, perhaps in Syria; but the Syrian region itself is almost impossible to define, since it stretched from the Mediterranean to the eastern parts of present Iraq and Iran" (*Markusevangelium*, 7). There are three possibilities for fixing a more definite place of origin. First, Mark's Gospel originated in western Syria, as H. Koester speculates: "Antioch or another city on the west coast of Syria" (*Einführung in das Neue Testament*, 602). Second, Mark comes from the part of Syria next to Palestine: H. C. Kee, *Community of the New Age*, 100–105; H. M. Schenke and K. M. Fischer, *Einleitung in die Schriften des Neuen Testaments* 2:80. Third, Mark's Gospel comes from Galilee, or is entirely focused on Galilee: W. Marxsen, *Der Evangelist Markus*. Berger (*Einführung in die Formgeschichte*, 202) locates it in Caesarea Philippi and its neighborhood.

4. Irenaeus *Adv. Haeres.* 3.1.1 is clearly based on Papias (Eusebius *Eccl. Hs.* 3.39.15). He could have concluded from it that Peter was already dead when Mark's Gospel was written, since Mark wrote everything from memory. But since Peter died at Rome, it was a natural conclusion that Mark's Gospel was written there, especially since this would correspond with the ecclesial importance of Rome in the eyes of Irenaeus.

He appears in connection with Peter only in 1 Pet 5:13.[5] I think it is probable that there was a "Mark" in early Syrian Christianity, an associate of Barnabas. The latter had ties to both Paul and Peter (cf. Gal 2:11ff.). Peter was a great authority in Syria as well (Mt 16:17ff.). In the Antiochene conflict, Barnabas's group broke with Paul and associated itself with Peter (Gal 2:11ff.). Thus, the close connection between "Mark" and Peter presumed by Papias could have originated in Syria.

The ascription of the oldest Gospel to this (?) "Mark" is found only in the *inscriptio*, which is not from the author of the Gospel: on the one hand, the introduction (ἀρχὴ τοῦ εὐαγγελίου Ἰησοῦ Χριστοῦ; Mk 1:1) is a satisfactory beginning for the book; on the other hand, the formula κατὰ Μᾶρκον presumes the existence of other gospels.[6] All we can conclude from the *inscriptio* is that the Gospel comes from a region and a tradition in which Mark was a significant authority.[7] It does not follow that the Mark who came from Palestine really wrote it, and in view of the geographic errors in Mark's Gospel, his authorship seems improbable.

But where does it come from? We will first examine the general milieu of Mark's Gospel with an eye to the question whether it points more toward Rome or toward Syria. Next, we will establish its location in the history of tradition and ask where the combination of various traditions observable in Mark would most probably have occurred. Finally, we will examine the explicit statements about places in Mark, especially its "geographical errors."

1. For the socio-ecological milieu of Mark's Gospel, the use of the term "sea" is revealing. Although it comes from individual pre-Markan traditions (cf. 4:39, 41; 5:13; 6:47-49), it is also found in transitional passages, which the author of Mark could formulate more freely. These probably redactional passages permit us to conclude that Mark has no problem about calling the Galilean lake a "sea." Here he is not handing on a traditional expression, but is following his own style.[8] We find θάλασσα six times in introductory phrases without augmentation (2:13; 3:7; 4:1a-b; 5:1, 21) and twice with a genitive attribute (θάλασσα τῆς Γαλιλαίας; 1:16; 7:31). This genitive attribute is also found in Jn 6:1, so that it is not Mark's

---

5. H. J. Körtner ("Markus der Mitarbeiter des Petrus") shows that "Mark" has been inserted from the Pauline into the Petrine tradition.

6. Cf. M. Hengel, *Die Evangelienüberschriften.*

7. This presumes that the book was already attributed to a "Mark" in oral tradition. "Otherwise, when it became desirable to give the book apostolic authority a more prominent man would have been chosen as its author" (P. Vielhauer, *Geschichte der urchristlichen Literatur,* 347).

8. E. J. Pryke (*Redactional Style in the Markan Gospel,* 136–38) regards it as redactional in twelve of nineteen passages.

creation. It does not correspond to Greek or Latin usage, in which lakes and oceans are usually described by an adjective. Thus, the eastern Mediterranean before the coast of Syria is called Συριακὴ θάλασσα (Strabo *Geogr.* 2.1.31), Συριακὸν πέλαγος (Ptolemy *Geography* 5.14.2, 3), or *Syrium mare* (Julius Honorius *Cosmography* 2.49). In contrast, the construction of a name with the genitive of a region is rare. The Vulgate calls the Red Sea "Aegypti mare" (Isa 11:15), and Pliny the Elder sometimes refers to the Dead Sea as "lacus Iudaeae" (*Nat. Hist.* 7.65).[9] On the other hand, the genitive attribute "Sea of Galilee" corresponds exactly to the common Hebrew and Aramaic construction for names, as in *yam ha kinnereth*. The genitive can describe a region: *yam ha'araba* is the "sea of the desert." We can therefore presume that the name θάλασσα τῆς Γαλιλαίας also goes back to a Semitic name or was constructed by analogy to such names. That points strongly to a milieu in which (as in the whole Aramaic-speaking East) Semitic names are familiar, and where the great Mediterranean world is not the center of everyone's experience. Anyone who knows the great sea would hardly call the little Galilean lake a "sea." In any case, Mark's talk of a "sea" would be hard to imagine in the cosmopolitan city of Rome.

This fits also with the fact that this evangelist retains the rural background of Jesus' activity better than any other. A word statistic can be used to illustrate this (Table 6), although we must keep in mind that the other Gospels are much longer by comparison.

A series of "neighborhood expressions," by which an event is often located in the neighborhood of a city or town, point in the same direction.[10] According to Mk 1:38, Jesus leaves the πόλις of Capernaum, because he wants to preach in the "neighboring towns" (κωμοπόλεις). In Mk 3:8, people come to Jesus in great numbers from the region "around Tyre and Sidon" (περὶ Τύρον καὶ Σιδῶνα). Mark does not say "from Tyre and Sidon," because he is thinking of the rural territories of those cities. In Mk 5:14, Gerasenes announce the news about Jesus "in the city and in the country" (Mt 8:33 has only "in the city"). In Mk 6:6, Jesus teaches in the villages around his home town. In Mk 8:27-29, Peter speaks, in representative fashion, the confession of faith of the Markan community in "the villages of Caesarea Philippi," that is, somewhere in the rural territories of that city. When we add that all the parables in Mark come from the agrarian world and deal with sowing and reaping, harvests, and vineyards, we find ourselves in a deeply rural milieu. If the world of the narrative reflects

---

9. On the Syro-Phoenician sea and the Egyptian sea, cf. V. Burr, *Nostrum mare*, 48–50. Other examples can be found in the index.

10. Kee (*Community of the New Age*, 103–4) even notices "a clear antipathy towards the city in Mark" (p. 103).

TABLE 6
Words Indicating Rural Background in the Gospels

	Mt	*Mk*	*Lk*
πόλις	25	7	37
κώμη	4	7	12
κωμοπόλεις	—	1	—
ἄγροι	—	3	2

something about the world of the narrators, it is hard to imagine the author of Mark's Gospel in the largest metropolis of the first-century world. It is more probable that rural Christianity is a familiar environment for both the author and the readers. Even if they live in a city, they know that Christianity is spreading throughout the countryside. This points more to Syria than to Rome.

2. Mark's Gospel forms an interesting "crossroads" in the history of tradition. Here, in the midst of the synoptic material, we find traditions stemming from early, pre-Pauline, and Pauline-influenced Hellenistic Christianity. At the very beginning of Mark's work, we encounter the concept of εὐαγγέλιον, which is traceable in many places to the evangelist himself,[11] including the beginning of the book (1:1), the introductory summary of Jesus' preaching (1:14-15), and the apocalyptic discourse, which is interrupted by the saying about preaching the gospel to all nations (13:10). Elsewhere it could be an addition: for example, Jesus' words in Mk 8:35 and 10:29 would be intelligible without it. It is a common term for Paul and his churches (cf. especially 1 Cor 15:1ff.) and certainly belongs to pre-Pauline tradition. The same is true of the Pauline version of the last supper, which Paul himself says he has received. Despite minor differences, this version is closely related to that of Mark (cf. 1 Cor 11:23-26 with Mk 14:22-25). These words, too, could have been introduced into the Passion account by the author of Mark; that they were not there originally can be surmised from the Passion account in John. Finally, we should mention the list of vices in Mk 7:21-22. This is a traditional genre, frequently found in the Pauline letters, but unique in the synoptic Gospels. In all these points, Mark's Gospel appears to be in contact with pre-

11. So Marxsen, *Der Evangelist Markus*, 77–101.

Pauline and Pauline-influenced traditions. Since Paul acquired these traditions in the place where he missioned for the longest time—among Syrian Christians—we may as a rule expect to find pre-Pauline traditions there. If the author of Mark includes such traditions in his Gospel, the easiest explanation is that his work was also shaped by Syrian Christianity.

In addition to these community traditions, he knows two from Jerusalem and Judea, the synoptic apocalypse and the Passion account, both of which play an important structural role in the Gospel. An overlap of influences derived from Syrian and Jewish Christianity at that early period is more likely in Syria than in Rome, especially since we know from Gal 2:1-14 that Syrian-Hellenistic and Palestinian traditions were in contact within the Christian community in Antioch.

Besides the community traditions, Mark's Gospel also contains popular tales and material stemming from Jesus' disciples. The court legend about the death of the Baptizer is, in my opinion, one of the popular traditions, together with the miracle stories, that leave a somewhat "secular" impression. In both cases Mark indicates that he has not received them from community tradition. His story of the death of the Baptizer follows the sending out of the disciples. On their return, Jesus asks them what the people think of him, and their first response is that he is said to be John the Baptizer. Here the author of Mark presumes Baptizer traditions among the people, which the disciples have encountered independently of their contact with Jesus and which have reached the ears of Herod Antipas (Mk 6:14). The story of the Baptizer's death would have been for Mark one of those traditions that one heard when traveling through the country, even outside the Christian communities. This is still clearer in the case of the miracle stories. Here Mark emphasizes repeatedly that they are told against Jesus' own wishes (cf. 5:20-21; 7:36)—in fact, the actions described in them are being imitated by strange exorcists, contrary to the will of the disciples (9:38-40). This can be "interpreted" in terms of tradition history by supposing that these stories were circulating independently of the Christian communities, and that they were not always gratified by the fact. Probably the author of Mark was still in contact with these circulating traditions about Jesus and the Baptizer. But such contacts are more likely in Palestine and the neighboring regions of Syria than in distant Rome, especially since some of these popular traditions were formed in the Palestinian region (e.g., Mk 5:1-21).[12]

---

12. Vielhauer emphasizes correctly that Mark's Gospel "was written in a city or region where the Palestinian Jesus traditions were still alive; Greek-speaking Syria presents these conditions in immeasurably greater degree than does Rome" (*Geschichte der urchristlichen Literatur*, 347).

Finally, Mark knows some disciple traditions, or more precisely, traditions that presume acquaintance with the life of Jesus' radical followers. Among these are the stories of the call of the disciples (Mk 1:16-20; 2:14), the missionary discourse (6:7ff.), and the story of the rich man (10:17ff.) with the question about the rewards of discipleship (10:28-30). All these traditions presuppose that the evangelist is acquainted with itinerant charismatics, and most of the evidence for these people points clearly to Palestine and Syria.[13] Here we are most likely to find followers of Jesus who have left house and land to preach the reign of God.

Mark's Gospel is a tradition-historical crossroads in still another sense. Where different influences collide, we find demarcations drawn and polemic added. Such a demarcation against other Jesus traditions is visible, I think, in some of Jesus' "secret teaching" to his disciples. These secret teachings could serve to maintain one's own point of view against others who called upon the same authority as a basis for different assertions. The secret nature of the teaching makes it plausible that the "others" have so far failed to see matters correctly, since anyone who introduces a tradition as "secret teaching" makes plain that that teaching is not current in all the places where it could be or must be known.

The first secret teaching has to do with food regulations. From the fact that purity is determined by internal rather than external factors, Mk 7:17-23 draws the conclusion that all foods are clean (7:19). It is well known that not everyone in early Christianity shared this opinion. It is close to that of Paul (and originally that of his associate, Barnabas), but it was attacked by others (Gal 2:11ff.). Matthew's Gospel does not take the same line as Mark: in taking over Mk 7:17ff., Matthew omits the declaration that all foods are clean. Hand-washing, in particular, is seen as neutral regarding cleanness or uncleanness (Mt 15:20). It is true that one could understand from the text that foods, too, are neither clean nor unclean, but this is not said *expressis verbis*. Those associated with Peter would have said something like: Peter first joined those who did not allow their association with gentile Christians to be limited by food laws, but then he changed his mind (Gal 2:11ff.).

The next secret teaching follows the healing of the epileptic boy (Mk 9:14-27), when Jesus warns against trusting in one's ability to cure serious diseases such as epilepsy: prayer alone is effective. Here, too, there are other voices in early Christianity. Matthew replaces this secret teaching of

---

13. Kee (*Community of the New Age*, 104–5), in locating Mark's Gospel in the regions of Syria near Palestine, refers also to contacts with early Christian itinerant charismatics. He emphasizes the similarity of these itinerants to Stoic and Cynic philosophers, whose traditions can be found in the Syrian cities and in the Decapolis.

Jesus with a quite different saying. When the disciples are unable to heal, it is because of their "little faith." Even a mustard seed of "faith" can move mountains (Mt 17:19-20).

In Mk 9:33ff., while teaching "in the house," Jesus addresses the disciples' quarrel about rank. Whoever among them wishes to be great must be prepared to be last of all and the servant of all. This refers to places in the community and is rendered concrete by the admonition to welcome children. Leading positions in the community are connected with readiness to give concrete assistance. Every group has problems about hierarchy. Early Christian writings offer enough examples of this (cf., e.g., 1 Corinthians 1–4; 3 John). Matthew's alteration is striking: for him the dispute is about positions in the "reign of God," and not so much in the present community (Mt 18:1ff.), and he has no hesitation in attributing a kind of "primacy" to Peter (Mt 16:17ff.).

The last secret teaching in the house is that about divorce (Mk 10:10-12), according to which the prohibition is equally binding on men and women. But it is limited in the sense that only remarriage constitutes adultery. Separation is permitted. Here again, Matthew's Gospel represents a different position: divorce is initiated only by the husband. It is forbidden in principle, but allowed in the case of "unchastity" (Mt 5:32; 19:9).

In conclusion, in the short "secret teachings" Mark draws a distinction against other Christian traditions. But that presumes that he had contact with them. Can it be accidental that Matthew usually represents a different opinion? It seems that Mark's Gospel must have been written in a place where he could encounter traditions and attitudes that were later recorded in Matthew's Gospel. That, too, would point to Syria—assuming that Matthew's Gospel should be located there.

3. The geographical statements in Mark's Gospel present us with a number of puzzles, whether we locate the Gospel in Syria or in Rome. Most remarkable are two geographical absurdities. The first concerns the location of Gerasa. According to 5:1ff., the town of Gerasa and its surrounding lands lie near the Lake of Galilee, although in reality Gerasa is about 65 kilometers southeast of the lake. In 5:20, the "land of the Gerasenes" seems to be identical with the whole Decapolis, which would make more sense, since some of the cities of the Decapolis really did border on the lake: certainly Hippos, and probably Gadara as well.[14] But de facto,

---

14. The territory of Gadara may have been cut off from the lake by Hippos, but there are two indications of a (temporary?) direct access to the lake. First, Strabo speaks once of an ἐν τῇ Γαδαρίδι ὕδωρ (*Geogr.* 16.2.45) meaning probably the Galilean lake. Second, the city of Gadara minted coins, often bearing a ship (E. Schürer, *History of the Jewish People* 2:136). M. Avi-Yonah, however, is skeptical (*Holy Land*, 174).

Gerasa was only one city among many. The second astonishing statement is in Mk 7:31, where Jesus goes "from the region of Tyre, . . . by way of Sidon towards the Sea of Galilee, through the region of the Decapolis," which makes about as much sense as traveling from Madrid by way of Paris and Vienna to Rome. Both these geographical anomalies are usually regarded as a certain indication that the author of Mark's Gospel did not know Palestine. But is that the whole truth? There are a number of ways of dealing with these geographical peculiarities.

First, one could try to prove that they are compatible with reality. For example, F. G. Lang has shown, with regard to Mk 7:31, that Damascus was part of the Decapolis (Pliny *Nat. Hist.* 5.16.74) and that Damascus and Sidon had a common border in the 30s (*Ant.* 18.153), so that a route from Sidon by way of Damascus (= Decapolis) to the Galilean sea would be imaginable.[15] That kind of proof in the case of Mk 5:1ff. is more difficult. One would have to postulate, without evidence, that Gerasa was regarded as the most significant city of the Decapolis in the first century, so that the whole territory could be called the "land of the Gerasenes," and at the same time that the city near the lake was another of the Decapolis cities. It would be easier to establish such a "realistic" interpretation for Gadara, which may have had access to the lake. But "Gadara" is the easier reading and "Gerasa," as the *lectio difficilior,* must be the original.

Second, by gathering examples of similar mistakes and false locations from contemporary literature, one could try to represent the geographical anomalies in Mark's Gospel as the "typical errors" of a time that had no precise maps. The remarkable route in Mk 7:31 is not quite so remarkable when we read Pliny the Elder's description of Phoenicia (*Nat. Hist.* 5.17.75–78). He describes Tyre, Sarephtha, and Sidon in that order; then his description turns sharply inland: behind Sidon is the Lebanon, and opposite it the Anti-Lebanon, "post eum introrsus Decapolitana regio praedictaeque cum ea Tetrarchiae et Palaestines tota laxitas" ("Behind Counter-Lebanon inland is the region of the Ten Cities, and with it the tetrarchies already mentioned, and the whole of the wide expanse of Palestine"; 5.17.77). Here again, if we line up the most important locations, we have a "curving path" comparable to that in Mk 7:31 (Table 7).

Is this agreement an accident? Or was it the usual thing to describe the country in a circular manner? Does Mk 7:31 correspond to such a "descriptive pattern"?[16] We can find mistakes among ancient geographers

---

15. F. G. Lang, "Über Sidon mitten ins Gebiet der Dekapolis."

16. We can also inquire about the perspective from which this "description" of the Syro-Palestinian region is drawn. In 77 C.E., Pliny the Elder dedicates his *Natural History* (Praefatio 3) to the prince, Titus, whom he may have accompanied on part of his military campaign

TABLE 7
The "Curving Path" in Pliny and Mark

Pliny Nat. Hist. 5.17.77	*Mk 7:31*
Tyre	Tyre
Sarephtha	
Sidon	Sidon
Lebanon	
Anti-Lebanon	
Decapolis	Decapolis
Tetrarchies	Sea of Galilee
Palestine	

similar to those in Mk 5:1ff. For example, Ptolemy (*Geography* 5.15) clearly distinguishes Samaria and Judea, but counts "Sebaste" among the Judean cities.

Third, we can ask whether the geographical "audacities" do not indicate a certain carelessness in Mark's attempts to drop some hints that "integrate" a region that is important to him into the story of Jesus. It is striking that both his major geographical "errors" (1) relate to the part of Syria neighboring Palestine, (2) foreshadow the movement of the gospel to the Gentiles, and (3) are found in places where we most expect to find redactional touches: at the beginning and end of a pericope. Even if Mark had taken them over from elsewhere, he could easily have altered them. Is he here deliberately breaking up the "geographical logic" of his narrative in order to bring the home of his communities into the picture? Matthew's Gospel also contains one mention of "Syria" (Mt 4:24), which we suppose to have been the home of Matthew's community. And the Fourth Gospel clearly brings the Diaspora—perhaps the location of the Gospel—into its story (cf. Jn 7:35; 12:20-21). It may have been the same with Mark's Gospel. If it originated in one of the nearby parts of Syria (perhaps in Chalcis,

in Palestine (though this is not certain). In 68–69, he was sub-procurator of Syria, and at his departure the inhabitants of Arad honored him with an inscription (*OGIS* 2:586), although we must infer certain letters in order to read his name. Thus, it is probable that Pliny the Elder knew Palestine and Syria, provided we combine the fragmentary dates of his life as K. Sallmann does in "Plinius," col. 929. In that case, his primary perspective would have been from the north of Palestine.

Damascus, or the southern Orontes Valley), Jesus' long detour over Sidon and the Decapolis in Mk 7:31 would have led him into the neighborhood of Markan Christianity. The talk about the southern Decapolis as "the land of the Gerasenes" would also be intelligible because, if one travels from north to south, the high road leads to Gerasa. As a mercantile and caravan city, it was the goal of many a journey.[17] This may explain why it could stand for the whole Decapolis, since anyone who traveled to the Decapolis really did enter "the land of the Gerasenes."

Thus, the geographical inexactitudes of Mark's Gospel do not speak against the supposition that it originated in Syria near Palestine. They could be based not so much on lack of knowledge as on the desire to mention those Syrian regions in the Gospel. That could also explain the appearance of a "Syrophoenician woman" (Mk 7:26). If the Markan community was located in Syria, it could have seen in Jesus' assistance to the Syrophoenician woman a foretaste of the entry of the gospel into that region. In fact, the expression "Syrophoenician" is often used as an argument against locating Mark's Gospel in Syria.[18] First of all, it is said to presume a distinction between Syrophoenicians and Libyphoenicians (cf. Diodorus 19.93.3; 20.55.4), and thereby to indicate a standpoint allowing a view of both the regions inhabited by Phoenicians. Second, the oldest examples of the expression "Syrophoenix" are said to come from Latin writers of the second century B.C.E. (Lucilius *Satires*, frag. 540–41) and the first century C.E. (Juvenal *Sat.* 8.158–62; Pliny *Nat. Hist.* 7.201). But the evidence can be read another way.

a. The Latin word "Syrophoenix" is probably borrowed from Greek, and thus was not coined by the Romans themselves. The Romans ordinarily spoke of "Punii" (*poeni*), but for the original Punii in the East, they borrowed the Greek designation "Phoenicians." Pliny the Elder uses both terms in the same text: "Phoenices" and related words (*Nat. Hist.* 7.192, 195, 197, 208–9) and "Poeni" (7.199). "Syrophoenix" is in any case a Greek construction, and the contrast it presumes between these and the "Libyphoenicians" is found for the first time in the work of the Greek author Diodorus of Sicily (Diodorus 20.55.4). The earliest literary evidence in Latin thus indicates a prehistory of the word in Greek, no instances of which have survived.

---

17. Cf. M. Rostovtzeff, *Caravan Cities*, 55ff. For the Roman road system, see the diagram in Avi-Yonah, *Holy Land*, 187, which shows that Gerasa could be reached from Scythopolis, from Damascus/Adra, and from Philadelphia. But the main road from Philadelphia went by way of Bostra to Damascus without touching Gerasa. On the roads leading out of Gerasa, see S. Mittmann, *Beiträge zur Siedlungs- und Territorialgeschichte*, 152–63. He rejects the notion of a direct Roman road from Gerasa to Bostra (pp. 162–63).

18. See esp. Hengel, "Entstehungszeit," 45; K. Niederwimmer, "Johannes Markus und die Frage nach dem Verfasser," 182.

b. The first Latin examples sometimes use "Syrophoenix" in a pejorative sense, in which contempt for Orientals is evident. In the *Satires* of Lucilius someone is insulted as "that devil of a money-grubber, that Syrophoenician, what did he usually do in a case like that?" (frag. 540–41). The same is true of the *Satires* of Juvenal:

> And when it pleases him to go back to the all-night tavern, a Syro-Phoenician [Syrophoenix] runs forth to meet him—a denizen of the Idumaean gate perpetually drenched in perfumes—and salutes him as lord and prince with all the airs of a host; and with him comes Cyane, her dress tucked up, carrying a flagon of wine for sale. (*Sat.* 8.158–62)

Even Lucian, who came from Syria, betrays a hint of condescension toward the eastern "Syrophoenicians" from the point of view of cultured westerners when he writes that the god Bacchus "on his mother's side . . . is not even Greek, but the grandson of a Syrophoenician trader named Cadmus" (*Deorum Concilium* 4). There is no trace of this Greco-Roman contempt for Orientals in Mk 7:24ff. On the contrary, the Syrophoenician woman is ingenuously identified as a "Greek." This identification is more readily imaginable from the perspective of ordinary people in the Orient (or from the Orient) than in the eyes of Roman readers.

c. In the first two centuries C.E., the contrast of "Libyphoenicians" and "Syrophoenicians" is not constitutive for examples of the term "Syrophoenician." Pliny the Elder mentions the Syrophoenicians as inventors of the ballista and the sling (*Nat. Hist.* 7.201), in a long list of inventions credited to individual nations or agents of culture. Here "Phoenicia" is mentioned six times: as the home of the alphabet (7.192), of stone quarrying (7.195), of gold mining (7.197), of commerce (7.199), of the skiff (7.208), and of astral navigation (7.209). No distinction is made between them and the "Syrophoenices" (7.201). The shift from "Phoenices" to "Syrophoenices" is not conditioned by any change in geographical context. Justin, in the middle of the second century C.E., uses the word "Syrophoenicia" without reference to Africa. Instead, he is distinguishing regions in the East when he writes: "That Damascus is and was part of the Arabian land, even if it now belongs to what is called Syrophoenicia, none of you can deny" (*Dial.* 78). There is a clearly Eastern perspective in an Egyptian papyrus from the first half of the second century C.E., describing the worship of Isis under various names: "among the Indians as Maia, among the Thessalians as Selene, among the Persians as Latina, among the Magi as Kore, Thapseusis, in Susa as Nania, in Syrophoenicia as God [ἐν Φοίνικι Συρ[ε]ίκε θεός]" (*P. Oxy.* 1380).[19]

---

19. The fact that "Syrophoenix" cannot be found in Egyptian papyri is not an argument for the "Western" character of the concept (contra Hengel, "Entstehungszeit," 45 n. 164); "Syrophoenicia" does occur in the papyri.

d. In 195 C.E., Syria was divided by Septimius Severus after the defeat of his opponent, C. Pescennius Niger, who had had himself proclaimed emperor at Antioch.[20] From this point the northern part was called Syria Coele, the southern part Syria Phoenice. These names were derived from local tradition. Septimius Severus had served in Syria and had been married since 185 to Julia Domna, the daughter of a priest from Emesa. She accompanied him in all his campaigns. When Justin uses the word "Syrophoenicia" for southern Syria circa 150–160 C.E., he is probably drawing on the same onomastic tradition that gave the province its official name under Septimius Severus.[21] The name "Syrophoenicia" must have spread quickly after 195 C.E., because two examples of it, found in Volubilis in Mauretania, at the western end of the empire, are dated after 194 C.E. A further instance of "Syria Foinicia" (*CIL* 6:228) comes from the period of the Severi.[22]

The "Syrophoenician woman" in Mk 7:26 is possibly the first example of an appellation that originated in Syria itself to distinguish southern from northern Syria. It is interesting to note where the Syrian Tatian locates this Syrophoenician woman (according to the Arabic *Diatessaron* 20.25–26). In his harmony of the Gospels, Tatian writes: "And at (the same) time a woman, a Canaanite, (whose) daughter had an unclean spirit, heard of him. And this woman was a believer from Homs in Syria."[23]

A further local note that could point to the neighborhood of Palestine may be the equation of two λεπτά with a quadrans in Mk 12:42,[24] even though this is often claimed as evidence for the Roman origin of Mark's Gospel because a Greek word is explained to the readers in Latin.[25] Moreover, it is a *terminus technicus* for the smallest Roman coin, which like all small change would have had only a local circulation. Although the quadrans did not circulate in the East,[26] its foreign name was probably

---

20. Cf. G. Winkler, "Septimius Severus."

21. E. Honigmann gives another explanation in "Συροφοινίκη," cols. 1788–89. Since the name "Syrophoenicia" would only be possible after the establishment of the province of Syria Phoenice in 195, he thinks that Justin *Dial.* 78 must be a later interpolation.

22. J.-M. Lassére (*Ubique Populus*, 398–99) offers four examples of "Syrophoenix" or "Syraphoenix" from Volubilis in Mauretania, two of which he dates to the period after 194, i.e., after the division of Syria. The other two are not dated.

23. Quoted from E. Preuschen, *Tatians Diatessaron*, 127.

24. It is occasionally supposed that Mk 12:42 wanted to equate one lepton with a quadrans: the text read ὅ ἐστιν rather than ἅ ἐστιν, and the parallel of Mt 5:26 ("quadrans") and Lk 12:59 ("lepton") indicated the identity of the two quantities. Cf. the discussion in F. Madden, *Jewish Coinage*, 296ff.

25. Cf. T. Zahn, *Einleitung in das Neue Testament* 2:241–42, 251. W. M. Ramsay ("On Mark 12,42," 232, 336) maintains this argument against the objections of F. Blass ("On Mark 12,42 and 15,16," 185–87, 286–87). (The latter was not available to me.) It has been taken up more recently by B. Standaert (*L'Évangile selon Marc*, 471) and Hengel ("Entstehungszeit," 44).

26. On the circulation of the quadrans, cf. H. Chantraine, "Quadrans," esp. 663–64. The quadrans was also minted in Sicily, Spain, and Gaul.

known there, since we find it in the Talmud[27] and in Matthew's Gospel, as a representation for the smallest amount of money: debtors must pay their debts to the last "quadrans" (Mt 5:26). The currency of the word "quadrans" in the absence of the coin itself can probably be explained by the fact that in many provinces the local copper coinage took the place of the quadrans and was sometimes called by the same name.[28] In Palestine these would have been the procurator's coins, which did on the average weigh a little less than the Roman quadrans.

There was a curious feature[29] of Palestinian coinage that might be explained on the basis of Mk 12:42. In addition to the procurator's coins (with an average weight of 2.08 grams)[30] there were also, in the late Hasmonean and early Herodian period, unusually small coins weighing only half as much. The average weight for a sample of this smallest type of coin made under Herod I is 0.89 grams.[31] These circulated even after the time of Herod I; they are still referred to in the rabbinic literature, where they are called "pruta." While a "quadrans" was one-fourth of an as, a "pruta" was worth only one-eighth of an as. "How much is a pruta? The eighth of an Italian assar" (m. Qidd. 1.1). There is good reason to believe that in their discussions about the value of a pruta the learned rabbis were talking about a past system of coinage that no longer existed for them, but had still been in circulation during the first century.[32]

These smallest Palestinian coins, two of which made a quadrans, were a relic of pre-Roman times, the result of a combination of local and imperial traditions of coinage. They would have circulated longest in those regions where Herodian princes continued to rule—that is, in northern Palestine—and would have been most common during the time when coins of Herod I were still circulating, and thus before 70 C.E. Their valuation in terms of the Roman coinage system was especially relevant in the places where people constantly had to translate local coins into the imperial values: in the provinces. In Rome, by contrast, the quadrans was *per definitionem* the smallest coin. Plutarch attests that for his own time: "the smallest copper coin was called a 'quadrans' " (*Cic.* 29.4). Roman readers would

---

27. E.g., *b. Qidd.* 12a; cf. P. Billerbeck, *Kommentar* 1:292.

28. Cf. K. Regling, "Lepton," 350–51; Chantraine, "Quadrans," 660: "Thus the κοδράντης = q. in the NT was possibly nothing other than the small brass coinage minted in Judea under Roman rule."

29. Cf. D. Sperber, "Palestinian Currency"; Schürer, *History of the Jewish People* 2:66 n. 208.

30. Calculated from the information in Y. Meshorer, *Jewish Coins.*

31. Sperber, "Palestinian Currency," 300.

32. This is the thesis of Sperber. "Our texts are referring to earlier monetary systems, no longer in use during the time of their traditionaries, but of crucial legal importance. They were local Palestinian systems (for they are mentioned in the Mishna) in use before the introduction of Roman currency into Palestine (hence the pruta)" ("Palestinian Currency," 283).

have needed an explanation of the fact that smaller coins than the quadrans existed at all.[33]

We come to the following conclusion: if we must choose between the hypotheses of a Roman or a Syrian origin for Mark's Gospel, it seems to me that the weight of the evidence is on the side of its having been written in the East. The culture of its milieu, its location with respect to tradition history, and its geographical references are more readily understood if it originated in the southern part of Syria, in the region that was later officially called "Syrophoenicia." This seems to be the goal of Jesus' imaginary journey (Mk 7:31). There, Galilee and Caesarea Philippi, the place of the disciples' first confession of faith (Mk 8:27-30), were relatively close by, while Jerusalem and Judea were far away. There we find those synagogues and councils, kings and governors, who create difficulties for the Markan community (Mk 13:9). The decisive question will be whether we can better understand the historical origins of Mark's Gospel against this local background. But before we turn to that question, let us take a brief look at Matthew and Luke.

There are some indications in Matthew's Gospel that it looks at Palestine from an Eastern perspective. The most informative of these is its highly individual use of the expression πέραν τοῦ Ιορδάνου. In the Old Testament, this phrase ordinarily refers to the land to the east of the Jordan, but its content really depends on the standpoint of the one using it. This is clear merely from the fact that the phrase "beyond the Jordan" sometimes is supplemented by the words "to the east" or "eastward" (Josh 13:27, 32; 1 Chr 6:78), or "to the west" (Josh 5:1). Furthermore, the absolute expression "beyond the Jordan" clearly refers to the land "west of the Jordan" (Deut 3:20; Josh 9:1, 12:7; Jdt 1:9). When Matthew says "beyond the Jordan," he also, in my opinion, means a region "west of the Jordan." First let us examine all three instances:

> Mt 4:15-16 "Land of Zebulun, land of Naphtali,
> on the road by the sea, across the Jordan,
> Galilee of the Gentiles—
> the people who sat in darkness have seen a great light,
> and for those who sat in the region and shadow of death
> light has dawned" (= Isa 9:1-2).[34]

---

33. R. Roller even thinks that Mark's Gospel was written in Rome under Claudius, "in any case, certainly before Nero, under whom the quadrans had long ceased and the drachma begun again, so that we must place it, at the latest, at the end of the 40s or beginning of the 50s" (*Münzen*, 28). The presumption is false: Nero also coined the quadrans; cf. Chantraine, "Quadrans," 659–60. It was minted as late as the second century.

34. In Isa 8:23 (9:1 RSV) *derek ha-yam* can mean (1) "westward" as a statement of direc-

Mt 4:25   "And great crowds followed him from Galilee, the Decapolis, Jerusalem, Judea, and from beyond the Jordan."

Mt 19:1   "When Jesus had finished saying these things, he left Galilee and went to the region of Judea beyond the Jordan."

The meaning of Mt 19:1 is unmistakable, since here Judea is located "beyond the Jordan." Matthew 4:15-16 is a quotation. The evangelist could have included it without connecting it with precise geographical ideas. All that is certain is that he identifies the "sea" with the Lake of Galilee, because shortly before this he writes that Capernaum lies on the "sea" (4:13). The expression "beyond the Jordan" is to be understood as attributive, a precision of "on the road by the sea." That would mean that "beyond the Jordan" is west of the Jordan. This is favored also by the fact that the land of "Zebulun and Naphtali," like "Galilee of the Gentiles," is west of the Jordan as far as Matthew is concerned. Galilee of the Gentiles is the Galilee mentioned just before, in Mt 4:12, which contains Nazareth and Capernaum and is identified with Zebulun and Naphtali (4:13). Matthew 4:25 should be evaluated differently. While in 4:15 and 19:1 "beyond the Jordan" is an attribute, it is here equally coordinated with other substantives and constitutes an idea in and of itself. In a series with Judea, it could refer to the region of "Perea." It is possible, but less likely, that in 4:25 "beyond the Jordan" means "Jerusalem and Judea and all the other regions beyond (i.e., west of) the Jordan"—for example, Idumea, which Matthew found in Mk 3:8 but omits at this point! The verse would then be comparable to Jdt 1:9, in which Nebuchadnezzar sends messengers to "all who were in Samaria and its towns, and beyond the Jordan as far as Jerusalem and Bethany and Chelous and Kadesh and the river of Egypt."

If these observations are correct, we must locate the evangelist in the east or northeast part of Palestine.[35]

Antioch is frequently mentioned as the place of the Gospel's origin. The first definite witness to Matthew's Gospel comes from Ignatius of Antioch, circa 110 C.E. (Ign. *Sm.* 1:1). In addition, the combination of Jewish and gentile Christian

---

tion, (2) a geographical region on the coast of the Mediterranean or Lake Gennesaret, (3) a province of the Assyrian Empire (so E. Forrer, *Die Provinzeinteilung*, 59–60), or (4) a road beside the Mediterranean or Lake Gennesaret. The last possibility can probably be eliminated, since we do not have evidence before the Middle Ages of a road called the *via maris*; cf. Z. Meshel, "Was There a 'Via Maris'?"

35. So also, referring to Mt 19:1, H. D. Slingerland, "Transjordanian Origin," 18–28.

theology fits the history and structure of that community.[36] But I do not find the two arguments convincing.

1. There are good reasons for thinking that the *Didache* is also dependent on Matthew's Gospel (cf. *Did.* 8:2; 11:3; 15:3-4).[37] The *Didache* probably originated in Syria, but certainly not in Antioch—the water shortage presupposed by *Did.* 7:2-3 is unthinkable on the Orontes, and the rural or village conditions in the *Didache* would scarcely be found in a city as large as Antioch. In addition, Matthew's Gospel is theologically much closer to the *Didache* than to the Antiochene bishop Ignatius, whose abstract paradoxes are out of harmony with Matthew. Thus, we need to ask whether we should not shift the location of Matthew's Gospel, both socially and physically, closer to the *Didache*—that is, to the interior of Syria—and away from the cosmopolitan city of Antioch.[38]

2. Matthew's Gospel contains traces of a struggle over the gentile mission (cf. Mt 10:6; 15:24), but the Antiochene community appears in the history of early Christianity from the very beginning as an advocate of the gentile mission: see Acts 15:1 and Gal 2:11ff., in which a stricter Jewish-Christian point of view is confronted by a community that is already open to gentile Christians. In Matthew's Gospel the reverse seems to be true: a community that originally was strongly Jewish-Christian in character opens itself, in the course of time, to Gentiles and depicts its own learning process in the form of a gospel, where we learn that Jesus himself at first worked only among Jews, and that it was not until after Easter that he sent his disciples to the Gentiles.

3. The following observation also fits a smaller city in Syria: only Matthew mentions forced assistance to soldiers (5:41). This particular problem is clarified by an inscription found at Hama in Syria, containing an edict of the emperor Domitian (81–96 C.E.),[39] in which the emperor confirms that cities are exempt from the duty to provide teams of horses for the public postal service. We may suspect that small towns found the requirement of providing services for public transportation more oppressive than did the large cities.

If we locate the Gospel in Syria it would be easy to explain why it can speak of a "Sea of Galilee" (4:18; 15:29), just as Mark does. The great sea is far away, and yet it is known: in Mt 23:15 the Pharisees and scribes are reproached for crossing "sea and land" (in that order!) to win converts. Here the author seems to have the Mediterranean in mind. But there is no specific place mentioned; this is simply a summary description of the whole world. In Mt 18:6, Matthew inserts a πέλαγος into the Markan text: those who lead others astray deserve to be drowned "in the depth of the

---

36. See the extensive arguments for Antiochene origin in B. H. Streeter, *Four Gospels*, 500–527; and more recently by J. Zumstein, "Antioche," 122–38.

37. Cf K. Wengst, ed., *Didache*, 24–32.

38. G. Schöllgen ("Die Didache") shows that the *Didache* would not have originated in a "village," but more likely in an average provincial city.

39. Cf. R. Monteverde and C. Mondésert, "Deux Inscriptions de Hama," 279ff.

sea." The concept of πέλαγος is otherwise found only in Acts 27:5, in reference to the open sea. No particular place is intended. If we imagine the Matthean community at some distance from the sea, we can understand the exaggerated threat of punishment for what it probably is: a completely unrealistic warning.

It appears that the Mediterranean is not beyond the horizons of the Matthean community, but neither is it part of their concrete environment. It is typical of Matthew's Gospel to give a symbolic character to the "sea." Here the story of the storm on the lake is a story of the endangered community. The disciples in the boat "follow" Jesus (unlike in Mark). Like them, all believers who follow Jesus experience both danger and security (Mt 8:23-27).[40]

On the whole we can perceive in Matthew's Gospel a certain "eastward shift" in perspective. The infancy narrative, which in Luke directs the readers' attention to the wide world between Rome and Jerusalem, in Matthew encompasses the East (2:1-12) and Egypt (2:13-15). We could easily imagine its author at some midpoint between these areas, that is, in Syria. When he relates the journey of the Magi to Judea, he may be writing from his own perspective, because for him and his community, a star over Bethlehem would stand in the (south)west. The statement that Jesus' reputation had spread throughout "all Syria" (4:24), which differs from the report in Mark, could also reflect the perspective of Matthew's community.[41]

Wind conditions in Palestine permit a kind of rough location of Luke's Gospel. Luke presumes in 12:54-56 that the west wind brings rain, while the south wind is hot: "when you see the south wind blowing, you say, 'There will be scorching heat'; and it happens" (12:55). But in Palestine it was primarily the east wind that brought desiccating heat, while in the Mediterranean world west of Palestine it was, in fact, the south wind. The author of Luke-Acts thus appears to be unacquainted with conditions in Palestine.[42] The situation is, of course, more complicated than that. For one thing, physical wind directions are not always identical with their labels. The biblical "east wind" is de facto a south wind. In addition, the

---

40. Cf. G. Bornkamm, "Die Sturmstillung im Matthäusevangelium."

41. Matthew here interprets Mk 1:28, "throughout the surrounding region of Galilee." For him, τῆς Γαλιλαίας is not an epexegetical genitive, but a possessive, referring to the lands bordering on Galilee. He probably equated those lands deliberately with Syria, because in Mt 9:26 he renders Mark's expression quite differently, as "throughout that district."

42. C. C. McCown (*Gospel Geography*, 16) had already reached this conclusion, a fact that often goes unrecognized. W. Grundmann (*Das Evangelium nach Lukas*, 273) speaks incorrectly of an "accurate weather observation" in Lk 12:55.

meteorological situation is not totally unambiguous, because in some parts of Palestine a hot south wind occurs from time to time.[43]

However, it is true of the traditions in the Hebrew Bible that the east wind (*ruach kadim*) brings scorching heat. In Pharaoh's dream, the heads of grain are blighted by the east wind (Gen 41:6, 23, 27). The plants wither as soon as they are touched by the "east wind" (Ezek 17:10, cf. 19:12). Jonah despairs because of a sultry "east wind" (Jon 4:8). Meteorological observations show that this east wind often comes from the southeast, out of the Arabian Desert. The compass rose in *1 Enoch* (76:5-13) shows desiccating south winds coming from ESE and SSE (see below). It would not be unthinkable for someone to classify this southeast wind as a "south wind" at some point, especially if this agrees with common usage in the rest of the Mediterranean world, where it is the "south wind" in particular that brings scorching heat in the form of hot air from the Sahara.[44]

The Greek translation of the Old Testament, which was done in Egypt, is revealing on this point. Egypt experienced the hot *chamsin* from the south. Therefore, the Septuagint translates the "east wind" of the Hebrew text either neutrally with "scorching wind," not mentioning any compass direction (ἄνεμος ὁ καύσων; cf. LXX Ezek 19:12; 17:10; Jon 4:8; Hos 13:15), or else it makes the Hebrew "east wind" a "south wind" (as in Exod 10:13; cf. Exod 14:21; Job 38:24; Ps 78:26; Ezek 27:26). Philo of Alexandria described this hot Egyptian south wind from his own point of view in his commentary on Exod 10:13:

> Then a violent south wind swooped down, gaining force and intensity throughout the day and night. This in itself was a source of much mischief, for the south wind is dry and produces headache and makes hearing difficult, and thus is fitted to cause distress and suffering, particularly in Egypt which lies well to the south, where the sun and the planets have their orbits, so that when the wind sets it in motion the scorching of the sun is pushed forward with it and burns up everything. (*Vita Moses* 1.120)

This *chamsin* can also be an unpleasant experience in the south of Palestine and in the coastal plain. It seldom comes directly from the south,

---

43. On wind conditions in Palestine, cf. F. M. Abel, *Géographie de la Palestine* 1:117–21; E.C.A. Riehm, ed., *Handwörterbuch des Biblischen Altertums* 2:1759–61; D. Schenkel, ed., *Bibel-Lexikon* 5:666–68.

44. On ancient usage, cf. "Notos," *KP* 5:168. The ancients knew three types of south wind: the winter wind that brought rain and storms, and capsized Paul's ship (Acts 27:14-44); a soft "south wind" that cleared the sky after midwinter, the one that drove Paul's ship from Rhegium to Puteoli in two days (Acts 28:13); and the fearful, dusty sirocco, the "pestilens Africus," blowing from the hot North African desert. This last is what Luke is thinking of in Lk 12:55-56. The Gospel and Acts show that he was well acquainted with wind conditions in the Mediterranean to the west of Palestine.

but often from the south-southwest. It is mentioned in Job 37:17. It is not so strong in the Palestinian hill country, where the "east wind" is the typical scorching wind.[45] The compass rose in *1 Enoch* (Fig. 6) thus correctly reproduces the wind conditions in Palestine when it shows the desiccating wind coming both from southeast and southwest (cf. *1 Enoch* 76:5, 7-13).[46]

What, then, does the "south wind" in Lk 12:55 tell us about the location of the Gospel? One thing is certain: this Gospel can scarcely stem from the interior of Palestine or Syria. If it was written anywhere in the East, it could only have been in a coastal region. Caesarea is not impossible,[47] but it is more likely that Luke views Palestine from a Western perspective.[48]

There are other reasons as well for presuming the Gospel's nearness to the great Mediterranean sea.[49] Luke consistently avoids calling the little inland lake in Galilee a "sea." He uses the more appropriate word λίμνη (Lk 8:22, 23, 33). Of nineteen places in which Mark writes θάλασσα, only two are retained in Luke (Lk 17:1, 6), and in both of those verses the word "sea" does not indicate a particular place, but is a generic reference to "the sea." The evangelist's motive is clear: for him the Mediterranean is *the* sea. The first time it is mentioned, in Acts 10:6, it can be called θάλασσα without further explanation. This absolute θάλασσα corresponds to normal Greek usage.[50] Beyond this, it is determined by Luke's more comprehensive local perspective. The author of Luke is the only evangelist we can

---

45. E. Wirth writes: "Under certain conditions . . . especially in the spring (February to May) in the warm sector a cyclone of continental-tropical air from the Sahara reaches as far as Syria. This strong, hot, dry south wind, called the samum or khamsin, . . . is feared throughout Syria. It brings especially strong and notable rises in temperature in the coastal stations" (*Syrien*, 85). In the rest of the Mediterranean, this wind is called the "sirocco," from Arabic *sharkija* ("east wind"). The adoption of the word "sirocco" for the hot south wind, even though *sharkija* really means "east wind," illustrates very well how the same phenomenon is connected with different compass directions in the various regions. On the subject of wind directions on the coast of Palestine, cf. J. Glaisher, "On the Direction of the Wind at Savona." According to this, in the summer months the wind most frequently blows from the southwest.

46. The compass rose is taken from S. Uhlig, *Das Äthiopische Henochbuch*, 654. It is very schematic, as shown by O. Neugebauer, "The 'Astronomical' Chapters of the Ethiopic Book of Enoch," 24ff. He believes it to be "far removed from empirical data," and yet the hot wind from south-southeast is quite obviously a break in the schema.

47. So H. Klein, "Abfassungsort der Lukasschriften," 477. For him the author is a "man from Caesarea."

48. Cf. H. Conzelmann, *Die Mitte der Zeit*, 62. He writes, "The whole country seems to be viewed from across the sea."

49. On what follows, see G. Theissen, " 'Meer' und 'See' in den Evangelien."

50. For Plato, θάλασσα can be simply the Mediterranean (*Phaedo* 109b, 111a). The same is true for Aelius Aristides (*Discourse on Rome* 16). But we also find this absolute usage in the works of Jewish authors (cf. 1 Macc 7:1; 13:29; 14:5; 15:1, 11; *Bell.* 1.409, 411, etc.). Just as in Greco-Roman antiquity the Mediterranean could simply be "the sea," so for the Babylonians the Persian Gulf was "the sea" (cf. Burr, *Nostrum mare*, 89).

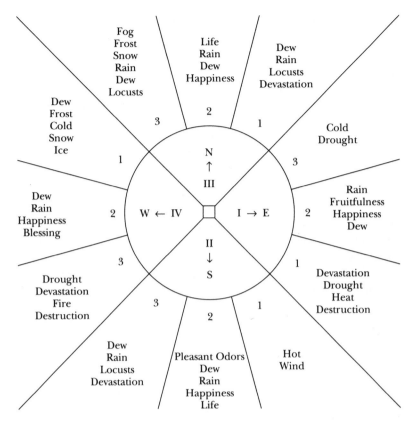

FIGURE 6
The compass rose in *1 Enoch*

be sure was well acquainted with the great Mediterranean world and its cities. This is evident from the stories in Acts and, in particular, the "we passages," which not accidentally begin with an ocean voyage (Acts 16:10ff.). With his "we," the author seeks to suggest to the readers that he has been an eyewitness to the events—an effort that has not succeeded with the majority of his historical-critical readers (with some notable exceptions).[51] But in any case the "we" leaves the impression that journeys by sea were part of the author's experience.

---

51. Among these exceptions is M. Hengel, "Der Historiker Lukas." I think Hengel has proved that the author of Luke-Acts had knowledge of Jerusalem that was probably acquired by a visit there. This does not necessarily mean that he was a companion of Paul. Many people visited the temple before 70 C.E.

If we only had Luke's Gospel, and not the Acts of the Apostles, we would still be able to guess at the author's perspective from some modest hints. Only in Luke is "distress . . . [at] the roaring of the sea and the waves" (Lk 21:25) part of the catastrophe of the last days. Only in his account do people from the "coast of Tyre and Sidon" (Lk 6:17) come to Jesus—as if he wanted to indicate how far the Christian message had penetrated.[52] Only Luke consistently replaces Mark's "sea" with "lake." It is true that one senses a broader local perspective from the start: the Gospel begins in Jerusalem, tells of an edict of the emperor that affects "all the world" (Lk 2:1), and mentions Syria (2:2) and several parts of Palestine (3:1). The mention of the emperors Augustus and Tiberius brings Rome indirectly into the picture, and it is in that city that Acts comes to a close. Thus far, Luke confirms our supposition: a broader local perspective means that Lake Gennesaret can no longer be called θάλασσα, but only λίμνη.[53]

The same distinction between inland lakes and the Mediterranean is found in the works of some Jewish writers whose life or work indicates a wider perspective. Josephus calls the Palestinian lakes λίμνη: the pool of Phiale (Bell. 3.511), Lake Semechonitis (Bell. 3.515; 4.3; Ant. 5.199), Lake Gennesaret (Bell. 2.573; 3.463, etc.), and Lake Asphaltitis (Ant. 1.174; 4.85; 9.7, 206; 15.168, etc.). However, he can call the Mediterranean θάλασσα without qualification (e.g., Bell. 1.409, 411; 2.14, 74, etc.).

The situation is similar in 1 Maccabees. The author is probably located in Jerusalem,[54] but his horizons are wider, for the Jewish alliance with the Romans and their conflicts with the Seleucids make the whole Mediterranean world the scene of action. The Mediterranean is simply "the sea" (θάλασσα; 1 Macc 7:1; 13:29; 14:5; 15:1, 11), but he calls Lake Gennesaret τὸ ὕδωρ τοῦ Γεννησαρ (1 Macc 11:67).[55]

These analogies confirm that Luke is writing from a wider local perspective, for readers who do not live in Palestine. And yet Luke is the only evangelist who has preserved for us the Galilean local name of the "lake of Gennesaret" (Lk 5:1). Mark's Gospel mentions the region of "Gennesaret" (Mk 6:53), but does not indicate that that is what the local people called the whole lake. It is certain that we have the common local name in this

---

52. In Mk 3:8, by contrast, it is clearly the territory of Tyre and Sidon on the landward side that is meant (see n. 48).

53. The importance of this wider local perspective for Luke is evident when he has Paul assert that "this was not done in a corner" (Acts 26:26).

54. Cf. K. D. Schunck, Das 1 Makkabäerbuch, 292.

55. The designation ὕδωρ is found in altered form in Josephus, as ὕδατα τῶν Γεννησάρων (Ant. 13.158), where Josephus is using 1 Maccabees as his source. But Strabo (Geogr. 16.2.45 = GLAJJ 1:298) and Dio Chrysostom (= GLAJJ 1:539) also speak of a ὕδωρ.

case. On the one hand, it corresponds most closely to the Hebrew *yam chinnereth* or *chinneroth* (cf. Num 34:11; Josh 12:3; 13:27),[56] translated in the Septuagint with θάλασσα Χεναρα, Χενερεθ, and Χενερωθ. On the other hand, we find this idea in Palestinian authors, including 1 Macc 11:67 (ὕδωρ Γεννησαρ) and Josephus.[57] Josephus expressly says that this name was used by the local people (cf. καλεῖται Γεννησὰρ πρὸς τῶν ἐπιχωρίων; *Bell.* 3.463). But non-Jewish authors also adopted this name. The oldest witness is Strabo (ca. 64 B.C.E.–20/30 C.E.), who speaks of the λίμνη Γεννησαρῖτις (*Geogr.* 16.2.16 = *GLAJJ* 1:288). Pliny the Elder (d. 79 C.E.) speaks of a lake "quem plures Genesaram vocant" (*Nat. Hist.* 5.15.71 = *GLAJJ* 1:469). Thereafter, the name disappears from ancient non-Christian literature and is replaced, beginning in the second century, by the name "Lake Tiberias."[58]

How should we interpret the evidence in Luke's Gospel? On the one hand, Luke writes from an external perspective; on the other hand, he is the only evangelist to record the local name of the lake, and he does so independently of his source document, Mark. This finding would fit admirably with the idea that Luke, while writing outside Palestine, has become familiar with the country through a journey to Jerusalem. This does not necessarily mean that he was a companion of Paul on his journeys. It is possible that he knows all the places mentioned in the "we passages" from his own experience; that he comes from the west coast of Asia Minor, where the "we passages" begin; and that he writes his two volumes in the place where the "we passages" end: in Rome. But unfortunately, those are only speculations.

Our reflections on the location of the Gospels have led to the following conclusions. Mark's Gospel was probably written in Syria near Palestine. It

---

56. Probably from the city of Chinnereth or Chinroth, which no longer existed in New Testament times (Deut 3:17; Josh 11:2; 19:35). Josephus clearly regards "Gennesar" as the description of a region (*Bell.* 3.506); in the same way in Mk 6:53, "Gennesaret" (v.l. Gennesar) is a region, as the word χώρα (Mk 6:55) makes clear. The transition from Old Testament *yam chinnereth* to Gennesar can be traced in *Targum Onqelos*, where Num 34:11 is given as *yam ginnesar.* Cf. Abel, *Géographie de la Palestine*, 495. J. R. Harris's interpretation of Gennesar as "garden of Osiris" in "Osiris in Galilee" is erroneous.

57. Cf. Josephus *Bell.* 2.573; 3.463, 506; 5.15; *Ant.* 5.84; 13.158; 18.28, 36.

58. The only exception is Solinus (third century C.E.), who bases his work on Pliny. The lake "Genesara" becomes a "lacus Sara," which he distinguishes from "lacus Tiberiadis" (*Collectanea Rerum Memorabilium* 35.3 = *GLAJJ* 2:418). It seems that he can no longer apply the mutilated name Genesara to the Lake of Tiberias, but thinks of it as a second lake. When we encounter the name "Lake Gennesaret" in later Christian writers, it is under the influence of Lk 5:1. Thus Eusebius, in his *Onomastikon*, along with the name current in his own time, "Lake of Tiberias" (*Onom.* 72.20; 74.14; 162.4–5), writes of "Lake Gennesaret" (*Onom.* 58.12; 120.2). Jerome, in his translation of *Onom.* 72.20, writes "stagnum Genezareth." The later pilgrim accounts usually call the lake, like the city, Tiberias; cf. H. Donner, *Pilgerfahrt ins Heilige Land*, 166–67, 180, 184, 188, 200, 263–64. They write either of the "lacum Tiberiadis" or the "mare Tiberiadis."

may view Galilee and Jerusalem from the north. Matthew's Gospel cannot have originated very far away. It looks at Palestine from an Eastern point of view, and could have been written in Damascus or in the Decapolis, possibly somewhere else in Syria. Luke's Gospel, by contrast, has a perspective that is clearly Western. Here the absolute distance from Palestine is greatest, but the author may have gotten to know Palestine from a visit there.

This view of matters is easily compatible with the two-source theory and the historical relationships of dependence it presupposes. The Sayings Source, originating in Palestine, and Mark's Gospel, written not far away, must have been accessible to the author of Matthew. The author of Luke could have acquired his two most important sources during a visit, without encountering the Gospel of Matthew, which had been written (or was being written) further inland. The discernible relationships are much more difficult to explain if Mark was written at Rome. He would have needed access there to Palestinian popular lore and Jerusalem community traditions, and his Gospel would have to have reached the East very quickly in order for Matthew to use it as a source. This is not impossible, but it is rather improbable.

THE THREAT OF WAR AND
THE AFTERMATH OF WAR IN THE GOSPELS
AS EVIDENCE FOR DATING

The purpose of dating is not the establishment of an external chronology; instead, it attempts to determine the historical situation a particular document is wrestling with. There is a consensus that Mark's Gospel is strongly affected by its proximity to the Jewish war of 66–74 C.E. Only a few authors argue for an earlier date.[59] But it is still debated whether the destruction of the temple (70 C.E.) has already happened or is still a prospect,[60] something that can only be decided on the basis of the interpretation given to Mark 13. However, a temporal determination for Mark 13 is made more difficult by the fact that it reworks traditions from the year 40 C.E. Conclusions about the situation of Mark's Gospel can be drawn most successfully

---

59. These include G. Zuntz, "Wann wurde das Evangelium Marci geschrieben?" As he emphasizes, his "dating of the Second Gospel to the year 40" depends "exclusively on an assessment of Mk 13:14" (p. 71). I agree with his interpretation of Mk 13:14 as referring to the Caligula crisis, but not with the conclusion that the redaction of Mark's Gospel can be dated in the same way, since Mk 13:14 belongs to an older tradition that has been adopted by Mark. J.A.T. Robinson (*Redating the New Testament*, 95, 107ff., 352–53) relies on Clement of Alexandria *Hypotypose* 6 (= Eusebius *Eccl. Hs.* 2.15.3–4), according to which Mark's Gospel was written in Peter's lifetime. Robinson thinks the date may have been between 45 and 60.

60. The most persuasive argument for a date shortly before the destruction of the temple is in Hengel, "Entstehungszeit," esp. 21ff.

at the point where redaction is most likely, especially in the framing of the apocalyptic discourse.[61]

The author of Mark has composed this discourse primarily as an esoteric instruction for the disciples, explicating the preceding public prophecy against the temple (Mk 13:1-2). This temple prophecy, in my opinion, presupposes the destruction of the temple, because it has been adapted to correspond to events that have already happened. Other variants of this prophecy have two parts: they predict both the destruction of the temple and its rebuilding (Mk 14:58; Jn 2:19). In the summer of 70, the temple had been destroyed and there was no prospect of its being rebuilt; consequently, Mark omits the positive half of the temple prophecy in 13:2. The precise description of the destruction is also revealing: "Do you see these great buildings? Not one stone will be left here [ὧδε] upon another; all will be thrown down" (Mk 13:2). The restrictive ὧδε could be a hint that only the buildings on the temple platform, but not its foundation walls, would be destroyed. The mighty stones of that foundation can still be seen today. Here again, the temple prophecy has been refined *ex eventu.*

The end of the apocalyptic discourse, like the beginning, has been redacted. The evangelist expects that heaven and earth will pass away within his own generation. No one knows the exact date; therefore, the only way to be prepared is to be constantly vigilant (Mk 13:30-37). Nevertheless, there are signs of its approach. Mark writes, "when you see these things taking place, you know that he is near, at the very gates" (Mk 13:29). This ὅταν ἴδητε ταῦτα can only refer to what the evangelist has announced in 13:14 (using an older source) with ὅταν δὲ ἴδητε τὸ βδέλυγμα τῆς ἐρημώσεως.[62]

Thus, the evangelist looks back to the destruction of the temple as an event within history, but expects within his own lifetime a universal, eschatological catastrophe. In this situation, he renews and revives the prophecy stemming from the Caligula crisis. With the same words in which that prophecy looks back to the Nabatean war in 36 C.E., the evangelist looks

---

61. While a dating of the received material in Mark 13 in terms of political history rests primarily on those parts that are generally regarded as traditional (esp. 13:6-8, 14-20, 24-27), a redaction-critical examination can begin at the point where the author of Mark has combined traditions in a new way. His work is a combination of the temple prophecy in 13:1-2 and an apocalyptic discourse, with the addition of individual logia at the end (13:28-37). The insertion of 13:9-13 also betrays a redactional purpose: here the author addresses the community directly. A redactional shaping of 13:21-23 is often posited as well.

62. Thus esp. F. Hahn, "Die Rede von der Parusie," 245ff. The detailed critique of Hahn by E. Brandenburger (*Markus 13,* 36ff.) has not convinced me. After we hear in 13:14ff. about two successive events—the "desolating sacrilege," followed by the Parousia of the Son of man—13:18-19 contains an appeal for understanding of the connection: when the former appears, then he (the Son of man coming in his Parousia) is at the door. The sign is not identical with the Parousia, but precedes it.

back at the Jewish war (66–70 C.E.). With formulae that at that time predicted the coming desecration of the temple by the emperor, he prophesies an unimaginable blasphemy standing in the place of the temple (13:14ff.). The most probable supposition is that he expects the same thing that had been feared in the Caligula crisis, that is, the establishment of a pagan cult in the place that had been sacred to Jewish worship. This makes it possible for him to revive the tradition from the year 40 C.E. without changing it in any essentials. Since we know from Tacitus (*Ann.* 12.54.1) that the fears aroused by the Caligula crisis were of long duration, we can be sure that the traditionists of the prophecy contained in Mark 13 would have known, even in the 70s, what the "desolating sacrilege" stood for. During the Jewish war, people probably expected the prophecy to come true. The temple was destroyed. But that could only be the "beginning of the birthpangs," for the final cultic desecration of the temple was still to come. What had mistakenly been expected in 40–41 was now about to be fulfilled.

> The proximity of Mark's Gospel to the war is evident not only from Mark 13, in which the evangelist deliberately concentrates on the life of the community after Jesus' death, but from the whole Gospel. It is not so noticeable because the Gospel focuses on past events that reflect the present of the author and readers only indirectly.
>
> In healing the withered hand, Jesus poses the alternative: "Is it lawful to do good or to do harm on the sabbath, to save life or to kill?" (Mk 3:4). This alternative sounds much more harmless in Luke's special material: "Is it lawful to cure people on the sabbath, or not?" (Lk 14:3). The question whether one may kill on the Sabbath arose during the war, and was discussed in the years 66–70. John of Gischala, arguing that it was blasphemy to take up weapons on the Sabbath, negotiated a truce during the siege of Gischala, and under its protection was able to escape to Jerusalem (*Bell.* 4.98ff.). Agrippa II protested against the war, saying that there could be no blessing on anyone who violated the Sabbath rest (*Bell.* 2.392ff.), as very soon happened (*Bell.* 2.517). In Mk 3:4, we may have a distant reflection of this debate,[63] especially because, after the alternative "to do good or to do evil," the second alternative "to save life or to kill" seems excessive.[64]

---

63. The debate goes back to the time of the Maccabees. After a group of rebels let themselves be cut to pieces on the Sabbath without offering resistance, the remaining revolutionaries decided: "Let us fight against anyone who comes to attack us on the sabbath day; let us not all die as our kindred died in their hiding places" (1 Macc 2:41; cf. *Ant.* 12.272–77). Josephus says that it has been an accepted custom ever since to fight on the Sabbath if necessary (*Ant.* 12.277). But Josephus also recognizes limits: thus, during Pompey's siege of Jerusalem the Jews resist direct attacks, but not mining and trenching.

64. Did the author of Mark make a redactional insertion of "to save life or to kill" in 3:4

When Jesus immediately afterward, in the dialogue about Beelzebub, says that a "kingdom" divided against itself cannot stand, readers probably thought of the Roman Empire, disrupted in 68–69 by civil wars. The divided βασιλεία in Mk 3:24 would be a reminder of those wars in 13:8, in which βασιλεία rose against βασιλεία.

Again in Mk 5:1ff., hearers of Mark's Gospel would have heard echoes of the war when a whole legion of demons is drowned in the sea. Palestine's gentile neighbors are alarmed by the aggressive action against the "legion" and banish the troublemaker from their territory.

The cleansing of the temple is justified in Mark by two quotations from the prophets. According to Isa 56:7, the temple is to be a house of prayer for all peoples, but as Jer 7:11 prophesies, it has been made a den of robbers. Even if the evangelist is using standard formulae, their combination could be determined by experiences during the Jewish war. The rebellion began when radical groups excluded Gentiles from any participation in the cult by refusing to accept any sacrifices or gifts from them (*Bell.* 2.409ff.). Then the temple was no longer a house of prayer for the Gentiles. Later, the radical revolutionaries took shelter in the inner temple. For Josephus, who likes to call the revolutionaries "robbers" or "brigands," that made the temple itself a robbers' den.[65]

The parable of the vine-dressers also contained for hearers of Mark's Gospel a clear echo of the war. At the end of the story, the narrator expresses the conviction that the lord of the vineyard will react harshly to the killing of his son: "He will come and destroy the tenants and give the vineyard to others" (Mk 12:9). The reference is to the high priests, scribes, and elders of the Sanhedrin. In reality, the Jewish war led to the destruction of the traditional power elite.

Finally, we should mention the Barabbas pericope, in which the text speaks of a certain στάσις at the time of Jesus. The author of Mark could adopt this expression without alteration because he knew that his hearers had experienced the great rebellion. For them, there had been a great στάσις in Palestine in the years 66–70; Barabbas is given a place within the prehistory of that revolt.[66]

The proximity of Mark's Gospel to the war is not often disputed. But it can be located precisely in space and time: Mark's Gospel was written in

---

in order to prepare for the plan of the Pharisees and Herodians to kill Jesus in 3:6? While Jesus is healing, his enemies are plotting his death. But deciding to kill someone is different from actually carrying out the plan. The alternative "save or kill" transcends the situation; after all, the opponents do not kill on the Sabbath.

65. G. W. Buchanan ("Mark 11,15-19"; idem, "An Additional Note") also supposes that the author of Mark was thinking of a historical occupation of the temple by Zealots (= "robbers" or "brigands").

66. Thus esp. Lührmann, *Markusevangelium*, 256.

Syria, near Palestine, shortly after the destruction of the temple.[67] This determination must be confirmed by Mark 13. The author of Mark is here incorporating a tradition that is thirty years older, but he would not have used it unless it had been plausible in his own circumstances. It is possible that he added to it in a few places, such as 13:9-13 and 13:21-24. In 13:9-13, he articulates, with the aid of traditional logia, the experiences of his community; in 13:21-24, he describes its expectations for the future. In both cases, we must ask whether these are plausible in the situation ca. 70–75. We can begin with the future expectations.

If our dating and location are correct, we should be able to explain why, despite the newly won stability in the Roman Empire, expectations of an imminent catastrophe remain vividly alive in Mark's Gospel. Three historical factors should be mentioned: (1) the postwar pangs, (2) the open question of the fate of the temple, and (3) the continuation of eschatological expectations.

1. With the capture of Jerusalem and the destruction of the temple the outcome of the war was decided, but the fighting was not over. "Sicarii" held out at Masada until 74 C.E. (*Bell.* 7.252–406).[68] Others had fled to Egypt and created unrest there (*Bell.* 7.409ff.). There was even a prophetic movement in Cyrenaica, where a weaver named Jonathan led his followers into the desert, promising to show them miracles and other phenomena (*Bell.* 7.437ff.). The expectations and energies kindled by the Jewish war were too powerful to be eliminated at a single blow. There must have been a good many people at that time who could not see the destruction of the temple as "the last word."

2. In particular, the fate of the temple was in doubt. The Romans not only had destroyed it, but had put an end to cultic worship.[69] This was done consciously, in order to break what they saw as the backbone of the resistance. That is the only explanation for the fact that they took the cultic vessels to Rome and set them up there in the newly built "Temple of Peace" (*Bell.* 7.158ff.). It also explains why the temple was not only burned, but razed, and why the temple in Leontopolis was destroyed for no evi-

---

67. The nearness to the war is still greater if we date Mark's Gospel between 68 and 70 C.E. The following considerations would also be valid, mutatis mutandis, under those conditions. With the elevation of Vespasian to the throne on 1 July 69, the East expected the civil wars to come to an end. Vespasian was recognized by the Senate as early as 22 December 69. At the beginning of the year 70, the "great war" was over. The suppression of the Jewish revolt could be regarded as certain, although it was not finally over until 74, when Masada fell.

68. Normally, the year 73 C.E. is accepted as the date of the capture of Masada, but since W. Eck ("Die Eroberung von Masada") more and more voices speak for the year 74. For this discussion, cf. H. Schwier, *Faktoren*, 48-52.

69. On this, see H. Schwier, *Tempel und Tempelzerstörung*, 273ff., 323ff. The following remarks on the Flavian propaganda are based on this work.

dent strategic reason (*Bell.* 7.420ff.). This is the only explanation, too, for the transformation of the temple tax into a tax paid to Jupiter Capitolinus (*Bell.* 7.218), which made abundantly clear that there was no thought of rebuilding the temple of Yahweh in Jerusalem. Instead, the money was to finance the rebuilding of the ruined temple of Jupiter in Rome, which the Flavians were partly responsible for burning. The fear that, after the building in Rome was finished, the funds could be applied to the construction of a pagan temple in Jerusalem was not far-fetched, especially since in the long term a country without a temple was unthinkable.[70]

Such fears were realistic, because Vespasian and Titus had probably taken over Jewish synagogues in other places and turned them to different purposes. Malalas's statements on that subject are, I think, trustworthy in their essentials, since the Antiochene is describing events in his own native city:

> Out of the spoils from Judaea Vespasian built in Antioch the Great, outside the city gate, what are known as the Cherubim, for he fixed there the bronze Cherubim which Titus his son had found fixed to the temple of Solomon. When he destroyed the temple, he removed them from there and brought them to Antioch with the Seraphim, celebrating a triumph for the victory over the Jews that had taken place during his reign. He set on an upper level a bronze statue in honour of Selene (the moon) with four bulls, facing Jerusalem, for he had captured the city at night by moonlight. He also built the theatre of Daphne, inscribing on it, "Ex praeda Iudaea" (from the spoils of Judaea). The site of the theatre had formerly been a Jewish synagogue but he destroyed their synagogue to insult them [πρὸς ὕβριν αὐτῶν], and made it a theatre, setting up there a marble statue of himself, which stands to the present day. Vespasian also built in Caesarea in Palestine out of the spoils from Judaea, a very large odeon, the size of a large theatre; its site too had formerly been that of a Jewish synagogue. (Malal. *Chron.* 260–61)

Malalas could well have known the cherubim, the theater with the Latin inscription, and the statue of Vespasian from having seen them himself. It is difficult to judge whether the story about when and how they were placed there corresponds to reality,[71] but there probably was a Jewish settlement at Daphne, which makes it clear why the high priest Onias fled to Daphne near Antioch (2 Macc 4:33-34). Evidence of a Jewish synagogue

---

70. This expectation was all the more justified since the Romans had destroyed only the temple buildings, but not the foundations, as if they wanted to retain them for use in a new structure. If this was not to be a temple of Yahweh, it could only be a pagan temple.

71. C. H. Kraeling ("Jewish Community at Antioch," 153) considers the erection of the cherubim at the city gate to be historical. He dates the destruction of the synagogue mentioned in Malalas *Chron.* 261, strangely enough, to the period of Tiberius (p. 140), although Malalas clearly attributes it to Vespasian. For the translation, see Elizabeth Jeffreys, Michael Jeffreys, Roger Scott, et al., trans., *The Chronicle of John Malalas* (Byzantina Australiensia 4; Melbourne, 1986). See also W. A. Meeks and R. L. Wilken, *Jews and Christians in Antioch*, 5.

there is from a later time (John Chrysostom *Adv. Jud. Or.* 1.6). The continuity of holy places in a cultic location is a well-attested phenomenon. Therefore, it is probable that Vespasian really did make a show of setting up his statue on the site of a synagogue or close by. The precarious situation of the Jews in Antioch after the Jewish war is well known to us from Josephus's account. Titus had to reject a petition that he drive the Jews out of Antioch and withdraw from them their customary rights (*Bell.* 7.100ff.). It is understandable that Josephus says nothing about humiliating actions taken against the Antiochene Jews.

This state of things must have revived the fear existing among the Jews and Christians in Syria since the time of Gaius Caligula that the (now destroyed) temple would be converted into a pagan sanctuary. Anyone who set up his statue in Antioch on the site of a synagogue could be expected to place it also in the most holy of all places—all the more so since the victorious Roman soldiers, after seizing the temple, had already sacrificed to their standards within its gates and acclaimed Titus as emperor there (*Bell.* 6.316). The temple had already been "cultically" seized by Gentiles once. Therefore, the author of Mark could incorporate the apocalyptic prophecy stemming from the Caligula crisis in his Gospel without changing it very much.[72] Everything indicated that what had been foreshadowed then was now about to be fulfilled. All that was necessary to bring the traditional prophecy up to date was to expand the saying about the temple (Mk 13:1-2) and to create a stronger reference to the present (13:9-13).

3. A further disturbing factor was the continuation of expectations of a decisive change that was about to take place. During the Jewish war, the long-standing Eastern hope that the East would recover its strength and rule over the West had played a role.[73]

> The majority firmly believed that their ancient priestly writings contained the prophecy that this was the very time when the East should grow strong and that men starting from Judea should possess the world. This mysterious prophecy had in reality pointed to Vespasian and Titus, but the common people, as is the way of human ambition, interpreted these great destinies in their own favour, and could not be turned to the truth even by adversity. (Tacitus *Hist.* 5.13.2).

---

72. Let us recall once more that, according to Tacitus *Ann.* 12.54.1, the expectation of a desecration of the temple remained active under Gaius's successors: "manebat metus, ne quis principum eadem imperitaret." The plural shows that he must have been thinking not only of Claudius, but of his successors as well. Only Vespasian was a serious candidate, because he alone had been active in the East. Second Thessalonians 2:4 is evidence for the fact that this fear was shared even by Christian groups for quite a long time—independent of the question of the age of this letter.

73. Cf. H. G. Kippenberg: " 'Dann wird der Orient herrschen und der Okzident dienen' "; Schwier, *Tempel und Tempelzerstörung*, 251ff.

The expectations described by Tacitus were attached to various "bearers of hope." Roman interpretation, of course, applied them to Vespasian and Titus, both of whom were in the East at the time of the civil wars. It was from the East that Vespasian appeared as the new emperor. Local "propagandists" lent an air of legitimacy to his usurpation: a priest on Carmel (Tacitus *Hist.* 2.78; Suetonius *Vesp.* 5) and Josephus himself, who prophesied world power for him (*Bell.* 3.400ff.; 4.623ff.; Suetonius *Vesp.* 5; Dio Cassius 65.1.4).

Besides this (secondary) *interpretatio romana*, there was a Jewish version, which interpreted the vague oracle in the sense of Jewish messianic faith. Tacitus alludes to this idea (*Hist.* 5.13.2), and Josephus confirms it:

> But what more than all else incited them to the war was an ambiguous oracle, likewise found in their sacred scriptures, to the effect that at that time one from their country would become ruler of the world. This they understood to mean someone of their own race, and many of their wise men went astray in their interpretation of it. The oracle, however, in reality signified the sovereignty of Vespasian, who was proclaimed Emperor on Jewish soil. (*Bell.* 6.312–13)

This text reveals the conjunction of two expectations: the common notion of a world ruler from the East and a Jewish prophecy that is "likewise" found in the "sacred scriptures." Probably, in the course of the war, these hopes were attached to a number of different figures, such as Menahem, who appeared at Jerusalem in royal attire (*Bell.* 2.444), or Simon ben Giora, who let himself be captured bearing the insignia of a ruler (*Bell.* 7.26ff.).

Finally, there was still a third variant of these expectations of the reversal of all things.[74] Nero had committed suicide on 9 June 68, but it was rumored that he was still alive. At the beginning of 69, a slave from Pontus appeared in the Cyclades, claiming to be Nero, but he was soon killed (Tacitus *Hist.* 2.8–9; Dio Cassius 64.9.3). Ten years later, a Nero *redivivus* from Asia Minor managed to flee to the Parthians (Dio Cassius 66.19.3; cf. Tacitus *Hist.* 1.2.1). The fourth Sibylline oracle, written shortly after the eruption of Vesuvius on 24–25 August 79, expects a Nero *redivivus* who will come from the Parthians to destroy the Roman Empire. He will restore power to Asia: "The great wealth is coming to Asia, that once Rome seized for itself and stored in its rich houses. Twice as much and more besides will Asia give back" (*Sib. Or.* 4.145–47).

When Mark's Gospel expects false messiahs and false prophets in this time (Mk 13:22), this fits the situation in the East after 70 C.E. The antici-

---

74. On Nero *redivivus*, see Hengel, "Entstehungszeit," 39–43; W. Bousset, *Die Offenbarung Johannis*, 410–18.

pation of a Nero *redivivus* shows that genuine expectations of the future (as in *Sib. Or.* 4.145–47) were shaped by concrete experiences. Without the historical Nero and his "imitators," there would have been no such prophecy. Thus, it is necessary and legitimate to seek a model for Mark's warning about pseudo-messiahs.

In doing so, we need to keep in mind that the number of predicted "pseudo-messiahs" (plural) is a sign of their lack of legitimacy. In reality, only one figure was anticipated, for the deceivers say: " 'Look! Here is *the* Messiah' [ὁ χριστός] or 'Look! There he is!' " (Mk 13:21). It is typical of the false messiah that he tries to use prophets and wonderful signs to seduce the elect. Here Vespasian's propaganda could be the concrete background, because it rested on both prophecies and miracles.[75]

There are a number of traditions, current among the people, according to which Vespasian had been promised the imperial rank by prophets:

> Between Judaea and Syria lies Carmel: this is the name given to both the mountain and the divinity. The god has no image or temple—such is the rule handed down by the [ancestors]; there is only an altar and the worship of the god. When Vespasian was sacrificing there and thinking over his secret hopes in his heart, the priest Basilides, after repeated inspection of the victim's vitals, said to him: "Whatever you are planning, Vespasian, whether to build a house, or to enlarge your holdings, or to increase the number of your slaves, the god grants you a mighty home, limitless bounds, and a multitude of [people]." This obscure oracle rumour had caught up at the time, and now was trying to interpret; nothing indeed was more often on [people's] lips. (Tacitus *Hist.* 2.78.3–4)

Suetonius (*Vesp.* 5.6) and Dio Cassius (65.1.4) reproduce the same propagandistic tradition, intended for the people of Syro-Palestine. For the Egyptian population another "prophecy" was set in motion: Vespasian was supposed to have gone alone into the temple of Serapis, but there he saw an Egyptian named "Basilides," whom he knew certainly to be in a town several days' journey away. He made sure that it was really Basilides who was there. "Then he concluded that this was a supernatural vision and drew a prophecy from the name Basilides" (Tacitus *Hist.* 4.82).[76]

A prophecy of special value to Vespasian came from Josephus himself. When, after being captured, he was brought before Vespasian, he said:

> "You imagine, Vespasian, that in the person of Josephus you have taken a mere captive; but I come to you as a messenger of greater destinies. . . . You will be Caesar, Vespasian, you will be emperor, you and your son here. Bind

---

75. For this section, see Schwier, *Tempel und Tempelzerstörung*, 307–22.

76. It can scarcely be accidental that the priest Basilides on Carmel had the same name as the prime Egyptian witness for Vespasian's rule. Does this not point to a clever arrangement of the "prophecies" and "signs"? Cf. ibid., 311–12.

me then yet more securely in chains and keep me for yourself; for you, Caesar, are master not of me only, but of land and sea and the whole human race." (*Bell.* 3.400–402)

This prophecy was also made public. Suetonius reports it in his life of Vespasian: "And one of his high-born prisoners, Josephus by name, as he was being put in chains, declared most confidently that he would soon be released by the same man, who would then, however, be emperor" (*Vesp.* 5.6). In the rabbinic tradition, it was credited to Rabbi Johanan ben Zakkai—another witness to its great "popularity."[77]

However, legitimacy was created for the new ruler not only through prophecies, but also by means of "signs and wonders." Suetonius speaks openly of their propaganda value:

> Vespasian as yet lacked prestige and a certain divinity, so to speak, since he was an unexpected and still new-made emperor; but these also were given him. A man of the people who was blind, and another who was lame, came to him together as he sat on the tribunal, begging for the help for their disorders which Serapis had promised in a dream; for the god declared that Vespasian would restore the eyes, if he would spit upon them, and give strength to the leg, if he would deign to touch it with his heel. Though he had hardly any faith that this could possibly succeed, and therefore shrank even from making the attempt, he was at last prevailed upon by his friends and tried both things in public before a large crowd; and with success. (*Vesp.* 7.2–3)

Tacitus also knew of these miracles. He agrees that they indicate "the favor of heaven" and "a certain partiality of the gods toward Vespasian" (*Hist.* 4.81.1).

We may also mention a series of "signs" that occurred during the siege of Jerusalem.[78] Tacitus writes of warring columns in the heavens, sudden lights around the temple, the bursting open of the temple gates, the exit of the gods. At the end of this series of signs stands the oracle that prophesied world rule for Vespasian (*Hist.* 5.13). Josephus, probably using the same Roman source, included this series of marvels in his account of the destruction of Jerusalem and added some additional signs (*Bell.* 6.296–314). In his story, they also lead up to Vespasian's ascent to world power.

Thus, Vespasian could be regarded in the East as a ruler who usurped messianic expectations and legitimated himself through prophets and miracles. It made no difference that he himself was a modest man. As a usurper, he had to rely on loud and vigorous propaganda. The warning

---

77. Cf. A. Schalit, "Die Erhebung Vespasians." P. Schäfer, "Die Flucht des Johanan b. Zakkais."

78. Cf. Schwier, *Tempel und Tempelzerstörung,* 313ff.

against pseudo-messiahs in Mk 13:21-22 could have been formulated against the background of such a "propaganda campaign" for the victorious new emperor, who created peace by subduing the Jews and whose legitimacy was supported by signs and wonders. In that case, the pseudo-messiahs would not have been leaders of the revolt against the Romans, nor would they represent expectations based on memories of those leaders. On the contrary, what was criticized was the usurpation of religious hopes by the Roman ruler who demolished the uprising. This interpretation is more in harmony with the traditions that have found their way into Mark 13, because even the prophecy from the year 40 warned against the hubris of power. The same is true of the whole Son of man tradition, especially Daniel 7: the reign of the Son of man destroys the rule of blasphemous world powers. It is his coming, and not the desperate efforts of native revolutionaries to achieve liberation, that puts an end to oppression.

The future expectations expressed in Mk 13:14ff. can thus be located with ease in the circumstances around 70 C.E. But in that case, Mk 13:9-14 must relate to the current situation of the Markan community. Certainly the evangelist has collected some traditional sayings here. But his inclusion of them in 13:9-13, and their connection with the saying about the spread of the gospel in 13:10, could depend on concrete events. We need to show, then, that it is likely that Syrian Christians could experience things in the period ca. 66–76 C.E. that correspond to the words of Jesus presented in 13:9-13: pressures from all sides (13:13), mutual betrayal of members of the same family (13:12), trials before Jewish and gentile courts (13:9), but also the certainty that the gospel would spread in the face of persecution.[79]

Although we have no direct evidence of the persecution of Christians in Syria, we can conclude indirectly from Josephus that Christians came under pressure at that time. They were close to the Jews and shared their fate, since they were also separated from the surrounding society by their rejection of the gods and by their restricted table fellowship (cf. Gal 2:11ff.). Because they did not adopt all the Jewish separatist rules, they appeared as a group somewhere between Jews and Gentiles. Josephus reports of them at the beginning of the Jewish war:[80]

> The Syrians on their side killed no less a number of Jews; they, too, slaughtered those whom they caught in the towns, not merely now, as before, from

---

79. On what follows, cf. C. Breytenbach, *Nachfolge und Zukunftserwartung*, 311–30; R. Kühschelm, *Jüngerverfolgung und Geschick Jesu*.

80. Breytenbach (*Nachfolge und Zukunftserwartung*, 327) also sees in the historical tensions described by Josephus the historical background for Mk 13:9ff.

hatred, but to forestall the peril which menaced themselves. The whole of Syria was a scene of frightful disorder; every city was divided into two camps, and the safety of one party lay in their anticipating the other. They passed their days in blood, their nights, yet more dreadful, in terror. For, though believing that they had rid themselves of the Jews, still each city had its Judaizers [τοὺς ἰουδαΐζοντας], who aroused suspicion; and while they shrunk from killing offhand this equivocal element in their midst, they feared these neutrals as much as pronounced aliens. Even those who had long been reputed the very mildest of men were instigated by avarice to murder their adversaries. (*Bell.* 2.461–64)

Of course, by "Judaizers" (ἰουδαΐζοντες), Josephus means primarily the so-called God-fearers who sympathized with the synagogue. But Christians could also fall under that label. Peter, as representative of Antiochene Christianity, is accused by Paul of "Judaizing" (ἰουδαΐζειν; Gal 2:14). Even a generation later, Ignatius of Antioch met Christians who, in his opinion, lived in "Judaismos" (Ign. *Magn.* 8:1) and whose thinking he characterizes as "Judaizing" (Ign. *Magn.* 10:3). It is possible that Ignatius's thinking has been affected by experiences in his Syrian homeland. In any case, it was not unthinkable that Christians in first-century Syria could be called "Judaizers." The fact that Josephus does not mention the Christians as a specific group does not argue against this proposal; even in describing the execution of James he does not speak of the other victims of execution as Christians, although it is fairly certain that they were (*Ant.* 20.200–201). Josephus does not yet differentiate between Jews and Christians as we do, nor even to the extent that some Christian groups were already doing at that time. What is critical for us is that a general situation of danger, in which Christians were "hated by all," both Jews and Gentiles, is readily imaginable in Syria at the time of Mark's Gospel.

These Christian communities must have experienced instances of betrayal within families. The apocalyptic *topos* of the decline of the family is not adequate to explain Mk 13:12, because the variant of that *topos* in Q sounds "milder." It talks about quarrels and strife within families (Mt 10:34–36 par.), not about delivering one another over to death, which is what Josephus witnessed among Syrian Jews at the time of Mark's Gospel. As the hatred of Jews reached its climax during the Jewish war, the son of the "chief magistrate of the Jews" in Antioch denounced his father for allegedly having plotted to burn down the city. The father and other Jews accused with him were burned to death in the theater as a result (*Bell.* 7.46ff.). This is not meant to show that this catastrophe in one Jewish family and one community is portrayed in Mk 13:12. But the story reveals what kind of dreadful events could be expected. Incidentally, at another point Josephus clearly echoes the apocalyptic *topos* of family decline:

"Between the enthusiasts for war and the friends of peace contention raged fiercely. Beginning in the home this party rivalry first attacked those who had long been bosom friends; then the nearest relations severed their connections" (*Bell.* 4.132).

If Mk 13:9-12 reflects Mark's communities in Syria, trials of Christians there before councils, synagogues, kings, and governors must have been possible (13:9). In fact, Syria was a province where we find those courts and individuals historically recorded. Here were some of the few client kings in the Roman Empire: Herod Agrippa II, Antiochus of Commagene and Cilicia (*Bell.* 7.219ff., 234ff.), Aristobulus of Chalcis (*Bell.* 7.226), and Soemus of Emesa (*Bell.* 7.226). There were more synagogues here than elsewhere in the empire; Jews were everywhere, but "particularly numerous in Syria, where intermingling is due to the proximity of the two countries" (*Bell.* 7.43). The province was ruled by an imperial legate, assisted by a procurator for Palestine.

In the midst of the sayings about persecution, which he applies to the difficult present situation of his community, the evangelist inserts the proud statement "And the good news must be proclaimed to all nations" (Mk 13:10). This would have had a special ring to it in Syria circa 70 C.E. Other εὐαγγέλια were known here. It was here in the eastern part of the empire, in its terrible crisis, that Vespasian had been proclaimed emperor—the man who succeeded in putting an end to civil war and rebellion and restoring peace. Josephus calls the news of his proclamation as emperor "good news": "Quicker than thought rumor spread the news of the new emperor in the east. Every city kept festival for the good news [εὐαγγέλια] and offered sacrifices on his behalf" (*Bell.* 4.618). Numerous embassies came from all over Syria to do him homage (*Bell.* 4.620). When Vespasian was recognized and acclaimed as emperor at Rome, Josephus again calls the news εὐαγγέλια (*Bell.* 4.656). In fact, the beginning of Vespasian's reign must really have seemed like an "evangel" to many people.

Consider merely the end-of-the-world mood in which Tacitus begins his depiction of these times:

> The history on which I am entering is that of a period rich in disasters, terrible with battles, torn by civil struggles, horrible even in peace. Four emperors fell by the sword; there were three civil wars, more foreign wars, and often both at the same time. . . . Italy was distressed by disasters unknown before or returning after the lapse of ages. Cities on the rich fertile shores of Campania were swallowed up or overwhelmed; Rome was devastated by conflagrations, in which her most ancient sanctuaries were consumed and the very Capitol fired by citizens' hands. (*Hist.* 1.2)

Vespasian had led the empire out of this, the most serious crisis since the civil wars of the late republic. No wonder he was revered as a savior sent from God. Josephus himself had prophesied world rule for him (*Bell.* 3.400ff.; 4.622ff.). Probably he transferred messianic expectations to Vespasian, who was acclaimed in Egypt as a god.[81] In this situation, the author of Mark is writing a kind of "counter-gospel": the message about the crucified one who is to be ruler of the world. It is not the consolidation of political affairs under Vespasian that is the "good news," but the story of the life and death of Jesus of Nazareth. The emphatic manner in which the author of Mark begins his book with the key word εὐαγγέλιον (Mk 1:1), calls the preaching of the coming kingdom εὐαγγέλιον (1:14), and connects this concept of "good news" with discipleship in suffering (8:35; 10:29)—all this could indicate that he consciously conceives his story of Jesus as an "evangel" of a different sort. Exaggerated religious propaganda for Vespasian was, for him, part of that "desolating sacrilege" that presaged the end of the world.[82]

Our conclusion, then, is that Mark's Gospel is marked by the proximity of war, both in its chronology and in its content. It was written during the Jewish war of 66–74 C.E., probably after the capture of the temple in August 70 and before all military activities and events in the immediate aftermath of the war had ceased. The war had passed its high point. It now appeared as the prologue to a greater catastrophe. In comparison to Mark, the other two Synoptic Gospels are characterized by their greater distance from the war. The exigencies from without in Mark are replaced in Matthew and Luke by intensified internal problems. We will describe the situation in Matthew's Gospel first.

A key to the Matthean view of history is the author's redaction of the parable of the "great banquet" (Mt 22:1-14). After the servants are sent out the second time, the evangelist inserts a remark about the destruction of Jerusalem: "The king was enraged. He sent his troops, destroyed those murderers, and burned their city" (Mt 22:7). Even if the description of the city's devastation is "topical"—since most of it could apply to the destruction of any ancient city[83]—its insertion into the parable cannot be

---

81. So P. Fouad, no. 8. On this, see Schwier, *Tempel und Tempelzerstörung*, 310ff.

82. E. Haenchen (*Der Weg Jesu*, 435–60, esp. 447) also sees in Mark 13 a counterposition to the imperial cult, but interprets the concrete indications in the text allegorically.

83. Among those who dispute the existence of a *vaticinium ex eventu* in Mt 22:7 is K. H. Rengstorf ("Die Stadt der Mörder"), who, with numerous citations, points out the topical character of Mt 22:7. Bo Reicke ("Synoptic Prophecies on the Destruction of Jerusalem") argues on the basis of the conflict with reality: Nero sent the armies against Jerusalem, and

explained on the basis of any literary tradition: war as a reaction against a rejected invitation is atypical and unrealistic. Only the Christian interpretation of the destruction of Jerusalem as punishment for the rejection of Jesus' message makes the connection plausible. For our purposes, it is important that the invitation of the "king" succeeds only after the destruction of the city, not among the original invitees, but with onlookers and outsiders who are brought in from everywhere. Readers of Matthew's Gospel must have thought of the Gentiles, too.[84] It must have been plausible to them that the invitation to the Gentiles (the third invitation to the "outsiders") had been extended by Matthew's community at a relatively late moment, after 70 C.E.—later than in other Christian communities. The resulting problems may also have arisen or first been recognized at that time. The community had become a *corpus mixtum*—the last invitation had been extended to "good and bad." Not all the new arrivals were worthy. That is why the author of Matthew adds the episode of the dismissal of the guest who has no wedding garment (22:11-14).[85] This episode sheds light on immediate and pressing problems in Matthew's community. Even if we cannot read the parables themselves as depictions of community situations, Matthew's version of the parable of the "great banquet" still suggests both a greater distance from the Jewish war and the emergence of internal problems in a community made up of Jewish and gentile Christians.

This greater distance from the year 70 C.E. can also be detected in a small change in the parable of the tenants in the vineyard. After the sending of the slaves and of the son has ended in the killing of the latter, there follows the judgment, according to which the owner of the vineyard will kill the tenants and give the vineyard to others. The author of Matthew adds to the Markan text that the new lessors of the vineyard "will give

---

the leap from Nero (in historical reality) to God (in the parable) is too great. See also S. Pedersen, "Zum Problem der vaticinia ex eventu."

84. L. Schottroff ("Das Gleichnis vom grossen Gastmahl") has shown, I think persuasively, that the original parable was not about the contrast of Jews and Gentiles or Pharisees and sinners, but about the difference between poor and rich. Still, in Matthew's redaction an interpretation in terms of an invitation to the Gentiles is probable. The argument that there is no tradition in which the image of poor people and beggars is equated with that of Gentiles is not, I think, compelling—anyone who can compare Gentiles with "dogs" who eat food scraps, as the author of Matthew does (Mt 15:26-27), could certainly think of the Gentiles as "poor people and beggars."

85. It can remain unclear whether the author of Matthew composed this addition or added it from an independent community tradition, as J. Jeremias (*Die Gleichnisse Jesu,* 62–63) thinks. The division of good and bad is typical of Matthew (Mt 23:24-30, 36-43, 47-50) and in any case expresses an idea that is important to him. The fact that this addition does not fit with the preceding parable—how should unexpectedly invited guests be able to provide themselves with clean festal robes?—does not bother the evangelist, since he already interprets the parable allegorically.

him the produce at the harvest time" (Mt 21:41), and this is reiterated in 21:43. While Mark has in view only the taking away of the vineyard, Matthew speaks of its renewed use. In order to bring fruit, the vineyard must be cultivated for a long time. That is certainly a feature of the "pictorial half" of the parable, which cannot simply be transformed into a statement about the community situation. But the addition, while appropriate in its context, would probably be more plausible if the author of Matthew could look back at a fairly long period of time since the "transfer" of the vineyard to new tenants.[86]

A greater distance from the Jewish war can also be sensed in Matthew's rendition of the apocalyptic discourse. Mark had composed his section on the time before the end in such a way that one could think of the periods of war and persecution (Mk 13:6-8, 9-12) as simultaneous. The "kingdoms" (13:8) that war against each other have something to do with the "kings" who will try to condemn the Christians (13:9). But Matthew makes a small addition that heightens the impression of a temporal sequence. After the saying about wars, he begins a new sentence in 24:9 with τότε ("then"), which is repeated in vv. 10, 14, 16, 23, and 30, sometimes in harmony with the Markan wording (e.g., vv. 16, 23). This τότε does not exclude simultaneity, but on the whole it gives the impression of a temporal sequence (esp. in 24:14).[87]

The decisive point is the internal distance of the present from the war. Matthew has redacted Mark's depiction of the present—that is, the time between the Jewish war (Mk 13:6-8 = Mt 24:6-8) and the expected "desolating sacrilege" (Mt 24:15ff.)—by incorporating the sayings about persecution (Mk 13:9-13) in his mission discourse for Israel (Mt 10:17-22) and omitting concrete examples of persecution from the apocalyptic discourse, so that it now applies to Christians all over the world.[88] Thus, Matthew emphasizes that Christians will be hated "by all nations." Conflict with the outside world continues. But at the same time, Matthew lays greater stress on internal difficulties: for example, the apocalyptic *topos* of the decline of the family (Mk 13:12) becomes in Matthew a warning about the collapse

---

86. Matthew's real interest here is parenetic. As the vineyard was taken from the leaders of Israel, it can also be taken from the Christian community if it does not bear fruit. Cf. H. Weder, *Die Gleichnisse Jesu als Metaphern*, 160–61.

87. N. A. Dahl (*Matteusevangeliet*, 286) thinks that Mt 24:9-14 does not announce persecution and suffering after the birthpangs already described, but at the same time as those pangs. But the sufferings now described are new in relationship to the Jewish war in 24:6-8, including the worldwide extent of the persecutions and the causes of the crisis within the community itself. J. Wellhausen, *Mt* 118, is correct when he says: "The threshold in 24:9-14 seems . . . in fact to have moved beyond the destruction of Jerusalem."

88. Matthew expands the situation beyond Palestine by speaking pointedly of "all nations" at the beginning and end of the section (cf. 24:9, 14). Cf. J. Wellhausen, *Das Evangelium Matthaei*, 118; W. Grundmann, *Das Evangelium nach Matthäus*, 502.

of the community.[89] Christians will betray one another. The "hatred" from outside has the result that, within the community, Christians "hate" one another (24:10). Such a divided community is open to being led astray. Matthew speaks of many false prophets, who for him are part of the community, as Mt 7:21-23 shows. Because of them, there will be an increase of "lawlessness" (cf. Mt 7:23) and the love of many will grow cold. Certainly, Matthew is aware of external pressures, but what really endangers the community is internal collapse: mutual hate and the cooling of love. Enduring to the end therefore means for him not only withstanding temptations from without, but steadfastness in the truth, despite false teachers within the community.[90]

Some new emphases in the anticipated future as we find it in Matthew's Gospel are in harmony with the observations just made. While the Sayings Source expects the Son of man to come into a world at peace, where everyone is going about his or her daily tasks, and whereas Mark's Gospel longs for the Parousia to rescue the community from a world at war, Matthew's Gospel combines both these images of the future by adding apocalyptic sayings from Q to Mark's discourse on the end time, beginning at Mt 24:15 (cf. Mt 24:26-28, 37-41). The result is not entirely smooth: the end comes after a time of terrible affliction (Mt 24:15ff.),[91] and at the same time it appears to break into a peaceful world (24:37ff.). Matthew expresses his real emphases in the great parables of the end time that he adds to the synoptic apocalypse. Even if the coming of the Lord is delayed (24:48), it is all the more important to be prepared for his return at any time. Constant watchfulness is demanded (25:1-13), as well as the use of the gifts that have been entrusted to each (25:14-30) and helpfulness toward every sister and brother (25:31-46). The end of the world is, for Matthew, not so much rescue from a desperate situation as it is a judgment of the world that should motivate all to ethical action. The greater distance from war and crisis situations leads him to place the topic of ethical conduct of life more in the foreground. Therefore, the inclusion of the Sayings Source is closely connected to his historical situation: Matthew, like Q, formulates a confident ethic in the wake of temptation successfully

---

89. Thus E. Schweizer, *Matthäus*, 294: "The real danger is within the community."

90. Ibid., 295.

91. Wellhausen (*Das Evangelium Matthaei*, 118) thinks that with the "desolating sacrilege" Matthew is referring to the destruction of Jerusalem, which has already occurred. But it is clear that, beginning with Mt 24:15ff., the subject is the real future, first, because v. 14 already points to the future. The worldwide preaching of the gospel is not yet complete. "The end" will come afterward. Second, the prayer that the flight may not occur on "the Sabbath" (only in Matthew) presumes that we are talking about a brief event taking place on a single day. In looking back at a historical event, one would speak of a longer period of flight.

resisted. The community has survived the Jewish war and has once more escaped the destructive machinery of warfare, just as Jesus escaped the murderous attempts of Herod. Now it is faced with its major task: to conduct its life in "normal times" according to Jesus' teachings.

In Luke we can observe some elements similar to those in Matthew. Here is an intensive reflection on the Jewish war. More than all the other evangelists, Luke expresses human compassion for the suffering of the Jewish people. Jesus weeps when he foresees the destruction of Jerusalem (Lk 19:41-44) and calls on the women of Jerusalem not to mourn for him, but for their fate and that of their children (23:28). The times will be so terrible that the childless will be called blessed (23:29) and "woe" will be invoked over women who are pregnant and nursing (21:23), because the war will fall hardest on them. Although Luke shares the opinion that the destruction of Jerusalem is a "punishment"—the siege is a time of "vengeance" (21:22)—the positive aspect of this thought is more important for him: the catastrophe need not have happened. Had the people accepted Jesus' message, this war could have been avoided. This is how we should understand 19:42: "If you, even you, had only recognized on this day the things that make for peace! But now they are hidden from your eyes." The promise to the Jewish people is valid now as then; Jesus is to be the future "Son of David" who will fulfill the hopes of his people (1:32-33).

In Luke, we do not yet find "internal" distance from the war, but we can recognize an effort to create an internal separation from the emotional shocks caused by it. This is most evident in Luke's redaction of the synoptic apocalypse.[92] The critical change is that Luke applies to the Jewish war the words about the "great tribulation" in Mark, and thus historicizes them. This gives a new structure to the traditional shape of the synoptic apocalypse (Table 8).

The "historicizing" interpretation of the great tribulation in Lk 21:20-24 disrupts the temporal sequence of events in the Lukan text, so that the introduction (21:8-11) becomes a reference forward to a later time. Consequently, the next section is introduced with πρὸ δὲ τούτων πάντων in order to place these events before those depicted in vv. 8-11. The persecutions described in 21:12-19 happened before the Jewish war and are, from Luke's perspective, in the past.[93] Therefore, at the end of this section we

---

92. Luke's discourse on the end time has been analyzed many times. The classic redaction-critical interpretation is that of Conzelmann, *Die Mitte der Zeit*, 116–24. Of more recent studies, let me mention only J. Zmijewski, *Eschatologiereden*, 43–325; idem, "Die Eschatologiereden Lk 21 und 17"; R. Geiger, *Die lukanischen Endzeitreden*, 149–258.

93. Luke has reported these persecutions in Acts. There are some connections between Lk 21:12-19 and Acts, esp. the martyrdom of Stephen. Cf. Zmijewski, *Eschatologiereden*, 166–67, 177.

TABLE 8
The Synoptic Apocalypse

In Mark's understanding	In Luke's understanding
13:5-8: Jewish war as "beginning of birthpangs"	21:8-9: warning against an eschatological interpretation of wars
	21:10-11: announcement of the Jewish war
13:9-13: time of persecution in and after the Jewish war as present	21:12-19: time of persecution before the Jewish war as past
13:14-23: desecration of the temple as feared future event	21:20-24: destruction of Jerusalem as fact. The "times of the Gentiles" as present
13:24-27: Parousia of the Son of man	21:25-28: Parousia of the Son of man

do not find the promise that "the one who endures *to the end* will be saved" (Mk 13:13), since the persecutions are not followed by the "end," but by the destruction of Jerusalem as a further event within history. If this interpretation is correct, the redactional changes in Lk 21:8-9 (10-11?) and 21:20-24 must have been made in light of the Jewish war. Let us examine them in turn.

Luke prophesies in 21:9 not only wars, but also ἀκαταστασίας, which means something like "insurrections" or "anarchy." This corresponds to the fact that the Jewish war occurred in a period of civil wars. For the first time in a century, the political institutions of the Principate failed to preserve the internal peace they had heretofore maintained. These "upheavals" were felt throughout the Roman Empire. Luke is thus speaking of events that may have been more immediate to his community than the Jewish war.[94]

---

94. Thus, H. Holtzmann *(Das Evangelium nach Lukas)* thinks of the "rapid alternations on the throne in the years 68–70." G. Harder ("Das eschatologische Geschichtsbild," 76) sees here on the contrary "a clear reflection of the Jewish revolt." The plural could indicate that

The distress that follows is separated from what has gone before by a new introductory phrase ("Then he said to them . . ."). It is more extreme than in the Markan source: not merely regional earthquakes, but "great earthquakes"; not only famines, but "plagues"; not only earthly catastrophes, but "dreadful portents and great signs from heaven." Does all this refer to the signs immediately before the end, things that for Luke are still in the future? The "great signs from heaven" (21:11) would then be identical with the "signs in the sun, the moon, and the stars" that Luke names as the introduction of the Parousia in 21:25.[95]

Another interpretation is possible. Luke first warns against giving an eschatological interpretation to the wars (21:8-9) and then surrounds these wars with circumstances that seem to invite an eschatological interpretation. But they should not be thought of in that way, because "the end will not follow immediately." The increased distress, compared with the text of Mark, in 21:10-11 would then be intended to avert an eschatological reading of even the most unusual signs. Could such signs be connected with the Jewish war, which is the subject of 21:8-9?[96]

1. Because we have no evidence of "great earthquakes" in the period from 66 to 74 C.E., Luke must have "synchronized" the Jewish war with earthquakes that were relatively close to it in time. In 62 or 63, the first earthquake struck Pompeii (Tacitus *Ann.* 15.22.2); in 79, both Pompeii and Herculaneum were buried by the eruption of Vesuvius (Pliny the Younger *Ep.* 6.16; Dio Cassius 66.21.1ff.). In 77, Corinth was destroyed by an earthquake (Malal. *Chron.* 261), and in the same year a number of cities on Cyprus were struck by earthquakes (*Oros.* 7.9.11; *Sib. Or.* 4.128–29). Luke may have been thinking of catastrophes such as these. The *Sibylline Oracles* also connect the destruction of Jerusalem, the earthquakes on Cyprus, and the eruption of Vesuvius (*Sib. Or.* 4.115–44). Luke 21:10ff. does not say that the wars and earthquakes must occur at exactly the same time.[97]

2. Famines are attested: the people trapped in Jerusalem suffered terri-

---

Luke is thinking of a number of instances of unrest—i.e., the overall situation in the Roman Empire at the time of the Jewish war, including the civil wars and the revolt of the Batavians.

95. So G. Schneider, *Evangelium nach Lukas*, 417. Luke separates 21:10-11, as events of the final days, from all the temporal happenings that have preceded them.

96. A. Schlatter (*Lukas*, 412ff.) believes that Luke is thinking of the Jewish war. This is also the opinion of Marxsen (*Der Evangelist Markus*, 131) and Zmijewski (*Eschatologiereden*, 122–25); the latter offers two arguments. First, Luke generally avoids doublets. Therefore the signs in vv. 11 and 25 could scarcely refer to the same event, since Luke could otherwise have easily avoided this "doublet." Second, Luke eliminates Mark's evaluation of the signs as "beginning of the birthpangs" and thus indirectly denies their eschatological character.

97. It would even be possible to see in Lk 21:10-11 the consequences of a political and cosmological dissolution in which "the end announces itself little by little" (Conzelmann, *Die Mitte der Zeit*, 109–10).

bly from the shortage of food (*Bell.* 5.424ff., 512ff.; 6.1ff.). Cases of cannibalism were known (*Bell.* 6.193–213). In the fragment of Sulpicius Severus on the destruction of Jerusalem (*Chron.* 2.30.3), starvation and cannibalism are seen as characteristic for the siege of Jerusalem, with sickness the consequence of starvation. The "plagues" mentioned by Luke are more difficult to account for, but we do find notice in Suetonius (*Titus* 8.3) of a "plague the like of which had hardly ever been known before" under Titus (79–81 C.E.).

3. "Dreadful portents and great signs from heaven" (Lk 21:11) are also attested for the time of the Jewish war. In the "propaganda battles" around Jerusalem, stories about signs in the heavens played a considerable role: "Contending hosts were seen meeting in the skies, arms flashed, and suddenly the temple was illumined with fire from the clouds. Of a sudden the doors of the shrine opened and a superhuman voice cried: 'The gods are departing': at the same moment the mighty stir of their going was heard" (Tacitus *Hist.* 5.13.1; cf. *Bell.* 6.288ff.). In this time of upheaval, people told of all sorts of signs of this type: "Besides the manifold misfortunes that befell [hu]mankind, there were prodigies [*prodigia*] in the sky and on the earth, warnings given by thunderbolts, and prophecies of the future, both joyful and gloomy, uncertain and clear" (Tacitus *Hist.* 1.3.2).

In 21:10-11, Luke probably had in mind a combination of political and "cosmic" catastrophes typical of the period of the Jewish war and the 70s. He touches the same dark, apocalyptic mood that can be sensed even in Tacitus's description of the times (*Hist.* 1.1.2–3). It is not important for us to fix each and every one of the crisis phenomena with historical exactitude, because it is not the events themselves, but people's ideas about them that are the focus of Luke's attention.

In Lk 21:20-24 we have an unmistakable portrayal of the siege and fall of Jerusalem.[98] Certainly, Luke paints his scene in Old Testament colors. But even if he is reproducing an independent tradition,[99] he has used it to replace Mark 13:14ff., and we must account for the fact that most of the deviations from the Markan text can be explained as adaptations to real events (or a plausible picture of them). Thus, we can gather from

---

98. This interpretation is seldom disputed, as it is by F. Flückiger in "Lk 21,20-24." He sees Lk 21:20-24 as a new interpretation of Mk 13:14-18 based on the words of Old Testament prophets. Cf. the pointed remarks of C. H. Dodd: "So far as any historical event has coloured the picture, it is not Titus's capture of Jerusalem in A.D. 70, but Nebuchadrezzar's capture in 586 B.C. There is no single trait of the forecast which cannot be documented directly out of the Old Testament" (*More New Testament Studies* [Manchester, 1968], 79).

99. There have been frequent attempts to find another source document besides Mark for Luke 21. Cf. V. Taylor, *Behind the Third Gospel*, 101ff. Schweizer (*Das Evangelium nach Lukas*, 207–11) also sees here the insertion of independent tradition. As a rule, however, Luke's deviations from the Markan text are explained redactionally.

Lk 21:20 that Jerusalem was surrounded by a number of legions. In fact, six legions, with their auxiliaries, encamped around the city, with their three stations on the Mount of Olives, near the Tower of Hippicus in the west, and near the Tower of Psephinus in the northwest (*Bell.* 5.130–35). Since a direct attack was unsuccessful, the Romans decided on a *circumvallatio* (*Bell.* 5.491–511), which is referred to in Lk 19:43-44. It was by no means so much a matter of course that Luke could have prophesied it without direct knowledge of the facts.[100] People had been fleeing from Judea since the beginning of the war (*Bell.* 2.556). Some of those besieged in Jerusalem also tried to go over to the Romans (*Bell.* 5.420ff., 446ff., 548ff.). We hear of people fleeing from Jericho into the hill country (*Bell.* 4.451).[101] But most people fled to Jerusalem (*Bell.* 4.106ff., 138ff.) where, like the Galileans around John of Gischala or the Idumeans, they composed parties that often attacked one another in bloody fashion. All these movements of flight make up the background of Lk 21:21. Luke knows about the desolation of Jerusalem (21:20). Titus had ordered "the whole city and the temple to be razed to the ground" (*Bell.* 7.1). Many Jews died in the war, and many more were sold as slaves (Lk 21:24).

If the interpretation of Lk 21:8-11 and 21:20-24 presented here is correct, we can gain from Luke's Gospel some important insights into the early Christian view of the Jewish war. Luke warns against eschatological expectations in connection with that war. Mark's admonition about false teachers who claim ἐγώ εἰμι is embellished with two descriptive statements: (1) they announce the approach of the end ("The time is near!") and (2) they entice the community to "go after them" (Lk 21:8). Then comes the assurance that "the end will not follow immediately" after the Jewish war (21:9). Luke omits the description of those events as the "beginning of the birthpangs." The most probable interpretation of this is that Luke knows that the Jewish war had at one time awakened eschatological expectations in the Christian communities. There was hope that Jesus would "restore the kingdom to Israel" (Acts 1:6) and "redeem Israel" (Lk 24:21). Probably people were already looking up to heaven to see Jesus

---

100. That was Flückiger's opinion: "At that time every fortified city was cut off and besieged before it could be destroyed by enemies. Luke could thus have presumed the same fate for Jerusalem, without being at all prophetic" ("Lk 21,20-24," 387). But both the legate Cestius Gallus (66 C.E.) and Titus (70 C.E.) tried first to conquer Jerusalem without a *circumvallatio*. The victory of Corbulo in Armenia was also accomplished by surprise attack, without a long siege (Tacitus *Ann.* 13.39). Still, it is true that a *circumvallatio* was the rule in Roman siege tactics, as at Carthage (146 B.C.E.), Numantia (133 B.C.E.), Alesia (52 B.C.E.), and Masada (73 or 74 C.E.).

101. I see nothing in favor of an allegorical interpretation of this flight as a call to "withdrawal from Judaism" and "turning toward the Gentiles," as Zmijewski suggests in *Eschatologiereden*, 211.

coming from there. That is why the angels ask, after the ascension, "Men of Galilee, why do you stand looking up toward heaven?" (Acts 1:11). Only when the Son of man comes with unmistakable cosmic signs will there be reason to "stand up and raise your heads, because your redemption is drawing near" (Lk 21:28). Possibly, some Christians went out with the "false leaders" to meet the returning Lord. That would explain Luke's specific warnings: "Do not go after them" (Lk 21:8); "Do not go; do not set off in pursuit" (Lk 17:23; contra Mt 24:26). Luke probably means to reject an intensified eschatological expectation resulting from the war. It was not the "lengthening time" that led Luke to correct immediate expectations of the end,[102] but an acutely inflamed anticipation that had proved erroneous. Luke does not completely give up hope that the end will soon come. He continues to believe that it could happen at any moment. But he no longer expects the end to arrive as the conclusion of a war.

For Luke, the war is over. These are "the times of the Gentiles" (Lk 21:24). As in the Sayings Source (= Lk 17:22-37), the Son of man will burst unexpectedly upon this peaceful age, and no one will be able to predict his coming. Thus, Luke's redaction of the apocalyptic discourse in Mark was carried out in light of the preceding "discourse on the end time" in the Sayings Source, which is better adapted to maintain early Christian expectations of the future in peaceful times than is the Markan apocalypse, shaped as it is by crises and war.

According to the interpretation presented here, Luke's Gospel could not have been written long after the Jewish war.[103] The author includes himself in the third generation after Jesus (Lk 1:1-3). He must still know people who were actively involved in the fate of Jerusalem. He may have visited the city before its destruction, which would explain his surprisingly accurate knowledge of the temple and its grounds.[104] He must at least have had contact with people who had seen the temple. He is writing at about the same time as Matthew, in the 80s or 90s.

We can now summarize our reflections on the situation and dating of the Synoptic Gospels. The Sayings Source was written in light of the recently surmounted Caligula crisis, sometime between 40 and 55 C.E. The circumstances of its origin are reflected in its structure: at the beginning, a satanic Temptation is overcome, and on that basis a confident ethic is proclaimed. Mark's Gospel, on the other hand, was written in the face of a threatening catastrophe, circa 70–74. Here Jesus' real temptation is at the

---

102. This is the classic thesis of Conzelmann, *Die Mitte der Zeit*, 5–6, 80ff., 112–13, etc.
103. See the discussion in H. Conzelmann, "Der geschichtliche Ort."
104. M. Hengel, "Der Historiker Lukas," 147ff.

end: in Gethsemane the Son of God suffers his crisis. The readers, like him, are approaching their critical test. Matthew and Luke combine both these views. Their circumstances are more like those of the Sayings Source, and they need this collection of Jesus-sayings for their revision of Mark's Gospel. A plan for active living has taken on more immediate significance for them than the conquest of conflict and suffering. Therefore, they describe not only Jesus' "end," but his whole life, from birth to the cross. The way to the cross is a long one. In Luke, it is full of ethical admonitions. The "travel account" contains the bulk of the material drawn from the Sayings Source. Matthew, in contrast, incorporates the sayings material in five great discourses within his Gospel. These are the critical content of his writing, in which the readers learn what must be taught to all peoples until the end of the world.

COMMUNITY TRADITIONS, DISCIPLES' TRADITIONS, AND POPULAR STORIES IN THE GOSPELS, AND THE QUESTION OF THEIR *SITZ IM LEBEN*

Mark's Gospel contains traditions drawn from a variety of life situations. Conclusions about the *Sitz im Leben* of Mark's Gospel can be drawn only from those traditions that are basic to the structure of the Gospel as a whole. At the heart of Mark's composition are the two "large units": the synoptic apocalypse (Mark 13) and the Passion account (Mark 14–16). The combination of the two reveals the intention of the author of Mark: the persecutions predicted for the disciples are the image of the story of Jesus. His Passion is a model of behavior for the Markan community.[105] Just as they are being pressured by Jewish and gentile authorities, so Jesus was rejected by both (cf. Mk 13:9; 14:55ff.). As they must reject any elaborate attempts to defend themselves, so Jesus dispensed with any defense and contented himself with confessing his majesty (cf. Mk 13:11; 14:62-63). As their members are being betrayed by their closest relatives, so Jesus was betrayed, abandoned, and denied by his own disciples (cf. Mk 13:12; 14:43ff.). Through the combination of two originally independent traditions, the Passion story is read as a "conflict parenesis," in light of a struggle with the world outside that threatens every disciple. This does not impose an alien meaning on the Passion story. On the contrary, from the very beginning, those who told the story of Jesus' suffering saw it as a reflection of their own fate. The whole of Mark's Gospel shares the purpose and perspective of the Passion story. It is thus decisive for the ques-

---

105. See the title of D. Dormeyer's book: *Die Passion Jesu als Verhaltensmodell.*

tion of the *Sitz im Leben* of Mark's Gospel to know that the two structuring "large units," the apocalypse and the Passion account, come from and address themselves to local communities. Mark's Gospel is shaped by community traditions. The most probable conclusion is that this entire Gospel is a record of Jesus traditions written for local communities, and that in this Gospel, popular tales and traditions from the disciples have been adopted and adapted in a new way for the use of these communities.

This adaptation took place with aid, among other things, of the motifs of secrecy that make of Mark's Gospel, despite the great variety of the individual traditions incorporated in it,[106] a compositional unity. These motifs of secrecy show as little unity among themselves as do the various individual traditions, but they can be classified in three basic types:[107]

1. Miracles as secret. Jesus tries unsuccessfully to prevent his miracles from becoming public knowledge.[108] The "secrecy of place" often belongs in this context: Jesus wants to remain hidden, in order not to attract the miracle-seeking crowds (Mk 1:45; 7:24; 9:30?).
2. Secret teachings that reveal the hidden meaning of Jesus' words for the disciples. The "parable theory" is only the first of these secret teachings, and serves as a fundamental justification for them.
3. Personal secret. Jesus' true dignity remains undiscovered. The disciples first recognize it at the time of Peter's confession of Jesus as Messiah. But it is the centurion at the cross who utters the first public (and still incomplete) confession of the "Son of God." The motif of the disciples' misunderstanding belongs in this context.

Miracles as Secret

The miracle secret serves in Mark's Gospel to integrate popular traditions about Jesus, including some of the miracle stories and the court legend

---

106. These individual traditions were probably to be found here and there in small collections, even if it is very difficult to prove their existence. On this point, see esp. the reflections of H. W. Kuhn, *Ältere Sammlungen im Markusevangelium.*

107. W. Wrede *(Das Messiasgeheimnis in den Evangelien)* distinguished three primary complexes: the admonitions to silence, the misunderstanding on the part of the disciples, and the parable theory. He was the first to recognize that the three belong together, but did not interpret them in terms of redaction criticism as an expression of the theology of the author of Mark. He regarded them as pre-Markan tradition.

108. The distinction between miracle secret and personal secret is that of U. Luz, "Das Geheimnismotiv." If we compare the three basic motifs of the "secrecy theory," we find they can be distinguished by the point at which the secret is revealed: miracle secrets are immediately violated, the personal secret is revealed only in the Passion, and the secret teachings remain secret. Only the post-Easter community learns of these teachings—which, in my opinion, is a sign that they belong to the present time of the community.

about the death of the Baptizer. The evangelist is sympathetic to these popular tales. For him, they are a sign of the inevitability of the spread of the Christian message, and they document the power with which the "new teaching" is proclaimed (Mk 1:27). But the evangelist has sensed that the popular image of Jesus was one-sided. Here Jesus is the successful wonder-worker. He puts an end to suffering; he does not lead people into it. Only Jesus' followers, who get into trouble because of him, are aware of this. By means of the secrecy motif, the evangelist probably wants to apply a certain corrective to the popular view. This, at least, is the opinion of most exegetes.[109] But we should not construct false alternatives: the story of the Baptizer's end also stems from popular tradition. Ordinary people knew that the "righteous" and the "holy" could come into conflict with the wielders of power. They had no illusions about the capricious rule of the mighty. According to Mark's Gospel, it is true that they made a different connection between the miracles and the Passion than did the evangelist himself: the miracles led to a rumor that he was the Baptizer risen from the dead, and for that reason mysterious powers were at work in him (Mk 6:14). Miracles are viewed as "God's protest" against the execution of God's prophet.

Secret Teachings

While the miracle stories spread quickly, Jesus' teaching falls on deaf ears: "they listen but do not understand" (cf. Mk 4:12). Jesus has to interpret the sayings tradition for the disciples in private. These teaching sessions are often, though not always, "in the house." This could indicate the groups that are addressed by these "additional teachings"—the local communities of house churches. For them, Jesus' teaching really did need reinterpretation. This connection with the local communities is especially clear in 9:33ff., where Jesus reacts to the disciples' disputes about rank. He is not content with a saying about the reversal of all positions, but illustrates it with an example. The model disciple is one who welcomes a child in the name of God. This benevolent action could not be done by an itinerant charismatic, but only by someone who lives in a house. A similar interpretation can be given to other secret teachings that take place "in the house." For example, the problem of food regulations was acute in the local communities. Itinerant preachers such as Peter and Barnabas could act differently according to the local situation (Gal 2:11ff.).[110] But a set-

---

109. T. Weeden has given the most extreme version of this thesis in his article "The Heresy That Necessitated Mark's Gospel": Mark is combating a heresy whose adherents were followers of Jesus the wonder-worker.

110. Paul accuses them of "hypocrisy" in Gal 2:11ff. because of their change in behavior,

tled community had to arrive at a long-term solution. The warning against too much confidence in one's own miraculous powers (Mk 9:28-29) was certainly appropriate for all Christians, but it could signal a certain dissociation from the itinerant charismatics: exorcisms were the business of traveling missionaries (Mk 6:12). If they failed to effect a cure, it was not a catastrophe for them, since they could go somewhere else and explain that the lack of faith in the last place had hindered the expression of their miraculous powers (Mk 6:5). Local communities, in contrast, had to reconcile realistic expectations and mere possibilities. Following the conflict dialogue about divorce, two topics relating to the family are dealt with in a private teaching "in the house" (Mk 10:10-16): toleration of divorce while, at the same time, both partners are forbidden to enter a new marriage; and the obligation to care for children. The "secret instruction in the house" thus expresses the fact that Jesus' teaching requires interpretation, especially for the concerns of the Christians who live "in houses." But both of the long private teachings "in the open air" have local communities in mind as well. The explanation of the parable of the fourfold yield is conceived from the point of view of the recipients of the word—that is, the local communities—because it is only there that people will be found in whom "the cares of the world, and the lure of wealth, and the desire for other things" will choke the word (Mk 4:19). The synoptic apocalypse is addressed to people who are conducting their ordinary business: they should drop everything and flee (Mk 13:15-16). If pregnant and nursing women are the particular victims of the tribulation, it is all the more evident that the audience lives in "normal" family relationships. The destruction of the family (Mk 13:12) is a catastrophe for them.

The Personal Secret

The secret about Jesus' identity is central to Mark's Gospel. Jesus does not wish that his dignity, which is known from the beginning only by non-human figures (God and the angels: Mk 1:11, 13; Satan and the demons: 1:13, 34), to be made public. The demons are silenced by an order (1:25; 3:11-12). But after a sharp division between the disciples and the people (Mark 4), Jesus permits a demon to acknowledge him (5:7) when only the disciples are witnesses. It seems that they must themselves recognize Jesus, but they remain blind. Their lack of understanding is repeatedly con-

---

but he is wrong to do so, since Paul himself had changed his mind on this question. Although in Antioch he argued for a consistent freedom from traditional food laws, in Corinth he brings all his eloquence into play (using different arguments; cf. 1 Corinthians 8–10) to persuade the Corinthians to respect those same laws for the sake of the weak. Paul, too, was an itinerant charismatic preacher.

demned (6:52; 8:14ff.), until finally Peter comes to a recognition of Jesus' messiahship (8:29) and is sharply rebuked because he connects it with "human things." From this point on, the disciples' lack of understanding gradually becomes misunderstanding. The disciples have to learn that Jesus is not a "messiah" in the worldly sense—the sense in which he is accused by the Sanhedrin (14:61) and which is indicated in his trial before Pilate with the title "king of the Jews" (15:2ff.). In reality, he is the suffering Son of man who will reveal himself to those who follow him in suffering (8:31-38) as the Son of God (9:2ff.). Jesus speaks of himself publicly as Son of God for the first time in the parable of the vine-dressers (12:1ff.). He also confesses his dignity publicly before his judges (14:62). He is publicly acknowledged as Son of God on the cross (15:39). But even the public witnesses are veiled: the parable of the vine-dressers speaks of the Son of God in the indirect form of the similitude. Jesus answers the question of his judges about his messianic identity by announcing the coming of the Son of man. The confession of the centurion is indeterminate, and is formulated in the imperfect. In all three places, a connection with the execution of Jesus is unmistakable: only in suffering is the personal secret made public, and it remains, in the humiliation of torture and death, all the more concealed.

The other motifs of secrecy should be understood in terms of this personal secret. The miracle secret shows that Jesus can only be authentically recognized when his way is accomplished to its end. The secret teachings underscore that he is not correctly understood in public, but only by those who, in following him, accept testing and persecution (cf. Mk 4:17; 13:9-13).

The first function of the personal secret relates to the community's external relationships. Worldly messianism had led to a catastrophe in the Jewish war. The rebel leaders Menahem and Simon had appeared as kings and were killed because of their pretensions, one of them by rival revolutionary groups (*Bell.* 2.444), the other in a Roman triumphal procession (*Bell.* 7.154–55). After the war, it was a matter of survival for both Jews and Christians to distance themselves from that kind of messianism.[111] Josephus did this by transferring parts of the messianic utopia to the Roman emperor; Mark's Gospel did the same by revising messianic expectations in the figure of the crucified one. At the end of the Gospel a representative of the Roman state honors in him the crucified "king of the Jews"—a direct counter-image to the reality in which Jews had to do homage to the

---

111. The analysis of the situation of Mark's Gospel presented here develops the direction suggested by L. Schottroff in her "Die Gegenwart." On aloofness from political messianism, see ibid., 715ff.

victorious Romans. The Gospel thus says that this "messiah" is, despite appearances, superior to the mighty Romans. His "gospel" is contrasted with the εὐαγγέλια of the confident world power. Those "gospels" proclaimed, after the great political crisis of the Principate, the arrival of a ruler who would restore lost stability, a man who was legitimated by prophecy and oracle and confirmed by miracles. This other gospel, by contrast, announced the beginning of the reign of God (Mk 1:14-15), and also legitimated itself by prophecy (Mk 1:2ff.) and miracles (1:23ff., etc.), but proclaimed an anti-lordship. Service to this ruler by surrender of one's life is the counter-image to the oppression of nations by the earthly wielders of power (10:41-45); his feeding of hungry crowds is a contrast to the frivolous banquet of a king (6:17ff.); his gospel spreads among all peoples not through military conquest, but through persecutions (13:10). His coming from heaven is a rejection of the blasphemous attempts of earthly powers to claim for themselves the worship due to the true God (Mark 13). Anyone who understands this ruler as a claimant to earthly power has misunderstood him (8:27ff.). It is only when his followers go with him to the cross and are themselves prepared to surrender their lives that they will recognize the majesty of this ruler (8:34ff.)—a majesty that relativizes every earthly power.

This describes the internal function of the personal secret: it concerns discipleship, that is, "following" Jesus. The concept of discipleship really comes from the traditions of the itinerant charismatic preachers (cf. Mk 10:28-31), but in Mark's Gospel it is expanded in such a way that every Christian can apply it to himself or herself. In the process, it acquires new accents: discipleship is carried out in suffering (see esp. 8:34-38; 10:32), in "service" (see esp. 15:41; cf. 1:31), and in table fellowship with Jesus (2:15).[112] These are features of Christian life that can be realized even by those who do not leave house and land to take up a homeless life of discipleship; in fact, service to others is more readily possible for them than for unpropertied wanderers. This application of Jesus traditions from the point of view of local communities explains why Mark's Gospel contains relatively little material from the sayings tradition, which had its

---

112. Mark inserts the key word "follow" in several places, probably with conscious intent. Thus, in the account of Levi's banquet (Mk 2:15) it seems somewhat excessive to write "for there were many, and they followed him" (the probable original reading). This "following" is similarly inserted at Mk 10:32. In Mk 8:34-38, the evangelist's composition joins discipleship and suffering: readiness to surrender one's life and to acknowledge Jesus before human authorities is an illustration of the saying of Jesus in 8:34 about following him to the cross. Mark 15:40-41 may be intended to combine "discipleship and service." We should probably imagine the women's service in Galilee in terms of Mk 1:31: women see to the needs of the preacher and his disciples for food and shelter. This very service, which can best be accomplished by those who have houses and money, is "discipleship."

original *Sitz im Leben* among the itinerant charismatics. Mark's Gospel is a "call to discipleship."[113] But the call is stated in such a way that it applies to everyone.[114] The common elements that unite all are the inevitability of persecution and the obligation to give assistance to the whole community. The disciples' lack of understanding consists in the fact that they have to learn both elements from Jesus: readiness to suffer and to serve.

In Matthew's and Luke's Gospels, this application of the Jesus traditions is further developed. While Mark's Gospel had incorporated and pre-served unadorned popular traditions in its story of Jesus, Matthew's and Luke's accomplishment was to integrate the Sayings Source in their Gos-pels and thus to retain traditions preserved by the disciples whose radical-ness often asks too much of "normal" life.

Matthew and Luke thus adopt the fundamental structure of Mark's Gospel. The Passion account is at the end, and all the events move toward that event. The parenetic character of the Passion story is preserved: being a Christian is tested and proved in a confession that leads one into con-flicts and even to martyrdom. In this all Christians are alike, whether they are itinerant preachers or members of a settled local community.

Both longer Gospels give a new framework to the Jesus tradition by adding infancy narratives that are independent of one another. In so doing, they are following a natural "biographical" tendency to complete-ness. At the same time, by doing this they both begin their narratives in the world of the family. An itinerant, homeless existence is not a chosen way of life for this family as it was for Jesus' radical disciples; it is a fate forced upon them from outside, the result of political persecution (Mt 2:13ff.) and the requirements of the census (Lk 2:1ff.). Jesus' family is protected by God in all dangers. This positive view of a family serves to soften the afamilial ethic of discipleship found in the Jesus tradition.

Between the infancy narratives and the Passion, these two Gospels incorporate the tradition of Jesus' sayings. In spite of modifications and adaptations, that tradition maintains its radical harshness. It does not offer a reality-oriented ethic for life in Galilee or in Roman society. But for that very reason it is not tied to its historical context. As a pragmatic program for living, its ethical radicalness is timeless. It is bearable only because it is embedded in a narrative. In the Sayings Source, demand followed demand and it was never clear how people could live with those requirements; we

---

113. Thus E. Stegemann's title: "Das Markusevangelium als Ruf in die Nachfolge."

114. This thesis is supported by Lührmann: "Discipleship on the way of the cross (cf. 8:34) can exist, according to Mark, even within existing structures" (*Markusevangelium*, 177). He is referring to the structures described in the excursus "Haus als soziale Grösse," pp. 176–77.

now learn how the disciples, who were the first audience of this teaching, came to terms with them. Here all the readers can relate the material to themselves, because all the disciples fail. All the disciples illustrate the difference between ethical demand and real life. And still they are all Jesus' disciples, whose lives are guided by his commandments.

Other forms are introduced to enable the readers to come to terms with the radical ethic of Jesus without being untrue to it. In Matthew we find hints of a two-level ethic. The rich young man needs only to fulfill the Ten Commandments; the call to a more thoroughgoing discipleship is conditional: "If you wish to be perfect, go, sell your possessions, and give the money to the poor, and you will have treasure in heaven; then come, follow me!" (Mt 19:21). Matthew knows teachers who fulfill the whole law, and others who "annul" certain commandments. But even the "moderate" teachers have a place in the reign of God, although it is the very last (Mt 5:19). This two-level ethic is not thoroughly developed, but there are some initial steps in that direction.

We find a different procedure in Luke. For him, the time of Jesus was a special period within history when certain norms were valid that at a later time can no longer be kept. These include the norms of the itinerant charismatics:

> He said to them, "When I sent you out without a purse, bag, or sandals, did you lack anything?" They said, "No, not a thing." He said to them, "But now, the one who has a purse must take it, and likewise a bag. And the one who has no sword must sell his cloak and buy one!" (Lk 22:35-36)

But these steps toward a certain "relativizing" of ethical radicalism should not cause us to forget that Jesus' ethical teachings are taken seriously in all the Gospels. They are to be called upon in regulating the daily life of the communities. In Matthew and Luke, that life occupies a more prominent place. Mark's Gospel was a Passion account with an extended introduction. The circumstances of the community behind it must have corresponded: a threatened situation in which attention was concentrated on conflict and suffering. In the same way, if in Matthew's and Luke's Gospels the time between Jesus' birth and his tomb is filled with sayings and teaching, the conduct of life must have moved into the foreground for the members of their communities. Matthew and Luke write Gospels intended to give their communities strength for their ongoing lives, a strength that is called upon in the fullest measure when they must face life-threatening conflicts.

We have come to the end of our examination of the Gospel redactions. The inquiry into indications of locality and date has not just yielded suggestions about those matters. Equally important, the historical motives that led to the writing of the Gospels have emerged more clearly. The Gospels preserve Jesus traditions in spite of all their changes in place, time, and life-situation. They are an attempt to create continuity and identity in the midst of historical change.

Unlike the Sayings Source, all the Gospels were written outside Palestine. For the author and readers of the Sayings Source, the land of Palestine and its history were still immediately present. Readers of the Gospels needed to have that context presented to them in a narrative framework before they could understand Jesus' words.

All the Gospels are marked by the upheavals of the years 66–74, when not only Palestine, but the whole world succumbed to crisis. All of them are concerned with that crisis, either in terms of the suffering to be expected in its aftermath (Mark) or the prospects for community life after the crisis had been overcome (Matthew, Luke).

All the Gospels are the expression of an altered *Sitz im Leben* for the Jesus traditions. The most important of these were originally preserved and handed on by itinerant charismatic preachers. Besides these, there were also community traditions and popular tales from a very early date. The Gospels were written for local communities and reveal the process by which popular material and traditions from the disciples were adapted and interpreted for the communities. The further development of the traditions preserved by the itinerant charismatics led more directly to the *Gospel of Thomas* than to the Synoptic Gospels.[115]

---

115. Cf. J. M. Robinson, "On Bridging the Gulf from Q to the *Gospel of Thomas* (or vice versa)," in *Nag Hammadi, Gnosticism and Early Christianity,* ed. C. W. Hedrick and R. Hodgson (Peabody, Mass., 1986), 127–75. I am grateful for important suggestions on this point from a dissertation in progress by S. Patterson, a student of J. M. Robinson.

Concluding Observations

The question of cultural context and political history in the synoptic tradition finds answers in only a few texts. Seldom can localizable information
be sifted out of the traditions. Only sporadically are concrete historical
situations visible. But if we connect the individual points, we discover a
"network of threads" that lets us discern broader connections. Taken
together, they do not yield a comprehensive "history of the synoptic tradition," but they do refute the skepticism that regards a recovery of the
prehistory of our Gospels as impossible. In closing, let me briefly sketch
these connections once more.

1. In the "history of the synoptic tradition" we can recognize some
dislocations of place. The oldest tradition was formed in Galilee and may
have spread very quickly within the neighboring regions. In any case, the
Galilean flavor of this tradition is to be expected because Jesus came from
Galilee; however, in the face of historical skepticism about the Jesus traditions, it cannot be taken for granted. We can also demonstrate a second
stage of Jesus traditions within Jewish territory, because some of these
traditions were shaped in and around Jerusalem. Here we are referring to
two "large units," the synoptic apocalypse and the Passion account. In
terms of literary history, this demonstrates that we are at a second stage,
when Jesus traditions were being transmitted not merely in "small units,"
but in longer complexes. This stage had been reached as early as ten years
after Jesus' death—the core of the synoptic apocalypse dates from the
Caligula crisis of the year 40 C.E., and the oldest Passion account could
have been shaped in the 40s as well. The Gospels themselves are a third
stage. None of them was written in Palestine, although we can detect a
"neighborhood perspective" in Mark. Mark could have been written north
of Palestine, in that part of Syria that was later called "Syrophoenicia," an
area that could be reached by popular tales about Jesus. In Matthew's

Gospel, an eastern perspective is discernible—Judea is "beyond the Jordan." The author of Luke, on the other hand, sees Palestine from the west and is familiar with the wide world of the Mediterranean cities. All the Gospels are marked by the knowledge that the Jesus traditions are to be spread throughout the whole world. The writing of these Gospels probably is meant to assist that dissemination.

2. The examination of the "political history" in the synoptic tradition also yielded some information applicable to all the Gospels. The history of the synoptic tradition was marked by two severe political crises. The Caligula crisis of the years 39–41 C.E., which shook the whole of Palestine, left deeper traces on the synoptic tradition than we had previously supposed. It was during those events that the apocalyptic prophecy that forms the heart of the great discourse on the end time in Mark 13 originated. The Sayings Source is also marked by the crisis, which in the meantime had passed away. Q introduces Jesus' preaching with the Temptation story, a narrative that reflects the conflict between the self-apotheosis of Gaius Caligula and Jewish monotheism. The Caligula crisis put great strain on the relations between Christian communities and their Jewish neighbors, as is clear from the persecution under Agrippa I immediately afterward. The Passion account may reflect these tensions. While the first political crisis thus affected the preparatory stages for the Gospels—that is, the "large units" and a "collection of sayings"—the reaction to the second crisis, the Jewish war (66–74 C.E.), led to the writing of the Gospels themselves. The author of Mark wrote the first Gospel in light of the destruction of the temple. He was able to take advantage of two "large units" shaped by the earlier crisis, both of which reflected the circumstances of his community in the newly critical situation. He incorporates the synoptic apocalypse because the fear of a desecration of the temple that had arisen under Gaius Caligula had been revived under his successors (Vespasian and Titus). And he uses the Passion account to prepare his community for the severe conflicts he expects in the near future. Conversely, Matthew's and Luke's Gospels reflect an increasing distance from the war. They were written to prepare Christian communities for life in times of peace. They integrate the Sayings Source into the Jesus traditions because this corresponds to their new situation. The Sayings Source proposed a confident ethic for daily living in the wake of the Caligula crisis; in the same way the authors of Matthew and Luke present their plan for life after the end of the Jewish war.

3. The question of the *Sitz im Leben* was only an auxiliary theme in this book, but the investigation of the context in which texts are situated led repeatedly to the question of ongoing social situations. We discerned three

groups that preserved traditions about Jesus: the disciples, the communities, and the people. The Jesus traditions are not the exclusive property of any one group; instead, some of them were handed on simultaneously by the disciples, in local communities, and among the general public. In this process we can presume a decreasing "density" of the traditions along the trajectory from disciples to the general public. Among the popular traditions are the legend about the death of the Baptizer and some miracle stories. Community traditions include the Passion account and the synoptic apocalypse, while the disciples preserved those sayings that approve a radical itinerant ethic that makes demands that are insupportable under "normal" conditions. The path to the Gospel literature is drawn especially by the community traditions. The first complexes of Jesus tradition to receive written form—the synoptic apocalypse and the Passion account—were found in local communities. They have shaped the composition of the oldest Gospel. This community Gospel incorporated other traditions of the disciples (Mark's Gospel is acquainted with the phenomenon of itinerant charismatic life), but especially the popular tales. The two later Gospels rewrite Mark by combining it with disciples' traditions derived from the Sayings Source, thus preserving those materials for their communities. The *Sitz im Leben* of all the Gospel redactions is thus the "local community." The Gospels were written in order to adapt traditions from the disciples and popular tales, all of them derived from a different social milieu, to the needs of local communities. In the Gospels, itinerant radicalism and popular belief in miracles were integrated in a story of Jesus in such a way that Christians living in settled communities could make this Jesus their guide for living.

The investigation of cultural context and political history was not part of the program of classical form criticism, which proposed to shed light on the oral prehistory of the Gospels in terms of history. Its methodological tools were the analysis of layers within the text, observations of tendencies within the transmission of texts, description of the structure of genres, and reconstruction of the *Sitz im Leben*. Thus, the basis for the historical reconstruction of the course of the synoptic tradition was primarily a text-immanent analysis. The investigations presented in this book took a different methodological course. They attempted to uncover historical developments by correlating the texts with external historical data and information about the land of Palestine. Three localizable stages in the development of the synoptic tradition were visible, in which two political crises left their traces. Also visible were three groups in which the tradition was preserved and whose life-situations shaped the synoptic tradition. Despite differences in detail, there is a remarkable similarity between the results achieved by following a methodological route immanent to the text and one outside the text—in particular, the discovery of a prehistory behind our Gospels, beginning with the first Jesus traditions in Galilee and finding its preliminary conclusion outside Palestine, in the Synoptic Gospels.

Bibliography

Abel, F. M. *Géographie de la Palestine.* Vol. 1, *Géographie Physique et Historique.* Études bibliques. Paris, 1933.

Albright, W. F., and C. S. Mann. *Matthew.* The Anchor Bible. Garden City, N.Y., 1971.

Alföldi, A. *Die monarchische Repräsentation im römischen Kaiserreiche.* Darmstadt, 1970.

Altaner, B., and A. Stuiber. *Patrologie: Leben, Schriften und Lehre der Kirchenväter.* 8th ed. Freiburg and Basel, 1978. Translated from the 5th ed. by Hilda C. Graef, under the title *Patrology.* Freiburg, 1960.

Annen, F. *Heil für die Heiden: Zur Bedeutung und Geschichte der Tradition vom besessenen Gerasener (Mk 5,1-20 parr.).* FTS 20. Frankfurt, 1976.

Avigad, N. "A Depository of Inscribed Ossuaries in the Kidron Valley." *IEJ* 12 (1962): 1–12.

Avi-Yonah, M. "Newly Discovered Latin and Greek Inscriptions." *QDAP* 12 (1948): 84–102.

———. "The Founding of Tiberias." *IEJ* 1 (1950–51): 160–69.

———. *The Holy Land: From the Persian Period to the Arab Conquests, 536 B.C. to A.D. 640: A Historical Geography.* Rev. ed. Grand Rapids, 1977.

Balsdon, J.P.V.D. *The Emperor Gaius (Caligula).* Oxford, 1934. Reprint, 1964.

———. "Notes Concerning the Principate of Gaius." *JRS* 27 (1934): 13–24.

Bammel, E. "Das Ende von Q." In *Verborum Veritas: Festschrift für G. Stählin,* ed. Otto Bocher and Klaus Haacker. 39–50. Wuppertal, 1970.

Barnett, P. S. "The Jewish Sign Prophets A.D. 40–70: Their Intentions and Origin." *NTS* 27 (1981): 679–97.

Batey, R. A. "'Is Not This the Carpenter?'" *NTS* 30 (1984): 249–58.

———. "Jesus and the Theatre." *NTS* 30 (1984): 563–74.

Bauer, W. *Das Leben Jesu im Zeitalter der neutestamentlichen Apokryphen.* Tübingen, 1909. Reprint, Darmstadt, 1967.

———. "Jesus der Galiläer." In *Festschrift für A. Jülicher,* 16–34. Tübingen, 1927. Reprinted in *Aufsätze und kleine Schriften,* ed. G. Strecker, 91–108. Tübingen, 1967.

Bauernfeind, O., and O. Michel, eds. *Flavius Josephus, De Bello Judaico—Der Jüdische Krieg, Griechisch-Deutsch.* 4 vols. Munich, 1959–69.

Beasley-Murray, G. R. *Jesus and the Future: An Examination of the Criticism of the Eschatological Discourse, Mark 13, with Special Reference to the Little Apocalypse Theory.* London and New York, 1954.

———. *A Commentary on Mark Thirteen.* London and New York, 1957.

Ben-David, A. *Jerusalem und Tyros: Ein Beitrag zur palästinensischen Münz- und Wirtschaftsgeschichte (126 a.C.–57 p.C.).* Basel and Tübingen, 1969.

———. *Talmudische Ökonomie.* Vol. 1. Hildesheim and New York, 1974.

Bengtson, H. "Syrien in der hellenistischen Zeit." In *Der Hellenismus und der Aufstieg Roms,* ed. P. Grimal. Die Mittelmeerwelt im Altertum 2. Fischer Weltgeschichte 6. Frankfurt, 1965.

Berger, K. *Exegese des Neuen Testaments: Neue Wege vom Text zur Auslegung.* UTb 658. Heidelberg, 1977.

———. "Hellenistische Gattungen im Neuen Testament." *ANRW* 2.25.2, pp. 1031–1432. Berlin, 1984.

———. *Einführung in die Formgeschichte.* UTb 1444. Tübingen, 1987.

Betz, O. "Probleme des Prozesses Jesu." *ANRW* 2.25.1, pp. 565–647. Berlin, 1982.

Bickermann, E.J. *Der Gott der Makkabäer: Untersuchungen über Sinn und Ursprung der makkabäischen Erhebung.* Berlin, 1937. Translated by Horst R. Moehring, under the title *The God of the Maccabees: Studies on the Meaning and Origin of the Maccabean Revolt.* Leiden, 1979.

———. "The Warning Inscriptions of Herod's Temple." *JQR* n.s. 37 (1946–47): 387–405.

Bietenhard, H. "Die syrische Dekapolis von Pompeius bis Trajan." *ANRW* 2.8, pp. 220–61. Berlin and New York, 1977.

Bilde, P. "Aufspejler Mark 13 et jødisk apokalyptisk forlaeg fra kriseåret 40." In *Nytestamentlige Studier,* ed. S. Pedersen, 103–33. Århus, 1976.

———. "The Roman Emperor Gaius (Caligula)'s Attempt to Erect His Statue in the Temple of Jerusalem." *STh* 32 (1978): 67–93.

———. *Josefus som historieskriver.* Copenhagen, 1983.

Billerbeck, P. *Kommentar zum Neuen Testament aus Talmud und Midrasch.* Vol. 1. 8th ed. Munich, 1982.

Blass, F. "On Mark 12,42 and 15,16." *ET* 10 (1898–99): 185–87.

Bleek, F. *Synoptische Erklärung der drei ersten Evangelien.* Leipzig, 1862.

Bornkamm, G. "Die Sturmstillung im Matthäusevangelium." In *Überlieferung und Auslegung im Matthäusevangelium,* ed. G. Bornkamm, G. Barth, and H. J. Held, 48–53. WMANT 1. 4th ed. Neukirchen, 1965. Translated by Percy Scott, under the title *Tradition and Interpretation in Matthew.* London and Philadelphia, 1963.

Bösen, W. *Galiläa als Lebensraum und Wirkungsfeld Jesu.* Freiburg, 1985.

Bosold, I. *Pazifismus und prophetische Provokation: Das Grussverbot Lk 10,4b und sein historischer Kontext.* SBS 90. Stuttgart, 1978.

Bousset, W. *Die Offenbarung Johannis.* KEK 16. 6th ed. Göttingen, 1906.

———. *Kyrios Christos.* FRLANT 21. Göttingen, 1913. Reprint, 1967. Translated by John E. Steely, under the title *Kyrios Christos: A History of the Belief in Christ from the Beginnings of Christianity to Irenaeus.* Nashville, 1970.

Bowersock, G. W. *Roman Arabia.* Cambridge, Mass., and London, 1983.

Brandenburger, E. *Markus 13 und die Apokalyptik.* FRLANT 134. Göttingen, 1984.

———, ed. *Himmelfahrt Moses.* JSHRZ 5/2. Gütersloh, 1976.

Brandon, S.G.F. *The Fall of Jerusalem and the Christian Church: A Study of the Effects of the Jewish Overthrow of* A.D. *70 on Christianity.* 2d ed. London, 1957.

———. *Jesus and the Zealots: A Study of the Political Factor in Primitive Christianity.* Manchester, 1967.

———. *The Trial of Jesus of Nazareth.* London, 1968.

Braumann, G., comp. *Das Lukas-Evangelium: Die redaktions- und kompositionsgeschichtliche Forschung.* WdF 280. Darmstadt, 1974.

Braund, D. *Rome and the Friendly King: The Character of the Client Kingship.* New York, 1984.

Breytenbach, C. *Nachfolge und Zukunftserwartung nach Markus: Eine methodenkritische Studie.* AThANT 71. Zurich, 1984.

Buchanan, G. W. "Mark 11,15-19: Brigands in the Temple." *HUCA* 30 (1959): 169–77.

———. "An Additional Note." *HUCA* 31 (1960): 103–5.

Bultmann, R. *Die Geschichte der synoptischen Tradition.* FRLANT 29. Göttingen, 1921. 9th ed., 1979. Translated by John Marsh, under the title *The History of the Synoptic Tradition.* Rev. ed. Oxford, 1968.

Burchard, C. "Jesus von Nazareth." In *Die Anfänge des Christentums: Alte Welt und neue Hoffnung,* ed. J. Becker, 12–58. Stuttgart, 1987.

Burkill, T. A. "The Syrophoenician Woman: The Congruence of Mark 7,24-31." *ZNW* 57 (1966): 23–37.

———. "The Historical Development of the Story of the Syrophoenician Woman (Mark VII 24-31)." *NT* 9 (1967): 161–77.

Burr, V. *Nostrum mare: Ursprung und Geschichte der Namen des Mittelmeeres und seiner Teilmeere im Altertum.* Würzburger Studien zur Altertumswissenschaft 4. Stuttgart, 1932.

Cancik, H. "Bios und Logos: Formgeschichtliche Untersuchungen zu Lukians 'Demonax.'" In *Markus-Philologie,* ed. H. Cancik, 115–30. WUNT 33. Tübingen, 1984.

Case, S. J. "Jesus and Sepphoris." *JBL* 45 (1926): 14–22.

Chantraine, H. "Quadrans." *RE* 24: 649–67.

Collins, M. F. "The Hidden Vessels in Samaritan Traditions." *JSJ* 3 (1972): 96–116.

Conzelmann, H. *Die Mitte der Zeit: Studien zur Theologie des Lukas.* Tübingen, 1954. 3d ed., 1960. Translated by Geoffrey Burwell, under the title *The Theology of St. Luke.* London, 1960; New York, 1961; Philadelphia, 1982.

———. "Geschichte und Eschaton nach Mk 13." *ZNW* 50 (1959): 210–21.

———. "Der geschichtliche Ort der lukanischen Schriften im Urchristentum." In *Das Lukas-Evangelium,* ed. G. Braumann, 236–60. WdF 280. Darmstadt, 1974.

Crook, J. A. "Titus und Berenice." *AJP* 72 (1951): 162–75.

Dahl, N. A. *Matteusevangeliet.* 2 vols. Oslo, 1962.

Dalman, G. "Zum Tanz der Tochter der Herodias." *PJ* 14 (1918): 44–46.

———. *Orte und Wege Jesu.* BFChTh, ser. 2, vol. 1. Gütersloh, 1919. 2d ed., 1921. Reprint, Darmstadt, 1967. Translated by Paul P. Levertoff, under the title *Sacred Sites and Ways: Studies in the Topography of the Gospels.* New York, 1935.

Daniel, C. "Les Esséniens et 'ceux qui sont dans les maisons des rois' (Mathieu 11,7-8 et Luc 7,24-25)." *RQ* 6 (1967): 261–377.

Dauer, A. *Die Passionsgeschichte im Johannesevangelium: Eine traditionsgeschichtliche und theologische Untersuchung zu Joh 18,1—19,30.* StANT 30. Munich, 1972.

Davies, W. D. *The Setting of the Sermon on the Mount.* Cambridge, 1964.

———. *The Gospel and the Land: Early Christianity and Jewish Territorial Doctrine.* Berkeley, 1974.

Deissmann, A. *Licht vom Osten.* 4th ed. Tübingen, 1923. Translated by Lionel R.M. Strachan, under the title *Light from the Ancient East.* London, 1910. Rev. ed., New York, 1927.

Delling, G. "Ehehindernisse." *RAC* 4: 680–91.

Demole, E. *Fluss- und Meergötter auf griechischen und römischen Münzen.* Geneva, 1923.

Dermience, A. "Tradition et rédaction dans la péricope de la Syrophénicienne: Marc 7,24-30." *RTL* 8 (1977): 15–29.

Dibelius, M. *Die urchristliche Überlieferung von Johannes dem Täufer.* FRLANT 15. Göttingen, 1911.

———. *Die Formgeschichte des Evangeliums.* 6th ed. Tübingen, 1971. Translated from the rev. 2d ed. by Bertram Lee Woolf, under the title *From Tradition to Gospel.* New York, 1935. Reprint, 1965.

———. "Das historische Problem der Leidensgeschichte." In *Redaktion und Theologie des Passionsberichtes nach den Synoptikern,* ed. M. Limbeck, 57–66. WdF 481. Darmstadt, 1981.

Dihle, A. "Die Evangelien und die griechische Biographie." In *Das Evangelium und die Evangelien,* ed. P. Stuhlmacher, 383–411. WUNT 28. Tübingen, 1983.

Dischon, D. *The Culture of Controversy in Israel* (in Hebrew). Tel Aviv, 1984.

Dodd, C. H. "The Fall of Jerusalem and the Abomination of Desolation." *JRS* 37 (1947): 47–54.

———. *Historical Tradition in the Fourth Gospel.* Cambridge, 1963.

Donner, H. *Pilgerfahrt ins Heilige Land: Die ältesten Berichte christlicher Palästinapilger (4–7 Jhdt.).* Stuttgart, 1979.

Dormeyer, D. *Die Passion Jesu als Verhaltensmodell.* Münster, 1974.

Duling, D. C. "The Eleazar Miracle and Solomon's Magical Wisdom in Flavius Josephus *Antiquitates Judaicae* 8,42–49." *HThR* 78 (1985): 1–25.

Dupont, J. *Die Versuchungen Jesu in der Wüste.* Translated by Andrea van Dälmen. SBS 37. Stuttgart, 1969. Originally published as *Les tentations de Jésus au désert.* Paris, 1968.

Duprez, A. *Jésus et les dieux guérisseurs: A propos de Jean 5.* Paris, 1970.

Dussaud, R. "Inscription phénicienne de Byblos d'époque romain." *Syria* 6 (1925): 269–73.

Eck, W. "Die Eroberung von Masada und eine neue Inschrift des L. Flavius Silva Nonius Bassus." *ZNW* 60 (1969): 282–89.

Enslin, M. S. "Bethsaida." *BHH* 1: 234.

Ernst, J. "Die Passionerzählung des Markus und die Aporien der Forschung." *ThGl* 70 (1980): 160–80.

Fauth, W. "Proskynese." *KP* 4: 1189.

Feldmeier, R. *Die Krisis des Gottessohnes.* WUNT, ser. 2, no. 21. Tübingen, 1987.

Finegan, J. *The Archeology of the New Testament.* Vol. 1, *The Life of Jesus and the Beginning of the Early Church.* Princeton, 1969.

Flammer, B. "Die Syrophönizerin (Mk 7,24-30)." *TThQ* 148 (1968): 463–78.

Fleddermann, H. "The Flight of a Naked Young Man (Mark 14,51-52)." *CBQ* 41 (1979): 412–18.

Flemming, W. *The History of Tyre.* New York, 1915.

Flückiger, F. "Lk 21,20-24 und die Zerstörung Jerusalems." *ThZ* 28 (1972): 385–90.

Flusser, D. "Das Wesen der Gleichnisse." Part 1 of *Die rabbinischen Gleichnisse und der Gleichniserzähler Jesus.* Judaica und Christiana 4. Bern, 1981.

Foerster, W. "βδελύσσομαι." *TDNT* 1: 598–600.

Forrer, E. *Die Provinzeinteilung des assyrischen Reiches.* Leipzig, 1920.

Frey, Jean Baptiste. *Corpus of Jewish Inscriptions: Jewish Inscriptions from the Third Century B.C. to the Seventh Century A.D.* Prolegomenon by Baruch Lifschitz. The Library of Biblical Studies. Vol. 1. New York, 1975.

Freyne, S. *Galilee from Alexander the Great to Hadrian, 323 B.C.E. to 135 C.E.: A Study of Second Temple Judaism.* Wilmington, Del., and Notre Dame, Ind., 1980.

Fuchs, A. "βηθσαϊδά(ν)." *EWNT* 1:515–16.

Gabelmann, H. *Antike Audienz- und Tribunalszenen.* Darmstadt, 1984.

Gaechter, P. *Das Matthäus-Evangelium.* Innsbruck, 1963.

Gärtner, H. "Progymnasmata." *KP* 4:1156.

Geiger, R. *Die lukanischen Endzeitreden: Studien zur Eschatologie des Lukas-Evangeliums.* Bern and Frankfurt, 1973.

Gerhardsson, B. *Memory and Manuscript: Oral Tradition and Written Transmission in Rabbinic Judaism and Early Christianity.* Translated by Eric J. Sharpe. ASNU 22. Lund and Copenhagen, 1961. 2d ed., 1964.

———. *The Testing of God's Son (Matt 4,1-11 and Par): An Analysis of an Early Christian Midrash.* CB. NT 2. Lund, 1966.

Glaisher, J. "On the Direction of the Wind at Savona, Recorded Daily by Herr Dreher, in the Ten Years 1880–1889." *PEFQSt,* 1892, 226–50.

Gnilka, J. "Das Martyrium Johannes des Täufers (Mk 6,17-29)." In *Orientierung an Jesus: Zur Theologie der Synoptiker: Festschrift fur J. Schmid,* ed. P. Hoffmann, N. Brox, and W. Pesch, 78–92. Freiburg, 1973.

———. *Das Evangelium nach Markus.* 2 vols. EKK 1/2. Neukirchen, 1978–79.

———. *Das Matthäusevangelium.* 2 vols. HThK 1. Freiburg, 1986–88.

Goguel, M. *Das Leben Jesu.* Zurich, 1934. Translated by Olive Wyon, under the title, *The Life of Jesus.* New York, 1933. Reprint, 1960.

Grant, M. *From Imperium to Auctoritas.* Cambridge, 1946.

Greeven, H. *Synopsis of the First Three Gospels: With the Addition of the Johannine Parallels.* 13th ed., rev. A. Huck. Tübingen, 1981.

Grégoire, H., and M.-A. Kugener, eds. *Marc le diacre: Vie de Porphyre, éveque de Gaza.* Paris, 1930.

Gressmann, H., ed. *Altorientalische Texte und Bilder zum Alten Testament.* 2 vols. 2d rev. ed. Berlin, 1926–27.

Grimm, W. "Zum Hintergrund von Mt 8,11f/Lk 13,28f." *BZ* 16 (1972): 255–56.

Grundmann, W. *Das Evangelium nach Markus.* ThHK 2. 2d ed. Berlin, 1959.

———. *Das Evangelium nach Lukas.* ThHK 3. 3d ed. Berlin, 1964.

———. *Das Evangelium nach Matthäus.* ThHK 1. Berlin, 1968.

Gunther, J. J. "The Fate of the Jerusalem Church: The Flight to Pella." *ThZ* 29 (1973): 81–84.

Güttgemanns, E. *Offene Fragen zur Formgeschichte des Evangeliums: Eine methodologische Skizze der Grundlagenproblematik der Form- und Redaktionsgeschichte.* BEvTh 54. Munich, 1970. 2d ed., 1971. Translated by W. J. Doty, under the title *Candid Questions Concerning Gospel Form Criticism: A Methodological Sketch of the Fundamental Problematics of Form and Redaction Criticism.* Pittsburgh, 1979.

Guttmann, J. "Ananos." *EJ(D)* 2:765–66. Berlin, 1928.

Haacker, K. "Leistung und Grenzen der Formkritik." *ThB* 12 (1981): 53–71.

Habicht, C., ed. *2 Makkabäerbuch.* JSHRZ 1/3. Gütersloh, 1976.

Haenchen, E. *Der Weg Jesu: Eine Erklärung des Markus-Evangeliums und der kanonischen Parallelen.* STö 2/6. 2d rev. ed. Berlin, 1968.

Hahn, F. "Die Rede von der Parusie des Menschensohnes: Markus 13." In *Jesus und der Menschensohn: Festschrift für A. Vögtle,* ed. R. Pesch, R. Schnackenburg, and O. Kaiser, 240–66. Freiburg, 1975.

Hahn, G. L. *Das Evangelium des Lucas.* Vol. 2. Breslau, 1894.

Hanslick, R. "Petronius," no. 24. *PRE* 19.1, cols. 1199–1201.

Hanson, R. S. *Tyrian Influence in Upper Galilee.* Meiron Excavation Project No. 2. Cambridge, Mass., 1980.

Harder, G. "Das eschatologische Geschichtsbild der sogenannten kleinen Apokalypse Markus 13." *ThViat* 4 (1952): 71–107.

Harnack, A. von. *Beiträge zur Einleitung in das Neue Testament II: Sprüche und Reden Jesu.* Leipzig, 1907. Translated by J. R. Wilkinson, under the title *New Testament Studies II: The Sayings of Jesus, the Second Source of St. Matthew and St. Luke.* London and New York, 1908.

Harris, J. R. "Osiris in Galilee." *ET* 40 (1928–29): 188–89.

Hartmann, L. *Prophecy Interpreted.* CB. NT 1. Lund, 1966.

Hassler, I. "The Incident of the Syrophoenician Woman (Matt XV,21-28; Mark VII,24-30)." *ET* 45 (1934): 459–61.

Hatch, E., and H. A. Redpath. *A Concordance to the Septuagint.* 2 vols. Oxford, 1897.

Hengel, M. *Die Zeloten: Untersuchungen zur jüdischen Freiheitsbewegung in der Zeit von Herodes I. bis 70 n. Chr.* AGJU 1. Cologne and Leiden, 1961. 2d ed., 1976. Translated by David Smith, under the title *The Zealots: Investigations into the Jewish Freedom Movement in the Period from Herod I until 70 A.D.* Edinburgh, 1989.

———. *Judentum und Hellenismus: Studien zu ihrer Begegnung unter besonderer Berücksichtigung Palästinas bis zur Mitte des 2. Jh. v. Chr.* WUNT 10. Tübingen, 1969. Translated by John Bowden, under the title *Judaism and Hellenism: Studies in Their Encounter in Palestine during the Early Hellenistic Period.* Philadelphia, 1974.

———. "Der Historiker Lukas und die Geographie Palästinas in der Apostelgeschichte." *ZDPV* 99 (1983): 147–83.

———. *Die Evangelienüberschriften.* SHAWPH, 3. Heidelberg, 1984.

———. "Entstehungszeit und Situation des Markusevangeliums." In *Markus-Philologie: Historische, literargeschichtliche und stilistische Untersuchungen zum zweiten Evangelium,* ed. H. Cancik, 1–45. WUNT 33. Tübingen, 1984.

———. "Jakobus der Herrenbruder—der erste 'Papst'?" In *Glaube und Eschatologie: Festschrift für W. G. Kümmel,* ed. E. Grässer and O. Merk, 71–104. Tübingen, 1985.

Hennecke, E. *Neutestamentliche Apokryphen in deutscher Übersetzung.* Edited by W. Schneemelcher. 2 vols. 4th ed. Tübingen, 1968–71. Translated by A.J.B. Higgins, et al., under the title *New Testament Apocrypha.* Edited by R. M. Wilson. 2 vols. London, 1963–65.

Hermann, A. "Erdbeben." *RAC* 5, col. 1104.

Hoehner, H. W. *Herod Antipas: A Contemporary of Jesus Christ.* SNTSMS 17. Cambridge, 1972.

Hoffmann, P. "Die Versuchungsgeschichte in der Logienquelle: Zur Auseinandersetzung der Judenchristen mit dem politischen Messianismus." *BZ* 13 (1969): 207–23.

———. *Studien zur Theologie der Logienquelle.* NTA, n.s. 8. Münster, 1972.

Hölscher, G. "Der Ursprung der Apokalypse Mk 13." *ThBl* 12 (1933), cols. 193–202.

Holtzmann, H. *Das Evangelium nach Lucas.* HKNT 1. Tübingen and Leipzig, 1901.

Holzmeister, U. "Wann war Pilatus Prokurator von Judaea." *Bib* 13 (1932): 228–32.

Honigmann, E. "Συροφοινίκη." *PRE* 4, A, 2, cols. 1788–89.

Horst, J. *Proskynein: Zur Anbetung im Urchristentum nach ihrer religionsgeschichtlichen Eigenart.* NTF 3. Gütersloh, 1932.

Hüttenmeister, F., and G. Reeg. *Die antiken Synagogen in Israel.* Beihefte zur TAVO B 12/1. Wiesbaden, 1977.

Hyldahl, N. "Die Versuchung auf der Zinne des Tempels." *STh* 15 (1961): 113–27.

———. "Paulus og Arabien." In *Hilsen til Noack,* ed. N. Hyldahl and E. Nielsen, 102–7. Copenhagen, 1975.

———. "Josefus som historieskriver." *DTT* 48 (1985): 51–64.

Imhoof-Blumer/Keller, O. *Tier -und Pflanzenbilder auf Münzen und Gemmen des Klassischen Altertums.* Leipzig, 1889.

Janssen, E. *Testament Abrahams.* JSHRZ 3/2. Gütersloh, 1975.

Jeremias, J. *Jerusalem zur Zeit Jesu: Eine kulturgeschichtliche Untersuchung zur neutestamentlichen Zeitgeschichte.* 2 vols. Göttingen, 1923–37. 3d ed., 1962. Translated by F. H. Cave and C. H. Cave, under the title *Jerusalem in the Time of Jesus: An Investigation into Economic and Social Conditions during the New Testament Period.* London and Philadelphia, 1969.

———. *Golgotha.* 'Αγγελος Archiv für neutestamentliche Zeitgeschichte und Kulturkunde, Beiheft 1. Leipzig, 1926.

———. "Sabbathjahr und neutestamentliche Chronologie." *ZNW* 27 (1928): 98–103.

———. *Die Gleichnisse Jesu.* Göttingen, 1947. 8th ed., 1970. Translated by S. H. Hooke, under the title *The Parables of Jesus.* New York, 1955. 2d rev. ed., 1972.

———. *Die Wiederentdeckung von Bethesda, Johannes 5,2.* FRLANT 59. Göttingen, 1949. Translated from the German by J. Vardaman, C. Burchard, D. Hume, and M. Zalampas; trans. rev. B. F. Meyer, under the title *The Rediscovery of Bethesda, John 5:2.* Louisville, Ky., 1966.

———. "Markus 14,9." *ZNW* (1952–53): 103–7.

———. *Jesu Verheissung für die Völker.* Stuttgart, 1956. 2d ed., 1959. Translated by S. H. Hooke, under the title *Jesus' Promise to the Nations.* Naperville, Ill., 1958.

———. *Heiligengräber in Jesu Umwelt (Mt 23,29; Lk 11,47): Eine Untersuchung zur Volksreligion der Zeit Jesu.* Göttingen, 1958.

————. *Die Abendmahlsworte Jesu.* 4th ed. Göttingen, 1967. Translated by Norman Perrin from the 3d ed., under the title *The Eucharistic Words of Jesus.* New York, 1966.

Jidejian, N. *Tyre through the Ages.* Beirut, 1969.

Jones, A.H.M. "The Urbanization of Palestine." *JRS* 21 (1931): 78–85.

Kaswaldek, P. "Corazim." *Terre Sainte* 3 (1985): 136–38.

Kee, H. C. *Community of the New Age: Studies in Mark's Gospel.* London and Philadelphia, 1977. Reprint, Macon, Ga., 1983.

Keel, O., and M. Küchler. *Orte und Landschaften der Bibel: Ein Handbuch und Studienreiseführer zum Heiligen Land.* 2 vols. Göttingen and Zurich, 1982–84.

Kelber, W. H. *The Oral and the Written Gospel.* Philadelphia, 1983.

————, ed. *The Passion in Mark: Studies on Mark 14–16.* Philadelphia, 1976.

Kennedy, G. "Classical and Christian Source Criticism." In *The Relationships among the Gospels: An Interdisciplinary Dialogue,* ed. W. O. Walker, Jr., 126–54. San Antonio, 1978.

Kertelge, K. *Die Wunder Jesu im Markusevangelium.* StANT 23. Munich, 1970.

Kinder, U. "Datierungsindizien für eine vormk Passionstradition anhand der Personenbezeichnungen in der Mk-Passion." Dissertation. Heidelberg, 1985.

Kindler, A. *The Coins of Tiberias.* Tiberias, 1961.

Kippenberg, H. G. " 'Dann wird der Orient herrschen und der Okzident dienen': Zur Begründung eines gesamtvorderasiatischen Standpunktes im Kampf gegen Rom." In *Spiegel und Gleichnis: Festschrift für J. Taubes,* ed. N. W. Bolz and W. Hübener, 40–48. Würzburg, 1983.

Klauck, H.-J. *Allegorie und Allegorese in synoptischen Gleichnistexten.* NTA, n.s. 13. Münster, 1978.

Klein, G. "Die Verleugnung des Petrus." In *Rekonstruktion und Interpretation,* 49–98. BEvTh 50. Munich, 1969.

Klein, H. "Zur Frage nach dem Abfassungsort der Lukasschriften." *EvTh* 32 (1972): 467–77.

Kloppenborg, J. S. "The Literary Genre of the Synoptic Sayings Source." Dissertation. University of St. Michael's College, Toronto, 1984.

————. "Tradition and Redaction in the Synoptic Sayings Source." *CBQ* 46 (1984): 34–62.

Klostermann, E. *Das Markusevangelium.* HNT 3. 4th ed. Tübingen, 1971.

Koch, D.-A. *Die Bedeutung der Wundererzählungen für die Christologie des Markusevangeliums.* BZNW 42. Berlin and New York, 1975.

Koester, H. *Einführung in das Neue Testament: Im Rahmen der Religionsgeschichte und Kulturgeschichte der hellenistischen und römischen Zeit.* Berlin and New York, 1980. Translated by the author, under the title *Introduction to the New Testament.* 2 vols. Philadelphia, Berlin, and New York, 1982.

Koester, H., and J. Robinson. *Entwicklungslinien durch die Welt des frühen Urchristentums.* Tübingen, 1971. = *Trajectories through Early Christianity.* Philadelphia, 1971.

Koestermann, E. *Cornelius Tacitus, Annalen, erläutert und mit einer Einleitung versehen.* WKLGS 3, Books 11–13. Heidelberg, 1967.

Köhler, L. "Archäologisches Nr. 16–19." *ZAW* 40 (1922): 15–46.

Kopp, C. *Die heiligen Stätten der Evangelien.* Regensburg, 1959. Translated by Ronald Walls, under the title *The Holy Places of the Gospels.* New York, 1963.

Körtner, H. J. "Markus der Mitarbeiter des Petrus." *ZNW* 71 (1980): 160–73.

Kraeling, C. H. "The Jewish Community at Antioch." *JBL* 51 (1932): 130–60.

———, ed. *Gerasa: City of the Decapolis.* New Haven, 1938.

Krieger, N. "Ein Mensch in weichen Kleidern." *NT* 1 (1965): 228–30.

Kuhn, H.-W. *Ältere Sammlungen im Markusevangelium.* StUNT 8. Göttingen, 1971.

———. "Die Kreuzesstrafe während der frühen Kaiserzeit: Ihre Wirklichkeit und Wertung in der Umwelt des Urchristentums." *ANRW* 2.25.1, pp. 648–793. Berlin and New York, 1982.

Kuhn, K. G. "Zum Essenischen Kalender." *ZNW* 52 (1961): 65–73.

Kühschelm, R. *Jüngerverfolgung und Geschick Jesu: Eine Exegetisch-bibeltheologische Untersuchung der synoptischen Verfolgungsankündigungen Mk 13,9-13 par und Mt 23,29-36 par.* Klosterneuburg, 1983.

Kümmel, W. G. *Verheissung und Erfüllung: Untersuchungen zur eschatologischen Verkündigung Jesu.* 3d ed. Zurich, 1956. Translated by Dorothea M. Barton, under the title *Promise and Fulfilment: The Eschatological Message of Jesus.* London and Naperville, Ill., 1957.

Kundsin, K. *Topologische Überlieferungsstoffe im Johannes-Evangelium.* FRLANT 39. Göttingen, 1925.

Künzi, M. *Das Naherwartungslogion Matthäus 10,23: Geschichte seiner Auslegung.* BGBE 9. Tübingen, 1970.

Lagrange, J. M. *Évangile selon Saint Jean.* Études bibliques. 5th ed. Paris, 1936.

Lampe, P. *Die stadtrömischen Christen in den ersten beiden Jahrhunderten.* WUNT, ser. 2, no. 18. Tübingen, 1987.

Lang, B. "Grussverbot oder Besuchsverbot? Eine sozialgeschichtliche Deutung von Lukas 10,4b." *BZ* 26 (1982): 75–79.

Lang, F. G. " 'Über Sidon mitten ins Gebiet der Dekapolis.' " *ZDPV* 94 (1978): 145–60.

Lassére, J.-M. *Ubique Populus.* Paris, 1977.

Laufen, R. *Die Doppelüberlieferungen der Logienquelle und des Markusevangeliums.* BBB 54. Bonn, 1980.

Lémonon, J.-P. *Pilate et le Gouvernement de la Judée.* Textes et Monuments. EtB. Paris, 1981.

Leon, H. J. *The Jews of Ancient Rome.* Philadelphia, 1960.

Liebenam, W. "Feldzeichen." *PRE* 6, cols. 2151–61.

Lietzmann, H. "Der Prozess Jesu." In *Kleine Schriften II: Studien zum Neuen Testament,* 251–63. TU 68. Berlin, 1958.

———. *An die Korinther I. II.* HNT 9. 5th ed. Tübingen, 1969.

Lightfoot, R. H. *Locality and Doctrine in the Gospels.* London, 1938.

Limbeck, M. "Ἰσχαριώθ." *EWNT* 2:491–93.

Linnemann, E. *Studien zur Passionsgeschichte.* FRLANT 102. Göttingen, 1970.

Loffreda, S. *Die Heiligtümer von Tabgha.* Jerusalem, 1978.

Lohmeyer, E. *Galiläa und Jerusalem in den Evangelien.* FRLANT 52. Göttingen, 1936.

———. *Das Evangelium des Markus.* KEK 1/2. 10th ed. Göttingen, 1937. 17th ed., 1967.

———. *Das Evangelium des Markus: Ergänzungsheft.* Edited by G. Sass. 2d ed. Göttingen, 1963.

Lohse, E. *Die Geschichte des Leidens und Sterbens Jesu Christi.* GTB 316. Gütersloh, 1979. Translated by Martin O. Dietrich, under the title *History of the Suffering and Death of Jesus Christ.* Philadelphia, 1967.

Loisy, A. *L'évangile selon Marc.* Paris, 1912.

Lüdemann, G. "The Successors of Pre-70 Jerusalem Christianity: A Critical Evaluation of the Pella-Tradition." In *Jewish and Christian Self-Definition*, ed. E. P. Sanders, 1:161–73. Philadelphia, 1980.

Lührmann, D. *Die Redaktion der Logienquelle.* WMANT 33. Neukirchen-Vluyn, 1969.

———. "Markus 14, 55-64: Christologie und Zerstörung des Tempels im Markusevangelium." *NTS* 27 (1981): 457–74.

———. *Das Markusevangelium.* HNT 3. Tübingen, 1987.

———. "Die Pharisäer und die Schriftgelehrten im Markusevangelium." *ZNW* 78 (1987): 169–85.

Luz, U. "Das Geheimnismotiv und die markinische Christologie." *ZNW* 56 (1965): 9–30.

———. *Das Evangelium nach Matthäus.* EKK 1/1. Zurich and Neukirchen, 1985.

McCown, C. C. "The Scene of John's Ministry." *JBL* 59 (1940): 113–31.

Macurdy, G. H. "Julia Berenice." *AJP* 56 (1935): 246–53.

Madden, F. A. *History of Jewish Coinage, and of Money in the Old and New Testament.* New York, 1967.

Mahnke, H. *Die Versuchungsgeschichte im Rahmen der synoptischen Evangelien.* BEvTh 9. Frankfurt, 1978.

Maier, J. *Jesus von Nazareth in der talmudischen Überlieferung.* EdF 82. Darmstadt, 1978.

Manns, F. "Marc 6,21-29 à la lumière des dernières fouilles du Machéronte." *Liber Annuus* 21 (1981): 287–90.

Marxsen, W. *Der Evangelist Markus: Studien zur Redaktionsgeschichte des Evangeliums.* FRLANT 67. Göttingen, 1956. Translated by James Boyce, et al., under the title *Mark the Evangelist: Studies on the Redaction History of the Gospel.* Nashville, 1969.

Matthiae, K., and E. Schönert-Geiss. *Münzen aus der urchristlichen Umwelt.* East Berlin, 1981.

Mayer Maly, T. "Vitellius" (7c). *PRE* Suppl. 9, cols. 1733–39.

Meeks, W. A., and R. L. Wilken. *Jews and Christians in Antioch in the First Four Centuries of the Common Era.* SBLbSt 13. Missoula, Mont., 1978.

Merritt, R. L. "Jesus Barabbas and the Paschal Pardon." *JBL* 104 (1985): 57–68.

Meshel, Z. "Was There a 'Via Maris'?" *IEJ* 23 (1973): 162–66.

Meshorer, Y. *Jewish Coins of the Second Temple Period.* Translated by I. H. Levine. Tel Aviv, 1967.

Meyer, P. D. "The Gentile Mission in Q." *JBL* 89 (1970): 405–17.

Meyers, E. M. "The Cultural Setting of Galilee: The Case of Regionalism and Early Judaism." *ANRW* 2.19.1, pp. 686–702. Berlin, 1979.

Meyshan, J. "The Canopy Symbol on the Coins of Agrippas I" (in Hebrew). *BIES* 22 (1958): 157–60.

Michel, O. "κύων." *TDNT* 3: 1100–1104.

Michel, O., and O. Bauernfeind. *Flavius Josephus, De Bello Judaico.* 3 vols. Munich, 1959–69.

Mittmann, S. *Beiträge zur Siedlungs- und Territorialgeschichte des nördlichen Ostjordanlandes.* Wiesbaden, 1970.

Mohr, T. A. *Markus- und Johannespassion.* AThANT 70. Zurich, 1982.

Mommsen, T. *Römische Geschichte.* 5 vols. Berlin, 1885. 3d ed. (7 vols.), Munich, 1894. Translated by W. P. Dickson, under the title *The History of Rome.* 4 vols. New York, 1894. Rev. ed. (5 vols.), 1911.

Monteverde, R., and C. Mondsert. "Deux Inscriptions de Hama." *Syria* 34 (1957): 278–87.

Morenz, S. "Das Tier mit den vier Hörnern." *ZAW* 63 (1951): 151–54.

Morgenthaler, R. "Roma—Sedes Satanae: Röm 13,1ff. im Lichte von Luk 4,5-8." *ThZ* 12 (1956): 289–304.

Musurillo, H. A. *The Acts of the Christian Martyrs.* Oxford, 1972.

Nauck, W. "Kapernaum." *BHH* 2:931.

Nestle, E. "Zu Daniel." *ZAW* 4 (1884): 247–48.

Neugebauer, O. "The 'Astronomical' Chapters of the Ethiopic Book of Enoch (72–82)." In *Det Koneglige Danske Videnskabernes Selskab.* Matematisk-fysiske Meddeleeser 40/10. Copenhagen, 1981.

Niederwimmer, K. "Johannes Markus und die Frage nach dem Verfasser des zweiten Evangeliums." *ZNW* 58 (1967): 172–82.

Otto, W. "Herodes," no. 24. *PRE* Suppl. II (Stuttgart, 1913), cols. 168–91.

Pedersen, S. "κύων." *EWNT* 2:821–23.

———. "Zum Problem der vaticinia ex eventu." *STh* 19 (1965): 167–88.

Pesch, R. *Naherwartungen: Tradition und Redaktion in Mk 13.* Düsseldorf, 1968.

———. *Das Markusevangelium.* 2 vols. HThK 2/1, 2. Freiburg, 1976–77.

———, ed. *Das Markus-Evangelium.* WdF 411. Darmstadt, 1979.

Pesch, R., R. Schnackenburg, and O. Kaiser. *Jesus und der Menschensohn: Festschrift für A. Vögtle zum 65. Geburtstag.* Freiburg, 1975.

Piganiol, A. "Observations sur la date de l'apocalypse synoptique." *RHPhR* 4 (1924): 245–49.

Pilgaard, A. "Jesus som undergører i Markusevangliet." *Bibel og historie* 3 (1983): 98–101.

Plummer, A. *A Critical and Exegetical Commentary on the Gospel according to St. Luke.* ICC 28. Edinburgh and New York, 1896. 5th ed., 1922.

Polag, A. *Die Christologie der Logienquelle.* WMANT 45. Neukirchen-Vluyn, 1977.

———, ed. *Fragmenta Q: Textheft zur Logienquelle.* Neukirchen-Vluyn, 1979 (Cf. Ivan Havener, *Q: The Sayings of Jesus: With a Reconstruction of Q by Athanasius Polag.* Wilmington, Del., 1987).

Porton, G. G. "The Pronouncement Story in Tannaitic Literature: A Review of Bultmann's Theory." In R. C. Tannehill, ed., *Pronouncement Stories, Semeia* 20 (1981): 81–100.

Pratscher, W. *Der Herrenbruder Jakobus und die Jakobustradition.* FRLANT 139. Göttingen, 1987.

Preuschen, E. *Tatians Diatessaron aus dem Arabischen übersetzt.* Heidelberg, 1926.

Pryke, E. J. *Redactional Style in the Markan Gospel: A Study of Syntax and Vocabulary as Guides to Redaction in Mark.* SNTSMS 33. Cambridge, 1978.

Rabin, C. *Hebrew and Aramaic in the First Century.* CJNT 1/2. Assen, 1976.

Ramsay, W. M. "On Mark 12,42." *ET* 10 (1898–99): 232, 336.

Regling, K. "Lepton." In *Wörterbuch der Münzkunde*, ed. F. v. Schrötter. Berlin and Leipzig, 1930.

Reicke, B. "Chorazim." *BHH* 1:301.

—————. "Synoptic Prophecies on the Destruction of Jerusalem." In *Studies in New Testament and Early Christian Literature: Festschrift for A. P. Wikgren*, ed. David E. Aune, 121–34. NT Suppl. 33. Leiden, 1972.

Reifenberg, A. *Ancient Jewish Coins*. Jerusalem, 1940. 6th ed., 1973.

Reinach, T. "Mon Nom est Légion." *REJ* 47 (1903): 172–78.

Rengstorf, K. H. "Die Stadt der Mörder (Mt 22,7)." In *Judentum, Urchristentum, Kirche: Festschrift für J. Jeremias*, ed. W. Eltester, 106–29. BZNW 26. Berlin, 1960.

Richter, W. "Hund." *KP* 2:1245–49.

Riehm, E.C.A., ed. *Handwörterbuch des Biblischen Altertums*. 2 vols. Bielefeld, 1884.

Riesner, R. *Jesus als Lehrer.* WUNT, 2d ser., no. 7. Tübingen, 1981. 2d ed., 1984.

—————. "Johannes der Täufer auf Machärus." *BiKi* 39 (1984): 176.

—————. "Die Synagoge von Kafernaum." *BiKi* 39 (1984): 136–38.

—————. "Essener und Urkirche in Jerusalem." *BiKi* 40 (1985): 64–76.

—————. "Golgata und Archäologie." *BiKi* 40 (1985): 21–26.

—————. "Neues von den Synagogen Kafernaums." *BiKi* 40 (1985): 133–35.

Rix, H. "Personennamen." *KP* 4:657–61.

Robinson, J.A.T. *Redating the New Testament*. London, 1976.

Roller, R. *Münzen, Geld und Vermögensverhältnisse in den Evangelien*. Karlsruhe, 1929. Reprint, 1969.

Roloff, J. *Das Kerygma und der irdische Jesus: Historische Motive in den Jesus-Erzählungen der Evangelien*. Göttingen, 1970.

Rordorf, W. "Die neronische Christusverfolgung im Spiegel der apokryphen Paulusakten." *NTS* 28 (1982): 365–74.

Rostovtzev, M. *Caravan Cities*. Translated by D. Rice and T. Talbot Rice. Oxford, 1932.

Rutherford, W. G. *The New Phrynichus, Being a Revised Text of the Ecloga of the Grammarian Phrynichus*. London, 1881.

Sallmann, K. "Plinius." *KP* 4:928–37.

Sanders, E. P. *The Tendencies of the Synoptic Tradition*. MSSNTS 9. Cambridge, 1969.

Schäfer, P. "Die Flucht Johanan b. Zakkais aus Jerusalem und die Gründung des 'Lehrhauses' in Jabne." *ANRW* 2.19.2, pp. 43–101. Berlin and New York, 1979.

Schalit, A. "Die Erhebung Vespasians nach Flavius Josephus, Talmud und Midrasch: Zur Geschichte einer messianischen Prophetie." *ANRW* 2.2, pp. 208–327. Berlin and New York, 1975.

Schenk, W. *Der Passionsbericht nach Markus*. Gütersloh, 1974.

—————. "Gefangenschaft und Tod des Täufers: Erwägungen zur Chronologie und ihren Konsequenzen." *NTS* 29 (1983): 453–83.

Schenke, H.-M., and K. M. Fischer. *Einleitung in die Schriften des Neuen Testaments*. 2 vols. Berlin, 1978–79.

Schenke, L. *Studien zur Passionsgeschichte des Markus: Tradition und Redaktion in Markus 14, 1-42*. FzB 4. Würzburg and Stuttgart, 1971.

—————. *Der gekreuzigte Christus*. SBS 69. Stuttgart, 1974.

—————. *Die Wundererzählungen des Markusevangeliums*. SBB 5. Stuttgart, 1974.

Schenkel, D., ed. *Bibel-Lexikon*, vol. 5. Leipzig, 1875.

Schille, G. "Die Topographie des Markusevangeliums: Ihre Hintergründe und ihre Einordnung." *ZDPV* 73 (1957): 133–66.

———. *Anfänge der Kirche: Erwägungen zur apostolischen Frühgeschichte.* BEvTh 43. Munich, 1966.

Schlatter, A. *Der Evangelist Matthäus: Seine Sprache, sein Ziel, seine Selbständigkeit.* Stuttgart, 1948.

———. *Das Evangelium des Lukas,* 2d ed. Stuttgart, 1960.

Schmidt, K. L. *Der Rahmen der Geschichte Jesu: Literarkritische Untersuchungen zur ältesten Jesusüberlieferung.* Berlin, 1919. Reprint, Darmstadt, 1964.

———. "Die Stellung der Evangelien in 'er allgemeinen Literaturgeschichte" (1923). In *Neues Testament, Judentum, Kirche,* 37–130. ThB 69. Munich, 1981.

Schmidt, W. "Der Einfluss der Anachorese im Rechtsleben Ägyptens zur Ptolemäerzeit." Dissertation. Cologne, 1966.

Schmithals, W. *Das Evangelium nach Markus.* 2 vols. ÖTK 2. Gütersloh, 1979.

———. "Kritik der Formkritik." *ZThK* 77 (1980): 149–85.

———. *Einleitung in die ersten drei Evangelien.* Berlin, 1985.

Schmitt, G. "Das Zeichen des Jona." *ZNW* 69 (1978): 123–29.

Schneider, A. M. *Die Brotvermehrungskirche in et-Tabga.* Paderborn, 1934. Translated by E. Graf, under the title *The Church of the Multiplying of the Loaves and Fishes, at Tabgha on the Lake of Gennesaret, and Its Mosaics,* ed. A. A. Gordon. London, 1937.

Schneider, G. "Die Verhaftung Jesu: Traditionsgeschichte von Mk 14, 43-52." *ZNW* 63 (1962): 188–209.

———. *Das Evangelium nach Lukas.* ÖTK ser. 3, no. 2. Gütersloh and Würzburg, 1977.

Schoeps, H. J. "Ebionitische Apokalyptik im Neuen Testament." *ZNW* 51 (1960): 101–11.

Schöllgen, G. "Die Didache—ein frühes Zeugnis für Landgemeinden?" *ZNW* 76 (1985): 140–43.

Schottroff, L. "Maria Magdalena und die Frauen am Grabe Jesu." *EvTh* 42 (1982): 3–25.

———. "Die Gegenwart in der Apokalyptik der synoptischen Evangelien." In *Apocalypticism in the Mediterranean World and the Near East: Proceedings of the International Colloquium on Apocalypticism, Uppsala, Aug. 12–17, 1979,* ed. D. Hellholm, 707–28. Tübingen, 1983.

———. "Das Gleichnis vom grossen Gastmahl in der Logienquelle." *EvTh* 47 (1987): 192–211.

Schottroff, L., and W. Stegemann. *Jesus von Nazareth, Hoffnung der Armen.* UTb 639. Stuttgart, 1978. Translated by Matthew J. O'Connell, under the title *Jesus and the Hope of the Poor.* Maryknoll, N.Y., 1986.

Schreiber, J. *Die Markuspassion: Wege zur Erforschung der Leidensgeschichte Jesu.* Hamburg, 1969.

Schulz, S. *Q: Die Spruchquelle der Evangelisten.* Zurich, 1972.

———. "Die Gottesherrschaft ist herbeigekommen (Mt 10,7/Lk 10,9): Der kerygmatische Entwurf der Q-Gemeinde Syriens." In *Das Wort und die Wörter: Festschrift für G. Friedrich,* ed. Horst Balz and Siegfried Schulz, 57–67. Stuttgart, 1973.

Schunck, K. D., ed. *Das 1 Makkabäerbuch.* JSHRZ 1/4. Gütersloh, 1980.

Schürer, E. *Geschichte des Jüdischen Volkes im Zeitalter Jesu Christi.* 4 vols. 4th ed. Leipzig, 1901–11.

————. *The History of the Jewish People in the Age of Jesus Christ (175 B.C.–A.D. 135)*. 4 vols. A new English version rev. and ed. G. Vermes and F. Millar. Edinburgh, 1973–87.

Schürmann, H. "Zur Traditions- und Redaktionsgeschichte von Mt 10,23." *BZ 3* (1959): 82–88.

————. "Mt 10,5b-6 und die Vorgeschichte des synoptischen Aussendungs-berichtes." In *Festschrift für J. Schmid*, 270–82. Regensburg, 1963.

————. *Das Lukasevangelium*. HThK ser. 3, no. 1. Freiburg, 1969.

Schwartz, E. "Über den Tod der Söhne Zebedäi" (1904). In *Gesammelte Schriften V*, 48–123. Berlin, 1963.

Schweizer, E. *Das Evangelium nach Markus*. NTD 1. 15th ed. Göttingen, 1978. Translated by Donald H. Medvig, under the title *The Good News according to Mark*. Richmond, 1970.

————. *Das Evangelium nach Matthäus*. NTD 2. 15th ed. Göttingen, 1981. Translated by David E. Green, under the title *The Good News according to Matthew*. Atlanta, 1975.

————. *Neues Testament und Christologie im Werden: Aufsätze*. Göttingen, 1982.

————. *Das Evangelium nach Lukas*. NTD 3. 2d rev. ed. Göttingen and Zurich, 1986.

Schwier, H. *Tempel und Tempelzerstörung: Untersuchungen zu den theologischen und ideologischen Faktoren im ersten jüdisch-römischen Krieg (66–74 n. Chr.)* Freiburg and Göttingen, 1989.

Silviae, S. "Peregrinatio ad loca sancta 47,4." In *Itinera Hierosolymitana saeculi IIII–VIII*, ed. P. Geyer. CSEL 39. Prague, Vienna, and Leipzig, 1898.

Slingerland, H. D. "The Transjordanian Origin of St. Matthew's Gospel." *JSNT 3* (1979): 18–28.

Smallwood, E. M. "The Date of the Dismissal of Pontius Pilatus from Judaea." *JJS 5* (1954): 12–21.

————. *The Jews under Roman Rule: From Pompey to Diocletian*. SJLA 20. Leiden, 1976.

————, ed. *Philonis Alexandrini: Legatio ad Gaium*. 2d ed. Leiden, 1970.

Snyder, G. F. "The Tobspruch in the New Testament." *NTS* 23 (1977): 117–20.

Sowers, S. "The Circumstances and Recollection of the Pella Flight." *ThZ* 26 (1970): 305–20.

Sperber, D. "Palestinian Currency Systems during the Second Commonwealth." *JQR* 56 (1966): 273–301.

Spitta, F. *Die Offenbarung des Johannes*. Halle, 1889.

Standaert, B. *L'Evangile selon Marc: Composition et Genre littéraire*. Nijmegen, Neth., 1978.

Stauffer, E. "Entmythologisierung oder Realtheologie?" *Kerygma und Mythos* 2 (1952): 13–28.

————. *Christus und die Caesaren*. 4th ed. Hamburg, 1954. Translated by K. Smith and R. Gregor Smith, under the title *Christ and the Caesars: Historical Sketches*. Philadelphia, 1955.

————. *Jesus: Gestalt und Geschichte*. DTb 332. Berne, 1957. Translated by Richard Winston and Clara Winston, under the title *Jesus and His Story*. New York, 1960.

Steck, O. H. *Israel und das gewaltsame Geschick der Propheten: Untersuchungen zur Überlieferung des deuteronomistischen Geschichtsbildes im Alten Testament, Spätjudentum und Urchristentum*. WMANT 23. Neukirchen-Vluyn, 1967.

Stegemann, E. "Das Markusevangelium als Ruf in die Nachfolge." Dissertation. Heidelberg, 1974.

———. "Von Kritik zur Feindschaft: Eine Auslegung von Markus 2,1–3,6." In *Der Gott der kleinen Leute: Sozialgeschichtliche Bibelauslegungen*, ed. W. Schottroff and W. Stegemann, vol. 2, *Neues Testament*, 39–57. Munich and Gelnhausen, 1979. Translated by Matthew O'Connell, under the title *God of the Lowly: Socio-Historical Interpretations of the Bible*. Maryknoll, N.Y., 1984.

Stegemann, W. "Die Versuchung Jesu im Matthäusevangelium, Mt 4,1-11." *EvTh* 45 (1985): 29–44.

Stendahl, K. *The School of St. Matthew and Its Use of the Old Testament.* ASNU 20. Uppsala, 1954.

Stern, M. *Greek and Latin Authors on Jews and Judaism.* 2 vols. Jerusalem, 1974–80.

Storch, W. "Zur Perikope von der Syrophönizierin: Mk 7,28 und Ri 1,7." *BZ* 14 (1970): 256–57.

Strack, H., and P. Billerbeck. *Kommentar zum Neuen Testament aus Talmud und Midrasch.* 6 vols. 8th ed. Munich, 1982.

Strecker, G. *Der Weg der Gerechtigkeit: Untersuchung zur Theologie des Matthäus.* FRLANT 82. 3d ed. Göttingen, 1971.

Streeter, B. H. *The Four Gospels: A Study of Origins.* London, 1924.

Strobel, A. *Die Stunde der Wahrheit.* WUNT 21. Tübingen, 1980.

Sullivan, R. D. "The Dynasty of Judaea in the First Century." *ANRW* 2.8, pp. 296–54. Berlin and New York, 1977.

Sydenham, E. A. *The Coinage of the Roman Republic.* London, 1952.

Tagawa, K. *Miracles et Évangile, la pensée personelle de l'évangeliste Marc.* EHPhR 62. Paris, 1966.

Tannehill, R. C. "Types and Function of Apophthegms in the Synoptic Gospels." *ANRW* 2.25.2, pp. 1792–1829. Berlin, 1984.

Taylor, V. *Behind the Third Gospel: A Study of the Proto-Luke Hypothesis.* Oxford, 1926.

———. *The Gospel according to St. Mark.* London, 1952. 2d ed., 1966.

Teeple, H. M. "The Oral Tradition That Never Existed." *JBL* 89 (1970): 56–68.

Theissen, G. "Wanderradikalismus: Literatursoziologische Aspekte der Überlieferung von Worten Jesu im Urchristentum." *ZThK* 70 (1973): 245–71. Reprinted in *Studien zur Soziologie des Urchristentums*, 79–105. WUNT 19. 2d ed. Tübingen, 1983.

———. *Urchristliche Wundergeschichten: Ein Beitrag zur formgeschichtlichen Erforschung der synoptischen Evangelien.* StNT 8. Gütersloh, 1974. 5th ed., 1987. Translated by Francis McDonagh, under the title *The Miracle Stories of the Early Christian Tradition.* Edinburgh, 1982; Philadelphia, 1983.

———. *Studien zur Soziologie des Urchristentums.* WUNT 19. 2d ed. Tübingen, 1983. Edited, translated, and with an introduction by John Schütz, under the title *The Social Setting of Pauline Christianity: Essays on Corinth.* Philadelphia, 1982.

———. "'Meer' und 'See' in den Evangelien: Ein Beitrag zur Lokalkoloritforschung." *SNTU* 10 (1985): 5–25.

Tödt, H. E. *Der Menschensohn in der synoptischen Überlieferung.* Gütersloh, 1959. Translated by Dorothea M. Barton, under the title *The Son of Man in the Synoptic Tradition.* Philadelphia, 1965.

Trocmé, É. *La formation de l'Evangile selon Marc. EHPhR* 57. Paris, 1963. Translated by Pamela Gaughan, under the title *The Formation of the Gospel according to Mark.* Philadelphia, 1975.

Uhlig, S., ed. *Das Äthiopische Henochbuch.* JSHRZ 5/6. Gütersloh, 1984.

Vanhoye, A. "La fuite du jeune homme nu (Mc 14,51-52)." *Bib* 52 (1971): 401–6.

Vermes, G. *Jesus the Jew: A Historian's Reading of the Gospels.* London, 1973; Philadelphia, 1981.

Vielhauer, P. "Tracht und Speise Johannes des Täufers." In *Aufsätze zum Neuen Testament,* 47–54. ThB 31. Munich, 1965.

———. *Geschichte der urchristlichen Literatur: Einleitung in das Neue Testament, die Apokryphen und die Apostolischen Väter.* Berlin and New York, 1975.

Violet, B. *Die Esra-Apokalypse (IV Esra).* GCS 18. Berlin, 1910.

———, ed. *Die palästinischen Märtyrer des Eusebius von Cäsarea.* TU 14/4. Leipzig, 1896.

Vögtle, A. *Das Evangelium und die Evangelien: Beiträge zur Evangelienforschung.* Düsseldorf, 1971.

Volz, P. *Die Eschatologie der jüdischen Gemeinde im neutestamentlichen Zeitalter.* Tübingen, 1934.

Vouga, F. "Pour une géographie théologique des christianismes primitifs." *EThR* 59 (1984): 141–49.

Waetjen, H. "The Ending of Mark and the Gospel's Shift in Eschatology." *ASTI* 4 (1965): 114–31.

Walter, N. "Tempelzerstörung und synoptische Apokalypse." *ZNW* 57 (1966): 38–49.

Weder, H. *Die Gleichnisse Jesu als Metaphern: Traditions- und redaktionsgeschichtliche Analysen und Interpretationen.* FRLANT 120. Göttingen, 1978.

Weeden, T. J. "The Heresy That Necessitated Mark's Gospel." *ZNW* 59 (1969): 145–58.

Weege, F. *Der Tanz in der Antike.* Halle, 1926.

Wegner, U. *Der Hauptmann von Kafarnaum.* WUNT 14. Tübingen, 1985.

Weinel, H. *Die Wirkungen des Geistes und der Geister im nachapostolischen Zeitalter bis auf Irenäus.* Freiburg, 1899.

Weiss, J. *Die drei ältesten Evangelien.* SNT 2. Göttingen, 1906.

———. *Der erste Korintherbrief.* Göttingen, 1910. Reprint, 1970.

Wellhausen, J. *Das Evangelium Marci.* 2d ed. Berlin and New York, 1909.

———. *Einleitung in die drei ersten Evangelien.* 2d ed. Berlin, 1911.

———. *Das Evangelium Matthaei.* 2d ed. Berlin and New York, 1914.

Wendling, E. *Die Entstehung des Markusevangeliums.* Tübingen, 1908.

Wengst, K. *Bedrängte Gemeinde und verherrlichter Christus: Der historische Ort des Johannesevangeliums als Schlüssel zu seiner Interpretation.* Biblisch-Theologische Studien 5. Neukirchen-Vluyn, 1981.

———, ed. *Didache.* Schriften des Urchristentums. Darmstadt, 1984.

Wenning, R. *Die Nabatäer—Denkmäler und Geschichte.* NTOA 3. Fribourg and Göttingen, 1987.

Windisch, H. "Kleine Beiträge zur evangelischen Überlieferung 1: Zum Gastmahl des Antipas." *ZNW* 18 (1917–18): 73–83.

Winkler, G. "Septimius Severus." *KP* 5:123–27.

Winter, P. "Simeon der Gerechte und Gaius Caligula." *Jud* 12 (1956): 129–32.

———. *On the Trial of Jesus.* SJ 1. Berlin, 1961.

Wirgin, W. "A Note on the 'Reed' of Tiberias." *IEJ* 18 (1968): 248–49.

Wirth, E. *Syrien: Eine geographische Landeskunde.* Wissenschaftliche Länderkunde 4/5. Darmstadt, 1971.

Wrede, W. *Das Messiasgeheimnis in den Evangelien: Zugleich ein Beitrag zum Verständnis des Markusevangeliums.* Göttingen, 1901. 4th ed., 1969. Translated by J.O.G. Greig, under the title *The Messianic Secret.* Greenwood, S.C., 1971.

Zahn, T. *Einleitung in das Neue Testament.* 2d ed. Leipzig, 1900.

———. *Das Evangelium des Matthäus.* KNT 1. 2d ed. Leipzig, 1905.

Zeller, D. "Das Logion Mt 8,11f/Lk 13,28f und das Motiv der 'Völkerwallfahrt.' " Parts 1, 2. *BZ* 15 (1971): 222–37; *BZ* 16 (1972): 84–93.

———. "Die Versuchungen Jesu in der Logienquelle." *TThZ* 89 (1980): 61–73.

———. "Wunder und Bekenntnis: Zum Sitz im Leben urchristlicher Wundergeschichten." *BZ* 25 (1981): 204–22.

Zmijewski, J. *Die Eschatologiereden des Lukas-Evangeliums.* BBB 40. Bonn, 1972.

———. "Die Eschatologiereden Lk 21 und 17." *BiLe* 14 (1973): 30–40.

Zumstein, J. "Antioche sur l'Oronte et l'évangile selon Matthieu." *SNTU* 5 (1980): 122–38.

Zuntz, G. "Wann wurde das Evangelium Marci geschrieben?" In *Markus-Philologie,* ed. H. Cancik, 47–71. WUNT 33. Tübingen, 1984.

Index